VIDA'S *CHRISTIAD* AND

VERGILIAN EPIC

MARIO A. DI CESARE

VIDA'S *CHRISTIAD* AND VERGILIAN EPIC

COLUMBIA UNIVERSITY PRESS

New York and London 1964

For Emily

The Stanwood Cockey Lodge Foundation has generously provided funds to assist in the publication of this volume

Library of Congress Catalog Card Number: 63-9870
Printed in Italy

POLEMICAL PREFACE

THE YOUNG John Milton, surveying poems written about Christ, praised Vida's *Christiad* thus in 1630:

> Loud O'er the rest Cremona's trump doth sound.
>
> ("The Passion," 26)

Three quarters of a century later, Alexander Pope, surveying the halcyon days of Renaissance Italy under Leo X, went further:

> Immortal Vida: on whose honour'd brow
> The Poet's bays and Critic's ivy grow;
> Cremona now shall ever boast thy name,
> As next in place to Mantua, next in fame.
>
> (*Essay on Criticism*, 705-708)

The praises were not isolated. Sometimes for epic, sometimes for poetic, often for both, Vida was lauded extravagantly from Leo's time to the end of the last century—lauded by people as diverse as Ariosto, Sadoleto, Bembo, Tasso, Klopstock, Dryden, Vico, Goldsmith, and Carducci.

But the history of Vida's fame is bizarre. In the eighteenth century, for instance, the pious irrelevance of Italian translators and eulogizers, the assiduity of German commentators, and the myopia of English disciples virtually killed off the poet of the *Christiad* while reconstructing him into the "prophet" of the *Ars poetica*. John Cranwell's translation of the epic (1768) conformed with

disturbing rigor to the rules of the *Ars poetica* as Christopher Pitt's heroic couplets had interpreted those rules in
1725. No one indeed seemed aware that Vida had actually
put aside the rules when he composed his epic. In effect,
Vida was mustered into neoclassicist ranks, just as his
master was transformed into an English gentleman. The
difference is that Vergil survived the metamorphosis.

Saintsbury, enemy of Pope's school, took out his enmity
on the Italian humanists. Those who came after, perhaps
innocent of the enmity, have perpetuated Saintsbury's
follies. Thus the commonest modern view makes out Vida
as prophet of neoclassicism and one-book poet: the *Ars
poetica*, of course. The fact is, Vida's *Ars poetica* was the
inheritance of *Quattrocento* Vergilian humanism; in many
ways, it was a mistake, the undeveloped product of un-
reflective years, but subsequent generations of poets and
theorists found many of their own notions neatly embedded in the *Ars poetica*, and the critics thought they
discovered in it the key to the *Christiad*. The result of
such compounded confusion is that the *Christiad*, the
poem which apparently had the largest part in shaping
the Vergilian tradition of the sixteenth, seventeenth, and,
to a lesser extent, eighteenth century, has now been virtually cast into oblivion. This is indeed a footnote to chaos,
when one considers that the most casual reader might
have found, in the less dreary passages of the *Ars poetica*,
explicit views of tradition, the individual talent, and the
objective correlative.

It is not the aim of this book to rescue Vida and his
epic from oblivion, however merited or unmerited. My
major concern is to do something which, even in the
heyday of Vida eulogies and studies, almost no one has
tried—that is, to examine the *Christiad* critically as an
epic poem and to appraise critically Vida's Vergilian
humanism. This seemed a worthy endeavor when Pro-

fessor Moses Hadas suggested it some years ago as a thesis-subject, and it seems an even worthier endeavor now as I rework the matter. There is always the justification that the *Christiad* lurks in the background of *Paradise Lost*— indeed, I believe it is one of the most important works in that background; but I am also convinced that it can stand on its own merits when once those merits are perceived. My point of departure has been not the theoretical poem but the epic itself; the texts for my discourse are the *Christiad* and the *Aeneid*. My major concern is the *Christiad* as an epic poem and as a Vergilian poem.

It seemed worthwhile to begin the book with a sketch of Vida's life and works, since no adequate biography of the man exists in any language, least of all in English. In the opening chapter, I have attempted to combine the reliable data of extant works with all the available documents, published and unpublished, and to provide materials for a future biographer. The second, or background, chapter surveys cursorily the thought and practice of the *Quattrocento* in what I have called Vergilian humanism. The following chapters, III, IV, and V, re-examine the canonical elements of epic composition—diction, rhetoric, narrative, and structure—in order to clear away the mechanistic fallacies foisted on us by those who know only one definition for *imitatio*. In these three chapters, I try to distinguish substantially the modes of apprenticeship and the forms of creative imitation and transformation. In the sixth chapter, I attempt to get at the essential Vergilianism of Vida, the area of creative imitation where he succeeded best in outgrowing his master— thematic design. There was little to go on here, few critics to agree with, build on, or eruditely quarrel with. Yet this part of my study is the most crucial, not only for Vida's *Christiad* but for any sound approach to Vergilian poetry in the Renaissance and to the whole tradition of epic which is called Vergilian.

Unless otherwise indicated, all quotations from Vida's works are from the two-volume quarto of 1731, Padua, known as the Cominiana edition. Quotations from Vergil are from the Oxford Classical Text edition by Arthur Hirtzel. Quotations from Homer are given in English translation. Longer Latin passages are followed by translations, generally my own, though occasionally they lean on other sources as the notes indicate. These renderings are intended to do nothing more than assist the reader to comprehend the sense of the Latin so that he may pursue its other qualities.

It is pleasant to record some debts.

Professor Moses Hadas of Columbia, the original guiding spirit of this work, has always been a gentle master, a helpful mentor, and an understanding friend. I owe a good deal of this work, and much else besides, to him.

The Samuel S. Fels Fund granted me a fellowship to pursue Vergil and Vida without interruption at least for a year, and the Stanwood Cockey Lodge Foundation is generously subsidizing the publication of this volume. To the Trustees of both I would express my deep gratitude.

I am very grateful also to Professor Marjorie Hope Nicolson, for generous support and trust; to William Nelson and Maurice Valency who kept me from many pitfalls; to Paul Oscar Kristeller for his liberal suggestions and assistance; to William York Tindall, who contributed in ways he may not know; to Gilbert Highet, who stimulated me in many discussions of Vergil both in and out of the seminar room.

The kindness, patience, and efficiency of a host of librarians must not go unnoticed. Miss Janet Brown of the Harpur College library performed countless services for me. So also did the librarians of Butler Library, Columbia; Pratt Institute Library; the New York Public Library; the Library of Congress; the British Museum; and the Cornell University Library. My friends Professor Charles T. O'Reilly and Father John Donaghey, S.V.D., obtained important documents for me. Mrs. Hazel A. Bell exercised faith, hope, and charity in assisting me in many stages of the work. The best of all debts is acknowledged where it should be.

Harpur College   MARIO A. DI CESARE
Binghamton, New York
July, 1962

CONTENTS

CHAPTER ONE

LIFE AND WORKS

THE EXTENT of Vida's contemporary reputation as *Vergilius Christianus* is indicated by Lilio Gregorio Giraldi's description of Vergil: "Corpore fuit et statura grandi, colore aquilino, hoc est, subfusco, facie rusticana: adeo ut nostro Vidae non adeo absimilis videri fuisse posset." The large frame, dark complexion, and leathery countenance probably miss Vergil, but Giraldi's remark provides a good description of *noster Vida* and suggests his stature in the 1540s. The underlying assumption, however, and the casual tone of the remark indicate the biographer's problem. Vida was well known indeed. As early as 1530 the Cremonese academician Paolo Tartessio prefaced a course on the *Ars poetica* with a lengthy disquisition on Vida's life and works, but omitted details; assuming everyone knew these, he concentrated on the embellishment.[1]

Vida himself offers little help. When Bartolomeo Botta set out in 1540 to be Servius to the new Vergil, he petitioned Vida for biographical data suitable to an introduction. Vida disarmed him by disavowing any desire for glory, particularly in connection with an opus—the *Christiad*—so fraught with peril for a good Christian: "Rogo ne a nobis vitae nostrae, aut rerum nostrarum ... commentarios exspectes ullos.... Ego certe opus tam arduum, atque adeo periculosum non spe immortalitatis, aut gloriae adortus sum." (Cominiana ed. II, ii, 130) After

Vida's death legend confused history. The lyric flights of aspiring disciples provided substance for the one and frustration for the other. Most of the biographies from his time to the end of the nineteenth century are simply uncritical elaborations of this mixed legend and history. They were aptly characterized by Novati as "ciance retoriche..., scipiti libercoli..., panegirici [e] memorie..., in cui la sciatteria si nasconde sotto il mantello ... d'una pretenziosa erudizione." All this gossip and coarse eulogizing, all this pretentious erudition, derives from the same meager factual sources.[2]

He was born Marcantonio Vida between 1480 and 1485, to Guglielmo Vida and Leone Oscasale of Cremona.[3] Though the once noble family was in reduced circumstances, Marcantonio received a thorough humanistic education, first at Cremonese schools under Niccolo Lucari, disciple of Vittorino da Feltre, and later at Mantua, where the tradition of Vittorino was prevalent.[4] Novati's suggestion that Mantuan society had a broadening effect on the young scholar seems accurate enough when we recall that, besides the Vergilian humanists of Vittorino's tradition, Mantua boasted the erudite court of Isabella d'Este Gonzaga and the prevailing *Vergilius Christianus*, Battista Spagnuoli. There Vida wrote his first poems—an elegy and two epigrams in memory of Serafino d'Aquila, who died in 1500.[5]

Returning to Cremona, he entered the Order of Canons Regular of St. John Lateran and took the name Marco Girolamo. Early in the pontificate of Julius II Vida went to Rome for studies in philosophy, law, and theology, but the truancy from poetry did not last long. One large work, *Felsinaidos libri*, is recorded as having been in Julius's library.[6] Vida wrote also a vigorous patriotic poem, *Tredecim pugilum certamen*, celebrating the combat at Barletta in 1503 between thirteen Frenchmen and thirteen Italians; the combat arose during a truce in one of those interminable struggles between the invading French and the Spaniards allied with the Italians, out of a slur cast on the valor of the Italians. Vida apparently attempted to destroy the work later, though it is difficult to know whether this was because of the shift in the political line during the 1520s, or because the problems of composition, particularly structure, were too great.[7]

By early 1511 Vida was well advanced on another large work, an epic *Juliad* dealing with the Pope's martial accomplishments. Our knowledge of this derives mainly from two letters, the first to Vincenzo Caraffa, accompanying the *Epicaedion*, a tedious panegyric in hexameters to the deceased Cardinal Oliviero Caraffa; and the second, two years later, accompanying the *Quercens*, a pastoral eulogy in honor of the dead Pontiff. By 1513 Vida was engaged in revision of the epic and was suggesting that Leonardo della Rovere, the Pontiff's brother, might subsidize publication: "tuis fortasse auspiciis in publicum exibit."[8] Again, nothing more is known of this work, and the fate of the *Quercens* may help to explain why.

In this pastoral eulogy three shepherds, Vitiscus (Vida), Myrtilus, and Coriletus, lament the death of Quercens. The main speaker, Vitiscus, calls attention to his achievements—he had restored liberty to Rome, he was generous and just; under him, there was no place for avarice, intrigue, or cowardice. But Quercens dead, the barbarians will overrun Rome, the infidel threat will become more dangerous. All creation and heaven itself lament his untimely death. The imagery of the poem is predominantly animal—flatterers and would-be poisoners are described as serpents; hangers-on from the reign of Alexander VI are cast as bears, wolves, or lions; Julius and his followers are the shepherd and his flock. But despite the clear command of hexameter and the control over structure, the poem was excluded from the canonical editions. With the accession of the Medici, a quite different breed was inheriting the earth. The quiet fury of the tribute and its harsh contemporary relevance may well have been the main reasons for suppression both of it and of the *Juliad.* If so, it is a pity.

In 1524 two small pieces were published in the *Carmina Coryciana,* a collection of lyrics for "Corycius," Johannes Goritz, a Luxembourger turned Roman and a kind of patriarch to the Roman Academy.[9] Of these pieces little need be said except that it was fortunate Vida could get away to Frascati for work on the *Christiad.* The style of both is precious; the first, celebrating Corycius and the "maximi Marones ... qui ... meritum evehunt ad astra," is trivial. The second, also on Corycius, his hospitality, his circle, attempts to be recondite but is merely insipid. The Vergilian allusion in

> Tu tamen o, quamvis mensis assuetus opimis
> Pontificum, contemnere opes, et vivere parvo
> Aude, hospes, rebusque veni non asper egenis.
> (63-65)

may seem like the Vergilianism of the *Christiad,* but it is not. The difference between these pieces and the epic poem is very much the difference in perception, understanding, and maturity between the view of Vergil in the *Ars poetica,* which is contemporary with them, and the results of a profounder study of Vergil as these results are seen in the *Christiad.*

None of these early works passed muster when Vida assembled the first edition of his poems in 1527, a handsome quarto volume which included the *Ars poetica, Bombyx, Ludus scacchiae, Hymns, Bucolics, Odes,* and an

Epistle to Giberti.[10] By then, he was a widely recognized poet, his fame resting mainly on the three large works. The latter poems, mostly occasional, have less staying power.

Carducci thought highly of the *Bucolics*: it is difficult to agree.[11] The first, *Daphnis*, on Gianmatteo Giberti's absence from Rome because of a diplomatic mission, has neat unity and honest feeling. But *Corydon*, lamenting the premature death of Celso Mellini, the young patrician associate of Christophe de Longeuil, seems almost satirical; and *Nice*, to Vittoria Colonna on her husband's death, is too lush.

Diis coelitibus, a hymn seconding Henry VIII's desire for a son, has merely historic interest: it was excluded from later editions because of Henry's defection. The hymn to Saint Margaret is redeemed from bathos by the intensity of its patriotic feeling; here are the closing lines:

> Civibus o tandem lucem da cernere nostris:
> Et populis redeat vetus in praecordia virtus.
> Inter se positis ultro civilibus armis
> Pacem agitent, unaque velint occurrere pesti
> Communi, atque ferum divellere finibus hostem.
>
> (70-74)

Grant our countrymen light that at last they may see, and bring pristine virtue back to the hearts of our people. Let them put aside, uncoerced, the arms they have taken up against each other, and wage peace, and yearn to battle together against the common enemy and to drive from our borders the fierce foe.

Divo Stephano Protomartyri, written when Vida assumed the Priory of St. Stephen, is interesting for the heroic image of Stephen facing the elders; the breadth with which the images is worked out suggests that Vida may have composed part of it originally for the *Christiad*.

There is, further, a suggestion of inner conflict, as cleric faces saint: "hominum curas rides miseratus inanes." (73)

In the first of the odes, to Giberti, Vida establishes the pointed contrast between the harassed life of the young diplomat and his own ease in the retreat at Frascati, and then he injects a gently ironical reminder that it was Giberti's intercession which won him the rural retreat. The second ode, to Leo X, expressing the enthusiastic hopes stirred by the projected crusade against the Turks, is vigorous and earnest. Written probably in 1517-1518, it provides fit setting for the closing lines of *Ars poetica* II, where the shattered dream is recounted in despairing and unresigned tones.[12] The third ode, again to Giberti, and one of the latest of all the short poems, is more philosophical than the rest, and neater in design and execution. Stanzas balance each other, as do pairs of lines. Giberti's encouragement of Vida's poetry is not well received; Vida musingly explains why. To the younger man he points out that it is time to put aside "plectra et artem."

> Mollem senectam me deceat magis
> Traducere intra Socraticam domum,
>   Dum cogito, quae sit beatis
>   Post cineres animis voluptas.   (37-40)

It would be far more fitting that I pass my weak old age in Socrates' cell, while contemplating the joys of beatified souls beyond the grave.

While the first and second ode show the craftsman and the patriot, the last is contemporary in spirit with the postscript to the 1527 edition, disclaiming impious intent in the use of "antique superstition," and asking that judgment be deferred until the *Christiad* is published:

QUISQUIS es, rogat te Vida, ne impietati sibi ascribas, quod quaedam ex antiquorum superstitione homo christianus versibus suis insperserit, neve ab iis animum suum metiare... Iudicium autem de se... differri vult, dum ea ediderit, quae nuperrime de Christo Deo et Homine gravissime scripserit.

(113r)

Since he himself asserts that the *Christiad* is not a "flight of the imagination," this last ode shows us the man grown older, partly because of many years of work on his high argument, and reflecting that, if the poetic impulse is gone, it may be just as well.[13] A score of years later, he judged the *Ludus scacchiae* as "meae adulescentiae lusus... de re ludicra" (*De reipublicae dignitate dialogi*, p. 47); but it must be borne in mind that, when he wrote that frivolous poem, he was approaching the height of his poetic powers. To that game, along with the other major works, we now turn.

The setting for the game of chess is the court of Memnon in Ethiopia, where Jupiter and the other gods are celebrating the nuptials of Oceanus and Terra. Oceanus brings out a board and boxwood figures, briefly explains the ground rules of the game, and suggests a first trial. The contenders, chosen by Jove, are Apollo and Mercury, playing white and black men, respectively. The early stages of the game are enlivened by the contrast between Apollo's wholesale assaults and Mercury's apparent clumsiness—he moves at random and blunders badly. But Mercury has been planning a broad strategy, and the ensuing setbacks make Apollo more cautious. Then confusion over the protocol regarding the queen throws Mercury off balance; his vindictive counterattack failing, he attempts a bluff, unsuccessfully. He cheats, until Apollo detects him. Having angered and confused Mercury, Apollo manages nearly to corner the king with his white queen, when the black queen races in to the defense. At this point Mars attempts clumsily to interfere by reactivating some of Mercury's pieces, but, caught by Vulcan, he is reproved roundly and Mercury must retract some illegitimate moves. Shortly Apollo's white queen slays the black queen; in the nick of time maiden pawns join the regal ranks, a successful ruse by Mercury upsets Apollo's calculations—he has just been boasting complacently—and a series of shrewd moves gives Mercury the game.[14]

The illusion of action is maintained perfectly, in a fresh and sprightly style which never wavers in its self-confidence. Vida solves the structural problem of accounting for each of the chess figures by focusing attention on the players and the onlookers. To complain, as some do, that the poem is not didactically adequate seems ungracious.[15] Indeed, the reader is never aware that he is not being taught how to play chess. The whole poem is genially mock-heroic, though never self-consciously so. Subtly ironic, the work seems to operate in a vacuum: no explicit satire disturbs the blend of gentle mockery, cordial burlesque, and delight in the action for its own sake.[16] The contrast between the impetuous, disorganized, often overheated Apollo and the sly calculating Mercury is adroitly handled. Mercury's outburst does not disturb this contrast: Vida is here thoroughly enjoying his capricious deities. Certainly that outburst induces a complacency in Apollo which hastens his downfall. But neither is Mercury Vida's hero; the tone is preserved by the absence of protagonist. There are intrigues on both sides, only Jupiter remaining properly impartial. The gods shift allegiance easily; their antics, particularly those of the coquettish Venus, the excitable Mars, and the pompous Vulcan who recalls Uncle Poseidon of *Odyssey* VIII, all correspond admirably to the unpredictable activities of the boxwood figures. The whimsical, half-serious tone of the following suggests to the reader the right attitude:

Continuo exoritur magnum certamen, et ingens
Hinc atque hinc rabies, dum fixum vincere utrisque.
Audentes in tela ruunt. stat multus ubique
Terror, ubique pavor, mortisque simillima imago.

(554-557)

Suddenly, a great conflict arises, as well as enormous frenzy on every side, as each is determined to conquer. Boldly, they rush for their arms. Everywhere there is terror, everywhere fear, and the very image of death.

Vida's growing dependence on Vergil becomes evident in this poem, as the above lines suggest. Cicchitelli indiscriminately cites "imitations":

Huc illuc agitans campo insultabat aperto   (577)
Campoque atrum rapit agmen aperto.
                                 (*Aeneid* XII. 445)

late et loca milite complent.   (207)
late loca milite complent.   (*Aeneid* II. 495)

emicat ense stricto eques.   (244)
micat aureus ensis   (*Aeneid* VII. 743)[17]

But such correspondences are, without exception, incidental to the genial argument. For all the Vergilian flavor, they contribute nothing to the poem's texture except by indirection. For his original myth Vida used language that is quite experimental. What is not drawn from a vast classically pedigreed lexicon is simply adapted to the needs of the moment. The poem cannot be read slowly and ponderously; that would, quite simply, spoil it. Vida's control of narrative pace and of illusion, for once, is quite striking, particularly when one considers that narrative is not a strong feature of the *Christiad*. Further, it may be pointed out thus early that the attention paid to diction and to varieties of figurative language, to simplicity and coherence of structure, to verisimilitude and propriety in characters and action, like the attention to narration, is fully in keeping with the precepts in the second and third books of the *Ars poetica.*

Julius Caesar Scaliger ranked the *Ludus scacchiae* below the *Bombyx*, which he called in his arbitrary way "rex librorum Vidae."[18] A didactic poem in two books, Vida's *Bombyx* celebrates the silkworm and the industry of the Italians. Vida deals in detail with the nature of the silkworm, its breeding, care, and feeding. He discusses various aspects of sericulture—suggesting, for instance, how the leaves of the mulberry tree may be protected in case of rain, what new methods of curing the worm may be safely used, what is the proper period for breeding, and how the silk is to be spun. Firsthand information on all these matters was not difficult for Vida to obtain; in the early sixteenth century both Mantua and Cremona were relatively important centers of the silk industry.[19] Vida alleges, in a letter to Isabella d'Este, that his work is original—"materia fin hora non toccata da scriptore alcuno né Greco né Latino che io sappia"—and the similarities between his poem and two earlier ones, by Lodovico Lazarelli and Pierfrancesco Giustolo da Spoleto, may well be more coincidental than Cicchitelli allows.[20]

The poem is dedicated to Isabella d'Este, whom Vida admired for her profound culture, her excellent reputation, and her sincere devotion to Italy.[21] Isabella symbolized the idea of Italy as conceived by Vergil in the *Georgics.* At the head of Book I Vida called her

> Nympha Padi ... e regibus orta,
> Quae gentem pulchra auxisti pulcherrima prole
> Gonsagam.

And in the accompanying letter he was outspoken about his high respect for Isabella, "quella che fra tutte le gran

Signore di virtú, bontà et altri beni di corpo è la prima."
His sincerity can hardly be doubted when he calls her

> ...decus Italidum
> Quae vastas fessae Italiae miserata ruinas
> Haud dubias pulchra spes nobis prole tulisti.
>
> (II. 2-4)

But the patriotism of the poem is not heavy. The whole
is liberally sprinkled with brief and graceful stories—how
Serius, father of the Seriad nymphs, brought sericulture
to Italy; how Venus became interested in the silkworm.
Particularly charming is the story of Saturn's involvement
with the nymph Phyllira. Saturn is unable to make any
progress in his suit:

> Ah quoties precibus Nympham deus aspernantem
> Tentavit supplex, ingrataque munera verbis
> Addidit! ah quoties nimbosis montibus errans
> Matutinus iter tulit, et monstravit in agris
> Praesentes morbis herbas, usumque medendi!
>
> (I. 401-405)

Ah, how often the god made his advances on the reluctant
nymph, a suppliant beseeching her, and reinforced his words
with gifts—spurned! Ah, how often he would roam about
the cloud-topped mountains early in the morning and point
out in the fields the grasses withering and wasted, and the
way to heal them!

But finally with Venus' help, Saturn has his desire. As
a reward, he gives her "semina clausa," with which

> pulcherrima, texes,
> Diva, tibi insignes tunicas...   (I. 420-422)

Lines like the following, describing the god's possession
of the reluctant nymph, convey the quality of the tale:

> hinnitu Pelion altum
> Clausus equo deus implevit, votoque petitus

Vi tenuit frustra pugnantem, et multa recusantem.
                                                    (I. 416-418)

From his place of concealment inside the horse, the god
filled lofty Pelion with his whinnying, and, though she begged
him not to, he forcefully took the nymph, however reluctant.

Vida handles such stories skillfully enough, interlarding
them whimsically but with relevance and giving to the
whole difficult theme what Luzio and Renier appropriately
call "eleganza signorile."

Classical models are not obtrusive.[22] The diction and
imagery, while generally effective, are not as striking
as in the *Scacchia.* Vida apparently paid most attention
to structure, which conforms generally to the precepts
of the second book of the *Ars poetica.* The alternation
of minute observance and technical detail with the unob-
trusive tales or mythological references succeeds in main-
taining the reader's attention and moving the poem
fluently towards its goal.

On the whole, it may be said of both the *Ludus
scacchiae* and the *Bombyx* that they demonstrate poetic
ability. Vida shows command of Latin diction and metric:
in command of versification, he surpasses virtually all
contemporary or preceding neo-Latin poets. He shows
further ability to handle various themes and various tones,
to create absorbing narrative and original effects on the
one hand, and on the other to invest a subject not itself
fascinating with enough spirit so that the resultant poem
could be widely read and widely praised. These poems
are, in fact, primarily responsible for Leo's commission
to write a *Christiad* and for generous financial support
by both Leo and Clement VII. They are quite clearly
the concrete expression of the views on poetry elaborated
in the *Ars poetica*, which Vida composed around 1515.
The principles enunciated in the second and third books

of the *Ars poetica* were both drawn from his experience in writing the *Ludus* and the *Bombyx*, and themselves controlled the revisions made in both these poems a few years later.

The three books of the *Ars poetica* cover poetic education and exercises of youth, the disposition of material, and diction and style.[23] In the first book Vida makes clear that his special concern is teaching youth the prerequisites of heroic poetry; what he says is, however, applicable generally. He insists that the would-be poet must have a real feeling for poetry, and he emphasizes the necessity of choosing the best teacher. This teacher will start the boy on Vergilian tales of youth. As an aid, Vida rapidly summarizes the history of poetry—the greatness of Homer, close to the Muses; the supremacy of Vergil as artist; the restoration of elegant poetry by the Medici. Genius and hard work, he says, must go together; discipline, travel, wide knowledge, experience, and continual study of the classics are necessary, as is constant practice. When the would-be poet is ready for his great work, he should leave the noisy city. The first book closes with a severe attack on overbearing patrons and supercilious philistines and with a hymn on the origin and power of poetry.

The second book deals with *dispositio*. The poet, Vida says, should begin modestly and simply, *in medias res*, fostering suspense and building easily to a climax. Too much suspense is dangerous; hence the need for foreshadowing. The poet must re-examine his work constantly, revising under the control of a well-ordered plan. He should avoid digressions, indecorous characters, irrelevant erudition; in elaborating, using "little" images, or developing characters, he should always be decorous, avoid repetition, and be carefully selective. When inspiration comes, it should be welcomed. Imitate nature, Vida says:

study the traits of age and youth, war and peace, servants and kings. Do not discount the techniques of orators. Be tactful in delicate matters. Latin poets will teach decorum and show the novice how to exploit Greek *inventa*. Borrowing is good so long as one improves on the model— thus Italy became great in the arts. This leadership Italy must retain, for politically she is divided and humiliated.

Much of the second book consists of analysis of the practice of Homer and Vergil. Much of the third, dealing with *eloquentia*, consists of examples. For youth, Vida says, *eloquentia* is crucial. To avoid obscurity, one should take advantage of the riches of language; to avoid repetition, vary as nature does. Figures provide both vividness and variety; metaphor, the speech of the gods, belongs properly to poets. Figures like hyperbole, metonymy, apostrophe, irony, anaphora may be used, but without display or incongruity. Similes should be short and to the point. The style must always be appropriate to the genre, a skill which is best learned in the classics. Here, Vida urges the novice to study the style of one poet whom he particularly likes and to imitate it without, however, spurning others, even the second-rate. Imitation means borrowing both style and subject matter, adapting them to one's own purposes, infusing new meanings, and generally improving on the original. In his own practice, Vida says, he borrows openly. The touchstone of poetry is imitative harmony—that is, the evocation of nature and of particular characteristics of persons, places, incidents, atmosphere, feelings, by use of appropriate words, sounds, rhythms. Finally, after counseling careful revision, Vida emphasizes again that his precepts do not insure success unless Apollo is favorable. The poem concludes with the praises of Vergil.

Even a detailed summary cannot bring out the simultaneous richness and poverty of this treatise on poetry.

Though it purports to treat fully *carmen heroicum*, no definition of epic is ever given nor can one be inferred. Actually, there is very little theory to the poem; it abounds rather with praxis. The *Ars poetica* essentially emphasizes the value of the classics, especially Vergil, in forming poets to preserve Italy's cultural supremacy. It is an essay on poetry as Vida conceives Vergil might have written that essay. Effectively, it is an example of limited imitation of Vergil.

At the same time, the general structure, a process of connection or association by pseudological adverbs, allows Vida considerable latitude and reveals much about his attitude towards poetry. In the latter two books he insists that he can cover merely the formal aspects of his subject, that he cannot discourse fully on the nature of poetry because that nature is not wholly clear to him. Numerous passages on the mystery of poetry are too distinct and too intense to be conventional. These lines from Book I take fire from the mystery:

> Dulcis et alma quies, ac paucis nota voluptas!
> At nimium trux ille, ferisque e cautibus ortus,
> Qui sanctos, genus innocuum, populumque deorum
> Aut armis audet vates, aut laedere dictis.
>
> .   .   .   .
>
> Parcite, mortales, sacros vexare poetas.
> Ultores sperate deos, sub numine quorum
> Semper vita fuit vatum defensa piorum.
> Illi omnes sibi fortunas posuere volentes
> Sub pedibus; rerumque et opes, et sceptra superba
> Ingenti vincunt animo, ac mortalia rident.
> Non illi usquam scelerum mens conscia caecos
> Horrescit caeli crepitus, ignemve coruscum,
> Quum pater omnipotens praeruptas fulmine turres
> Ingeminans quatit, ac montes diverberat altos.
> Securi terrorum hilares ad sidera mentes

Arrexere, deumque agitant sine crimine vitam.
Dona deum Musae, vulgus, procul este, profanum.
                                    (496-499, 503-515)

Sweet and beloved peace, and joy known to but few! Surely
that man is excessively fierce, born amid the wild crags, who
would dare to trouble, either by force or by word, the holy
seers, a race particularly shielded, and the people of the
gods.... Mortals, refrain from vexing these sacred poets. Count
on the vengeance of the gods, under whose divinity the life
of holy seers has always been shielded. Willingly, they have
ground fortunes underfoot; in their great spirit, they overcome
the wealth of this world and the pride of scepters, and laugh
at mortal things. Their spirit has never been affrighted, as if
conscious of crimes, by the blind thunders of heaven or the
flashing lightning, when the almighty father, roaring, shakes
the steep towers with his thunderbolt and rumbles among
the mountain peaks. Safe from their terrors, they have
joyfully raised their minds to the stars, and they live the life
of the gods without harm. The Muses are gifts of the gods.
Keep far off, vulgar crowd!

In many passages, he reaffirms the need for genius—
auctor Apollo—and, more specifically, for spontaneity.
He stresses the necessity for consistent, thoughtful reading
and loving understanding of the classics:

                    ... adi monimenta priorum
Crebra oculis, animoque legens, et multa voluta.
                                    (III. 186-187)

And he emphasizes the importance of a deep love for
poetry:

                    ... mira operum dulcedine captus.
Musarum nequit avelli complexibus arctis.
                                    (I. 288-289)[24]

The whole method of instruction indicates clearly his
respect for Apollo. Vida is first of all a poet and only

incidentally a teacher. When he does teach, he does so by example rather than by precept. His precepts are generalized, but his examples and his praxis, exemplifying in the very process of stating, are quite specific. Here is a typical case:

> Nec vero hae sine lege datae, sine mente figurae,
> Sed facies sua pro meritis, habitusque, sonusque
> Cunctis, cuique suus, vocum discrimine certo.
> Ergo ubi jam nautae spumas salis aere ruentes   385
> Incubuere mari, videas spumare reductis
> Convulsum remis, rostrisque tridentibus aequor.
> Tunc longe sale saxa sonant, tunc et freta ventis
> Incipiunt agitata tumescere: litore fluctus
> Illidunt rauco, atque refracta remurmurat unda   390
> Ad scopulos, cumulo insequitur praeruptus aque mons.
> Nec mora, Trinacriam cernas procul intremere omnem
> Funditus, et montes concurrere montibus altos.
> Quum vero ex alto speculatus caerula Nereus
> Leniit in morem stagni, placidaeque paludis,   395
> Labitur uncta vadis abies, natat uncta carina.
>
> (II. 382-396)

These figures are not suggested without any law or purpose, for each of them, depending on its value, has its own peculiar form, its shape, its sound, according as the words are used. So when the sailors, driving the foam on before their prows, have pressed hard on the sea, you can see the deep all churned up and foaming under the vigorous oars and the speeding trident bows. Then, from far off, the rocks resound with the surf, and the sea begins to swell, higher and higher, under the force of the winds; the waves heave on the rough shoals, and the deep re-echoes as the waves recede, build up again, and suddenly a mountain of water bursts over them. Immediately you can see the whole of distant Sicily vibrating to its foundations and the high mountains being dashed against each other. But then Nereus, looking out over the deep from his throne, calms the sea and pacifies it so that it becomes like a gentle pond or a still pool. The well-tarred hull glides over the waters and goes on.

In this passage, after pointing out that a proper choice and order of words, and a proper "shape" of line, can evoke the one appropriate effect for one situation, he gives the example: *Ergo ... videas.* The example is taken from Vergil, almost in cento-style. This is, however, a strange way to make cento. Line 385 is drawn partly from *Aeneid* I. 35; 386 partly from I. 84, and the rest of 386-387 from VIII. 689-690. Lines 388-389 are developed from *Georgics* I. 356-357 and *Aeneid* V. 866; 390 partly from *Aeneid* X. 291; 391 partly from I. 105; 392 from III. 581-582; 393 mostly from VIII. 692; 395 mostly from VIII. 87-88; and 396 from a combination of VIII. 91 and IV. 398.

This passage is not only carefully devised; it is also highly effective. The pattern of sound is intricately worked out, changing slowly and unnoticeably from 385 to 388, and again from 392 to 396. The diction and much of the word order is Vergilian, but that fact hardly detracts from the value of the passage. What Vida has done here is to call attention to the marvelous way in which Vergil handled his storm and sea passages, by complex echoing of eight such passages. Thus, in illustrating his general statement, he also comments on the dazzling variety of imitative-harmony effects found in Vergil. For Vida this is an example of good poetry: it makes you *see* (*videas ... cernas*) by imitating nature closely, so closely

> Non tantum ut dici videantur, sed *fieri* res;
> Unde ipsis nomen Graji fecere poetis.
>
> (II. 380-381)

Vida realizes he can talk not about the nature of poetry but about its imitable characteristics. Apollo himself, we are told at the very beginning, dwells in a place difficult to reach (*inaccessae ... rupi*, I. 6). The same rock image opens the second and third books, and recurs frequently at the end of Book III: 533-538, 541, 550, 583. The poet himself is a *viator*, an image which itself turns up again and again throughout the poem: Book I. 313-314, 452-458; II. 5, 64-73, 150-155, 170-175; III. 64-69, 363, 533-541, 546-553. Toward the end Vida brings the two images together, speaking of himself as guide:

> Ipse viam tantum potui docuisse repertam
> Aonas ad montes, longeque ostendere Musas
> Plaudentes celsae choreas in vertice rupis,
> Quod me haud ire sinunt umquam fata invida, et usque
> Absterrentque, arcentque procul, nec summa jugi umquam
> Fas prensare manu fastigia.   (III. 533-538)

I myself could merely show the well-known route to the Muses' mountains, and point out from afar the Muses dancing on the summit of the high rock, since the fates in their envy will hardly allow me to climb there, and up to now they have kept me off and denied me the right to take hold of the topmost fastnesses of the ridge.

That he can show the way at all is due, of course, to Vergil, whom he saluted in the first book as *alumnus* of the Muses. Looking up to the heights, he exclaims:

> Virgilii ante omnes laeti *hic* super astra feremus
> Carminibus patriis laudes. decus unde Latinum,
> Unde mihi vires, animus mihi ducitur unde.
>
>   .   .   .   .
>
> Quodcumque hoc opis, atque artis, nostrique reperti
> Uni grata tibi debet praeclara juventus,
> Quam docui, et rupis sacrae super ardua duxi,
> Dum tua fida lego vestigia, te sequor unum,
> O decus Italiae, lux o clarissima vatum.
>   (III. 554-556, 581-585)

Here let us joyfully sing the praises of Vergil before all others in native strains. He is the source of the Latins' glory, he is the source of my strength, he is the source of my spirit.... Whatever there is of value or of art in my treatise, our outstanding youth owe it to you alone, these youths whom I have taught and led through difficulties to the sacred rock—but I have been successful only as long as I have followed faithfully your footsteps, O glory of Italy, O most brilliant light of poets.

The imagery comes full circle; following the trustworthy steps of Vergil, he can both lead towards the rock and perhaps attain it himself. The fervent closing lines sound like apotheosis:

> Te colimus: tibi serta damus, tibi tura, tibi aras,
> Et tibi rite sacrum semper dicemus honorem
> Carminibus memores. salve, sanctissime vates.
> Laudibus augeri tua gloria nil potis ultra,
> Et nostrae nil vocis eget. nos aspice praesens,
> Pectoribusque tuos castis infunde calores
> Adveniens, pater, atque animis te te insere nostris.
>
> (III. 586-592)

You do we worship; to you we present wreaths, frankincense, and altars; to you, as duty bids, in remembrance of your songs we will chant forever our sacred office. Hail, consecrated seer! Our praises can hardly increase your glory; you have no need for our song. Ever be with us and look upon us; come, father, and kindle our virgin hearts with your flames, and take your place in our souls.

The prayer for union almost makes Vergil out a Muse. But Vida is not fatuous. If Vergil is godlike, it is in a particular respect: *Verba deo similis* (III. 565). So far as the *Ars poetica* is a treatise, its central matter is the "altera cura arti obnoxia" (II. 15), those imitable and circumscribed qualities of a work of art

Unde solent laudem in primis optare poetae.

(II. 16)

To the Greeks, particularly Homer, goes the palm for "naturalness" and "inventiveness." So far as Vida's notions and his own compositions of the 1510s are concerned, Vergil is the artist par excellence who can teach elegance of diction, fluency in metrics, propriety and effectiveness in structure and characterization—in short, the external characteristics of poetry.

On the whole, Vida makes his points competently and clearly. His verse is appropriate, frequently elegant; at times, he manifests a striking virtuosity. The tone of the work is warm, sensible, moderate; for all the magisterial quality, Vida's manner is consistently genial. Frequently he speaks with tongue in cheek and even parodies his master. The treatment of hyperbole, metonymy, apostrophe, and irony is jovial. Saintsbury upbraided him bitterly for disapproving of images like

... crines magnae genitricis gramina dicat,

but the context of that line is humorous:

Haud magis imprudens mihi erit, et luminis expers
Qui puero ingentes habitus det ferre gigantis,
Quam siquis stabula alta, lares appellet equinos,
Aut crines magnae genitricis gramina dicat.

(III. 156-159)[25]

The one who clothes a mere boy with the huge garments of a giant will hardly seem more imprudent or senseless than one who would call a large stable an "equine temple" or speak of the grass as the "tresses of the mighty mother."

The *Ars poetica* enjoyed a great and bizarre success. It was known widely in Rome, as Giraldi, writing in 1516-1517, attests; in 1519 the Patres of Cremona wrote a formal letter to Vida asking permission to publish a

3.

special edition for use in Cremona's schools. The long-awaited 1527 edition was the first of many. The German humanist Eobanus Hessus had a special edition printed at Nuremberg for use in his course at Erfurt; Tartessio and others lectured on the poem at Cremona; soon other schools and other humanists were virtually sitting at Vida's feet.[26]

The success of the *Ars poetica* was Vida's undoing. It must be remembered that the poem was written around 1515, that it deals not with theory but with *dispositio* and *eloquentia*, that it does not attempt to define epic, that it was ostensibly written for schoolboys. But when the work was published in 1527, the battle over Aristotle's *Poetics* was already beginning, and when Vida's poem gained fullest currency in subsequent decades, literary theory was a far hotter subject for debate than it had been in the 1510s. As Toffanin pointed out, the *Ars poetica* was the first and last work of its kind. It looked backward to the Vergilian humanism of the *Quattrocento*; it was the first systematic attempt to treat the characteristics of Vergilian poetry; but it was out of date as theory by the time the first edition appeared. The adulation of aspiring neohumanists was very much beside the point.

Scaliger's remarks in the 1550s indicate the confusion: he called the *Poetic* of Vida superior to both Horace's and Aristotle's. But Vida's friend in the Rome of the 1510s, Pietro Bembo, knew better; reading Vida's *Ars* in 1529, he found it a pleasing poem which had nothing to do with theory.[27] It was part of that tradition beginning with Salutati and the pedagogues like Barzizza, Vittorino, and Guarino Veronese on the one hand, and with Sicco Polenton and Angelo Decembrio on the other. The tradition had done its work, as Bembo had taken pains to point out in the 1510s; it was now part of history.

Nonetheless, Vida's notes on his experience with the *Scacchia* and *Bombyx* continued to be treated as systematic theory. The neoclassicists, with translations like Pitt's heroic couplets and with pompous commentaries like Klotz's and Oudin's, certified Vida's neoclassicism. The literary historians compounded the error by yoking the poem to impossible contexts. Saintsbury, typical of most, roundly condemned Vida for Maronolatry and for "words, words, words," and confusedly equated Vida's works with the "theory," exalting him into the apostle of Vergilian imitation and suggesting that Vida and his contemporaries really believed the rhetorical excess they glorified.[28]

Vida's devotion to Vergil is clearly strong and unswerving; in diction, structure, narration, characterization, fantasy, and digression, his *Scacchia* and *Bombyx* proceed largely as the *Ars poetica* says they should. But not the *Christiad*; the Vergilianism there is of a kind Saintsbury could not recognize, nor the eighteenth century either. Further, Vida's Maronolatry must be viewed in its proper context—that is, in the tradition of Decembrio's *Politia Literaria*, Poliziano's *Sylvae*, and Pontano's *Actius*. Throughout the *Quattrocento* the predominance of Vergil in not only Latin but virtually all poetic expression is widely accepted. Neither Poliziano nor Pontano could be called "servile imitators," but both pay amazing tribute to the elegance of Vergil's rhetoric. It seems indeed clear that much of the Maronolatry is a convention, that these men attach far less importance than the historians do to rhetorical fluency in itself, that passages like the conclusion of Poliziano's *Manto* or of Vida's *Ars Poetica* are part of a widely understood alphabet. The alphabet was outdated in Scaliger's time, but he typically continued to use it. No wonder the confusion.

Vida's own education at Cremona and Mantua lay

behind much of what he said in the *Ars poetica*. In the
first book, particularly, the emphasis is on the practice
developed by Guarino Veronese and Vittorino; that book
is indebted quite as much to educators like Matteo Palmieri as to Horace and Quintilian. Emphasizing the rhetorical tradition, Vida looks backwards. Even though the
training instilled by the *Quattrocento* humanists was not
easily brushed aside, their notions and the implications
of their entire method—that poetry might be learned
mainly from models, that Latin poetry and Greek are
the only fit exercises for learned men—these were shortly
to be subjected to severe question, and gradually cast
aside.

The assumption that Vida's dicta in the *Ars poetica*
controlled his composition in the *Christiad* has been made
by virtually every critic. Such a notion is aprioristic and,
as I mean to show in this study, wholly mistaken. It
is true to say that the *Christiad* is a recast *Aeneid*. But
it is untrue to say, "The *Christiad* is the *Ars poetica* put
into practice."[29] The inability or the unwillingness to
make the important distinction has thrown out of focus
much critical study not only of the *Christiad* but of the
Ars poetica itself. The verse treatise is only hesitantly
and spasmodically about epic. Book I is about education,
Book II about certain compositional elements relevant
to long hexameter narratives, Book III about rhetoric
applicable to all forms of poetry. What carries over into
the *Christiad* is only the general feeling about the superiority of Vergil; the discussion of constituent elements
in long narrative rarely informs Vida's actual composition.
In short, the *Ars poetica* is a genial and facile running
commentary on Vida's early experiences with hexameter
verse, early understanding of the nature of Latin poetry
and of the exigencies of Latin narrative, and the apparent
greatness of Vergil. On the other hand, the *Christiad*,

which occupied Vida during the final years of the 1510s and throughout the 1520s, shows a mature and deepened understanding of Vergil and of epic.

More than the *Poetica*, the *Bombyx* and *Scacchia* brought Vida into the public eye at Rome. Recognition had been growing; he was well known to Bembo and Sadoleto, the secretaries of Leo X, and to other important figures like Castiglione, Calcagnini, and Egidio of Viterbo. The fame of the two works, Giraldi tells us, spread rapidly; the eventual result was a formal commission from Leo X to write the *Christiad*. Tartessio told the story as he knew it:

Leo X. Pont. Max. summa auctoritate, summo judicio, quum ad se a Lascare... allatum M. Hieronymi carmen quo ludicrum proelium describitur, accurate lectitasset, hominis ingenio, et scribendi tum facultate, tum dignitate allectus, persancte affirmavit hunc illum esse quem summis votis diu expetivisset, cuius sublimi, et eleganti stylo Christi res gestae mirae, et insignes a nonnullis jam tentatae, sed parum luculenter expressae, carmine celebrari possent; easque ut versibus attingeret, atque inchoaret, hortatu suo perfecit.[30]

The great and wise Pope Leo X, given by Lascaris Vida's poem narrating the mock battle, read it carefully and was very pleased by the author's talent, and by the facility and appropriateness of his style. He solemnly affirmed that this was the man whom he had prayed for so long, whose sublime and elegant style would be adequate for a poem celebrating the marvelous deeds of Christ—a work often undertaken but with little success. By his encouragement and help, Vida set himself to the project and began his poem.

The closeness of Vida's friendship with Giberti makes it likely that the young secretary of Giuliano de' Medici arranged with Lascaris, secretary to Leo X, for an audience.

Tartessio's observation that Rome had been waiting for Vida is not wholly hyperbolic; as Toffanin indicates, a great Christian epic was desired as the culmination of humanism: "la romanitas leonina diventa mistica." The ideal of the Christian Cicero and the Christian Vergil had not yet been fulfilled; the concurrent strivings of Bembo to clarify the ideals in theory, and of Bembo and Sadoleto to fulfill the first, Sannazaro and Vida the second, were among the central literary facts of Leo's era. Coincident was the growing need for reform, recognized but deferred; one of the few practical results of the Lateran Council was the establishment of the Oratory of Divine Love, which included two of Vida's closest friends and fellow humanists, Giberti and Sadoleto. For Leo, a central problem of the Lutheran heresy was the negation of Rome; thus an important desideratum in Vida's project was a reaffirmation of Rome. The story that, exulting in his expectations, Leo cried out,

> Cedite Romani scriptores, cedite Graji!
> Nescio quid maius nascitur *Aeneide!*

may well be apocryphal, but the spirit of it is true. "Tutta Roma attendeva la *Cristiade*," says Toffanin succinctly —as if by such performances, by the rededication to "latinità cuore del mondo," the German discontent might be pacified.[31]

Vida began work on the *Christiad* around 1518. He resided mainly at the priory of St. Sylvester in Frascati, amid the Tusculan vistas which had delighted Cicero.[32] When he stayed away from Rome for long periods, his friends came to see him and to hear passages from the epic—not only Giberti, Castiglione, and Sadoleto, but also Tebaldeo, Molza, and Paolo Giovio, whom the Medicis considered the new Livy. Vida's contemporary Sannazaro had been composing his own epic, *De partu virginis,* since 1506; circulating in parts, that poem began to appear to many as a new *Fourth Bucolic,* not a new *Aeneid.*[33] For various reasons, furthermore, it had fallen into official disfavor. But Leo, publicly disaffected with Sannazaro, did not live to see either poem completed. His cousin Giuliano, as Clement VII, reaffirmed interest in Vida's epic.[34] By 1530 enough of the *Christiad* was ready for public readings at Bologna before Pope and Emperor. The completed manuscript was delivered to Clement in 1532; the first edition appeared at Cremona in 1535.

That the poem was eagerly awaited is clear from numerous contemporary references to it.[35] The years of expectancy had brought fame to the poet, and the publication of the poem itself increased that fame. Multiple editions appeared shortly after the first; within a decade the poem was being used as a text for courses theological and literary not only in Italian schools but even in Germany. Botta's massive commentary, the best of its kind, was not the only one. The inevitably fulsome praises of humanists all over Europe were more fulsome than ever. Melanchthon's son-in-law, Sabinus, went out of his way to praise Vida, though many like Lutheran Eobanus Hessus confined their praises to the poet's nonreligious work; Lotichius wrote typically:

> Caesaris est vates Maro: Vida sed esse Jehovae
> Et Christi vates maluit esse sui.

Erasmus's garrulous correspondent, Viglius Zuichemus, while he spread gossip about Vida's opportunism, had to admit the greatness of his reputation. From Padua he wrote, "Vida ... ob Christeida Pontifici dicata episcopatu donatus est. Huius ac Fracastorii cuiusdam carmina primam laudem apud Italos obtinent."[36]

While the fame of the *Christiad* is not open to question, the accuracy of this gossip is. Nothing in Vida's life justifies this charge; in the present instance, the charge, if anything, should have been obtuseness, for the diocese Vida was "donated" was poor, badly managed, and seething with political and theological volcanoes. At any rate, on February 7, 1533, he was consecrated Bishop of the diocese of Alba in Lombardy.[37]

As Novati suggests, Vida was at last able to break "i legami dorati d'una servitú che gli si è fatta incresciosa .... Eccolo vescovo ... e libero."[38] Even before leaving Rome in 1535 he sounded new notes: the adaptable views of his younger years had changed radically. His ode to Clement VII, while cheering the beset Pontiff, called sharply for a less political, more spiritual view of the Church's mission. His activity upon his arrival in Alba and during the next few years has little to suggest the poet laureate. In the first of his *Hymni de rebus divinis* he speaks of himself as the poet who did what others had tried; but "novo nunc ore canendum."[39] His 1540 letter to Botta indicates that he has done with the Muses and that, in a sense, he did not regard his great epic as a poetic flight. An earlier letter to Bembo is severe in its distinction between the frivolities of that newly made Cardinal's earlier life and the serious conversion reported of him. Later documents consistently view Leo's commission as a burden; indeed, the autobiographical excursion in the *Republic* makes clear that the *Christiad* had spoiled him for poetry:

poetae quae canunt, scribuntve, ea suapte sponte, atque animi libera quadam oblectatione faciunt. ego vero ista [scil. *Christiad* and *Hymns*], qualiacumque, jussus, ne dicam coactus, scripsi: rectiusque fere Leonis Decimi poemata, quam mea dici possunt. Tandem, restincto in me calore illo....

Poets sing and write spontaneously and with a kind of joyful liberation of spirit. But I wrote these poems actually by commission, not to say by coercion; and they may almost be more accurately called the works of Leo X rather than my own. Finally, when that fire had been extinguished in me ....

No one who is not completely his own master and completely free of external pressure—"nullius obnoxius imperio"—can be considered worthy of the name of poet.[40]

For the greater part of Vida's tenure as bishop, political problems plagued him. Lombardy was ravaged by wars between French and Spaniards, wars which inflicted famine, disease, and death on a region not particularly flourishing anyway. At the death of Francesco Sforza, November, 1535, Francis I and Charles V both laid claim to the duchy of Milan. Francis's attack in the spring of 1536 won the provinces of Savoy and Piedmont; a counterattack gave Alba to the Spaniards. In July, 1537, it fell again to the French, only to be reconquered in September by the Spaniards. The truce of November left Alba in Spanish hands, though the rest of Piedmont was in French control. When famine spread, the French viceroy, Guillaume du Bellay, left Alba out of his efforts to alleviate the misery. Vida's letters to Francis brought no result, and only his provident campaign to plant a large crop at his own expense forestalled catastrophe.[41] Vida gained some further aid in ensuing years by constant personal intercession with the viceroy, but the murder of two French ambassadors revived the fighting in July, 1542. When the French attacked Alba, the aging bishop led the spirited defense which saved the city. This action destroyed Vida's diplomacy. Reconciliation no longer possible, Vida returned to Cremona.[42]

The political situation seriously aggravated the problems of the Lutheran heresy, problems more serious

than he had suspected. During the earlier years, at Rome
and Frascati, he had tried to win some French favor; for
example, even at the cost of offending some friends, he
had, in 1525, altered the dedication of his *Ars poetica* in
favor of the Dauphin. It seems clear also that, at the time,
he was not sharply aware of the implications of Luther's
heresy, though it is highly questionable that he was indifferent.[43] In the altercations with the French, he singled
out Francis's support of the heretics in contrast to the
professedly religious concerns of Charles V, characterizing
the French monarch's motive as "amor sceleratus habendi."

Clearly the poet of the *Christiad* did not perceive
with the acuteness of, say, Dante the relationship between
his epic subject and the problems besetting the Church.
But personally he maintained a purity of life and doctrine
unusual in his times; as Novati suggests, the ideal of the
reformed clergy could have been found in the younger
Vida.[44] What the Sack of Rome meant to him personally
may well be suggested by passages such as that in his
ode to Clement VII. The hope is expressed that God
will mitigate His severity,

> Sed ante mens est cuique latentibus
> Purganda morbis. sunt quoque luridi
>   Mores retractandi, nec ultra
>   Progrediendum iter institutum.   (53-56)

But first each one must purge his spirit of hidden vices.
Furthermore, there are evil practices which must be reversed;
nor can we pursue any further the road we are now on.

To Charles V Vida wrote a hymn some years later—
Jesu Christo Opt. Max., de Carolo V. imperatore—in
which the emperor's valor is considered less important
than the excellence of his motives; he is indeed "decus ...,

verae gloria militiae"; but most crucially, his mission is to reunite the Church:

> Jam jam unum duce te reget unus pastor ovile.
> Disjectas cogi te duce oportet oves.
>
> (VII. 63-64)

Vida's own zeal could be a little disconcerting, as he himself recognized. In a long letter written around 1540 to Pope Paul III he outlined his views on the urgent necessity for internal reform. Luther he calls a "portentum teterrimum," and his movement "amentia" and "pestis illa." They will not rest until they have utterly destroyed the Christian world. The strongest measures are necessary, including the "secular arm," against such a diabolic evil: "non enim ... errore peccant, sed de industria, animis volentibus, cum sint ingenio malo et pravo." If his recommendations seem too severe, he is forced to them: "Momordit me atque impulsit reipublicae charitas et iustus ... dolor."[45]

Paramount was internal reform. In his letter to Paul III as in many other letters Vida states bluntly that it is high time the Bishops returned to their dioceses and their appointed duties. He was called to the Council of Trent "specialiter ob probitatem."[46] He attended every session of the council, however briefly, but he was impatient with the convolutions of theological debate and with the obvious political intrigues which dictated so many of the council's actions. Disappointed at the meager results of the first session, he walked out on it and addressed a lengthy explanation to the Papal Legates, Reginald Pole, Marcello Cervini, and Gianmaria Del Monte.[47] Sharply, he pointed out that too much time was being wasted, that nothing new was being said, that the points of debate were mainly legalistic and trivial since Pope and Curia possessed broad powers already. With impassioned courage, he insisted on the crucial fact, the duty of the clergy:

Sunt enim pastores populorum, nec eos aequum est tam diu nulla causa abesse a gregibus suis; cumque iidem Ecclesiarum sponsi dicantur, haud eos fas est a suis sponsis secubare. Cuius rei utinam iam multos annos habita fuisset a nostris ratio, ut, inquam, pontifices, lectissimi viri, in suis dioecesibus domicilium haberent; nunc proculdubio haud tantum laboraremus.

For they are the pastors of the people; it is not right that they should be absent from their flocks so much without reason. And since they are called spouses of their churches, it is hardly just that they live apart from their spouses. If only our colleagues had held this view these many years past that bishops, presumably the most excellent men, should live in their dioceses! Doubtless, we would hardly have so much trouble now.

Such forthrightness was not yet respectable; Vida knew well that it would cut him off from future honors. But, as Novati has pointed out, his fierce integrity would hardly permit him to compete for a more comfortable diocese or the red hat. He did not amass riches; indeed, he gave away what he had. He won the respect of both humanist popes like Leo, Clement, and Paul III and of the unimpeachable St. Pius V and the idealistic young Cardinal Carlo Borromeo.[48] In matters touching the Church, he stood closest not to his fellow poet Marcantonio Flaminio or his fellow Ciceronian Jacopo Sadoleto, but to the earnest cleric and reformer, Gianmatteo Giberti.

The definitive edition of Vida's collected poems appeared in 1550, published by Girolamo Muzio and Antonio Lucheta of Cremona, under the personal supervision of the author.[49] The first volume contained the *Christiad* and *Hymni de rebus divinis*; the second contained most of the 1527 edition, the elegy on the death of his parents, the ode to Clement, and a few other lyrics and epigrams.

The elegy, *Gelelmi Vidae et Leonae Oscasalae: Parentum manibus*, is one of his finest lyrics. His subject is himself, but he treats it in an oblique manner: the recollections of childhood, the bond with his parents, his plans for them—ripe for fulfillment when old age and sickness took them away. Though the poem is intimate, even here the light is focused off-center. Suggestions of distance temper the warm sentiment and provide perspective. A feeling for age recalls the "Socraticam pacem" of the ode to Giberti, written not long before at Frascati.[50]

The epigram *Roma discedens*, similarly personal, has an unusual roughness of tone. The harsh third line—

Nec jam egeam addictus nulli, mihi id est satis abs te.

—is balanced by the honest recognition in the fifth, and the ambiguous declaration of independence in the sixth:

Plusque meis oculis absens te semper amabo,
    Et procul, ut colimus numina sancta, colam.

The epigram *Telluri* allows momentary intimacy and shows his deep compassion for his people. It is almost indecorous, allowing a subject so simple—"Has tibi, terra, fabas ... Dat Vida"—to bear such strong feeling.[51] But the ode *Paci*, contemporary with it, while conveying similarly circumscribed compassion, attains universality.

Less varied, less interesting, nonetheless powerful and important are the Hymns.[52] Their intent is clearly devotional and apologetic. Many are doctrinal, supplementing somewhat the *Christiad*—II, III, IV, addressed to individual members of the Trinity; VI, *In Eucharistian*; V and VIII, on the Crucifixion; IX, to the Virgin; XV and XVI, to the Apostles John and Andrew; XI, *Ex*

Cantico Moysis. These present feelings and ideas relevant
to the material but not to the form of the epic poem.
Their imagery may inevitably recall the epic, but their
main interest lies in the light they shed on artistic motives
of selection and arrangement. Some are intolerably long
—II, *Deo*, runs to 814 hexameters—but their shape is
controlled not by any dramatic or epic view, but by the
development and interplay of particular theological or
religious ideas.

Other hymns are tributes to saints. Hymn XXXI,
Divo Thomae Aquinati, is remarkable for its subtly
worked theme of *pietas docta*, achieved less by statement
that by collocation of various aspects of the Saint's career.
Hymn XXVII, to Augustine, disappoints by never rising
above its occasional nature. In many, contemporary
subjects receive due attention—the Council of Trent is
almost embarrassingly stressed in IV, *Spiritui Sancto.*

References to Rome occur frequently, suggesting perhaps a running theme. This Rome is not, however, the
idealized Rome of the earlier years. The harsh realities
—from the Sack of Rome to the Council of Trent—forced
on Vida a more durable but less tangible feeling for that
city. He is always orthodox, solid, substantial, in the
hymns; there are clearly defined boundaries of spiritual
and temporal powers. The enthusiasm is gone, along with
the easy adherence to the Medici line; if the Latinity
remains apparently the same, the dreams of the humanist
have evaporated. Vida's verse is workmanlike and ef-
ficient, often too much so; many lines sound too facile
to have been chiseled with the calm patience and struggling control which makes some of the earlier works
massive in their classical purity. What power the best
of the hymns have—such as the excellent ones to the
Virgin and to the Eucharist—is virtually dissipated by
the ease with which, in others, he seems to pile on hex-

ameters. His mastery of Latin verse has become too complete for his own good.

Of Vida's abundant prose, the best known is *De reipublicae dignitate*, two long dialogues on political philosophy, written in the mid-1540s.[53] The republic in question is a qualified city of God, the Christian state. Vida suggests the breadth of his undertaking when he reviews past thought and points out that the discussion must include all nations and peoples who know Christ or will know Him in the future. The focus of the state will be Christ, "ipsa justitia," and its organization, Vida argues, must be based both on the principles of the ancients and on the Christian development of these. Its purpose will be to foster the happiness and well-being of men: "bene et beate vivendi."

Vida's opponent, Marcantonio Flaminio, points out the dangers of highly organized society. He favors a qualified natural state, with no interference from government and without emphasis on civilization and progress. A decent pastoral life is his goal: "Ubi paucitas, ibi beatitas." This he pursues at length in the first book, only to have it demolished by Vida's historical and logical arguments for a state based on the will of the people and safeguarded against the alleged dangers of tyranny. Praising nature, Vida avers, "Natura hominem inchoavit; doctrina [that is, leges] deinde perficit, et absolvit." His rationalism seems thoroughgoing: "Lex est recta ratio." The state he identifies with the will of the people, invoking the authority of Aristotle and of Cicero's Scipio Africanus. For Flaminio's good man, Vida substitutes the man of enormous potential for good and evil: "Homine bono nihil melius, malo autem nihil pejus esse posse."[54] The whole work closes with Vida's fervent peroration on the good life and the virtues of the good society, emphasizing both progress and the elevation of man and the word and playing down material advantages in favor of the Christian ideal of charity.

In March, 1549, Vida was called upon by his native city to defend it in a continuing quarrel with Pavia. The occasion was bizarre: the subject of debate was the precedence of delegates in public functions at Milan. But Vida rose to it, and above it, composing the *Orationes tres*.[55] The appeal of these vigorous Ciceronian invectives is limited by the subject matter. Nonetheless, they provide interesting details of Cremonese history and of Vida's own life; the headlong style reaches heights in the exultant description of the artistic, literary, and scientific achievements of Cremona, and in the details of Cremona's martial vigor or of its arrangements for charities and the welfare of the poor.[56]

Vida's final large prose work, the *Constitutiones synodales* (1562), is written in simple Latin, so that even the least learned clerics would understand:

De industria autem stylo, et dicendi genere admodum familiari, humilique, et interdum prope vulgari eas confecimus, ut facile planeque ab omnibus tam doctis, quam indoctis percipi possint.[57]

So much of this work deals with intellectual incapacity, that one wonders whether the remark is as snobbish as it seems. The scope is broad, taking full account of matters spiritual, liturgical, civil, judicial, and economic in the diocese of Alba, analyzing and reorganizing, anticipating virtually all eventualities, and establishing clear limits and clear goals. Gentle firmness, severe kindness, an abiding concern for his priests and people all come through in the disconcerting logic of the work. The humanist speaks in the linking of ignorance and moral turpitude; the whole, as Osimo has pointed out, shows the "piissimo e zelantissimo sacerdote," and the "vescovo accorto e animoso."[58]

On the whole, Vida's prose is both more and less impressive than the critics suggest. Cicchitelli's argument on behalf of the *Republic* assumes that Vida intended Flaminio to win and that the work anticipates Rousseau as well as Montaigne; it is impossible to agree.[59] The second book quite thoroughly demolishes the first. At that, the arguments on both sides are thin. The Ciceronian style, sometimes pleasant, becomes monotonous. Finally, the whole work is incomplete and only partly relevant to the questions it raises. Vida's deliberate avoidance of theological issues seems to have taken the reality out of the work.

The style of the *Orationes* is more successful. In them, the invective is sharp but always controlled, recalling not the *Quattrocento* invectives of Poggio and Valla, but the more carefully forged invectives of Petrarch and Cicero. The vigorous and precipitate style gains from subtle understatement and restraint. Contemporaries of Vida, trying to outdo the panegyrics of the humanist poets, spoke of these as new Verrines which rivaled Cicero's; one, wilder than the rest, seized upon the versatility of style displayed in Vida's prose and lauded him as equal to Cicero and Vergil together.[60] But fortunately, when Borromeo requested Vida, in 1564, to write a short oration for the opening of the Synod of Milan, what he had in mind was the simple and honest style of the *Constitutiones*. This final oration was not published in Vida's time, but it should have been; it is brief and admirably eloquent.[61]

The style of Vida's letters varies considerably, from the barely tolerable Italian of his administrative notes, to the elevated Latin of his 1545 letter.[62] In this remarkable document elegance is counterpoised with the sharp-

4.

ness and unmitigated honesty of his suggestions and criticisms. Less elegant but more striking is a letter in Italian, written apparently in white heat, to Fernando Gonzaga. Vida valued the Gonzagas' friendship highly, as many of his letters show, but when in 1552 the report reached him that Alba was to be assaulted again, by Fernando's army, he wrote thus in part:[63]

Come Vescovo d'Alba, le protesto in nome di Dio, se va alla suddetta impresa ..., non avrà onore .... Se potessi sperare, che l'asprezza del tempo permettesse all'età mia già fiacca e precipitata, di potermi reggere, e durare in cammino, non mi terrebbe alcun rispetto, che io non venissi alle mura d'Alba ..., non già per conservare quelli pochi stracci e reliquie assegnate al viver mio, quali volentieri con tutto 'l Vescovado lascerei per la salute di qualsivoglia minimo di quelli cittadini, tutti miei figliuoli cari ..., ma per morire insieme con essi, venendo 'l caso, perché lo spirito mio potesse ire in compagnia di quelle anime tribolate, e maltrattate avanti il tribunal di Dio, e chiedere vendetta alla divina giustizia del sangue innocente contra chi l'avesse sparso con mano, con consiglio, e con commissioni.

As Bishop of Alba, I assert in the name of God, if you carry out this undertaking, you will not have honor .... If I could hope that the harshness of the season would allow me, in the weakness of old age, to make the journey, nothing could prevent me from coming to the walls of Alba ... not, indeed, to safeguard those miserable rags and tatters consigned to my livelihood—which I would willingly surrender, along with my entire bishopric, for the safety of the least of these citizens, all my dear children..., but rather to die together with them, if such should be the outcome, so that my soul might go in the company of these tormented and persecuted souls before the throne of God and there seek from Divine Justice vengeance for the shedding of innocent blood, vengeance on all who shed it, whether personally, by counsel, or by commands.

Gonzaga's reply, which shortly reached Vida, perfunctorily professed innocence, and was suitably courteous and humble. But the aging prelate's fiery words had had their effect; the siege was virtually bloodless, looting was strictly forbidden, and the long and fruitful friendship between Vida and the Gonzaga family continued.

One of Vida's last acts was to acquire Giulio Campi's "Martirio di San Lorenzo" for the Cathedral at Alba. He had commissioned the painting some years before; in the heat of July, 1566, he went to Cremona, to personally oversee its completion. Shortly after he returned to his diocese with the painting, he died, on September 27, 1566. He was buried in the Cathedral Church at Alba, near the epistle side of the altar. The epitaph was simple and austere: "Hic situs est M. Hieronymus Vida Cremon. Albae Episcopus." In 1870, his bones were transferred to a marble tomb at the entrance to the sanctuary which bears this elaborate inscription:[64]

M. Hieron. Vidae
Cremonensis
Ab anno MDXXXIII ad MDLXVI Alb. episc.
Christiano carmine Virgilii famam
Aemulati
Reliquiae olim ad laevam arae max.
Depositae
Ne tanto viro debitus honos
Plane deficeret
instaurato templo
Hoc monumento conditae sunt
Anno MDCCCLXX

CHAPTER TWO

VIDA'S *ARS POETICA* AND

VERGILIAN HUMANISM

JULIUS CAESAR SCALIGER credits Vida's *Ars poetica* with organization and thoroughness superior to Horace's.[1] But the praise is faint; indeed, Vida's major weakness is his lack of thoroughness. The *Ars poetica* discusses fully neither poetry nor the poet, does not define epic or treat it comprehensively, subordinates such matters as characterization to the passion for decorum, and ignores many problems in Vergilian epic. It is a very commonplace piece of work, drawn from common sources.[2]

The most important source is Quintilian's *Institutiones oratoriae*. For Book I, Plutarch is of some importance, as are Vergerio's *De ingenuis moribus*, the *De educatione liberorum* of Piccolomini and that of Vegio, and Matteo Palmieri's *Vita civile*.[3] Any attempt to place the *Ars poetica* in its proper context and to assess both what it says and what, relative to the *Christiad*, it omits to say, must deal with the thought and practice of the fifteenth century.

In the *Ars poetica*, Vida presents his Vergil as almost a muse. Without Vergil, there would have been neither *Christiad* nor *Ars poetica*. If Quintilian, Cicero, Horace, and the humanists supplied the general framework and many of the particular precepts and turns of phrase, Vergil's example supplied the controlling attitude and the controlling ideas. Vida testified to this in his letter to the senate of Cremona:

Hujus ego quoties, Patres optimi, divinum Poema lego, videtur mihi vir ille ... de ea ipsa Arte praecepta tradere voluisse, ut ostenderet, quantum Graecis ipsis, a quibus hanc Disciplinam accepimus, defuisset, quodve de hac Arte est, quod de ceteris omnibus dici posset, nostros videlicet quae ab aliis accepere ea semper meliora reddidisse. (Cominiana ed. II, v.)

Whenever I read his divine poem, Fathers, it seems to me that this excellent man ... wished to hand down precepts on the Art itself, to demonstrate how incapable were the Greeks themselves—from whom we have received this Discipline—and how in regard to this art as to all others, it can well be said that our poets have always improved what they took over from others.

Thus the prescription that the poet begin with a small work and gradually prepare for a greater is based on the practice of Vergil;[4] the suggestion about making a prose sketch first comes partly from Donatus:

Aeneida prosa prius oratione formatam digestamque in XII libros particulatim componere instituit ... ac ne quid impetum moraretur, quaedam inperfecta transmisit, alia levissimis versibus veluti fulsit, quae per iocum pro tibicinibus interponi aiebat ad sustinendum opus, donec solidae columnae advenirent.[5]

His practice was to work out the *Aeneid* first in prose, and to arrange the parts of it into twelve books.... And in order not to lose his momentum, he left some things incomplete, others he propped up, as he jokingly put it, with light verses to sustain the work, while he continued revising, until the solid pillars were ready.

Books II and III are mostly Vida's reading of Vergil's practice, a reading which became for many *the* reading and which exerted curious and widespread influence.[6]

The commonplaces of the *Ars poetica* may be conveniently divided into two categories, humanism and Vergil.[7] Vida the humanist seems most concerned with per-

fection of the form. Poetry does not have to say a great
deal; it gives pleasure by technical excellence, by propriety
and decorum, by virtuosity of diction and style, by proper
use of figures, and by capturing in imitative harmony the
qualities of external nature and of human nature. An epic
is a long narrative, elevated in style, featuring only
heroes—low characters, like Thersites but not Drances,
are inadmissible. To be successful, epic must be conducted
with mastery of suspense, plot development, characterization, pleasing variety, and style. Since these qualities
are found at their best in the classics, poets will imitate
the classics.

Vida's Vergil is of course the Prince of Poets, but he
is also the best of men—Vida's suggestions in Book I on
discipline and moral safeguards are clearly based on the
legendary as well as the literary Vergil. As poet, Vergil is
great because of Apollo's favor: he could turn amorphous
matter into high art. Homer is slighted, thus, because he
is repetitious, garrulous, disorganized, and blind to the
real possibilities of verse. Vergil's verse is fluid, proper,
"harmonious." As both poet and man, he is tender and
humane, noble and elevated; he understands men—and
women too. And he is a patriotic Roman, who perceived
and exalted the eminent destiny of Rome.

In its main lines, this Vergilian humanism developed
from the humanistic currents of the fourteenth and
fifteenth centuries, i.e., the political views of Dante and
Petrarch, the notion of *humanitas*, the reconciliation of
Christian material with pagan forms through, for instance,
allegory and elegance, and the practice of Christian epic
poetry. To these matters we now turn.

With some modifications, Vida's Vergilian humanism
is founded on the idea and ideal of the rebirth of antiquity. Composed originally of patriotic, moral, and rhe-

torical elements, that idea becomes in Vida a quest for cultural superiority—a quest made poignant by the parlous state of Italian politics in the early sixteenth century. The boast of Ciriaco of Ancona, "I go to awaken the dead," is almost a prayer for Vida, a prayer with something of resignation in it: how radically the "rebirth dream" had changed is made bitterly clear in Erasmus' sadly scornful *Ciceronianus*, published the year after Vida's *Ars poetica*.

For Dante and Petrarch, hope in the Holy Roman Empire was still possible. In them existed in a relatively pure form the "patriotic motive of the classical revival in Italy." Cicero's *humanitas* was for Dante a thrilling ideal, and Vergil became his symbol of perfected humanity. His feeling for classical antiquity demanded a rebirth, a re-establishment of the temporal order; the Vergil of the *Comedy* is his personal illustration of fully developed humanity and of the contribution such perfection could make to religious rebirth. "Quel savio gentil, che tutto seppe…, mar di tutto 'l senno" is the model on whom Dante, in the poem, perfects his own humanity. For Dante, as for the Renaissance as a whole, the *Aeneid* has as one end "to fashion a gentleman or noble person in vertuous and gentle discipline."[8]

Dante, however, had comparatively little of what became the Renaissance enthusiasm for Latinity. The patriotism of Petrarch, hardly less ardent than Dante's, was modified by his Latinity. In him, Dante's *bello stile* becomes style in the strict sense; the ecstatic praise of Cicero's style is typical: "Sola me verborum dulcedo quaedam et sonoritas detinebat, ut quidquid aliud vel legerem vel audirem, raucum mihi longeque dissonum videretur." Admitting and even insisting on his own practice of imitation and allusion—virtually second nature, as he declares in an *Invectiva*—he draws the line only at clichés.[9]

His generally dull epic, *Africa*, rises to high lyrical pitch
when Petrarch contemplates Rome, its greatness, its fate.[10]
The choice of Scipio Africanus as hero, and the theme
of conflict between *virtus Romana* and Carthaginian
treachery, derived from Livy and *Aeneid* IV, bear further
witness. As classicizer, he is not reluctant to name his
models—Vergil, Lucan, and Statius; but though in subject
and intent the poem aspires to Vergil, it owes most to
Lucan.[11] Thus Dante's broad and free service to antiquity
becomes something else, an enthusiasm for Latinity:

In Petrarch's Latin, ancient Rome speaks again. In language,
at least, he by himself inaugurated a real renaissance, embodied
an actual rebirth, of classical antiquity. Speaking like antique
Romans is not quite indeed being reborn into their life. Still,
to renounce one's own language for that of another people
is a long step towards naturalization among that people....
Petrarch's life aim was to satisfy that prime requirement for
citizenship in ancient Rome revived—to satisfy it in himself
and to induce his compatriots to satisfy it also.[12]

For nascent humanism, there was always the problem
of the use of pagan literature by Christian scholars and
poets. Petrarch asserts forcefully in his *Invective contra
medicum* Vergil's integrity: he was *the poet*, who wrote
only "de virtutibus, de naturis hominum ac rerum omnium,
atque omnino de perfectione humana, stilo mirabili et
quem frustra tibi aperire moliar." At length, he expounds
both the poet's function and his mode of discourse:

Quis miretur ante veritatis adventum licuisse aliquid errori,
cum post agnitam veritatem quidam quoque catholici magni
viri ita deviarint, ut ipsa veritas unquam acrius oppugnata
non fuerit, quam ab eis fuit? ... Siquis autem, veritatis
amicus—sine qua nichil verum dici potest, quoniam, ut ait
Augustinus, omne verum a veritate verum est—siquis ergo
talis, pio instigatus affectu, ad ipsius veritatis ornatum musarum presidio niteretur, et vel stilo clarissimo Cristi vitam

vel sacrum aliud vel prophanum etiam, modo non vetitum, celebraret—quod nostrorum quidam fecerunt quamvis preter
legem carminis nullo poetico artificio usi sint—, quis putas
id melius posset implere?

Who would wonder that before the advent of Truth, al-
lowance was made for error, when even after Truth was
known, certain great men, Catholics among them, deviated so
far from it that Truth itself was never so bitterly opposed as
it was by them? ... But if someone, a friend of Truth—without
which nothing true can be said, since, as Augustine says,
everything that is true is true because of Truth—if then such
a man, moved by a sublime feeling, should attempt to ornament Truth itself with the help of the muses, and in an
admirable style should celebrate the life of Christ or something
sacred or even profane, as long as it is not forbidden—which
certain of our poets have done even though they have used
no poetic device beyond the law of poetry—who do you
think would best be able to carry out such a task?

The question indeed answers itself. Later, he buttresses
his defense further with Augustine's praises of Vergil:

"Quem ... parvuli legunt, ut videlicet poeta magnus, omnium-
que praeclarissimus atque optimus ..."[13]

For Coluccio Salutati and the humanists of the fifteenth
century, the problem became somewhat more acute, and
the response, though effectively similar to Petrarch's,
slowly began to diverge and ramify. Salutati's views on
Vergil in particular were attacked bitterly; when he requested from Giuliano Zonarini, Chancellor of Bologna,
a volume of Vergil, Zonarini curtly refused him on the
grounds that Vergil was *vates ... mentificus*, and offered
instead some volumes of pious literature. In his reply,
Salutati asserted that his delight was not in the fables,
but in the style, the majesty of language, the harmony of
verses, the elegance of composition.[14] A few months later,

in the spring of 1379, Salutati wrote again, further defining his position:

Sanctius, plane, fateor, et utilius lectioni sacrae paginae sine intermissione temporis insudare; sed haec inventa gentilium, ac etiam, quos adeo horres, carmina poetarum, si quis ea alta mens libraverit, non parvum aedificant atque prosunt ad ea quae fidei sunt....
Sic igitur ego christianus Virgilium lego, quod non sim ibidem semper aut aliquandiu mansurus, sed indagine diligenti perscrutor si quid ad honestatem et mores optimos, Maronica legens, valeam reperire.

I admit that it is clearly more pious and more useful to apply oneself unremittingly to the study of Scripture; but these inventions of the pagans, and even these songs of poets, whom you find so repugnant—if one ponders them with noble intent, they can be quite edifying and profitable in matters of our religion....
It is thus that I, a Christian, read Vergil, not indeed with the intention to stick here all my life or even for a very long time, but I study his works carefully to see if, reading Vergil, I can discover things that contribute to religion and morality.

Truth, he maintained, derives from God, whether found in the Bible or in the pagan writers, in theology or in poetry; it should not be despised.[15]

Not untypical of the attacks on the humanists was the violent letter which Giovanni da San Miniato dispatched to Angelo Corbinelli, Salutati's pupil. Here is a sample:

Placet "iudicium Paridis spreteque iniuria forme," placet et Didonis cum Anna sorore familiare lamentum, et te video in eius iusta morte iniuste dolere. Sed et Augustinus tandem in se reversus incomparabiliter plangit se in Didonis morte flevisse. Si illo tu melior ... sis, nescio.

The "judgment of Paris and the anguish of beauty scorned" pleases; the lament of Dido with her confidante-sister Anna pleases, and I see you grieving improperly over her proper death. But Augustine himself, in the end, came to his senses and wept bitterly for the tears he had shed over Dido's death. I do not know whether you are a better man than he was.

A list of references to favorite classical passages is followed by this:

Haec omnia non solum vanitas et vanitas vanitatum sed in ore Christicole pene blasfemie sunt idolorumque ignota cultura, que velut monstruosa portenta mentem inquinant, mores dissipant, et si quid boni animo possides, huius peste veneni perimetur. Nam quid non mali tibi suadent hec studia repetita?

All these things are not only vanity and vanity of vanities, but in the mouth of a follower of Christ, they are virtually blasphemies and the blind worship of idols, which, like monstrous nightmares, contaminate the mind and dissipate morals; whatever spiritual qualities you possess will be undermined by this poison. For what wickedness is there which such studies do not foster?

The letter was obviously intended for Coluccio, who read it and answered with a long defense of poetry. Repeating previous arguments, he goes on to point out how freely Jerome, Ambrose, and Augustine quoted from pagan poets in their most sacred writings; and as for disturbing stories, what about the Bible—which is itself poetry?[16]

A worse storm was brewing; apparently in response to Coluccio's defense, Giovanni Dominici wrote *Lucula Noctis*, a closely reasoned treatise and one of the most extended attacks on the reading of pagan poets. First, Dominici presents all the possible reasons for reading Vergil and the other classics; then he advances the thesis that such reading is wrong and harmful, and demonstrates that thesis by refuting all the alleged "benefits." The arguments are presented in articles and questions and follow the syllogistic method, organized by acrostics and

embellished with extensive rhetorical devices. Giovanni
is by turns scornful, prolix, and pithy; in one remarkable
passage, he declares ignorance superior to pagan knowledge and sees far more value in ploughing the fields than
in reading Vergil.[17]

The treatise was composed with a carelessness that offended Salutati. Ullman's study of the dedication copy
and of Salutati's marginalia indicates some of the errors
Salutati is concerned with—not only errors of grammar
and style, but inaccurate and distorted quotations, apparently from memory or from the encyclopedic works
of Vincent of Beauvais and John of Salisbury. Salutati
insists on accurate quotation as a necessity for avoiding
obscurities and misunderstandings.[18]

In his lengthy response, Salutati vigorously defends
humanism on the understanding, as always, that humanism
can strengthen rather than subvert religion. All the arts,
he asserts, are handmaidens to poetry; poetry teaches
virtue and abhors vice: what better activity for a
Christian?[19] Indeed, Giovanni himself points out the value
and the innocence of the classics. The distinction made by
Giovanni between *res* and *verba* is disputed fiercely by
Salutati, as it will be later by Leonardo Bruni and the
other humanists: their position is that the two cannot
be separated without doing violence to both.[20]

Coluccio's defenses of poetry established firmly for the
humanists the supremacy of Vergil as poet—"omnium
divinorum vatum divinior Maro noster;" "celestis ingenii
vatem, quem nec divinarum, nec humanarum rerum scientia latuit"—and as moral guide.[21] If in 1400 it was difficult at times to justify Vergil as a school text, by 1450
Vergil was standard reading for all schoolboys, for many
indeed the core of their education. The controversy in
mid-century between another friar, Giovanni da Prato,
and Guarino Veronese shows the change; Giovanni does

not consider the question of truth or falsehood and can find the only real problem in Dido.[22]

The change came about not only because of the continued dialogue but also because of the work of the pedagogues. Gasparino Barzizza, Pietro Paulo Vergerio, Guarino Veronese and his son Battista, Vittorino da Feltre, Maffeo Vegio, Enea Silvio Piccolomini—their names are history.[23] Their approaches to education, whether in classroom or in treatise, were diverse, but on two things they agreed—the central function of moral philosophy in classical rhetorical education and the supremacy of Vergil as poet and as moral guide for young and old alike.[24] Bruni's translation of St. Basil's letter, *De legendis libris gentilium*, was, as Kristeller points out, widely circulated and no doubt extensively used in the classroom.[25]

With the emphasis on sound Latinity, occasional exaggeration of elegance was inevitable; Monnier, however, distorts the context when he remarks: "Leur style fut, en effet, leur préoccupation dominante. On peut même affirmer qu'il fut leur préoccupation unique."[26] These men placed most stress on moral values; Woodward says, rightly, that the humanists intended a "reconciliation of the ancient learning with the Christian life, thought, and polity" of their own time. Before all else, they were Christians. Thus, Guarino's translation of Plutarch, *De educatione liberorum*, was comparable in importance to Poggio's discovery of the complete text of Quintilian in 1417 and of the complete *De oratore* of Cicero in 1422. All of these works supported the humanist emphasis on the dignity of the educated man, the status of the teacher, the inherent value of learning, and the breadth of the educational aim. When, later, Vida uses Quintilian and Plutarch as bases for *Ars poetica* I, he is approaching these men in the *Quattrocento* spirit, seeing them, that is, as molders of perfect gentlemen, perfecters of the

human spirit, and witnesses to high moral values. The
aristocracy which he seeks in the *Ars poetica* and exemplifies in the *Christiad* is the aristocracy of the spirit; on it
is based his notion of decorum.[27]

There is little doubt about Vergil's stature. He becomes
in the *Quattrocento poeta* as Aristotle was *philosophus*
and Paul *Apostolus.* Vergerio admired Homer from a
distance, but could not rank him above Vergil. "Virgilium ... alterum in terris Deum esse arbitrabar," said
Vegio in later years; as a boy, he had memorized long
passages from the *Aeneid.* The practice was not at all
unusual; many of Vittorino's students memorized the
entire poem, as did Battista Guarino's. After all, the
Aeneid was the poem which contained the whole of moral
truth. Piccolomini prescribed the *Aeneid* both as excellent
material to begin with and as the subject of fruitful
contemplation in maturer years.[28] Leonardo Bruni ranks
Vergil with Cicero in a context discussing authors to read
for stylistic purposes; discussing poets, he declares that
Vergil surpasses the philosophers themselves in his penetration of the secrets of nature and man. Bruni more than
others is concerned with the defense of poetry. He
counsels against reading these fictions too literally, or
making too much of disturbing passages: they are, after
all, rare. He attempts to distinguish between the fictional
matter and the genius of the poet, but the distinction
fails when it is placed against his earlier prescription that
Vergil be read with the greatest attention to style and imagery, read, that is, with a full critical sense, observing
the range of diction and the force of individual words.[29]

Piccolomini finds Vergil quite beyond criticism, while
Battista Guarino declares that, as a subject of deep and
regular study, Vergil must stand not first but alone. And
on Vergil's supreme claim to our lifelong companionship,
he cites the authority of Augustine. But in these praises,

the younger Guarino is following his father without full understanding. His attempts to analyze the form and function of poetry are meager and inept, unable to go beyond minor literary effects—comparison of passages in Homer and Vergil, for instance. Similarly, his distinction between the artist and the moralist, seeming to promise something beyond the superficial criticism the century abounds in, peters out in a limp and disappointing partial definition of decorum.[30]

The praises of Vergil in which the pedagogues abound are the more remarkable since they were generally training men of affairs and since they frankly regarded history as the primary subject of study. A work more directly concerned with literary art and generally representative of its own time—the mid-*Quattrocento*—is the little known but highly important *Politia literaria* of Angelo Decembrio. A lengthy dialogue of seven books, it was apparently composed during the 1440's and 1450's, and enjoyed a wide circulation in the next century and a half; it has, however, received little critical attention, so that its bearing on developments in the sixteenth century—especially Vida's *Ars poetica*—has gone unnoticed.[31]

The discussion ranges from the general qualifications of *bibliotheca politior* to lectures on Greek diphthongs.[32] Book I turns into a lengthy examination of authors, particularly Vergil. Book II covers literature in general, with special attention given, after Vergil, to Terence. III, IV, and VII are filled with matters of philology. Book V discusses texts, history, and civil affairs, and then returns to literature and moral philosophy.

Naturally, the *politia* proposed is to be moral as well as literary. Since history is true and poetry false, Feltrino Boiardo proposes that they agree on Livy's superiority to Vergil. But Leonello d'Este argues Vergil's wide range of subjects, concluding:

... notaveris consiliis, prodigiis, auguriis, exercitibus, ducibus, proeliis, iocosis atque funebribus, aethereis atque terrestribus, sacris atque profanis, denique supernis et infernalibus: nullus Latinorum aeque subtilis disertusve, nullus ad naturalium conformitatem accomodatus, ac in Livio tuo, Feltrine: etsi eius omnes historici quatuordecim (ut aiunt) Decadas evolveris, nequaquam tot generum exempla comperias.

You will have remarked his councils, prodigies, auguries, armies, generals, battles, scenes light and grim, heavenly and earthly, sacred and profane, and even supernal and infernal: no Latin has been equally simple or eloquent, none so remarkably in harmony with nature, not even your Livy, Feltrino; even if you were to search through all fourteen Decades, as they are called, of his history, you would never find so much wonderful variety.

The argument about truth, he points out, is not the main thing:

In quo quidem poeta tanta dicendi copia gratiaque a diis data, tantaque elegantia erat, ut quo magis legatur, eo plus commoveat ad legendum: doctissimosque nonnullos dicendi solitos acceperim, sese quodcunque orationis genus edere vellent, tam ex hujus operibus quam Tullii quamque Homeri commodissime posse deligere, neque mirandum, si quod in Graeco poeta floridum, frugiferum, iucundissimumque sit, in eodem Latino comperis aemulatum, cum tamen ille libros octo et quadraginta, ut Graecorum est multa eloqui, hic nedum illorum dimidium explicuerit.

The gods lavished such abundance and such grace of eloquence on this poet, so much elegance, that the more he is read, the more one is moved to read him. I know for a fact that some of the most distinguished speakers, no matter what the type of speech they are working on, can find it, most appropriately, quite as easily in Vergil's works as in those of Cicero or of Homer; nor is it surprising that whatever is flowery, fruitful, and most pleasant in the Greek poet, can be found equally in the Latin poet, even though Homer wrote forty-eight books—Greek authors are always long-winded—while Vergil wrote barely half that total.

Thus the norm is to be elegance-with-virtue, and the discussion turns to other poets whose elegance and moral probity pass muster—Terence, Horace, Statius, Juvenal. But vernacular writers, however upright, are relegated to a shed outside the library.[33]

Like the earlier Greekless humanists, these men find Latin authors preferable. Plato and Aristotle are commended, as Homer was: "Cicero ... ex Graecis ita aemulatus est, ut ab eis inventa meliora reddiderit, qui etiam per se sapientius excogitavit." Leonello has indeed no doubts that Cicero's lost *De republica* must be better than Plato's! The Christian authors to be preferred are those whose classicism is indeed most intensively Ciceronian; certainly the *Civitas Dei* is a great work, but they put before it "praecipue Hieronymi, cuius omnia divina, praeclara, Tullianaque sunt opera."[34]

Philology gradually usurps the stage. The thirtieth chapter, for instance, is entitled "De Latinae linguae facultate ... ac de his sermonibus homonymis seu aequivocis commendatio, qui apud Virgilium praecipue et elegantissime scribentem, non unam tantum ... sed alias insuper habent significationes opportunas." (A commendation of the range of the Latin language ... and of those homonymns or ambiguous words which, particularly in the magnificent works of Vergil, have not just one meaning, but also others which are peculiarly appropriate.)

The whole of Book IV is a lecture by Guarino on individual words, consisting of minute examinations, sometimes critical analyses, of Vergilian texts.[35] If questions of allegory arise, they are dealt with by scrupulous explication of literal meaning. The literalism of Guarino and

5.

Leonello, and the corresponding exertions of many humanists in establishing exact texts, had far-reaching effects.[36]
I refer not only to Valla's exposé of the Donation of
Constantine, but also, and more particularly, to the development of a large body of classics and to the constant
insistence on close and thorough reading. The possibilities
of richness and even of ambiguity depend on such close
reading, and while the "Nizolian paperbooks" of the
sixteenth century may be one outcome of Guarino's
method, more important is the influence on Vida's thought
and practice.

In the *Politia*, literary genres are frequently not distinguished. Leonello, eloquently refuting Boiardo, asserts
about the *Aeneid*: "Dissolve carmen ... in prosam, fac
pedestrem orationem, tam eloquenter ut Livius, rhetorice
tantum ut Cicero dissertabit." (Turn his poem into prose,
rewrite it straightforwardly—he will be as eloquent as
Livy, as elegant as Cicero.) (p. 21)

This confusion, never questioned, underlies most of the
discussions; they move easily from genre to genre, the
transitions effected by similarity of content, questions of
moral value, or the comprehensive notion of *elegantia*.
What distinctions are made are based externally—excellence in hexameter, for instance, as compared to pentam-
eter poetry.[37]

A lengthy discussion of Dante, petulantly pursued by
Tito Strozzi, brings up interesting problems. The moral
values eloquently championed a few chapters earlier are
here beside the point. Strozzi admits that Dante's style
is not comparable to Vergil's; still, Dante did write admirably about nether and upper regions. Ironically, Guarino replies:

Exhorruistine magis ... o fili, inferorum poenas, quae a Dante
tuo Florentino, quam quae a Mantuano praedicantur? eo sci-

licet, quod verbosiores sint, et ad vulgarem consuetudinem magis accommodata, quae ab eo referuntur?

My boy, were you more frightened by the infernal punishments described by your Florentine Dante than by the ones Vergil describes? That would be, naturally, because the things he relates are wordier and more suited to vulgar taste?

Guarino will grant that Dante copied Vergil, but not that he copied him well. He labels Dante's work a *curiosum opus*, patched together from hack works of piety replete with meaningless riddles; anyone acquainted with poetry and theology sees through it readily. As for discussion of hidden meanings—that is frequently an excuse for sloppiness; those writers turn theology into verse "qui vere rudes sint et indocti, ut a vulgo scientiores existimentur." Guarino excoriates Dante at length for his misinterpretation of *auri sacra fames* and other errors, and concludes:

Et miramur poetam nostrum a quibusdam ita solere contemni, qui nullum eius versum intelligant, nec intelligi ab aliis velint: cum qui eum maxime scire iudicantur, eius scripta studiose persequentes, talia peccata commiserint?

And are we surprised that our poet is commonly contemned by certain people who do not understand a single line of his and who prevent others from understanding, when even those who, because of their diligent and persevering study of him, are considered to best know him, even these have committed such faults?

Overwhelmed, Strozzi capitulates and, incidentally, points the moral:

Satis ab eo sentire videor, praeceptor mi, cum ea Maronis altitudo, praestantia, majestas sit, ut aut vulgariter scribentibus non tuto effingi possit: aut certe, ut Macrobius ille subtilissimus indagator excepit, tantum adeo Virgilium esse constat, ut neque major fieri possit a laudantibus, tametsi peritissimis, neque reprehendentium imperitia comminui.

My master, I retract that original opinion; for Vergil is clearly
so profound, so excellent, so majestic, that he cannot be
properly imitated by vernacular poets. And certainly, as that
very perceptive commentator Macrobius said, Vergil is so great
that praise, even the most skilled, does not increase his stature,
nor does the clumsiness of his detractors diminish it.

The supremacy acclaimed seems less glorious.[38]

Most of the remainder alternates between grammar and
philology on the one hand and further attempts at literary
criticism on the other. The whole work generally exemplifies many of the currents of mid-century: the abiding
concern with virtue and the increasing concern with elegance and rhetoric; the attempts at literary analysis,
buttressed by close and careful reading; the inferiority of
the vernacular; and the exaltation of Vergil. Vergil is
made the norm for admission "in hanc quam nunc strui-
mus politiorem bibliothecam."[39] The fact that more than
half of this large work is devoted to Vergil indicates their
affection. It is something more than Vida's, though less
than Scaliger's. Quite clearly, this book is one of the
major sources, along with Landino's work, of the developing Vergil cult; for all his interest both in allegory and
in the vernacular, Landino in his *Commentary* on the
Aeneid adds significantly to the school of elegance.[40]

The *Politia's* exaltation of Vergil is quite precise. The
fervent statements consistently derive from explication,
analysis, comparison. Vergil's qualities are singled out,
carefully and in detail: because of his *gravitas*, the elevation of his style, the breadth of his range, he is a worthy
model for youth. Most impressive is his art. They cheerfully admit that he imitated—not only Homer but other
poets as well; *mutua imitatio* was common among the
Latin poets. His achievement is the important point:
"Adeo Homerum Virgilius praeter ceteros aemulatus est,
ut apud Latinos quod notissimum, apud Graecos quod

admirabile, quantum Maro, nemo tam perfecte effinxerit."
Homer's greatness is not denied; he simply happened to
live before Vergil: Vergil is "Homero aetate inferior, eloquentia par, etsi quidam Graeculi id negent." The *Graeculi* is symptomatic, preluding the conventional sniping at
Homer—for example, he is indecorous, garrulous, careless
of diction, repetitious.[41]

Vergil's art subsumes all else. His poems are the supreme achievement of all poetry. The *Aeneid*, his best
work, covers all aspects of life, with a sense of economy
and order which is remarkable. Thus, Vegio's attempt to
write a thirteenth book was a piece of folly; apparently,
Vegio did not understand that the funeral of Turnus and
the marriage of Lavinia would be superfluous.[42]

The *Aeneid* is to these men a profound work which
deserves the most careful reading and meditation—a valuable lifelong companion. But primarily, "art" means style:
aptitudo sermonum and *styli magnificentia.* Statius used
Vergilian matter, but he sang *inferiore lyra*.[43] Lengthy
discourses discuss not only words but also rhythm, sound,
metrical effects, juxtaposition, the order of words, the use
of vowels and consonants, and the various ways harmony
can be achieved in verse. Whatever the merits of other
poets, Vergil is master in all these.[44] One who wants to
compose will imitate the better authors, especially Vergil;
he will begin young, practice much, and make his own
the ancients' manner of speech. He will strive *aemulari ...
et effingere, permutare, transcribere.*[45] Though imitation
is discussed only in scattered passages, its central importance for the would-be poet is constantly implied.
Traditional enough in statement, the doctrine of imitation
is presented in the *Politia* in almost precisely the terms
Vida will use a half-century later.

The discussion of allegory in the *Politia* is curious. In
the thirty-second chapter, Guarino takes up the reference

in Vergil's *Bucolic* IV to the Golden Age: "nonnulli poetam volunt ... tamquam alterum Platonem divinorum vatum prophetias non ignorasse, etiam asserente Hieronymo."[46] He demonstrates for such poetry the crucial importance of philological study and analysis, so that, while not wholly discounting allegory, he shows and elicits little sympathy. The discussion of Vegio's *Supplementum* never refers to the allegorical intent; that book is useless because the "major events" have already been anticipated. No attention is paid to the apotheosis of Aeneas, the event which Vegio considered central in his addition. And the discussion of Dante virtually considers allegory an excuse for bad poetry.[47]

For Petrarch and Boccaccio, allegory was a mode of discourse which contained the essential justification of poetry. Thus, in the *Africa*, Petrarch emphasized the possibilities:

> Non illa licentia vatum est
> Quam multis placuisse palam est ...
> Scripturum iecisse prius firmissima veri
> Fundamenta decet, quibus inde innixus amoena
> Et varia sub nube potest abscondere sese
> Lectori longum cumulans placidumque laborem,
> Quaesitu asperior quo sit sententia, verum
> Dulcior inventu. Quicquid labor historiarum est
> Quicquid virtutum cultus documentaque vitae,
> Naturae studium quicquid, licuisse poetis
> Crede: sub ignoto tamen ut celentur amictu,
> Nuda alibi, et tenui frustrentur lumina velo,
> Interdumque palam veniant, fugiantque vicissim.[48]

Poets do not have as much liberty as many would have liked ... The would-be poet must first lay soundest foundations of truth, on the basis of which he can conceal himself in a pleasant and many-faceted cloud, thus offering to the reader a lengthy but also a tranquil labor, so that while his meaning is harder to search out, it is also sweeter when found. Be assured that within the province of the poet falls whatever pertains to history, whatever to the promotion of morals, whatever to the experience of life, whatever to the study of nature: but with the condition that these things elsewhere revealed, are concealed under a veil of mystery, that they elude our eyes because of this light veil, and that sometimes they are made clear and sometimes they are hidden.

Salutati, no less certain of moral justification, makes that justification paramount; freely admitting that he derives his allegorical notions very much from Boccaccio as well as Petrarch, he shows less of the poet's understanding of allegory as mode of discourse. All poets allegorize, he points out, whether they know it or not; one must indeed be a *misticus interpres* to understand them properly.[49]

Et sicubi forte dicatur verum aliquid, ut multi cogitant, divinasse, non fuit illa Maronis intentio sed dei revelantis etiam per gentiles misteria sua et vis erumpentis etiam inter mendacia veritatis. (p. 14)

And if anywhere he may be said to have divined, as many think, some truth, that was not the intention of Vergil, but rather the intention of God Who reveals His mysteries even through the gentiles, and the power of truth which breaks out even amid lies.

The pious opponents of Vergil are, Salutati declares, being somewhat arrogant; their charge of *mendacium* appears wholly arbitrary.[50]

Poetry is necessarily allegorical:

Est enim proprium poete sermone metrico et figurato imaginativam cum delectatione movere ita quod ipsa dicta cum intellectis videat simul taliter ordinari quod similitudine quadam intellectus noster et id percipiat quod dicitur et aliud intelligat quam narretur.

For the poet may properly move the imagination with pleasure by means of rhythmic and figurative language, so that it can see that the things said and the things meant are simultaneously ordered in such a way that, by a kind of analogy, our intellect both perceives what is said and understands something other than what is said.

Officium erit ... prodesse ... et iuvare cum immutatione verborum et rerum, ut cum unum dicere videantur, aliud tamen secreto sensu relinquant omnibus intelligendum. (p. 70)

It will be his duty to profit and to please by a mutual interaction of words and things, so that when they appear to say one thing, they nonetheless leave something else to be understood by all in a secret sense.

Salutati's word order—*prodesse, iuvare*—indicates the necessity that an obvious moral be present; he insists on the goodness of poets, calling up as his clinching argument "Maronem nostrum" who was particularly remarkable for his "mundicitia vitae, integritate morum, conversationisque nitore."[51]

Though he devotes prime space to Vergil, Salutati does not treat the *Messianic Eclogue*; Bruni does, in quite medieval manner, in his *De Studiis*. The term *vates*, he points out, indicates the "possession" poets experience. Following Salutati on the unwitting prophet, he discourses unhesitantly on the precise relevance of this poem to the Sibylline prophecies of the Nativity.[52] More committed than Bruni, Maffeo Vegio attempts to work out a fuller allegorization of Vergil's work. In his *De educatione*, he spends a good deal of time on the moral-allegorical significance of Vergil's characters; through Aeneas, for instance, Vergil showed the virtuous man—"virum omni virtute praeditum, nunc in adversis, nunc in prosperis casibus."[53] About the famous *o socii* passage, Vegio declares that even a Christian poet could not have written more fitly or more religiously. "We are here taught to remember the past with joy, to bear the present bravely, to hope for a better future, and finally to cultivate perseverance at all times with a hero's might ..." For Latium, he would substitute "heaven" and for Troy, "life"—"why might the passage not have come from the pen of the Apostle Paul?"[54] As Anna Cox Brinton remarked about the *Supplementum*:

To Vegius, Vergil's epic was above all an allegory of the soul. For this reason he could ill spare what was to him the climax of its narrative—the crossing of the river where the mortal garment was left behind and the swift ascent through regions of air to a place of glory among the stars. Aeneas' westward voyage, his war in Italy, his marriage, and his apotheosis all lent themselves to symbolic interpretation.[55]

But the most important *Quattrocento* allegorizer and critic of Vergil is Cristoforo Landino, whose commentary on the *Aeneid* and *Disputationes Camaldulenses* are in many ways distinct advances over all previous work.[56] The four books of the *Disputationes* cover four days of discussion by Lorenzo and Giuliano de' Medici, Leon Battista Alberti, Marsilio Ficino, and Landino. In the first book, Lorenzo and Alberti dispute the merits of the active and the contemplative life, agreeing in the end that the perfect man is he who recognizes the superiority of the contemplative and its function of providing norms for directing the active, and who joins both and reconciles them in himself. In the second book, Alberti and Ficino attempt to define the *summum bonum*. This is God, identified by man with supreme felicity, which can be achieved by the human intellect. On the last two days, Alberti exemplifies the discourses of Books I and II by a detailed allegorization of the *Aeneid*. This allegorization Landino considered the first complete one—"quae quidem vix a paucis pauca, a

nullo autem omnia interpretata videremus."[57] Furthermore, the adumbration was to be concerned not with
moral philosophy, but with art; for Landino, Vergil's art
is not subjected to moral philosophy. The poet's purpose
was an embodiment of Platonic doctrine in poetic figments
—just as Homer had, unconsciously, adumbrated the reality which Plato would later describe.[58]

In the allegory, Aeneas proceeds from the life of the
senses (Troy) through political activity (Carthage) to the
summit of contemplation which directs the good life
(Latium). Abandoning Troy or the life of worldly pleasure
was the first step; gradually, through his adventures, his
perils, his obstacles, he grows stronger against sensuality.
The mistake he makes at Carthage is less his affair with
Dido than his surrender to the active life as a *summum
bonum*, but Aeneas' reason, guided by conscience, leads
him back to his destiny.[59] In this framework, the experience in the Sibyl's cave is a Platonic vision of reality;
the monsters at the gates symbolize temptations or trials;
the golden bough which fortifies him is wisdom, with
the help of which he moves through hell unharmed. The
trials themselves are part of the purifying process necessary for the mystical heights he will achieve, and the
minor gods are agents of the power controlling the Trojan
destiny.[60]

When Landino wrote the *Disputationes*, philological
trends were repudiating, directly or indirectly, the work
done by Petrarch, Salutati, Filelfo, and the others. Landino did not wholly rescue them; as Zabughin points out,
he did not believe unconditionally in Vergil as prophet of
Christ, but he did consider him apostle of Plato. Landino
succeeded at least in making allegory more respectable;
his contribution was to unify the principles of art with
the allegorical reading. A combination of philologist, phi-
losopher, and poet, he brought all his interests to bear

on Vergil.[61] His interpretations rely heavily on Plato, Aristotle, Cicero, Augustine, Aquinas, and Marsilio Ficino. The *Disputationes*, as Rossi suggests, is a graceful exposition of philosophic doctrines applied to poetry and an eloquent attempt to unite the notions of Platonism and Aristotelianism, classical antiquity and Christian revelation. Landino does not hesitate to adopt the attitudes of Petrarch or Dante, or to follow the authority of Macrobius and Servius, but he rejects specifically Fulgentius and Probus among the older authorities and Filelfo among the more recent interpreters.[62] But important as his synthesis may have been in minor philosophic currents of his time, his major influence was upon the criticism of Vergil and imitation of the *Aeneid* during the next century and a half; what he did in effect was reunite, at the height of the *Quattrocento*, the Vergil of Dante with the master of language and feeling of ancient Rome. Landino's interpretations "penetrated the conception of epic poetry held by all thinking men."[63] More than that, they helped crystallize at least some of the disconnected notions of epic and give the struggling form a semblance of coherence. Vida will virtually reject allegory, but the following passage from the *Disputationes* would not be amiss in the author of the *Christiad*:

Nam quae ad allegoriam referre volumus inde solum accersenda censeo, unde ducentem sua sponte sequantur. Sin autem et ingenij invita eruantur, tantum de gravitate sua amittunt, ut ridicula pene reddantur. Itaque omittamus anxias interpretationes, eaque solum assumamus, quae non modo in abdito non latent, sed ultro sese quaerentibus offerunt.

For the things we wish to interpret allegorically can be derived only when they spontaneously follow the lead. But if they are dug out incongruously, they lose so much of their substance, that they are rendered virtually ridiculous. Therefore let us avoid forced readings, and attend only to those things which, far from concealing themselves, actually proffer themselves unsought to the reader.

When Landino praises Vergil for creative imitation of Homer, one might hear Vida's voice, and while the designer of the *Christiad* is more interested, apparently, in Vergil as *historicus* than as moralist, he would not dispute Landino's fervent,

O divinum ingenium! O virum inter rarissimos viros omnino excellentem, et poetae nomine vere dignum, qui, non Christianus, omnis tamen Christianorum verissimae doctrinae similima proferat...[64]

O divine genius! o man altogether outstanding even among the most excellent men, and truly worthy of the name of poet; while not a Christian, nevertheless you proffer everywhere matters most like the deepest belief of Christians.

Vida's contemporaries focused their sights on elegance rather than on allegory. One reason for this may be that the independent status of poetry was assured in the age of Julius II, Leo X, and Clement VII. Since at least the *Politia literaria*, there was less and less explicit need for justifying poetry, and, in the abundant confusion of poetry with philology, criticism with personal stylistic development, there was a more pronounced emphasis on formal elegance. Even before the *Politia*, the conventional attitudes towards the *Trecento* Latinists were symptomatic. When Niccolo Niccoli attacks Dante, Petrarch, and Boccaccio, for their "butchers' Latin," Salutati's attempts to defend them do not suffice; Niccolo can afford to smile condescendingly on the barbarous age these men represented.[65] Gradually, it becomes a cliché to point out that Petrarch's Latin style, while generally inadequate, was at least superior to Dante's and even Dante's was at least superior to that of his predecessors.[66] The balanced views of the pedagogues are distorted by those who made rhetoric a hobbyhorse; Poggio's dispute with Alberto da Sarzano is typical, or Trepezuntius' with Guarino. In his *Rhetorica* (1437) Trepezuntius dissects mercilessly a eulogy delivered by Guarino Veronese almost a decade earlier; selecting three major passages, he writes them as they should be written—in "pure" classical Latin. And Valla, who took a strong stand against the purism of Poggio, is himself quite as extreme in his emphasis on elegance.[67]

While moral values continue to predominate in the thought and practice of the earlier *Quattrocento*, in the latter half of the century they are overshadowed. Poliziano's quarrels with Bartolomeo Scala on the one hand and with Paolo Cortesi on the other, and the subsequent quarrel over imitation between Bembo and Giovanfrancesco Pico della Mirandola—these are among the major documents at the turn of the century. Cortesi's literary "history," better than Sicco Polentone's, shares this quality with his predecessor: a view of poetry that recognizes almost nothing but music and erudition. Valla's prefaces to his *Elegantiae* made of the Latin language a *sacramentum, magnum numen*, and there were many who lost the numinous in sound and forgot the orthodox meaning of "sacrament." One hundred and eighty Latin versifiers celebrated the coronation of Leo X, while the greatest living poet of Leo's decade, Ariosto, chose to write his major work in Italian rather than Latin because he could not cope fully with elegance—an ironic footnote indeed to Valla's declaration, "Romanum imperium ibi esse, ubi Romana lingua dominatur."[68]

Among all those who wrote dialogues, invectives, or manifestoes, two men stand out—Poliziano, for his brilliant statements on imitation and for his definition of Vergil's stature, and Giovanni Pontano, for crystallizing certain important tendencies in Vergilian criticism. It is no accident that these two are the finest Latin poets of the Renaissance. Both were original and independent men, sometimes insisting fiercely on their originality. They differ on various points, but are agreed on the superiority of Vergil's art and its efficacy for the would-be poet; the direction they sought to give to Latin letters was lost, however, by the too literal-minded and mechanical imitators who followed.

When Poliziano chose Statius for his prolusion, *Oratio super ... Statii Sylvis* (1480), he did so because Statius could lead the student to Vergil, the master. His enthusiasm for Statius is generous, but he never lets his hearers or readers forget that Vergil is *the* poet. Of his own *Sylvae*, or verse prolusions, two are devoted to the poetry of Vergil: *Manto* (1482) and *Rusticus* (1483). *Nutricia* (1486), a brief history of poetry from Homer to Lorenzo de' Medici, asserts that only *veneranda senectus* places Homer above Vergil.[69]

Most striking of Poliziano's praises of Vergil is the conclusion of the *Manto*, whose epithets on the Vergilian style—*facundia dives, tanti eloquii, ubere largo*—echo Dante's *bello stile* and *parola ornata*. Poliziano singles out not so much elegance as the power of style which renders everything true and moving; the poet rather than the philologist is here speaking of style which encompasses total poetic activity. Poliziano's eulogy restates Vittorino's *mens sana in corpore sano*, and reaffirms the pedagogues' identification of *res* and *verba*. It is very close to Vida's *verba deo similis*, as indeed much of the *Manto* may be taken as text for the *Ars poetica*.[70]

Poliziano's commendation of Vergil in the *Manto* recalls Vida's hymn closing the *Ars poetica*. He says in part,

> Semper erit magni decus immortale Maronis,
> Semper inexhaustis ibunt haec flumina venis,

Semper ab his docti ducentur fontibus haustus,
Semper odoratos fundent haec gramina flores,
Unde piae libetis apes, unde inclyta nectat
Serta comis triplici juvenalis Gratia dextra.   (345-350)

Ever will the immortal glory of mighty Vergil endure. Ever will these rivers flow abundantly. Ever will poets drink deep draughts from these fountains. Ever will these fields blossom with sweet flowers, which the sacred bees may suck, and with which the lovely Graces may weave beautiful garlands for their hair.

The image of the bee, recalling also Petrarch, is a clue to his thought on imitation. In the epistolary debate with Paolo Cortesi, spokesman for the purists, Poliziano takes up another image, that of the ape, once applied to Salutati as a compliment, and turns it into biting rebuke. If the ape's visage is "homini similior..., honestior tauri facies aut item leonis quam simiae videtur." Pointing out that Quintilian and Horace ridiculed barren imitation, he adds:

Mihi certe quicumque tantum componunt ex imitatione, similes esse vel psittaco vel picae videntur, proferentibus quae nec intelligunt. Carent enim quae scribunt isti viribus et vita; carent actu, carent affectu, carent indole, iacent, dormiunt, stertunt. Nihil ibi verum, nihil solidum, nihil efficax. Non exprimis, inquit aliquis, Ciceronem. Quid tum? non enim sum Cicero; me tamen, ut opinor, exprimo.

For my part, I consider those who compose exclusively by imitation to be nothing more than parrots or magpies who repeat what they do not understand. Their writings lack sinews and life; they have no energy, no feeling, no character; they lie prostrate, they sleep, they snore. Nothing will you find there true, nothing substantial, nothing moving. Someone will say, you do not portray Cicero. What of it? I am not Cicero. But I do, I think, portray myself.

Cortesi's long and involved answer is only partially relevant to the problems raised and the charges made. Though
he also attempts to invoke Petrarch's prestige with his,
"Similem volo ... non ut simiam hominis, sed ut filium
parentis," his rhetorical hairsplitting confounds him:
"malo assecla esse et simia Ciceronis quam alumnus aut
filius aliorum." After all, he concludes lamely, the imitator who strictly follows a good author shows sound
judgment![71]

In the excesses of Cortesi and his colleagues, the patri-
otic-humanistic dream of Dante and Petrarch becomes a
dead letter. The logical development may be seen in
Bembo's debate with Giovanfrancesco Pico della Mirandola. Pico asserts that the purists wantonly neglect
substance, and points out that various interpretations and
estimates of the ancients make the proponents of rigid
imitation self-contradictory: the good poet is he who
grows out of the ancients in the sense of outgrowing
them. "Ex ipsa varietate totius universi pulchritudo con-
stituatur." It is impossible to imitate decently in every
particular; the attempt itself becomes barren, a con-
ditioned reflex.[72]

Bembo's reply depends on rhetorical distinctions and
sophistry too much of the time. Allowing the archetype
Pico defined—"ideam ... recte loquendi ... et pulchritu-
dinis"—he refers it not to Plato but to "maxime omnium
Cicero." Bembo denies the necessity of various grades of
perfection and therefore of style: some of the ancients
at least achieved complete perfection. As to Pico's "divi-
nas illas imagines spetiesque," he argues,

Ac ego quidem sic existimo, in ipso mundi ac rerum omnium
auctore et effectore deo; ut iustitiae, ut temperantiae, ut alia-
rum virtutum; sic etiam recte scribendi spetiem quandam
divinam illam quidem, et cui nihil desit, atque omnino absolutissimam existere.

And I do indeed think that there exists, in God Himself, Creator and Mover of the world and of all things, a Form— just as there is a Form of justice, of temperance, and of the other virtues—a Form of good writing, definite and divine, lacking nothing whatsoever and altogether absolute.

This *spetiem ... absolutissimam* Bembo identifies clearly with Cicero for prose, Vergil for poetry.

Nam de Virgilio quidem nemo ambigit, omnes in uno illo omnium poetarum ... inveniri posse virtutes summa singulari- que dignitate ..., ut si natura ipsa hominum rerumque omnium parens, ea loqui versibus voluisset, quae ab ipso perscripta sunt; nec melius ..., nec omnino aliter fuisse loquuturam.

In regard to Vergil, no one doubts that in him alone of all poets can be found all the virtues in their highest perfection and dignity; ... so that if Nature herself, the Mother of men and of all things, had wished to write the poems he wrote, she would not have written any better than he did, or in any other way.

That he inconsistently suggests the possibility of sur- passing these absolute masters is a small matter; at all costs, he must lay down forever and irrevocably his rules of imitation, rigid and unrelenting.[73]

Poliziano's contemporary, Giovanni Pontano, may be less articulate on the general principles and less concerned with the controversies; nonetheless, he contributes quite substantially to the tradition of Vergilian criticism culmi- nating in Vida's *Ars poetica*. In *Actius, de numeris poeti- cis*, a dialogue composed around 1499, the major speaker, Sannazaro, asserts the purpose: to select "eam partem quae tota versatur in *numeris* ... quibus eminere videtur Virgilius." The examination of "numbers" proceeds "nec minus docte quam copiose," and, despite an occasional confusion about quantities, covers thoroughly and admi- rably almost every conceivable possibility of rhythm. Text

6.

after text is analyzed at length, in an attempt to penetrate
quintessential Vergilianism; alterations are suggested, to
show why the verse had to be written just so. The discussion of many texts sounds as if the speakers were
anticipating Bembo's *spetiem absolutissimam*. For instance,

> "multum ille et terris iactatus et alto,"
Plenus hic quidem est versus, sonorus, gravis, numerosus;
quae laus tota existit de collisione vocalium statim repercussa
eaque ingeminata. Quodsi dictionem eam subtrahas quae est
ille et dicas
> "multumque et terris iactatus et alto,"
mirum est quantum de versus ipsius dignitate, gravitate, mag-
nitudine detrahatur. Quod quidem ipsum fit etiam ob accen-
tus unius detractionem. Etenim pars ea quae est *multumque*
unum tantum secum adducit accentum eumque subinclinatum,
at *multum ille* duos, quos utique collisio ipsa et coniungit
simul ambos et eos efficit tum pleniores tum etiam magis
sonoros.

The verse "multum ille et terris iactatus et alto," is full,
sonorous, weighty, rhythmical; and all this excellence stems
from the conflict of vowels immediately re-echoed and re-
doubled. But if you were to drop the word "ille" and say,
"multumque et terris iactatus et alto," it is amazing how
much of the dignity, gravity, and grandeur of the line is lost.
And this happens also because of the removal of one accent.
"Multumque" has only one accent, and that a grave; but
"multum ille" has two, and the conflict itself simultaneously
unites them and makes them both more full and more sonorous.

A partial end is variety, "cuius natura ipsa videtur fuisse
vel in primis studiosa."[74]
      Much of the dialogue elaborates expertly and with ex-
quisite taste the points touched on in the *Politia*, and is
also the basis for Vida's discussion of imitative harmony.
Pontano's statements on imitation, similarly recalling the

Politia, point to Vida. Pontano deprecates imitation of a single author, while allowing for specific models in specific genres—primarily Vergil for epic, pastoral, and didactic. He counsels broad and through reading in all the classics, and imitation of whatever is best,

ut similes, ut pares, si superare illos minus valuerint, aut imitatores saltem boni ut evadant laudemque si non primi aut secundi loci, aliquam quoque et ipsi certam propriamque ac studiis suis dignam consequantur.

so that they may be similar, so that they may be equal, if they are not able to surpass them, or at least that they may emerge as effective imitators and thus may win some praise, if not of the first or second order, at least some that is proper and worthy of their efforts.

While this advice is conventional enough, and seems even to reflect the views of the purists and advocates of rigid imitation, it must be remembered that this hinges on close analysis, constant reading and meditation, and the kind of critical understanding demonstrated by the dialogue. The gentle indulgence at the end is for those who simply cannot do any better. For Pontano, however, as for Vida, poets cannot be imitators in the strict sense; they will have to re-create or be forgotten.[75]

Vida seems close to Bembo in equating Vergil with the archetype or idea. At the same time, Vida's insistence on moderation, the breadth of his definitions of imitation, the advice to emulate, and the notion of style in its broadest sense—the sense given it by Poliziano, and the details as worked out by Pontano—all these elements seem to place him closer to the group including Petrarch, Poliziano, Pontano, and the younger Pico, and including Landino for his critical understanding of Vergil's own imitative processes and for the liberating qualities of his aesthetic insights. It would be a mistake to force Vida

into the exact pattern of the 1510s and 1520s, to discover
the secrets of the *Christiad* in the *Bombyx* or the *Ludus
scacchiae*, or even to expect him to adhere to his own
precepts. In changing times, Vida harks back to the past,
to the elusive dreams of the earlier humanists, to their
struggles and their frustrated attempts at defining Vergil's
poetry and its significance. The confusions of the *Ars
poetica* were bred in the confusions of the *Quattrocento*,
but it may also be said that the achievements of the
Christiad are a synthesis of many of the best elements
from the *Quattrocento.*

Christian epic poetry, both Latin and Italian, abounded
in the *Quattrocento*; very little of it is of any importance.
The epics most obviously imitative of Vergil were con-
ditioned generally by a number of factors—the problems
of pagan mythology, the strands of elegance and allegory,
the practice of earlier Christian poets, the influence of the
secular chronicle-epics, and the lack of any definition
of epic.

Those who attempted Latin epics modeled on the
Aeneid found the problem of pagan mythology more acute
than Salutati and the pedagogues had. Dante's solution was
not wholly relevant—he had created a sacred poem out
of epic materials; it is not unremarkable that neither
Petrarch nor Boccaccio had assayed the form. For the
would-be rivals of Juvencus and Sedulius, the crucial
problem was how to compose an epic poem that would
be orthodox aesthetically, that is, authentically Vergilian
in form, as well as orthodox theologically. As history
shows, the obvious solutions did not work—the solutions
of sticking close to the Gospel text, even paraphrasing
that text in hexameters redolent of Vergil; of combining
the typological approach of Biblical exegetes with the
allegorical readings of the Vergilian critics; or of dis-

pensing with the strictly pagan elements and writing chronicle poems in the Vergilian style. What was necessary was a full-scale transformation of the *Aeneid* into a style and structure completely relevant to the times.

The achievements of the post-Classical Christian poets were not properly suitable for the *Quattrocento*. Prudentius composed the *Psychomachia* in a time of struggle and defense, but the defense was concerned not with poetry but with Christianity. His strength partly lay in the energy with which his allegory addressed itself to contemporary crises. Those two lights of Christian epic, Juvencus and Sedulius, had much the same purpose. Juvencus was the first who attempted to "provide for educated Christian readers a substitute for the perilous beauties of the classical poets." His *Evangeliorum Libri Quattuor*, officially Vergilian in diction and style, rigorously followed the Gospels; in the *Carmen Paschale*, one of the finest of Christian poems, Sedulius took more liberties with the text but never yielded his apologetical purpose. Juvencus' literal adherence to his source and Sedulius' insistence on his message sometimes made for strain; neither was wholly at his ease as poet. But their particular achievement cannot be gainsaid. Juvencus in his hexameter translation of the Gospels and Sedulius in his more eclectic poem—drawn from selected events of the Old Testament and of the life of Christ, and bristling with typological elucidation—succeeded in creating a kind of Christian mythology which found enormous favor with subsequent generations of poets. They contributed enormously to the remodeling of Vergil for the literary Christian world.[76]

Allegory in the fifteenth century, however, was not generally the personification or the typology of the fifth. Maffeo Vegio's *Supplementum* intends to complete an allegorical scheme; commentary is wholly absent. But in

one curious work, the *Crisias* by Hilarion, Benedictine
protegé of Cardinal Bessarion, there is a cross between
making a type and explaining it. In this poem, Vergil is
not only model but also character; the antichrist is described as partially a product of humanistic education who
learns wickedness from the other pagan poets; and this
in the 1460s.[77] Vergil, however, is different from the
pagans; his *Fourth Eclogue* is identified with the Sibylline
prophecies and the Sibyl who guided Aeneas is turned
into a guardian of Vergil himself:

> redeunt saturnia regna,
> Ecce nobis foetus summo descendit olympo.
> Tu quae magnanimum aeneam per regia ditis
> Perque lacus stygios traxisti patris ad umbras:
> Dic quae de christo cecinisti oracula quondam.[78]

The reign of Saturn returns; behold a child descends to us
from high heaven. You, who lead greathearted Aeneas through
the kingdom of Dis and through the Stygian lake to the shade
of his father: sing to us again the prophecies which once you
sang of Christ.

Now while this inchoative celebration of the *Fourth
Eclogue* may lead to Sannazaro's *De partu virginis*, the
assumptions point towards Vida. For humanists like Hilarion who could not easily square the practice of pagan
poetry with their Christian material, there was at least
no doubt about the suitability of Vergil and his poetry.

The best and most authentic Christian allegory of the
period was written not by an Italian but by a Croatian
humanist, Marko Marulic, towards the end of the fifteenth
century. His *Davidias* may be noticed here, however, since
it was well known in Italy.[79] It is an epic in fourteen
books treating the life of King David as a prefiguring of
the life of Christ; Marulic explains his intent at the beginning of his "Tropologica Davidiadis Expositio":

Sub veteris instrumenti historiis novi latere mysteria apostolus
testatur dicens: Omnia illis contingebant in figuram. Osten-
dere igitur aggrediar spiritu sancto adjuvante ... Davidis res
gestas, quas, ut potuimus, nostra poesi complexi sumus, quo
spectent quosve typos in se habere mihi videantur novitatis.
In omnibus fere Davidem puto personam gerere Christi; Sau-
lem autem Iudeos, qui Christum persequebantur, significare.
Tum sub prophetarum dictis factisque contineri utriusque legis
auctoritatem.[80]

The Apostle himself bears witness that in the narratives of
the Old Testament are concealed the mysteries of the New,
when he says: All these things happened to them as a pre-
figuration. Therefore, I will attempt to show, with the help
of the Holy Spirit, the deeds of David which I have narrated
in my poem as best I could, to what end they point and
what types of the New Testament they seem to me to contain.
In almost all details, I consider David to foreshadow Christ,
while Saul signifies the Jews who persecuted Christ. Then,
by the words and deeds of the prophets, I consider the authority of each Testament to be contained.

But while this poem, fully Vergilian in style and imagery,
operates in precise allegory—each book is preceded by
an expository headnote—the narrative follows the chroni-
cle-history structure of most *Quattrocento* epics.

The practice of Petrarch in the *Africa* did not have a
great deal to do with the *Quattrocento* preference for the
annalistic form; few of the epics, sacred or secular, attempted the scope and design of the *Africa*. They were
not, indeed, free to; poets like Naldi and Filelfo, in attempting to give their contemporary heroes stature by
imposition of the classical frame and by imitation of
heroic figures, were attempting to please their patrons.[81]
The practice was not new; the chronicle epic which assayed heroic proportions through the use of Vergilian
style and Vergilian machinery had been common for cen-

turies—for example the *Carmen de laudibus Berengarii*
in the tenth century, *Liber Majolichinus* in the eleventh,
Gesta Roberti Wiscardi, Gesta Federici, and *De rebus
Siculis* in succeeding centuries.[82] All these masquerades
of Vergil are confused gropings in the direction of the
Africa; classical machinery, diction, similes are all there—
even to plagiarism of lines and passages.[83] But they are
better history than poetry; their only importance for
literature is that they indicate the continuing attraction
to literary men of Vergil's style and Vergil's epic
achievement, and the complete lack of distinction between
epic and *annales*. Their occasional hyperbolic suggestions
of significance or scope are wholly artificial.

In *Quattrocento* Christian epic the formula seems to
have been a combination of Juvencus' paraphrase with
Sedulius' breadth, without however the straitness of the
one or the philosophizing of the other. Typical failures
of the quasi-historical sort were the vulgar epics of Gra-
denigo, *I quattro vangeli*, Candido de' Buontempi, *Libro
del Salvatore*, and Francesco Filelfo's life of John the
Baptist, which bears some relationship to Paulinus of
Nola's hexameter paraphrase of the Gospel on the same
subject.[84] Among Latin epics, the works of Lorenzo Buonincontri of San Miniato may be mentioned; in the 1470s
he wrote first a kind of Christian *Fasti, Dierum solem-
nium Christiane Ecclesie*, in four books, and then an
incomplete epic on the life of Christ. This latter stretches
from the rebellion of the angels to the spread of Christianity; almost free of pagan myth, it suggests a Christian
mythology in the manner of Juvencus and Sedulius, but
its attempts at a purified Vergilian style are wooden and
dull. A contemporary, Domenico di Giovanni da Corella,
composed a *Theotokon, seu de vita et obitu beatae Virginis Mariae*, in four books (1468); its pseudochronology
does not make up for lack of structure. Of the four

books, only the first is properly concerned with the
Virgin's life and death; the others treat various scenes
of her glorification and her miracles. A Dominican prior,
Corella rejected both Muses and *numina ficta*; he should
also have rejected Vergil, for his style seems as unap-
propriate as his structure. Giulia Calisti cites the descent
of Christ into Hell as an anticipation of Muzio and Sannazaro, but sees no other worth in the poem.[85]

The Christian epics of Maffeo Vegio, Girolamo Dalle
Valli, Battista Spagnuoli, and Macario Muzio share in
varying degrees the chronicle form. Vegio's *Antonias*,
written in 1437, deals with an episode in the life of
St. Anthony the Abbot—his visit in his declining years
to Paul the Hermit. It seems a sharp change from the
secular earlier work, but, as critics have noted, humanist
and Christian march hand in hand. Despite the fine Vergilian flavor of the style, the poem does not succeed
mainly because the character of the hero has neither
stature nor life: temptations are not conquered but simply
disposed of by divine decree.[86] Less than a decade later,
Girolamo Dalle Valli, a Paduan doctor, composed his
Jesuida, intended as part of a vast poem about the life
of man. The little work was surprisingly popular; its imitation of Vergil is mechanical and dull, and the structure
is flabby, though it does at least succeed in pointing up
some of the dramatic possibilities of Christ's life and
death.[87]

Battista Spagnuoli's *Parthenice Mariana*, first published
at Bologna in 1481, enjoyed at least ten reprintings in
the next twenty-five years; it is difficult to say why. The
first of seven *Parthenicae*, this one is about the life and
miracles of the Virgin; the others treat the legend of
St. Catherine and similar religious topics. The *Parthenice
Mariana* has intermixed a generous portion of mythology
in unexpected ways: "ora a guisa di reminiscenza, ora

come termine di confronto, ora per sostituire le divinità
pagane all'elemento fantastico demoniaco cristiano." ("at
times as a kind of reminiscence, at times as a term of
comparison, or at times by substituting the pagan deities
for the fabulous Christian demons.") Spagnuoli's handling
of Latin style is similarly peculiar and idiosyncratic; by
freely adapting Vergil as well as other classical poets, he
sought to create a style of his own. But the result is
neither fish nor fowl, as is the result of his meddling
with structure. Here his eccentricity produces a devotional rather than a dramatic or narrative structure: the
Parthenice is controlled not by the Gospel, not by organized narrative, but by the mysteries of the Rosary.[88]

The most authentically Vergilian of Spagnuoli's longer
poems was his *Trophaeum pro Gallorum ex Italia ex-
pulsione*, in five books, delicated to Francesco Gonzaga;
this work may represent in a small way the triumph of
what Zabughin calls the neoteric school of *Quattrocento*
history-epic poets.[89] The victory might have been final for
Latin epic, except for the abortive success of Muzio and
the subsequent supremacy of Vida and Sannazaro. Mantuan did not have the patience or the craftsmanship to
carry through a really great work; his career abounds
with large projects which came too hot off the presses.
His admirer Zabughin notes: "Il Mantovano non ebbe
il grado necessario di euritmia e lima artistica per con-
durre a termine un'opera grande, veramente organica e
rappresentativa." ("Spagnuoli had neither the necessary
sense of harmony nor the willingness for patient revision
to bring to completion a great work, truly organic and
representative.") The next generation was quick to note
this; Spagnuoli was hardly dead when Lilio Giraldi was
writing about him,

Nam ut ubique Maro perfectus, ita hic immodica et paene

temeraria usus est licentia, quam et magis atque magis in dies auxit...

For as Vergil is everywhere finished, so this fellow has used immoderate and uncalled-for license, which he relied on more and more as time went on.

His earlier work was satisfactory, but as he got older he wrote in a mixed and undisciplined style:

Vix enim ea legere possumus, quae longius ille aetate provectus carmina scripsit.

We can hardly read those poems which he wrote in his more advanced years.

While here the voice of the devotees of elegance plainly speaks, the censure is clearly justified; Mantuan's achievement in the *Eclogues* is never equaled by the epics. What was a real transformation of the bucolic Vergil becomes in the longer poems arbitrary and sometimes pompous trifling.[90]

Macario Muzio's *De triumpho Christi*, a short epic of 317 hexameters, was first published at Venice in 1499; in ways other than chronological, this little work is the final word in *Quattrocento* religious epic. Christ's descent into Limbo and His ascension are told in Vergilian verses which have uncompromisingly dispensed with all traces of pagan mythology. While the author intrudes too much —witness the closing prayer—Christ's description of how and why He became man and of His death is set dramatically against the background of the exultant souls of the just. The decision to reject pagan mythology and all its trappings is justified by Muzio in an admirable introduction, which set the tone for much of the following decades, Sannazaro excepted; and the general freedom from strict chronology suggests the shape of Vida's epic.[91]

Sannazaro's *De partu virginis*, epic only by the loosest
kind of definition, must be passed over here; the suggestion of Lorenzo Gatta that Vida picked up where
Sannazaro left off is utter nonsense. As Moroncini has
demonstrated conclusively, the connections between Vida's
Christiad and Sannazaro's poem are tenuous at best.[92]
Perhaps Sannazaro was attempting epic, but what he
achieved was a "poemetto mitologico"—beautiful in many
of its passages but disturbing in the confusion of tones
and in what Zumbini characterizes as the artificial service
of mythology. *De partu virginis* belongs loosely in the
genre of Pontano's *De laudibus divinis*.[93]

For many of the Christian epic poets of the *Quattrocento,* Rossi's comment is accurate:

Le anime cui era tormento il dubbio tra la fede nelle verità
transcendenti del cristianesimo e la fede nella onnipotente
virtú umana, e le anime ingenuamente pie, incapaci di pensare
una vita priva di fede, eppure prese nella loro intimità dal-
l'ideale operoso del rinnovamento classico, non potevano scan-
dalizzarsi come d'una profanazione perché ad un fine pura-
mente ornamentale paganesimo e cristianesimo si trovassero
giustappositi in un medesimo componimento.[94]

Those spirits who were tormented by the conflict between
faith in the transcendental truths of Christianity and faith in
the all-powerful human virtue of man, and those naively pious
spirits, unable to conceive of a life without faith, and still
seized in their hearts with the active ideal of the classical
revival—these could not be scandalized (as if by a profanation) at the fact that, for purely ornamental reasons, paganism and Christianity were collocated in one and the same
whole.

The essential problems of Christian Latin epic were not
solved either in theory or in practice during the fifteenth
century. Virtually all the Christian epics lacked real relevance. Spagnuoli felt it necessary to excuse his mythol-

ogizing and to write a poem, *De sacris diebus*, in which
the gods and demigods of myth are contrasted with sacred
history; in one scene, while Gabriel descends for the
Annunciation, Mercury shoots from Carmel to Olympus
and proclaims Gabriel's activities to the gods in solemn
council met.[95] As Flamini comments about Mantuan's
general attitude, "Le finzioni poetiche del paganesimo
apparivano agli occhi del buon carmelitano quasi trofei
da offrire a Dio della vittoria riportata dalla verace fede
sopra la falsa e bugiarda."[96] (The poetic figments of paganism seemed, in the eyes of this good Carmelite, like
trophies to offer to God, of the victory won by the true
faith over falsehood and lies.)

But the attempts did not succeed; this private conflict
of many humanists received its conclusive reproof in the
Hagiomachia of Folengo, which celebrates at tedious
length the triumph by death of nineteen Christian martyrs
over paganism.[97] One wonders if any of these poets, their
eyes turned towards devout Prudentius, Juvencus, and
Sedulius, their hearts set on elegant Vergil, ever perceived
the anachronism of their performance.

Marulic's success did not generate a school; his friend
and colleague, Jacobus de Bona, forgetting the success
his allegorized myth had enjoyed, produced in the 1510s
and 1520s a long chronicle epic with lyric infusions, *De
vita et gestis Christi*. Its sixteen books are loosely organized around the nine choirs of angels and the seven
gifts of the Holy Ghost, but the narrative proceeds
chronologically, from the Incarnation to Pentecost.[98] Another Mantuan humanist, Battista Fiera, intensely interested in allegory, also produced a chronicle epic, *De deo
homine*, in 1522.[99]

The possible influences on Vida of many the earlier
works have been suggested, but little direct connection
shown. What Cessi says about Dalle Valli's *Jesuida* and

its place in Vida's background is accurate enough: Dalle Valli marked out

i contorni piú drammatici.... Al Vida fu riconosciuto il merito di averne concepita la complessa costruzione e di averne disegnato i lineamenti con fine arte.

the most dramatic lines.... But it remained for Vida to gain the distinction of having conceived the complex structure and of having worked out its details with high art.

Vida's poem is far grander in design and obscures its predecessor

coll'accoppiare il pensiero religioso e l'azione mistica all'espressione classica.... Vida ha interpolato lo svolgimento mistico della concezione divina nella vita umana.[100]

in its union of religious thought and mystic action with classical expression.... Vida injected the mystic development of the idea of the divine into human life.

Spagnuoli's medievalizing may have helped Vida shape the infernal scenes in the *Christiad*, while Vida was rejecting the mythologizing; and Muzio's suggestions of scope were of some importance, as was Muzio's successful veto of the pagan tone.[101]

    It must be noted, however, the predominantly annalistic epics which preceded Vida are Vergilian only at a distance. Diction and style are certainly there, but virtually all of these poets saw Vergil through the medium of Statius and other classical imitators. What was considered Vergilian composition, what was indeed common to all the imitative epics, was the canonical practice developed by Statius and Silius, Juvencus and Sedulius. Invocations, prophecies, banquets, heroes and their epithets, dreams and visions, all the celestial machinery— these were canonical because the *imitators* of Vergil had made them so. The practice of Vergil himself, which seemed to be canonizing what Homer had done, was no doubt considered sanction enough. But never in the practice and rarely in the theory of the *Quattrocento* is there any hint either of the Vergilian design or of the essential relationship between the elements Vergil used and their specific functions in that design. The scholars and critics compared Vergil to Homer and found that Vergil wrote more smoothly, more artistically, albeit with less invention; but no one suggests that the relationship between these poets is critical rather than imitative. The one exception to the poetic mediocrity of Christian Latin epic, Marulic's *Davidiad*, is impressive not for its inherent design or structure, but for the lucidity of its allegorical framework, the superiority of its narrative to that of Statius or Juvencus, and the beauty of its imagery

While it worshiped the *Aeneid*, the *Quattrocento* supplied Vida with neither a viable definition of epic nor any exemplary practice of Christian epic. As Cicchitelli suggests, the fact that no great epic emerged cleared the way for Vida.[102] It is no coincidence that any meaningful study of the *Christiad* must go directly whither the *Ars poetica*, in its general configuration, points—to Vergil's *Aeneid*, rather than to the derivative poems or commentaries. The *Ars poetica*, bred of the gropings of *Quattrocento* humanists, performs its most vital function for the *Christiad* not in what it prescribes but in what it clarifies. In synthesizing the dominant elements of *Quattrocento* thought, the *Ars poetica* suggests the possibilities of advancing beyond prior epic practice. The emphasis on Vergil indicates that the fuzzy epic form may be clarified, that the intuitive leap may be made from the sterility of elegant chronicling to the grand design of the *Aeneid*.

Negatively, the fifteenth century solved the problem of

Christian use of pagan poetry at least for scholars and
readers, and partially for poets; with the undisputed
supremacy of Vergil in all forms, secular and sacred, the
need for allegory and its practical application to composition was minimized. Further, with elegance dominant,
the notion in Vida's time of morals making not so much
the Christian as the gentleman reduced temporarily the
inherent dissensions among Latinists. But elegance did
not solve the more pressing problem of how to make a
Christian epic relevant. It is worth noting that all three
attempts at the great Christian poem—Marulic's, Sannazaro's, and Vida's—were demanded less by the failure of
the *Quattrocento* than by the *ambiente* of humanism
victorious: *romanità cuore del mondo*; and that each of
these attempts defined a Vergilianism bordering on the
mystical—Marulic with his allegory varnished by Vergilian elegance, Sannazaro with his enshrining of the
Messianic Eclogue, and Vida with his effort at grand
design. The question that remains is whether Vida's effort
at grand design goes far enough beyond the dull aes-
theticism of his *Ars poetica* to become truly the Christian
Aeneid.

Like the practice, criticism in the *Quattrocento* remained on the primary level. Extraneous aims, moral or
stylistic, often decided methods and conclusions; it is
curious, indeed, that the allegorizations by Petrarch, or
Salutati, or Landino could be joined so easily with concerns for philology and style, and enjoy a common patron-
age in the name of civil or spiritual good. It is curious
too that a funeral elegy could be subjoined to a rhetorical
treatise whose ramifications suggest post-Empsonian ambiguity.[103] But at the same time, we must not be deceived
by the humanist convention. Poliziano's apparently excessive praise of Vergilian rhetoric or Vida's *verba deo
similis*, for instance, must be read in terms of the union

between *res* and *verbum* maintained by the leading humanists. Vittorino's *mens sana in corpore sano* was no empty slogan; it would be historical suicide to associate the rhetoricians of the humanist movement with the symbol-manipulators of our own time.

Taken with its background in the Vergilian humanism of the *Quattrocento*, the *Ars poetica* does not indicate clearly what sort of progressive imitation the *Christiad* will be, only that it will be progressive. Certain traits the epic will not have—obscurity or fantasy, for instance. The ambiguous remarks on imitation suggest both extremes—a *cento* of Vergil or something wholly new. The pitiless attack on barbarism, seen as prevailing from Vergil's death to the advent of the Medici, indicates a bias for elegance, so that one would expect the greatest attention to diction in the epic.

Vida's casual remarks on *sententiae* themselves lead nowhere, but the unity of feeling in the closing hymns of each book may be a clue. *Ars poetica* I closes with a hymn to poetry and a fierce defense of the poet's integrity; Book II with a patriotic paean calling for cultural rebirth; Book III with a fervent rededication to Vergil. Together, the three passages hint at a depth of poetic conviction and a forcefulness of purpose which may elevate the *Christiad* above anything the *Ars poetica* could directly engender or the previous tradition suggest. Vida's insistence on the necessity of genius and on constant, thorough, contemplative reading of the classics, is, like the hymns, less prescriptive than descriptive. But it is safe to say that these elements of the *Ars*, and not its precepts, will be the most important in our study of the poet at work.

We must conclude without neat statements of the relationship of the background or of the theory to the *Christiad*. No formula can be imposed. The suggestions

7.

I have made about the tradition of Vergilian humanism
up to Vida, and including the *Ars poetica*, must be
retained as background; significant criticism of the
Christiad as epic must begin with, and perhaps end with,
Vergil and the *Aeneid*.

CHAPTER THREE

THE VERGILIAN FRAMEWORK

THE TRADITION of Vergilian poetry was a hard taskmaster and a capricious one. It established canons by which every poet must needs abide if he would be respectable. These canons, apparently engendered by Vergil, were defined less by the practice of the *Aeneid* than by the hallowing of time. Furthermore, individual talent was less important than the poet's devotion to the tradition. To some extent, the *Ars poetica* adheres to this view: its second and third books suggest canons and rubrics necessary for authentic Vergilianism as Vida understood it at the time, modified by the Idealism of Bembo and the elegance of the *Quattrocento* Latinists. In general framework, the *Christiad* itself seems squarely in the tradition. Our inquiry in this and the following chapters must determine to what extend the strategy and tactics of Vida's epic are indebted to Vergil; whether in them Vida merely observed the canons or transcended them; whether Vida mechanically imitated his master or, understanding the original functions of what had become canonical in the tradition, transformed him. We must discover if the *Christiad*, growing out of the elegance-modified Vergilian tradition, managed also to outgrow and perhaps to reshape that tradition.[1]

Vida's epic appears to have everything canonically demanded. It opens *in medias res*; it has catalogue, historical background, and enhanced characters; it has some species of wars, councils, and banquets. Easily enough, the poem abounds in supernatural machinery—infernal and celestial scenes, numerous demonic and angelic personages, extensive and resounding prophecies. But these and other elements can be called canonical only to the extent that they are divorced from significant function and used merely because the tradition says they must be.

In proposition and invocation, Vida inverts the Vergilian practice. He attempts Vergil's compressed and stately manner while eschewing a bold announcement like *Arma virumque cano.* The *Christiad* begins modestly with a prayer to the Holy Spirit. Then Vida states the ineffable and moving subject, hints at some of the major episodes, and concludes with a suggestion of higher argument:

> Qui mare, qui terras, qui caelum numine comples
> Spiritus alme, tuo liceat mihi munere regem
> Bis genitum canere, e superi qui sede parentis,
> Virginis intactae gravidam descendit in alvum,
> Mortalesque auras hausit puer, ut genus ultus
> Humanum eriperet tenebris, et carcere iniquo
> Morte sua, manesque pios inferret Olympo.
> Illum, sponte hominum morientem ob crimina Tellus
> Aegra tulit, puduitque poli de vertice Solem
> Aspicere, et tenebris insuetis terruit orbem.
> Fas mihi, te duce, mortali immortalia digno
> Ore loqui, interdumque oculos attollere caelo,
> Et lucem accipere aetheream, summique parentis
> Consilia, atque necis tam dirae evolvere causas.
>
> (I. 1-14)

Spirit of love, Whose divinity fills the sea, the earth, and the sky, grant me Thine aid to sing the twice-born King Who, leaving the throne of His heavenly Father, came down into the womb of the undefiled Virgin and, as a child, breathed our mortal air, to vindicate the human race and to rescue it from the darkness of its miserable prison by His death, and to bear the souls of the just to heaven. As He died of His own will, for the sins of men, Nature groaned, and the sun, reluctant to look on, plunged the world into terrifying unnatural darkness at high noon.

Grant me the grace under Thy guidance to fix my eyes on heaven and to receive its spiritual light, so that my mortal tongue may utter worthily things immortal and unfold the design of the Almighty Father and the reasons for this death so cruel.

Lucretius' opening hymn to Venus offers a precedent for the order, though Vida has obviously dispensed with both the sceptical tone and the suggestion of sugarcoating. Vida's conclusion also differs in some respects from Vergil's: the summary of the Apostolic age at the end of the *Christiad* stresses the universal significance of Christ's redemption. In this, as in the highly reverent references to the redemption in his opening lines, Vida clearly suggests the higher argument of his poem.[2]

Multiple invocation was traditional in epic. Its commonest purposes were to mark off the narrative into major sections, to point up important passages, and to call on the gods as witnesses to the truth of the tale.[3] Thus, Homer calls on the gods before narrating the battle of the ships; Apollonius invokes Erato, patroness of love, at the beginning of his Jason-Medea episode; Vergil invokes the proper gods before the descent into Hades, at the Trojans' arrival in Latium, and before narrating the exploits of Turnus. Vida has new invocations before the catalogue, in Book V when Christ's condemnation seems imminent, and in Book VI before the Harrowing of Hell.[4]

The invocation before the Harrowing of Hell is particularly interesting:

> Aura veni afflanti patris omnipotentis ab ore:
> Aura potens caeli numen, superumque voluptas,

> Quicquid adhuc superat mihi dira e caede dolorum
> Mente fuga, laetosque animi nunc reffice sensus,
> Et placidos per membra riga mihi numine motus.
> Sit fas laetitiae sentire in pectore lapsus,
> Laetitiae, qua gens fruitur felicis Olympi,
> Larga ubi latifluo passim torrente redundat
> Gaudia, nec fines novit diffusa voluptas.
> Vertitur hic rerum facies, hic gaudia nostra
> Incipiunt: longe in melius versa omnia cerno.
>
> (VI. 110-120)

Come, Spirit, from the life-giving breath of the Father
Almighty, mighty Spirit, Godhead of heaven, joy of the angels.
Cast out whatever tinges of sorrow still remain in my mind
from this grievous death, and refresh the senses of my soul
and divinely wash my limbs in the dew of Your peace. Grant
me to feel in my heart the advent of joy, of the joy in which
the blessed delight in heaven, where great happiness abounds
as in a mighty torrent, and where pleasure continues endlessly.
Now the face of things is transfigured; now our joys begin.
I see all things turned to the good.

The possible examples in Vergil—the invocation before
the descent into Hades or upon the arrival of the Trojans
in Latium—are only partially appropriate. The first is
awesome: "Di, quibus imperium est animarum, umbrae-
que silentes ..." (*Aen.* VI. 264); the second, announcing

> maior rerum mihi nascitur ordo,
> maius opus moveo.   (VII. 44-45)

is weighed down by what has preceded:

> dicam horrida bella,
> dicam acies actosque animis in funera reges ...
>
> (VII. 41-42)

What Vida's invocation does is to change the tone
unobtrusively, introducing a quiet but genuinely religious
joy.[5] The patterned repetitions of key words like *voluptas,*

laetitia, and *gaudium* are part of the movement, but one is not fully aware of the shift until the last two lines. In the long episodes which follow, the feeling of joy expands, to reach its fullness at the Ascension.

Though Vida uses invocations more sparingly than Vergil does, he is lavish with his apostrophes. Vergil has only one clear apostrophe, that to Nisus and Euryalus.[6] Lucan, however, discarding many of Vergil's techniques, used apostrophe extensively, a practice followed by Petrarch in the *Africa.* But frequent as Vida's apostrophes are, they derive almost as much from Vergil as from Lucan. The mournful quality of the apostrophe to deicidal Judea has none of Lucan's indignation; this chantlike rendering of the *Improperia* recalls fleetingly Anchises' lines on Marcellus.[7] The apostrophe on the goodness of Christ suggests Lucan's reflections on Pompey, as that on Judas suggests Lucan's on Caesar.[8]

Whatever other purpose the invocations and apostrophes serve, they aid substantially in providing epic proportions. The same purpose is served more distinctly by other canonical elements, such as the catalogue, the use of historical background, suggestions of etymological derivation of names, and the use of wars, councils, and banquets. In varying degrees, these elements help to suggest what Tillyard has called "amplitude and breadth."[9]

The catalogue in Book II is roughly canonical, with this difference: it serves mainly as setting and as amplification. It has a special invocation; this is common enough from Homer on, a guaranty that the list is valid.[10] Vida adapts both invocation and the catalogue itself to his own purposes. The occasion is the Paschal feast, but the tribes and cities catalogued do not play an important role in the action. Vida's justification is reverence for the land where the angels walked and Christ lived. By emphasizing this in the invocation, he discards the fiction of listing

"combatants" and suggests forthrightly the real function
of a catalogue. In the catalogue itself, Vida includes interesting tales or allusions, such as the story of Sodom and
Gomorrah, of the sun standing still, of the tribe of Dan
—sad because of a prophecy that a false Christ would
spring from their line—, and the prophecy about one
youthful member of the crowds converging on Jerusalem,
Saul, who would do great things.[11] But the list does not
masquerade as the roster of an army; had Vida considered
such to be the function of the catalogue, he would have
used the twelve Apostles on the one hand and the Jews
or devils or both on the other.[12]

Vida does make more conventional use of the historical
background of people and places. In Book I, he gives the
legend of the founding of Jerusalem by "Semes ... vitisator
pater," and of the temple:

> Hic templum Solomon, per terras omnibus aris
> Eversis, ope barbarica rex condidit olim,
> Templum opulentum, ingens, eductam ad sidera molem.
>   (I. 384-386)

Here Solomon, after destroying all the altars throughout the
land, long ago founded a temple, rich with foreign spoil and
mighty, and rising massively upwards towards the heavens.

He adds the history of the sacrifice:

> Hic gentis rex, atque omni cum gente sacerdos
> Sacra ferens pecudum fundebat rite cruorem:
> Victima non alias maculabat sanguine sedes.
>   (394-396)

Here the king and the priest, with all the people, bearing the
sacred vessels, ritually shed the blood of sheep. Nowhere else
was victim's blood spilled.

Passages like these, and their prototypes in the *Aeneid*,
providing interest or relief, also suggest heroic pro-

portions.[13] The etymology of names may be similarly enlarging, but Vida employs this only to explain—with symbolic intent—*Jesus* and *Christus*. Wary of meddling with history, he very likely would not permit himself the creation of facts out of whole cloth, however much he might countenance the adaptation of details. The catalogue and the compressed details provided about the places passed during the flight into Egypt are generally orthodox, as the detailed notes of Botta and Perrone show; so too is the history of the pool in Book I.[14]

The washing of the feet at the Last Supper is an instance of the appeal to tradition:

> Hinc genibus positis, Petro, reliquisque suorum
> . . . .
> Dat pedibus lymphas, et molli siccat amictu
> Accurvus, sociis linquens imitabile factum.
>
> (II. 676, 678-679)

Then, going down on His knees, He bent over and washed the feet of Peter and of the other Apostles, and dried them with the towel, leaving them an example which they were to imitate.

As with the Mass and the veneration of the Cross, the connection between the epic event and contemporary practice enlarges both. Vergil's example[15] is easily adapted here, and Vida can be even more precise—his historical information is obviously more accurate than his master's was.

Like Vergil, Vida attempts epic size in the council scenes—of the devils in hell and of the priests in Jerusalem—and in the mobilization of the angels in Book V. He has no opportunity for massed battles, but he exploits specific hand-to-hand conflicts, like that between Christ and the devils who possessed the Gerasene youth, that between Pilate and the Jews, and the incident of the adulteress whom the Jews dragged before Christ to trap Him. These and others Vida narrates with vigor that emulates Vergil's. Both can only suggest the proportions which Homer more directly achieved, but they have their best moments in the single conflicts—perhaps mainly because these are open to extended significance.

Banquets are cited in the *Ars poetica* (II. 255 ff.) as an attractive feature of epic, but the *Christiad* shows little trace of them. Neither in the episode of Zaccheus' conversion, nor the dinner at Simon's house, nor the marriage feast at Cana, does Vida provide any semblance of a banquet. The Last Supper has little connection with the feast in Dido's palace; Vida's scene and the relevant circumstances combine elements from the whole of *Aeneid* I with parts of *Aeneid* VIII. Simon the bard is also host, with the manner of Evander. Despite the clearly impoverished circumstances, Vergil cannot give up the insistence on *cerealia liba*; nor can Vida. But the narration of the Last Supper is primarily shaped by the impelling reverence Vida the cleric has for so sacred an incident; the scene is denuded to strictly necessary details and brief reference to contemporary customs. While Vida foregoes many opportunities to develop full-scale banquets, his poem gains in the Last Supper scene with its brevity and yet its power.[16]

The canon of supernatural machinery is easy for Vida to follow; given the divine subject as well as the classical exemplars, there is surprisingly less than might be expected. There are councils in heaven and hell, movements of devils and angels, prophecies, a bard, a sibyl, and dreams—but all carefully subordinated. Vida took pains to avoid the excesses of Statius, for instance, or of Sannazaro.

In Vergil, as in Homer, the bard belongs to the celestial machinery only because of his heaven-sent inspiration; in

Vida, he has a prophetic function. The song of Simon
before the Last Supper recalls only generally the song of
Iopas in Dido's hall.[17] The bard Iopas, otherwise un-
identified, sings a Lucretian song which provides a setting
for Aeneas' long narrative. Vida's Simon is given a complete history and is clearly certified as a proper *vates*;
before the entry of Peter and John, he had been singing
of nature and of ancient times. His subsequent song, given
in detail by Vida, concerns the exodus from Egypt, the
manna, the water from the rock, and the sacrifice of
Melchisedech—all prophetic in the context.

The role of sibyl is filled by Anna, mother of Mary;
her prophetic function is decidedly minor. Here, Vida's
adaptation is awkward, only a little less bizarre than
Sannazaro's Proteus, who, at great length, performs a
similar function. The dignity Cicchitelli claims for Vida's
Sibyl is difficult to perceive in the frenetic Anna.[18]

Vida's handling of dreams is happier. With adaptations
from Vergil he combines scriptural suggestions and psychological truth. At a crucial point in the action, Pilate's wife
narrates to him her dream of the "candidus agnus,"

> Quem circumfusique canes, sudibusque petebant
> Pastorum globus omnis. cum mox omnia ademtum
> Pascuaque, et notis flebant cum saltibus agri.
> At pater altitonans manifesta percitus ira
> Desuper auctores caedis saevibat in ipsos.
> Turbatum extemplo visum ruere undique caelum,
> Et campos late, ac silvas quatere horrida grando.
> Tum subito audita ex alto, voxque acta per auras:
> Parce Deo, Romane, hominum compesce furorem.
>
> (V. 287-295)

whom the dogs were closing in on and the whole band of
shepherds harassed with pikes: soon all things were weeping
over the death of the lamb—the pastures and fields, and the
dales so familiar to it. But the father who thunders on high,

moved by wrath, was furious against those who had brought
about its death. Suddenly the whole sky was seen to shiver
with turmoil, and fearful hail rained far and wide on field
and wood. Immediately a voice was heard from on high, borne
on the winds: "Roman, spare God and curb the anger of
men!"

The symbolism of the dream derives clearly enough from
the words both of Christ and of John the Baptist which
had just been cited by the Apostle John in his narrative
to Pilate; the conclusion Pilate's wife draws—

> Parce manus scelerare, pio, vir, parce cruori.—

is the accurate, unqualified conclusion she might well
have drawn from seeing Christ captive and hearing the
narrative of John. Though Vida does not suggest that she
heard the story, she knows well enough what is going
on; the elements of her dream need not be supernatural.[19]

At least two other dreams in the *Christiad* have this
psychological aspect. Joseph's first dream, in which an
angel reveals to him the truth of Mary's claim, is scriptural
in origin. Vida's arrangement of the details, however, suggests the likelihood that meditation on the prophecies of
the Old Testament had contributed to his understanding
and that the emphasis Joseph places on the angel is attrib-
utable to modesty on his part and to the desire to con-
vince.[20] Judas' dream, completely unscriptural, is predicated
primarily on his readiness to reshuffle the arguments for
and against the betrayal. Nothing that Satan says to him
is really new to Judas. The result of his dream is a
rationalization of his decision.[21]

For these dreams, Vergil provides a precedent in three
dreams of Aeneas—the dream of Hector, of the Penates,
and of Mercury. None of these needs a nonhuman explanation; each of them has certain elements highly suggestive of ordinary subconscious processes; and each has,

as content, matter which is somehow or other already known.[22] Other dreams in the *Aeneid*, however, involve definite information not otherwise available, as in the apparition of Allecto to Turnus in VII, or of the river-god to Aeneas in VIII. Resembling these are the dreams Anna has early in *Christiad* III, when she is urged to find a husband for Mary, and Joseph's later dream, when the angel reveals Herod's intent and orders him to take the child and His mother to Egypt. While such dreams are clearly part of the celestial machinery of Vida's epic, they are not as effective as either his more realistic dreams or any of Vergil's.

When we turn to the more actively supernatural elements of the *Christiad*, the activities of devils and angels, the crucial question arises of the use of mythology in a Christian poem. In rendering hell and the devils, Vida seems to resort extensively to mythology. Here is his description of the devils in the infernal council scene: there gather

> Lucifugi coetus varia, atque bicorpora monstra
> Pube tenus hominum facies, verum hispida in anguem
> Desinit ingenti sinuata volumine cauda.
> Gorgonas hi, Sphingasque obscoeno corpore reddunt,
> Centaurosque, Hydrasque illi, ignivomasque Chimaeras.
> Centum alii Scyllas, ac foedificas Harpyias,
> Et quae multa homines simulacra horrentia fingunt.

... various twin-bodied monsters of the light-shunning band, in the shape of men down to their middle, but with bristly tails convoluted in huge coils and ending in the form of snakes. Some have the look of Gorgons or Sphinxes with their revolting torsos, and others of Centaurs, Hydras, or fire-spewing Chimaeras. Many others take the shape of Scyllas or of putrefying Harpies, or of the many other repulsive shapes which men depict ...

Satan, "igne tricuspide ... armatus," appears,

> ... centumgeminus flammanti vertice supra est
> Arbiter ipse Erebi, centenaque brachia jactat
> Centimanus, totidemque eructat faucibus aestus.
>
> (I. 140-149)

But above the blazing peak is the emperor of hell himself, hundredfold, his hundred hands flailing his hundred arms about, and his hundred mouths belching forth seething flames.

Satan and his crew are, elsewhere, *infernae vis effera gentis*; *furiae*; *Erynnis*; *Erebi legio*.[23] On the other hand, the regions of hell presented in the council scene, in the ekphrasis, and in the Harrowing of Hell scene are quite medieval, deriving less from Vergil and Statius than from Dante. To some extent, of course, Christian tradition supported Vida's procedure, holding that the coming of Christ not only toppled the idols of Egypt but also clarified the identification of the mythological deities as colleagues of Satan.[24]

But for all the mythological flavor, neither the devils nor hell ever become ghoulish, mainly because Vida never leaves the character of the devils and their activities in doubt. Against the purplish background of hell, he limns the huge irony of Satan's campaign—

> ... non inscius illam
> Jam prope adesse diem, superi qua maximus ultor
> Imperio patris infernis succederet oris
> Manibus auxilio, ac sedes vastaret opertas,
> Sollicitus partes animum versabat in omnes,
> Siqua forte potis regno hanc avertere cladem,
> Molirique Deo letum meditatur ...
>
> (I. 122-128)

He was not unaware that that day was fast approaching on which the great Avenger, at His Father's command, would descend to the shores of hell to help the souls of the just and to destroy the infernal prison. Anxiously, he pondered all the possible ways to ward off this disaster from his kingdom, and he lays plans to have the Lord killed ...

—as of Satan's interpretation of their fall from grace, and his proposals for doing away with this Christ. The dragon-like devil who tempts Eve is medieval in appearance and orthodox in character. The activities of the demons when they organize the priests and force matters to a head, when they lash on the mob and subvert Pilate's good intentions, when they try to tempt Christ or possess luckless youths—all these are clearly orthodox in motive and procedure.[25] These demons are clearly St. Paul's "principalities and powers," briefly individualizing the antagonist force of evil in the poem.

The council of devils recalls only distantly the council of the Latins in *Aeneid* X; in Vida's scene, there are some suggestions of Vergil's Tartarus, though Claudian and Dante are clearer sources. The Harrowing of Hell in Book VI differs from the conventional descent scene in both form and function. Vida's description of the underworld, with the differentiation between the abode of the damned and the abode of the just, has affinities with Dante's *Inferno* and *Paradiso*.[26] The demeanor of the just, their songs, their expectation are a distillation of the Old Testament and suggest, by their yearning, the minor modes of the Advent liturgy. Unlike the underworld episodes of Homer and Vergil, Vida's is vivid and energetic; it has, further, telling contrasts, dramatic detail, and subtle patterns of imagery. The function of the episode is quite unlike that of *Aeneid* VI, where revelation to Aeneas and confirmation of his mission are both important and major themes of the poem are underlined. Vida has transferred these functions in large part to his fourth book, the apocalyptic discourse by John on the nature of God and the mission of Christ Incarnate. The Harrowing of Hell dramatizes only partially the import of the redemption.

What resemblance the angels bear to mythological figures like Mercury or Iris is incidental. Frequently, Vida uses overblown epithets, like *superi* or *coetus aligeri*. But his angelology is consistent; there is no real confusion of the nine choirs with the various deities of the ancient world. In Book V, a lengthy preparation for battle suggests Homer's Hera and Athena meddling in the Trojan War. Christ has just reached Calvary and, shuddering at the Cross, has cried out to His Father. The angels, watching from all points of the heavens, are called to arms by one who has not lost the taste for battle. Flocking together, they take on corporeal form and arm themselves with their long-unused armor and with the spoils of a "former war." Behind the magnificent Michael, they march to destroy the Jews and save Christ. At the portals of heaven, Clementia and Pietas of the choir of Virtues meet them, sent by the Father to halt this march. The angels assemble about God's throne and receive a rebuke, an explanation of the divine will, and a prophecy of the destruction of Jerusalem.

Vida may have intended here to evoke the ancient deities interfering in the wars of mortals and being rebuked by Zeus and Jupiter. But aside from the nice question of the angels' exact motive, Vida is orthodox. His contrivance obscures the central question of obedience: Vida implies that the angels are taking for granted the propriety of their action, but he also suggests, by recalling that former battle with the rebels, that these angels are not inquiring too closely into the divine will. Similarly, God's rebuke is clear, but tempered by the prediction of the impending destruction of Jerusalem.

The mobilized angels and especially Michael are terrible in their righteous wrath yet luminous of aspect; Vida's description conveys enormous and frightful power, covered by a gentleness, and boundless strength ordered by their allegiance to the just and meek Christ. When, chastened, they submit, it is without muttering or casting wistful looks at the shining gear they were almost able to use again. Their ancestry, then, is rather the angels who destroyed Pharaoh's army and did battle against the Amalecites and the Assyrians than the willful and insubordinate deities of the Trojan War, Latium, or Thebes.[27]

The whole angels' scene of Book V has been subjected by the critics to extravagant praise and blame. Typically, Cicchitelli suggests that the scene enhances the Crucifixion but excoriates Vida for drawing his God too faithfully on the model of Homer's Zeus. But he wrenches both out of context: the motif is Vergilian; the angels bow to Destiny, as does the humanity of Christ. The similarities of form emphasize the difference of meaning. Homer's Zeus is tricked easily; Vergil's Aeneas and Juno are less capricious than their Homeric counterparts, and his Jupiter more serenely majestic. Vida's God is not any of these, nor is He the God of the Israelites any longer; that God might well have sent down His angels to destroy Jerusalem: witness the significant contrast in the ekphrasis and the Sodom and Gomorrah tale, a striking pendant to the angels' scene.[28] The whole passage is further enriched by allusion and parody. As Vergil's Jupiter, in *Aeneid* XII, gains stature by the allusion to Homer's Zeus, so, by the unhesitant and ungrudging submission of the angels, Vida underlines God's absolute supremacy in contrast to the fitful and short-lived fears of Hera and Athena and the sullen compromise which Juno extracts. Finally, it may be pointed out, there is a large and telling gap between the pronouncements of Zeus and Jupiter on the one hand and of Vida's God on the other.[29]

The whole matter of the use of mythology is too easily obscured by romantic preconceptions. Petrarch stated

8.

the position of most of the humanists in his *Contra Medicum*:[30]

... siquis ergo talis, pio instigatus affectu, ad ipsius veritatis ornatum musarum presidio niteretur, et vel stilo clarissimo Cristi vitam vel sacrum aliud vel prophanum etiam, modo non vetitum, celebraret ... quis putas id melius posset implere?

... if then such a man, moved by a sublime feeling, should attempt to ornament Truth itself with the help of the Muses, and in an admirable style should celebrate the life of Christ or some other sacred subject or even profane, as long as it is not forbidden ... who do you think would best be able to carry out such a task?

To the humanists, the answer is clear enough: the classically trained poet. But against the humanist conception of literature, the outcry is "pagan profanation." A typical confusion, which finds echoes in Symonds, is that of Saint-Marc Girardin, who went to great lengths to demonstrate the corroding influence of pagan literature on Vida's epic, while also attacking Vida's classical polish. As romantic, he must assert the movingly lyrical quality of Sannazaro's *De partu virginis*, while as latter-day Christian he complains bitterly of Vida's pagan diction. As romantic, he accepts warmly Sannazaro's tributes to gods and goddesses and rivers, and rejects the marblelike quality of Vida's style; while as Christian again he asserts the religious quality of Sannazaro's Joseph and David, and the pagan quality of Vida's God and angels. This confusion of romanticism and its brand of paganism with Christian orthodoxy on the one hand, and the paganism of antiquity with the classical purity of certain ancient poets on the other, is all the more remarkable when we note that the combination of antique paganism with antique purity rarely occurs: Vergil is hardly pagan in that sense. This kind of confusion makes criticism impossible.[31]

Perhaps part of the celestial machinery but nonetheless functioning in their own right in Vida's epic are prophecy and the use of ekphrasis. The prophecies of the Father during the Transfiguration in the first book and after the Ascension in the last book are evidently intended to emulate Jupiter's prophecies in the opening and closing books of the *Aeneid*. In the first Christ has been praying for the frail Apostles, indicating His worries about the trials ahead and particularly His concern about the Church. Though the whole prayer is founded on John 17, the rhetorical arrangement of Christ's questions, contrasted to Venus' indignant passion, suggests contrivance. But the Father's reply is grand prophecy, broadly asserting the Apostles' perseverance and the miraculous spread of the Church, and proclaiming Rome's destiny as center of Christendom. Difficulties there will be, among even the elect; yet despite "nepotes degeneres,"

> ... per dura, laboresque
> Exercens lapsam revocabo in pristina gentem.
> Illa malis semper melior se tollet ad astra.
>
> (I. 921-923)

... with hardship and travail will I visit them and recall the erring people to its proper goodness. That city will always arise from its miseries more glorious than before.

The final prophecy is similarly prepared for by Christ's leading questions; again, the contrivance is awkward, though based on John and the epistles of Paul. Christ asks the Father to send the Paraclete so that the timorous disciples may proceed courageously with their mission. In response, the Father predicts that, fortified by the Paraclete, the Apostles will go forth, preaching and teaching in Christ's name; the Gospel will be spread to the ends of the earth and these timid men will not be deterred by either torture or martyrdom:

> Implebunt terras monitis, et cuncta novantes,
> Templa pererrato statuent tibi maxima mundo,
> Ad tua mutatae properabunt nomina gentes,
> Divisae penitus toto orbe per aequora gentes,
> Seclaque conversis procedent aurea rebus.
>
> (VI. 863-867)

They will fill the world with Your teaching, and, making all things new, they will establish great churches to You as they traverse the earth. Converted nations will hasten at Your name, nations in the far corners of the earth; and with this great change, the golden age will begin.

Both of these passages gain by allusive contrast to Vergil. Christ's filial demeanor and serene confidence are crowned by the Transfiguration, in which, shining like the sun,[32] He is joined by the symbolic figures of Elias and Moses. The contrast with the volatile and plaintive Venus is effective, and even more, the contrast of the Father with the half-mocking Jove. Vida's daring allusion, *oscula libavit nato*, is followed by these words of the Father, retaining the simplicity of the Gospel:

> Hic mea progenies, hic est mea magna voluptas:
> Uni huic, mortales omnes, parete volentes.
>
> (I. 957-958)

This is My Son, this is My greatest joy.
To him alone, all ye mortals, bow down in humble
[obedience.

The prophecy itself, when it seems most distinctly to echo Jove's, is most significantly different: for the empire of peace to be achieved by bloody conquest, Vida's God defines a Rome where greatness is predicated on trials and tribulations. A similar passage in the final prophecy tells indeed of blood necessarily spilt, but the blood is that of martyrs. There too the contrast of circumstances is sharply underlined: Juno's peevish exaction of a compro-

mise is a foil for Christ's showing the Father the insignia
of His passion. For Jupiter's history of Rome, which
includes a vague forecast of adjustments involving lineal
descent, customs, tribal name, and language, Vida's God
speaks of the wonderful and universal merits of Christ's
death, the peaceful conversion of the world, and the end
of distinctions between Chosen People and Gentiles:

> Tanta tuae merces, ea vis, ea gratia mortis.
>
> (VI. 873)

Vida is suggesting that everything that came of Jupiter's
Rome was merely the groundwork for its true destiny as
center of Christendom.

Both of these prophecies are exalted and impressive;
both derive from Vergilian models and gain by significant
contrast. At the end of the last, however, a provincial
element, from a post-Vergilian tradition, badly mars the
sublime quality. "As the centuries roll on," the Father
promises Christ,

> ... tuis omnes resonabunt laudibus urbes,
> Praesertim laetam Italiae felicis ad oram,
> Addua ubi vagus, et muscoso Serius amne
> Purior electro, tortoque simillimus angui,
> Qua rex fluviorum Eridanus se turbidus infert,
> Moenia turrigerae stringens male tuta Cremonae ...
>
> (VI. 884-889)

... all the cities will resound with Your praises, particularly
in the happy area of Italy where the winding Adige and the
Serius with its mossy stream, purer than amber, glides like
a coiling serpent, where the Po, lord of all rivers, rushes on,
threatening the walls of towered Cremona ...

There, after fifteen hundred years, poets will arise to sing
Christ's glory! Statius' modest advertisement closing the
Thebaid may have suggested the practice:

> Durabisne procul dominoque legere superstes,
> O mihi bissenos multum vigilata per annos
> Thebai? iam certe praesens tibi Fama benignum
> stravit iter coepitque novam monstrare futuris.
> iam te magnanimus dignatur noscere Caesar,
> Itala iam studio discit memoratque iuventus.

Will you endure in the years to come, and survive your master, and be read, O *Thebaid*, for twelve years the object of my laborious toil? Indeed, Fame has already been kind to you and has begun to hold you up, young as you are, to future times. Already, greathearted Caesar acknowledges you, and the youth of Italy study and recite your lines.

Petrarch's audacious imitation of this is less direct; in the ninth book of the *Africa*, Homer prophesies in his lengthy dream discourse with Scipio the advent of a Florentine poet:

> Ille diu profugas revocabit carmine Musas
> Tempus in extremum, veteresque Elicone Sorores
> Restituet, vario quamvis agitante tumultu;
> Francisco cui nomen erit; qui grandia facta,
> Vidisti que cunta oculis, ceu corpus in unum
> Colliget: Hispanas acies Libieque labores
> Scipiadamque tuum: titulusque poematis illi
> AFRICA. Quin etiam ingenii fiducia quanta,
> Quantus aget laudum stimulus! seroque triumpho
> Hic tandem ascendet Capitolia vestra...

He will at long last recall the long-exiled Muses, and will restore the venerable sisters on Helicon, even though he faces great difficulties. This will be Francis, by name; these great deeds which you have witnessed he will gather up as into one body: the war in Spain, the Libyan campaign, and your Scipio's—and the title of the poem will be AFRICA. What confidence in his native talent, what stimulus of glory will move him—until finally he will ascend, in a belated triumph, your Capitol ...

But in Homer's mouth, and to a hero whose desire is glory, the lines are not badly inappropriate.[33] Vida's reference to himself is periphrastic and plural, including other poets of his region. It announces a new era in poetry, when Greek fictions will have been abandoned:

> Tum veri, Grajum obliti mendacia, vates
> Funera per gentes referent tua carmine verso....
>
> (VI. 882-883)

Then the true poets, forgetting the falsehoods of the Greeks, will with new song sing your death to the peoples ...

But the length of the passage and its anticlimactic effect inevitably adduce a sense of trivialization.

Other prophecies, large and small, abound in the work. In his use of prophecy in general, Vida follows his predecessors. In Homer and Vergil, particularly, and to a lesser extent in Apollonius of Rhodes and the minor Latin poets, prophecy serves to focus attention on particular characters and incidents; to heighten suspense; to unite the narrative proper with matters relative to it but not strictly in its compass; to expand the legitimate scope of the action beyond the poem's conclusion and thus suggest broader implications; and finally to suggest larger areas of the heroic world by the projection of the divine connection with human life.[34] Many of the prophecies in the *Christiad* perform one or more of these functions. Christ's death, for instance, is predicted or foreshadowed again and again, while events directly related to that act, such as the betrayal by Judas and the denial by Peter, and indirectly related to it, such as the marriage of Mary and Joseph or the events attendant on the birth of Christ, also receive clear attention.[35] Enlargement and expansion are provided by the prophetic implications of the ekphrasis, by the legends embedded in the catalogue of the tribes and cities of Israel, by Christ's predictions of the future awaiting the Apostles.[36] Similarly, Vida follows his models by interweaving prophecies, developing the veiled suggestions of one in the clear statements of a later one, or using prophecy as pendant to action.[37]

Some of the prophecies in the *Christiad*, particularly the two major ones, cannot be satisfactorily accounted for in these functions. The reason is a unique practice of Vergil in which, as so often, he departs from tradition and creates something entirely new. That is the use of prophecy for cosmic expansion of theme. Jupiter's prophecies and the supporting revelations by Helenus, by Venus, by Hector and Creusa, by oracles and omens, and especially in Hades, are Vergil's major means for expanding the person of Aeneas into a symbol and his mission into a vision of transcendent Rome.[38] This is not only a matter of the apocalyptic technique, by which the interweaving of prophecies which are fulfilled with prophecies which project into the future creates the illusion that these latter must also be fulfilled. Also, and more, this is a spiritual vision, delineated and made concrete in prophecy, imagery, incident, and character, and pervaded by Vergil's profound feelings for it.

Vida perceived and attempted to make use of this. The cosmic implications of Christ's death are suggested again and again in the poem—in Christ's prophecies about the destruction of Jerusalem and the transfer of the center of worship; in the prophecies of the archangel to Mary; in the outcry of the Jews to Pilate and in the song of the just at the Harrowing of Hell; and also in Christ's prophecies in Book IV about the end of the world, and in Book VI about the sending to the Apostles of the Paraclete.[39] Each of these, and others, supplement and enlarge the earlier explanations, so that between the Father's prophecy at the Transfiguration and His final prophecy,

Vida provides an expanding thematic exegesis which comprehends virtually all time and space.

But all of these adroitly handled prophecies, hints, suggestions lack the human element. Vida's prophecy is so infallibly right and so unmistakably clear that it becomes almost tiresome. The pathos of Laocoon or Cassandra, the fright induced by the Harpies, the troubling omen of the fiery arrow, or the mysterious sign of the white sow, even the virtuoso clairvoyance of Dido—these provide elements of mystery or of human interest which do not fit, and perhaps are not possible, in a poem whose hero is a God-Man. Vida attempted to mitigate the defect by providing ambiguity and misinterpretation on the part of Joseph and Mary, and stupefaction on the part of the Apostles; however, the difference between his central character and Vergil's, and the truncation of his other characters, weaken these effects. Far from being baffled or confused, Christ Himself prophesied frequently. The unexpected is a minor element in the *Christiad*.

The technique of ekphrasis, virtually canonical after Vergil, serves a partially prophetic function in the *Christiad*. Vida uses ekphrasis three times: in Book I, the story of the creation and the fall, with episodes and types from the Old Testament, is found engraved on the walls of the temple; in Book V, the story of the War in Heaven is on the towers at heaven's portal; in Book VI, the story of Jonas in the whale's belly is on the walls of Christ's tomb.[40] The second is part of the celestial history; its function in the narrative is to remind the angels, who have taken up arms and are marching forth to destroy the Jewish nation and save Christ, that their act is not perfectly in tune with the Father's will, that other angels once flaunted that will and they themselves had done battle against the rebels. The last presents one of the many types of Christ and provides Magdalene with a clue to the

Resurrection. But these two, however functional in narrative and theme, are awkward and contrived; it is difficult
not to consider grotesque the bronze towers at the gate of
heaven on which the story is carved—and in gold!—or the
suggestion that someone had worked, on the marble walls
of Christ's tomb, a representation of Jonas.

But the major ekphrasis is highly impressive. In the
scene immediately preceding it, Christ had driven out the
vendors, and, rejoining the Apostles who were marveling
anew at the wonders of the temple, had prophesied its
destruction and gone on thus:

> Ipse tuos quoties, praesens ut vera monerem
> Tentavi cives incassum cogere in unum.
> . . . .
> Longe alias pater omnipotens sacra transtulit oras:
> Longe alia vult ipse coli, et placarier urbe.
> . . . .
> Sic fatus, monstrat miras in marmore formas,
> Argumentum ingens, senum monimenta dierum,
> Magna quibus magni compacta est machina mundi,
> Et veterum eventus, et prisca ex ordine avorum
> Facta, haud humanis opus enarrabile verbis.
> Non illic hominum effigies, simulacrave divum,
> Arcanis sed cuncta notis, signisque notavit
> Obscuris manus artificis, non hactenus ulli
> Cognita: non potuere ipsi deprendere vates.
>   (I. 570-571, 579-580, 582-590)

How often I have tried—in vain—to unite your people in
one mind that I might teach them the truth....
To far distant shores has the Almighty Father transferred His
sacred rites; in another city, far off, does He wish to be
worshiped and adored....
Speaking thus, He pointed out the wonderful scenes in the
marble, the high argument, monuments of those ancient times
when the vast frame of the world was constructed, and of the
deeds of the ancients, and of those things that had happened

long before in the days of their forefathers—a work to which human tongue is not equal. No pictures of men or images of gods were there; but rather, the hand of the sculptor had chiseled everything in secret details and symbols, which had heretofore not been fathomed by anyone: the very prophets themselves could not interpret them.

The references to the Incarnation, to the Jews' rejection, and to the "other city" provide an appropriate setting for the *argumentum ingens*. The lines introducing the ekphrasis are rich in texture; we may note very briefly, in the first five lines, the alternation of long *a* and *e* sounds in lines weighty in spondees, the predominant *m*, the interlocking onomatopoeia, and the variation of consonant combinations, all suggesting the solemn atmosphere, as well as the hints of mystery in the following lines, particularly in the striking oxymoron, *arcanis...notis.*

The scenes of the ekphrasis depict God looking on chaos; the creation of heaven and earth; the separation of land and water, mountains and valleys; the first fish, birds, and animals, and finally man in his garden. Scenes representing the fall of man and its consequences follow. To the wondering Apostles, Christ comments briefly on the import of these scenes. Then He directs their attention to five more: the ark of Noah, the sacrifice of Isaac, the selling of Joseph and the sorrow of Jacob, Moses and the brazen serpent, and the pelican feeding her young with her own blood.

It is a long passage, but it is replete with sharp descriptive touches, as well as manifold allusions, skillful compression, and effective detail, virtually all in a style of sustained elevation. The parts are so rich in meaning that the whole is almost a symbolic miniature of the entire *Christiad*. In the final five scenes, for instance, Vida presents among other things major types and figures of Christ, the mission and fortunes of the Chosen People,

and the difference between the Old and the New Covenant.
The closing image of the pelican—

> Parte alia rostro terebrans sibi viscera acuto
> Foeta avis implumes pascebat vulnere natos.
> Stant olli circum materno sanguine laeti,
> Et pectus certatim omnes rimantur apertum.
>
> (I. 721-724)

In another part, a generous pelican, plucking out its vitals
with its sharp beak, was feeding its young from the wound.
All the little ones, nourished by their mother's blood, stand
close up and vie with each other to devour the opened breast.

—derived from Psalm 101 and Augustine's commentary
on it, suggests not only the Eucharist and the Crucifixion
but also the future history of the Church.[41]

The external setting of the ekphrasis resembles that of
the ekphrasis on the portals of the Carthaginian temple in
Aeneid I, but the differences between the two are more
striking. Vida's scenes are quite as mysterious to the
Apostles as they were to the prophets. No particular
achievements of theirs are recalled, nor is there any sign
of the world's recognition or sympathy. Like the Trojans
in Carthage, the Apostles are exiles, but they do not yet
comprehend this either. Nor has Vida used the organization of Vergil's ekphrasis. Vergil's has eight scenes in
four parallel pairs; Vida's progresses in interwoven and
highly complicated scenes of creation and fall to five distinct and highly symbolic scenes from the Old Testament.
In the earlier part, there are some suggestions of Achilles'
shield, though with quite different intent; there are reminiscences of Anchises' philosophical discourse in *Aeneid*
VI, and of Lucretius; the stylistic flavor is also somewhat
Lucretian. The five later scenes have some traces of
Vergil's other ekphrasis, the shield of Aeneas. But no
model or group of models is quite satisfactory.[42]

More than the other canonical elements, Vida's ekphrasis is, in structure, development, and relationship to the rest of the poem, very much his own. In this he has succeeded best. The framework of his epic is ostensibly Vergilian; his fidelity in observing the rubrics leads at times to grotesque results. His epic proportions are sometimes badly askew; sibylline Anna is a pathetic figure. But the major ekphrasis demonstrates that he is capable of creative imitation, of transforming his original into an effective vehicle for his own vision.

CHAPTER FOUR

THE VERGILIAN STYLE

THE HIGHER argument of Vida's Christian epic called for *verborum suppellex digna*. Such was part of Leo's original commission; Vida himself broadcast this unreservedly. That his poem had grown out of the *Aeneid* he was the first to admit. The diction of the *Christiad* is generally Vergilian; the rhetoric is recognizable and the abundant similes clamor to be identified in the original; the style seems almost cento. But the important question is, did the *Christiad* manage to outgrow the *Aeneid*?

The critics who have read, or claim to have read, the *Christiad* are quick to assert that this overrated epic is a good example of the inevitable catastrophe wrought by adherence to formulas laid down in *Ars poetica* Book III. Yet as has been indicated, in the quite recognizably Vergilian framework of his epic, Vida played fast and loose with his own precepts of *Ars poetica* II and frequently applied to the Vergilian model an untraditional, transformative process. Did he do the same in matters of style? Are there clearly creative elements in his linguistic imitation? The questions can be answered only by close examination of Vida's *eloquentia*, by determining to what extent he adheres to his own prior precepts, to what extent he disregards them, to what extent he is simpleminded imitator or poet transforming his model.

The generally Vergilian stamp of Vida's diction applies at one extreme to phrases that seem almost clichés—*tendit ad sidera palmas, dira cupido*—and at the other to some unusual words used exclusively or almost exclusively by Vergil, like *reboare*. At the same time, Vida is not completely tied down; he can borrow from prose writers or from other poets, provided decorum be not violated. Thus he uses non-Vergilian or rare-Vergilian but clearly appropriate words like these samplings: *clivus, lunatum, bisuleus, teter, pernix, accipiter.*[1] For Vida, these words are well-bred, falling into the same category as derived words, for example *diriguit, nubicolor*. But such words remain in the minority, unable to disturb the Vergilian surface or make their author seem an adventurer.

The familiar Vergilian tags occur—*mirabile dictu, si vera est fama*—sometimes with a slight variation, as in *visu lacrimabile*. One verse is wholly exclamatory: *Ecce (incredibile auditu, mirabile visu!)* (IV. 383) Vida's usage of such certified tags is generally conventional; yet one must note how such tags help to characterize Joseph in Book III:

Plena Deo tota (visu venerabile!) in aede ...
(191)

Impatiens exorsque viri (mirabile dictu!)
(309)

(Mira loquar) video medium discedere caelum ...
(321)

(Mens adeo mihi laeva fuit) tam mira ferenti ...
(400)

Inventam (portentum ingens!) in montibus altis ...
(467)

Vix primum attigeram limen (mirabile dictu!)
(478)

These tags and similar exclamations all through the third book help to convey Joseph's lingering bewilderment as

he recounts to Pilate the events of thirty-odd years before.
The patterned tags and exclamations are subtly counter-
pointed with Joseph's solemn and grave assurances that
gradually he "understood" the Old Testament prophecies,
the import of the events, and the meaning of the prophecies uttered by the angel and by Simeon.

Like Vergil, Vida uses archaic forms occasionally to give
something of the flavor of *sancta vetustas*.[2] To suggest the
venerable age of Manasses, the old man to whom the
youthful Susanna was forcibly wed, he writes:

> Pallida longaevi conjux Susanna Manassei,
> Quoi pater egregiam forma, et florentibus annis ...
> (I. 729-730)

The use of *quoi* may even be intended to counterbalance
the sympathetically-presented adulteress. About the Magi,
Joseph says:

> His vis astrorum, ac ratio volventis olympi
> Monstrarat regem nostris in finibus ortum,
> Quoi caeli, terraeque paterent debita sceptra.
> (III. 743-745)

The *quoi* here, referring to Christ, evokes not only the
solemn majesty of God but also the antiquity of the three
kings themselves. A few lines later, Vida attempts to
capitalize on archaism again, combining it with metrical
irregularity:

> Jamque urbem ingressi sedes adiere tyranni
> Herodis, caussamque viae docuere, rati olli
> Hanc sobolem, quod erat rex his in finibus, ortam.[3]
> (III. 753-755)

Used at times for metrical convenience, the archaic
genitive serves other functions as well. In II, referring to
the soldiers who have come to arrest Christ, it suggests
an eerie quality in the whole scene:

Longius aera micant tremulai lumine lunae.[4]

(II. 769)

Similarly, while the extra syllable in the archaic infinitive
form may help the meter, its use in general is confined
to passages where particular effects are sought, as in the
hint at Rome:

Longe alia vult ipse coli, et placarier urbe.[5]

(I. 580)

In all of this, what Vida is attempting is that quality
Quintilian remarked in certain passages of the *Aeneid*:
" 'Olli' et 'quianam' et 'miis' et 'pone' pellucent et asper-
gunt illam, quae etiam in picturis est gratissima, vetusti-
tatis inimitabilem arti auctoritatem."[6] (Forms like "olli"
and "quianam" and "miis" and "pone" are quite con-
spicuous and provide for art that inimitable dignity of
venerable age which is most pleasing also in painting.)

But the Vergilian veneer which Vida attempts is not
so uniform in the case of the conventional epithet. Vida's
fidus Joannes hardly raises an eyebrow because John
himself has as little clearly defined character as his proto-
type Achates. For God, there are instances which are quite
Jovian: *omnipotens sator, pater imbripotens, nimbipotens
genitor.* But the impression is fleeting; Vida's God is
clearly the First Person of the Trinity; most frequently
He is referred to simply as *Deus* or *Pater omnipotens.*
When God is called *Pater superum*, or the angels *superi*,
there is no confusion between the "spirits of the upper
air" and the members of the Olympian hierarchy. Similarly, the Holy Ghost is *Spiritus almus*, and Mary usually
virgo or *mater.*

Some of the appellations of Christ raise a larger
problem. *Vera Dei suboles*, an allusion to the Messianic
Eclogue, is well chosen, though *regis supremi satus* may

9.

seem awkward. *Deus*, used most commonly, need cause
no comment. However, the use of Christ's names and of
the epithet *heros* is striking. *Jesus* occurs only twice,
Christus only twenty-three times, and *heros* thirty-three
times with reference to Christ. Not only is Vida quite
sparing with these three, but he also places them very
carefully; the difference from Vergil's practice is remarkable. *Heros* occurs only nineteen times in the singular in
the *Aeneid*, eighteen of which occurrences come at the
end of a hexameter;[7] the name *Aeneas* or an oblique form
of it occurs 237 times.

Critics have objected to the use of *heros*, suggesting
artificial classicizing. But some considerations are in order
here. In a few cases, *heros* serves metrical convenience:
in II. 651, Vida takes advantage of initial elision. Similarly in II. 66, the oblique form *Christi* permits final
elision. Except for III. 2, *heros* always occurs in the
nominative while the oblique forms of *Christus* are used
several times.[8] Metrically, Vida is not fully consistent with
either, using both generally as spondees, occasionally as
trochees.

Beyond these circumstantial matters, there is a general
pattern in the poem to which Vida adheres in using these
two appellations. *Heros* most commonly indicates the
active Christ, the epic hero in the conventional sense.
Thus, when Christ raises Lazarus, enters Jerusalem tri-
umphantly, drives the vendors out of the temple, or
descends from Tabor, He is the *heros*.[9] Some of the priests
fear to move against Christ because the *heros* is beloved
of the people; when the soldiers come to make the arrest,
the *heros* addresses them forthrightly; in John's narrative
of the public life, Christ's activities are those of the *heros*;
to the Apostles and Magdalene in VI, Christ is *heros*.[10]
On the other hand, *Christus* indicates the passive Christ,
the Redeemer and Savior. The first and last references in

the poem are to *Christus*; in his narrative, Joseph defines
for Pilate the meaning of Christ's names:

> Addimus et nomen, memoresque vocamus Iesum,
> Ut quondam admonuit puer actus ab aethere praepes.
> Idem etiam, quod sit regum de stirpe sacerdos,
> Gentibus est Graio dictus de nomine Christus.
>
> (III. 643-646)[11]

And giving Him a name, we called Him Jesus, remembering
the counsel of the young man who had suddenly visited us
from the sky; and because he comes of royal and priestly
stock, the gentiles call Him also by the name, as it is given
in Greek, of Christ.

It is *Christus* who sends the Apostles to prepare the Last
Supper and who tells Pilate that His kingdom is not of
this world. Though in the account of Christ's public
activities, John often refers to his master as *heros* or *dux*,
in the highly symbolic incident of the loaves and fishes,
where Vida seeks to stress Christ's sacerdotal character,
John refers to Him only as *Christus*. The Apostles and
Magdalene thought only of their "leader" in VI, but the
mysterious figure who speaks to the two disciples on the
way to Emmaus and who is recognized in the breaking of
the bread, speaks of the resurrection of *Christus*.[12]

In III. 2, Vida calls attention to this distinction between
the use of *heros* and of *Christus* by the clearly deliberate
choice he makes, emphasized by metrical roughness:

> Fama volans jam finitimas impleverat urbes,
> Exceptum insidiis heroa dolisque suorum.
>
> (III. 1-2)

This solitary oblique usage occurs in an irregular form.
For the crowd, Christ is the *heros*.

Clearly enough, Vida's practice involves more than
casual classicizing. Decorum, the basis of much of Vida's

attitude toward language and style, includes not only
elegance but also appropriateness. This can be in relation
to the poem as a whole, to a particular incident or a
particular personage within the total context, or to the
style of an individual episode or passage. It is the character
of the entire work as well as of the single section which
determines the style. Thus, it is not inappropriate in the
Christiad to have low characters, though it is repugnant
not only to the poem but to the whole epic genre to use
lowly images to describe such characters. But when
judgment is passed on the "appropriateness" of style or
imagery, the poem must not be confused with the material
on which the poem is based, in this case the Gospels. C. S.
Lewis' castigation of Vida for embellishing his characters,
"even Lazarus," was bred of such confusion.[13]

In one very awkward line, Mary, usually called *virgo*
or *mater*, is referred to quite otherwise. The line occurs
at the beginning of Book III; Joseph has been hesitating,
but John, urging him to tell all he knows to Pilate,
addresses him thus:

> Regia progenies, Nymphae dignate superbo
> Conjugio ...   (III. 101-102)

The critics who pick up "Nymph" as typical of Vida's
classicizing surely overstate their case; the epithet is never
again used in reference to Mary, and its usage here is
partly justified as John's attempt to assure Joseph of a kind
of equality with Pilate.[14] At the same time, the line is
clearly offensive. It is relevant to this inquiry to note the
possible reasons for such offense. Awkward and troublesome, "Nymph" has little point in the context of the
whole poem. It is like Vergil's *fidus Achates*, an epithet
widely scorned, for the good reason that Achates is rarely
anything else, that his relationship to Aeneas is a poor
attempt at the Odysseus-Athena relationship, or the

Achilles-Patroclus friendship. At the same time, the complaints of critics about the trivializing effect of *fidus Achates* or the paganizing effect of Vida's *Nymphae* indicate how far irrelevant considerations can intrude, particularly in criticism of the *Christiad*. Vida's rendering of the Pater Noster is a case in point:

> Omnipotens genitor, sedes cui lucidus aether,
> Sic nomen, laudesque tuae celebrentur ubique,
> Et promissa orbi incipiant procedere lustra,
> Quum tua non minus in terris gens jussa facessat
> Mortalis, quam caelicolae tibi in aethere parent.
> Nos divina hodie caelo dape reffice ab alto.
> Parce dehinc bonus, ut nostris ignoscimus ipsi
> Hostibus, ac nullis adversis objice inermes
> Tentando: prohibe a nobis sed cuncta pericla.
>
> (IV. 972-980)

For many, this rendering is an inflated distortion of sacred lines. But which is the essential consideration—the inflation or the sacred lines? The sacred lines, after all, are extrapoetic matter; to judge by them is to assert that the *Christiad* is a translation of familiar and emotionally connotative texts, not a poem. One must attend to the parts of the poem in their own context, not judge the work with a Vulgate or a King James in one hand. The only really relevant comment to be made about Vida's passage is that the attempt at exalted language is indifferently successful.

The use of classical "poetic diction" here is very much a matter of choice; in other passages, Vida is strictly conventional:

> Jamque heros puras fruges properataque liba
> Accipiens, frangensque manu partitur in omnes:
> Inde mero implevit pateram lymphaque recenti,
> Et laticis mixti divum sacravit honorem....
>
> (II. 651-654)

Then the Hero took unleavened bread, which had been hastily
prepared, and broke it in His Hands and gave of it to all of
them; and He filled a chalice with wine and with fresh water,
and consecrated the sacred mixture of liquids ...

> Hic heros palmas in caelum sustulit ambas,
> Concipiensque preces genitorem in vota vocavit.
>
> (IV. 492-493)

At this point, the Hero raised both His palms in prayer to
heaven and called upon His Father.

> Ut primum fruges tostas cerealia liba ...   (VI. 554)

As soon as (He touched) the baked bread, the grain-cakes ...

Such circumlocutions, traditional and limited, are under-
standable enough, but that referring to the dead Lazarus
is egregious:

> ... quem faucibus haustum
> Telluris quarto jam Sol non viderat ortu.
>
> (I. 258-259)

... whom already the sun had not seen in four risings, swal-
lowed up as he was by the jaws of the earth.

The process involved in all these passages includes both
enhancement for the sake of decorum and glossing for the
sake of elegance alone. On this latter count particularly,
the charge that such a style is nourished by clichés is not
unjust. The style, we may recall, was not original with
Vergil; the Alexandrian scholars, particularly the scholar-
poet Apollonius of Rhodes, made embellishment a *sine
qua non* of epic when they substituted static elegance for
the Homeric "crudities." But in the *Aeneid*, thanks to
the exaltation Vergil is able to achieve, such periphrasis
is not usually obtrusive. Vergil stands in a certain relationship to his material which makes enhancement by
periphrasis less a matter of external decoration than of
internal necessity. His lines opening *Aeneid* X—,

> Panditur interea domus omnipotentis Olympi,
> conciliumque vocat divom pater atque hominum rex
> sideream in sedem ...

—are solemn and majestic. Neither the enlargement by word-choice or sound, nor the anthropomorphizing of the description can really be caviled at; the Olympus suggested there is certainly not a carbon copy of Homer's, just as the Jupiter who calls the other gods to council is not a copy of Zeus. Vergil is trying to convey, in this and similar passages, the solemnity with which his deities are to be considered; his gods form a hierarchy, subject to the Supreme Power which rules the universe, and Jove himself has many features of a monotheistic god.

Driven by the internal necessity of his material, Vida attempts the Vergilian style but hardly attains it. But his style is effective. The language is consistent, clear, and quite appropriate; Vida has mastered Vergil sufficiently so that the borrowed language never interferes with the movement of his poem; and he is able to adapt the Vergilian language broadly. Often he manages to catch just the right note, as in the following periphrasis from John's narrative. The crowds flocking after Christ had grown to such huge proportions that, in order to address them, Christ had to enter a boat and pull away from shore; the winds had been blowing—

> Ipse loquebatur, circum sedata silebant
> Aequora, ubique modo spirantibus incita flabris,
> Frondiferaeque domus avium sine murmure circum
> Stabant immotae procurvo in litore silvae.
>
> (IV. 870-873)

He began speaking: all around Him the waves grew calm, which just previously had been rocking under the gusty breezes, and along the curving shoreline, the motionless trees, their bird-infested branches silent, did not stir.

The indirect description of the spreading silence gives more prominence to the *loquebatur*, and the filled-in background conveys more effectively the sense of Christ's voice being heard more and more clearly.[15]

Vida's description of the water turned to wine at Cana is what one would expect:

> Fontis aquam latices Bacchi convertit in atros.
>
> (III. 982)

It is quite conventional, this elevation of wine into the dark liquids of the Bacchic fount; the process is the consistent one, generally indifferent, rarely so flagrant as to draw attention to itself. Compare with these lines the English version by J. Cranwell:

> Beneath the magic of his pow'r divine,
> The bashful water blush'd to purple wine.[16]

Here the conventional phrase, noted primarily for its good breeding and its suitability in heroic poetry, becomes something else—a "turn," drawn perhaps from a Nizolian paper-book. One might well question both Cranwell's padding and his diction, but what is most troublesome, and, in the final analysis, quite different from Vida's elegance, is the attempt to capitalize on every possible occasion by the use of a "sounding phrase." Here the source is Crashaw; elsewhere, it is Milton, Donne, Jonson, Marlowe, Dryden. Cranwell's heroic couplets have no consistency, no style. Vida at least attempted to make Vergil's style his own; though he does not attain Vergil's heights, he generally has a respectably unified, adequate, and appropriate style.

For all the circumlocution, Vida is capable of striking brevity, also Vergilian. Christ's words to the adulteress, *I melior*, are adequate; the Transfiguration is effectively climaxed by the Father's

Hic mea progenies, hic est mea magna voluptas:
Uni huic, mortales omnes, parete volentes.

(I. 957-958)

To the devils who plead for permission to enter the swine,
the response is a mixture of dignity and scorn: *Annuit.*
The final line of Book V hides its brevity by appropriate
metrical variation:

Supremamque auram ponens caput expiravit.

(V. 995)

In his choice of words, Vida uses, like Vergil, thematic
patterns of key words—*labor, supplicium, pax,* for
instance, functioning like *pietas* and *fatum* in the *Aeneid.*
But Vida's vocabulary is far more limited than his master's.
He can make words do full service; *gravido* in

Atque procul gravido tremefacta est corpore tellus,

(I. 138)

referring to hell and its incumbents, takes on a monstrous
quality. These two lines describe the Apostles after the
descent of the Paraclete:

Jamque pudet metuisse omnes, animosaque lethi
Spes magis atque magis viget acris numinis haustu.

(VI. 966-967)

Animosa conveys the quality of their *spes,* while *acris*
gives appropriate edge to the whole passage. So, too, when
Elias is described in the Transfiguration scene as *equis
insultans,* the detail is sharpened. In some lines, Vida
compresses effectively:

Remivaga siccum cupidi tenuere carina. (VI. 624)

The elliptical *cupidi* suggests the excitement of the
Apostles and their desire to be near Christ again. In
the line,

Undeni proceres, omnisque effusa juventus,
(VI. 802)

proceres might well go unnoticed; it is slipped into the
passage narrating the Apostles' return to Jerusalem from
the mountain whence Christ ascended, and suggests the
change that has taken place: *they* must now be leaders.[17]

In some descriptions, Vida attends to his words
carefully; here is the presentation of the sinner Maria:

Ingreditur forma insignis, cultuque puella,
Picta peregrinas tunicasque, sinusque crepanti
Argento saturos, atque auro intertexto:
Cui caput implicitum gemmis; it flexile collo
Aurum ingens mixtis onerosa monilia baccis,
Propexique nitent electro molle capilli,
Nexilibus quos in nodos collegerat hamis;
Aureaque ex humero demissam fibula vestem
Eois opibus gravidam, et Gangetide gaza
Subnectit, media micat ardens fronte pyropus,
Crebraque consertis pendent redimicula gemmis ...
(I. 305-315)

The young woman enters, striking in figure and appearance,
arrayed in exotic raiment. Her bosom was rich with rustling
silver and gold, finely interwoven, and her head was crowned
with gems. About her neck was a heavy gold band, a heavy
necklace studded with pearls; her bright hair, which she had
gathered into knots with pins, shone like soft amber. A golden
brooch bound the glistening Oriental cloak which dropped
gracefully from her shoulders, and on her forehead flashed
a brilliant ruby, and numerous fillets, hung with countless
gems.

The general tenor of the passage suggests the exotic; this
Maria is, indeed, almost more oriental than Vergil's Dido.
Not only the individual words, but their organization into
various patterns of sound and rhythm, combined with
special metrical variations—in the second and third line,

for instance, the intertwined sounds culminating in the slow and suggestive *intertexto* imitate what they describe. But even beyond the words, sound, and rhythm, Vida's arrangement of detail is noteworthy. He presents the whole as it would strike a viewer in the process of seeing it, dwelling on details in the order in which one would take note of them.[18]

At the same time, it is curious that Vida's attempts at description are almost apologetic. He relies primarily on the impression or the suggestion, rarely on the concrete detail. Jerusalem is a connotative name, hardly a solid city. The court of Pilate has no definite outlines. The hell of the council scene is presented in purplish tones which suggest *Odyssey* XI, while heaven is described in varying ways as an abode of light. For all the excellent details, descriptive and psychological, employed in passages like the above or that describing the Israelites fleeing from Egypt, the pattern which virtually controls the style is an oratorical pattern, a tendency to arrange the details, whether concrete or impressionistic, whether specific or general, into pleasing harmonies of verse, sound, and, perhaps, thematic structure. Lorenzo Gatta censures Vida severely for never giving us solid ground to stand on. Cicchitelli suggests that the temple of Jerusalem recalls more of Juno's temple at Carthage than of the real temple of Solomon. True, Vida has not gotten near

quell'opera meravigliosa dell'antichità ebraica, lo splendido edificio con le sue guglie d'oro, con l'urna di bronzo, sostenuto da leoni, con la vita gigantesca d'oro puro, simbolo d'Israele; ci sforziamo invano di ravvisare la degna casa di Dio, illuminata da preziosi candelabri, vivificata dalla fede.

that marvelous achievement of Hebrew antiquity, the splendid edifice with its golden pinnacles, its bronze urn, its gigantic vine of pure gold, symbol of Israel; we try in vain to discover the House of God, illuminated by precious candelabra and vivified by faith.

But Cicchitelli has forgotten that the temple described in *Aeneid* I is more Roman than Carthaginian, and that the palace of Priam, which Vida also draws on for his temple, is hardly Phrygian. In Vida's hands, the temple of Solomon becomes neither Carthaginian nor Trojan nor Jewish, but something vaguely Roman.[19]

It is clear that Vida is not as concerned about diction as the third book of the *Ars poetica* would suggest. The confusion between *vatem* for Messiah in

> Aereas vatem venturum lucis ad auras ...
>
> (IV. 799)

and *vates* in

> Id patribus promissum, omnes id volvere vates
>
> (IV. 802)

is disconcerting enough, but it is compounded by the awkward repetition of *lucem* in different meanings in IV. 799, quoted above, and in the following:

> ... quibus atris
> Non datur in tenebris praesentem agnoscere lucem ...
>
> (IV. 803-804)

Another kind of imprecision can be seen in these two lines, from a simile:

> Ac velut in pastus celsa quae sede columbae ...
> Tecta petunt, celeresque cavis se turribus abdunt.
>
> (V. 528, 533)

Neither *celsa sede* in the first line nor *cavis turribus* in the last line of the simile conveys anything very definite. In the particular passage, the defect is not grave since the point of the simile comes across, but lack of precision is

not uncommon in Vida's descriptions. He varies very
carefully his descriptions of morning or evening, as Vergil
does, while at the same time he gives no impression of
that meticulousness of style which demands endless variety of expression.[20] Here are lines describing Christ's
setting out with His cross:

> Et jam purpureos habitus ...
> Exutum, vinctumque manus clamore trahebant
> Dirum ad supplicium ...
> ...... plagisque cruentus
> Nocturnis, humerosque trabem duplicem ipse gerebat
> Praecisis gravidam nodis, ac robore iniquo,
> Qua super infando mortales linqueret auras
> Supplicio, et duros finiret morte labores.
>
> (V. 423-425, 427-431)

Now stripped of His robe, His hands bound, they dragged
Him forth with a shout to His fearful doom ... Bloody from
the wounds of the previous night, He carried on His shoulder
the crossbeams, full of sharp knots and rough splinters, on
which He would take His leave of mortal earth in unspeakable
torment, and would end His laborious toils in death.

The words are common enough, some are repeated,
some—like *cruentus*, *infando*, and *duros*—have obviously
been overused. In the succeeding lines there is some relief
from the beat of heavy, oppressive words, in the more
specific description of the soldiers and in the variations
of the rhythm:

> Armati circumsistunt, clypeataque juxta
> Agmina densantur: collucent spicula longe,
> Spiculaque et rubis capitum cava tegmina cristis,
> Aereaque alterno conspirant cornua cantu.
>
> (432-435)

The soldiers stand about Him, their shields crowded together
in formation, their spears gleaming far off—their spears and

their helmets crested with scarlet; and the bronze trumpets blared in alternating rhythm.

Vida's diction, it may be said in general, is undistinguished, serviceable, appropriate, and effective. The Vergilian surface is apparent, but heights and glaring improprieties are rare. My conclusion is that Vida did not take the pains attributed to him or called for by *Ars poetica* III; his diction is far more limited, and far less inventive or precise, than Vergil's. Examination of his rhetorical devices would generally suggest the same conclusions, with some important qualifications in regard to Vergilian similes, of which the prior theory says little but which Vida uses with interesting freedom. In the similes, indeed, we will find some significant features of his service to his master.

In *Ars poetica* III Vida leans very heavily on Quintilian. He makes no attempt, however, to adhere to that Roman's careful definitions and schematization of individual tropes, his definitions of individual figures, or his distinctions between tropes and figures, between figures of thought and figures of speech, and, among figures of speech, between grammatical figures and rhetorical figures.[21] *Ars poetica* III begins with a general discussion of metaphor, paying only brief attention to a miscellaneous group of tropes and figures of thought and, later, to a small group of grammatical figures.[22] But even this, as schematization, is distinctly lax.

What is generally clear about the figures in the *Christiad* is their lack of schematization. Vida uses there all the figures mentioned in *Ars poetica* III and others not mentioned; besides those which have already been cited, the following may be pointed out: metonymy, synecdoche, and antinomasia; personification, anaphora, hendiadys, oxymoron, hysteron proteron, hyperbole, hypallage, and imprecation.[23] But in utilizing them, Vida played by ear, depending rather on his reading of Vergil and other poets than on his study of Quintilian.

Even in the *Ars poetica* he shows unconcern for such matters. He blurs the distinctions between figures and tropes, or between various kinds; he refers offhandedly to the teacher for technical details; he blithely disregards the lists common to handbooks of poetic and rhetoric. When he turns from figures to that talent without which one may be a versifier but certainly not a poet—namely, imitative harmony—, it is especially noteworthy that he does not go into technical details:

> Haud satis est illis utcumque claudere versum,
> Et res verborum propria vi reddere claras;
> Omnia sed numeris vocum concordibus aptant,
> Atque sono quaecumque canunt imitantur, et apta
> Verborum facie, et quaesito carminis ore.
>
> (III. 365-369)

They are not satisfied to end their lines in any fashion and to make their points by simply an apt choice of words; but they adapt their words with the harmonious rhythm of the sounds, and in the sound they reproduce their subject, both by an appropriate shape of the words and by the special character of their verse.

What he stresses is the principle:

> ... facies sua pro meritis, habitusque, sonusque
> Cunctis, cuique suus, vocum discrimine certo.
>
> (383-384)

... each, depending on its value, has its own peculiar form, its shape, its sound, according as the words are used.

On that principle he elaborates, showing that he means far more than onomatopoeia, more than sound-with-sense; what he specifies is the embodiment of the quality or feeling or shape of an incident, character, scene, atmosphere, by all the resources of diction and metrics. But nowhere does he stipulate the use of a particular trope or figure for a particular effect. His discussion of metaphor at the beginning of Book III is a discussion of figurative language in general; without getting too technical, he says, one can observe what diverse but interrelated meanings can be derived from individual images:

> Nam diversa simul datur e re cernere eadem
> Multarum simulacra animo subeuntia rerum.
>
> (62-63)

Figurative language is delightful; it opens up various meanings inherent in the things under consideration; it amends the poverty of everyday language and is a very valuable aid to clarity of expression; it engages the mind and the senses on at least two levels at once. Through metaphor, he says, the poet may surprise his reader with *diversas rerum species.*

About the simile, Vida's *Ars poetica* says simply that it should be brief, precise, and appropriate; if it is too long, it may easily distract the reader from the matter at hand:

>   ... paucisque
> Includas numeris, unde illa simillima imago
> Ducitur, et breviter confer. ne forte priorum
> Oblitus sermonum alio traducere mentem,
> Inque alia ex aliis videare exordia labi.
>
> (III. 165-169)

In the *Christiad*, Vida uses seventy-four similes of three or more lines, and more than forty short ones.[24] Most of them seem Vergilian.

The first simile compares the crowds following Christ to the tributaries which join the river Po as it rushes to sea. Several other river and sea similes occur. More frequent are similes of flowers—the rose especially, and the hyacinth, lily, marjoram, and narcissus; and similes of birds and animals, tame like the dove, sheep, or deer, fierce like the hawk, wolf, or lion, as well as animals whose tameness or fierceness is irrelevant, such as the cow, dog, bees, and horse. Human and natural phenomena are used also—storms and floods, various aspects of the sun, moon, or stars, conquering armies, fierce or peaceful rustics, athletes, drunks, and sleeping men. And these are not all; smoke and smouldering fires, bright gems, little boys' games, mountain peaks—the list could go on. Obviously, Vida took pains to avoid repetition or overuse of a particular kind, as well as to bring into the compass of his poem as much as possible.

The similes are scattered more or less evenly through the six books; their total bulk—some 400 lines out of 6000—is not excessive.[25] What gives the impression of extensive usage is the spacing of the similes in some passages. In the first half of Book I precise and functional similes occur unobtrusively, but in the Jethro episode, three similes very close to each other produce a sense of clutter.[26] In the third of these the cured Jethro is compared to a frozen snake accidentally thawed by a shepherd collecting twigs and feeding his fire; the simile takes too long to make its point, and the possible symbolism of immortality is obscured by the strain in getting the simile in at all. A similar sense of clutter is induced by the spate of similes in the narrative of the possessed youth of Gerasa. Here, however, the similes function better, enlarging the scale of the conflict between Christ and the demons; the harsh rhythm and the skillful alliteration and onomatopoeia convey the rage of the demons and the quality of the struggle.[27]

While generally Vergilian, very few of Vida's similes are so specifically Vergilian that they can be traced, and

10.

none is so imitative as to use either the phrasing or the detail of a specific simile in the *Aeneid*.[28] The double simile illustrating the dead face of the widow of Nain's son—

> Qualis, quem pede pressit agro bos signa relinquens,
> Paulatim lassa languet cervice hyacinthus,
> Aut rosa, quam molli decerpens pollice virgo
> Vepribus in densis lapsam sub Sole reliquit ...
> (IV. 325-328)

So does the hyacinth droop languidly, when it has been trod underfoot and crushed by an ox in the field; or the rose, which a girl plucks gently, and then drops it, leaving it where it falls in the briars to wither under the sun.

—recalls the double simile used by Vergil for dead Euryalus:

> purpureus veluti cum flos succisus aratro
> languescit moriens, lassove papavera collo
> demisere caput pluvia cum forte gravantur.
> (*Aeneid* IX. 435-437)

As when, its stalk cut down by the ploughshare, the shining flower languishes and dies; or when poppies, weighed down by heavy rain, droop their burdened heads upon their stems.

But the differences here are significant. Vergil's flowers are destroyed in the course of daily work or the common phenomenon of rain; Vida's *arator* would seem parallel to the Rutulian who killed Euryalus. Vida's *bos* and particularly his *virgo*, emphasizing needless waste, add poignancy to the widow's lament. Similarly, Vida's simile for Christ driving out the vendors—

> Qualis ubi Arctois Boreas erupit ab antris,
> Aereos rapido perverrens turbine campos,
> It caelo ferus, et piceas toto aethere nubes
> Insequitur. dant victa locum, et cava nubila cedunt.
> (I. 521-524)

Just so does the north wind burst out of his arctic caves and, roaring, with fierce gusts through the fields of heaven, drives savagely through the sky, scattering the pitch-black clouds before him. The clouds yield, vanquished utterly.

—is related to Vergil's simile for Turnus breaking through the battle lines:

> Ac velut Edoni Boreae cum spiritus alto
> insonat Aegaeo sequiturque ad litora fluctus;
> quae venti incubuere, fugam dent nubila caelo.
> (*Aeneid* XII. 365-367)

As when the north wind roars out from Thrace over the Aegean and drives the waves to shore: the clouds which the blasts have hit flee through the sky.

Vergil's emphasis is on storminess, however, while Vida's is on the restoration of order and the brightening of the sky; the changes, particularly the addition of *piceas* and *victa*, account for the difference.

For some of the similes, Vida derives either content or technique—occasionally both—from the Scriptures. The sheep and goats of Matthew are transposed thus:

> Qualis post hiemem exactam, cum gramine molli
> Pascua laeta vocant stabulis armenta reclusis,
> Ipse greges pastor nitidos missurus in agros
> Sortitur: placidas primo legit ille bidentes
> Dinumerans, olidasque jubet procul esse capellas.
> (IV. 1010-1014)

So at the end of winter, when the meadows cheerful with swaying grass call the herds from their stalls and pens, the shepherd, about to send his flocks into the sunny fields, sorts them out. The gentle sheep he takes aside and separates, despatching the smelly goats to pasture farther off.

Not only has the shepherd been added from other sections of the Gospel, but specific details—the end of winter,

the joyful fields, the happy sheep, and the smelly goats—
adapt the original perfectly to the tone of Vida's context.
The conversion of Nicodemus is illustrated by this brief
simile:

> veluti de nocte profunda
> In lucem revocatus, ei se junxit amore ...
>
> (II. 157-158)

The suggestion of spiritual rebirth can be found only in
Christ's words to Nicodemus: "Nisi homo renatus fuerit
de aqua et Spiritu Sancto, non videbit ..." (John 3:1).
The comparison of Maria, the converted sinner, to a dog
at its master's table,

> Ut canis ad mensam procumbere suetus herilem
>
> (I. 358)

transposes another evangelical detail. The simile which
compares the effect of the Paraclete on the Apostles to
that of rain on parched earth alludes to Gideon's fleece,
a much-discussed type from the Old Testament; elsewhere,
Vida uses the type conventionally for Mary.[29]

Not only in his similes, but in many other passages,
Vida uses much scriptural material obliquely. There are,
in fact, only two passages in the entire *Christiad* in which
scriptural matter is utilized in a manner approaching the
Hebraic. The first is the lilies of the field passage, which
is almost directly translated from the Sermon on the
Mount. The other is the parable related by Christ to the
two disciples journeying to Emmaus, and even here the
parable has been transposed.[30]

Vida's liberality in the use of scriptural material has
not been understood by any of the critics except Zumbini, who perceived the necessity in such a work of developing "una vita interna da cui procedessero il movi-
mento e i caratteri epici, che altrimenti sarebbero del
tutto mancati." While this was a necessary undertaking,

it was not an easy one; "e quindi il suo merito consiste nel saper conformare ad essa la propria coscienza."[31] For any proper reading of the poem, Vida's liberality in this regard must be understood. He is not, after all, repeating the performance of Juvencus, though many critics seem to think so.

A few of Vida's similes are Homeric in the gap between the points being illustrated and the full content of the similes. Examples are the snake in the Jethro episode and the three similes in the middle of Book V. In the first of these, the angels, rushing from all parts of heaven and earth to answer the summons of the trumpet, are like doves driven from the fields by storm and flocking back to their turrets. In the second, the multicolored variety of the mobilizing angelic hosts is compared to nature's multicolored variety in autumn. In the third, the subdued angels watching the Crucifixion are like friends of an athlete who are prevented by the rules of the game from lending a helping hand.[32] In each, there is illustration, but the similes and the actions being illustrated jar with each other.

By and large, however, Vida's similes are precise and appropriate. Typical is the hind to which he compares Christ's anguished mother as she searches for Him; the homing birds which illustrate the feelings of the demons as they land in Jerusalem, and the scattered sheep to which he compares the terrified Apostles after Christ's arrest.[33] Like Vergil, Vida seeks to convey

the peculiar sentiment with which ... the situation is to be regarded. In the perception of these analogies, it is not merely intellectual curiosity that is gratified by the apprehension of the *touto ekeino* in the phenomena; but the imagination is enlarged by the recognition of analogous forces operating in different spheres, which separately are capable of producing a vivid and noble emotion.[34]

"Analogous forces ... in different spheres" may be seen in this simile from the *Aeneid*: Vergil is comparing the orderly advance of the Italian host after its tumultuous gathering from many quarters, to the movement of mighty rivers when their component waters have found their appointed bed:

> ceu septem surgens sedatis amnibus altus
> per tacitum Ganges aut pingui flumine Nilus
> cum refluit campis et iam se condidit alveo.
> > *(Aeneid* IX. 30-32)

Like the Ganges after it has risen silently in flood in its seven tranquil branches, or the Nile, when it withdraws its enriching stream from the lowlands and returns to its channel.

This simile and its effect are partly recalled by Vida's first simile, comparing the great crowds, flocking after Christ, to the Po, rushing down from Mount Vesulus and picking up size from rivulets which join it. The details, carefully chosen, are reinforced by sound and rhythm:

> Pinifero veluti Vesuli de vertice primum
> It Padus, exiguo sulcans sata pinguia rivo:
> Hinc magis atque magis labendo viribus auctus
> Surgit, latifluoque sonans se gurgite pandi
> Victor: opes amnes varii auxiliaribus undis
> Hinc addunt, atque inde, suo nec se capit alveo
> Turbidus, haud uno dum rumpat in aequora cornu.
> > *(Christiad* I. 25-31)

Just as the Po, when it first appears from the pine-covered peak of Vesulus, cutting between the rich fields in a thin stream, but gathering more and more might as it flows along, until it swells and, roaring in a wide-sweeping torrent, it shows itself a conqueror: from all sides, other streams join it with re-enforcing waters. Then the swollen current no longer remains in its bed, but bursts through many channels over the plains.

The poet's "subtle discernment of the conditions of inward feeling" is combined with a broad use of similes in supporting and developing tone. The similes which Joseph uses in Book III, for instance, have a gentleness and charm perfectly consonant with the narrative they illustrate; the similes in Book VI, on the other hand, are vigorous or exultant, expressing joy, excitement, hope, or strength. Individual similes illuminate specific aspects: Magdalene's joy at seeing Christ is compared to a rose which, drooping under the weight of rain, slowly lifts its face to the sun; the risen Christ is like the phoenix; the glorified Christ passing through closed doors is compared to the sun penetrating windows and chinks in the wall and brightening the entire house.[35] A kind of ordeal by fire, from which the Apostles emerge purified and strengthened, is suggested by the lines describing the descent of the Paraclete.[36]

One of Vida's finest similes, found in the center of his epic, is that comparing the Apostle John in ecstasy to an eagle:

> Qualis ubi alta petens terris aufertur ab imis
> Alituum regina, vagas spatiata per auras
> Dat plausum gyro, atque in nubila conditur alis.
> Aetherea jamque illa plaga levis instat, et acrem
> Intendens aciem, criniti lumina Solis
> Suspicit, obtutuque oculos fixa haeret acuto.
>
> (IV. 10-15)

Just so the queen of the birds, seeking the heights, swoops aloft from the low-lying earth; gliding among the roaming breezes, she circles and flaps her wings, and soars into the clouds. Lightly she pursues her way in the ethereal region, and fixing her sharp eye, she looks directly into the light of the blazing sun, with piercing and unremitting gaze.

In this, and indeed in many of Vida's similes, there is

not only an enlargement of the imagination but also a
Vergilian expansion of scope. In *Aeneid* I, Vergil compares Neptune calming the stormy waves to a *virum pie-
tate gravem*, who, in the midst of a riot, quiets the *igno-
bile vulgus*:

> ille regit dictis animos et pectora mulcet.   (153)

Not only are the salient details of the action precisely
illustrated, but also underlying themes, such as the conflict between the rational and the irrational, are suggested.
In the *Christiad*, for instance, it is not fortuitous that
John himself, early in his discourse, resorts to a sun[37]
simile to explain the nature and omnipresence of God:

> Lux humiles veluti perfundens lumine terras
> Solis ab orbe venit, suppostaque circuit arva,
> Non tamen aethereo divisa ab Sole recedit
> Illa usquam, quamvis longinquas ambiat oras:
> Nec sine Sole suo est lux, nec sine luce sua Sol.
>   (IV. 54-58)

In the same way light comes from the solar sphere and
pervades the lowly earth, circling the fields below; but that
light is never taken away from the heavenly sun, and never
parts from it, no matter how widely it is diffused. Never
is there light without its sun, nor sun without its light.

In the epic simile, then, Vergil's influence on Vida is
far larger than fleeting suggestions of content or phrasing.
It is also less tangible. Vida has outdistanced both his
own prescriptions in the *Ars poetica* and the hackneyed
practice of tradition; he adapts liberally both profane and
sacred masters to his own purpose. The possibilities he
finds in metaphorical language in general are derived from
his meditation on both the Scriptures and Vergil, and from
his actual practice of epic poetry. What happens in the
Christiad in terms of imagery, similes, or broad symbolism

does not depend on prior theory; to read the *Christiad* as practical application of the *Ars poetica* would be futile, as the pointless maunderings of too many critics have already demonstrated.[38]

Vida's direct imitation of the Vergilian style may be divided into three general categories: the commonplace phrase, the echo, and the evocative allusion. All three categories are suggested in the famous passage on imitation in the *Ars poetica*, though without perhaps as sharp distinctions as are suggested here.[39] Curiously, that passage is taken by many critics as a blanket endorsement of mechanical imitation, a conclusion which would necessarily make half of the passage self-contradictory. In it, Vida indicates some of the reasons for imitating—the perfection of style which some of the ancients attained and the qualities one might oneself gain by study of the ancients. Then he turns to the methods of imitation, from plagiarism—

> ... ordine falle legentes
> Mutato. nova sit facies, nova prorsus imago.
> (*Ars poetica* III. 219-220)

—through improving on the ancients or infusing new meaning into their phrases—

> ... dictis ordine verso
> Longe alios iisdem sensus mira arte dedere,
> Exueruntque animos verborum impune priores.
> (225-227)

—to broad allusions:

> ... aliud longe verbis proferre sub iisdem. (258)

He is so emphatic about being aboveboard and open in imitation that plagiarism is beyond him. However, when he speaks of improving on the ancients or alluding broadly to them, he is referring to his own practice, to his attempts both to incorporate the wisdom and perfection of the ancients and to approach their heights.

The commonplace phrase is most clearly suggested earlier in the *Ars poetica*. One of the youthful poet's first cares must be, Vida says,

> ... digna suppellex
> Verborum, rerumque paranda est: proque videnda
> Instant multa prius, quorum vatum indiget usus.
> (I. 63-65)

to make ready a covering of worthy language and of material, and to see to it that he has a store of phrases and words which poets commonly use.

As the term is used here, the commonplace phrase may be generally described as a convenient, ready-made, and suitably pedigreed manner of speaking which both facilitates the composition of passages of epic poetry and also lends to those passages an appropriate luster. It can be further characterized as being both distinctive and undistinctive— *tendo ad sidera palmas* is distinctively an inflated or enhanced phrase, but it occurs so frequently in epic that it is commonplace. Here are some examples from the *Christiad*:

> Tandem Romulides juvenum stipante caterva ...
> (V. 87)

> Tum magis atque magis curarum fluctuat aestu ...
> (III. 765)

> Horror iit; genua aegra labant; vox faucibus haesit.
> (V. 328)

> Hostis, civis ei nullo discrimine habentur:
> Multi impune ideo digna atque indigna ferenti ...
> (IV. 662-663)

Haud tamen abstinuit verbis, vocive pepercit.

(V. 356)

Jussa obeunt ludicra, ingens it ad aethera clamor.

(V. 384)

Phrases like these appear in many other passages, as do the similarly commonplace *dira cupido, non aequis passibus, mobilitate viget,* and *se tollit ad astra.* Most of these are not attached to any particular context in the *Aeneid* and do not bring over, to Vida's poem, either specific or general connotations. They are in the nature of "repeats," though it may sometimes be difficult to distinguish them from clichés. The "repeats" Vergil found in Homer, where they were born of the exigencies of oral composition; Vergil's usage, of course, is predicated on other bases, but after Vergil, such commonplace phrases and their like become a convention in epic poetry.

The Homeric style, as Richmond Lattimore points out, is generated by two mutually dependent demands. First, the poems were meant to be recited aloud; hence they drew on a "deep-piled tradition of oral recitations," especially in exact phrases. Second, all statement in the poems is dominated by meter; thus ready-made phrases which fit easily tend to be retained, while feasible innovations must be rejected if they do not fit. It is possible to find padding in almost any random passage from the *Iliad* or the *Odyssey*; rarely is the style cut down to the minimum meaning to be communicated. This lack of preoccupation with brevity, combined with a frank willingness to be unoriginal, creates what Lattimore calls a "leisurely style, and one that does not avoid saying a thing in a practically desirable way merely because the thing has been said that way before.... Repetition in Homer is a pattern so all-pervasive ... that it creates an essential texture of language without which Homer would not be

Homer." The operative principle for "repeats" is simply that a "thing once said in the right way should be said again in the *same* way when occasion demands."[40]

With some modifications, both Vergil and his pupil adapt the Homeric practice. Vida's severe castigation of Homer for repetition[41] reflects not on commonplace phrases and their extensive usage but on the repetition of whole lines without justification, and the repetition of groups of lines and entire speeches. This was the kind of repetition that Vergil avoided; the development and use of the commonplace phrase, elegant, appropriate, and metrically right, seemed probably to Vergil a perfection of the Homeric practice. Vida's imitation here is clearly a minor matter; those critics who have drawn up comparative lists of phrases Vida "stole" from Vergil might as well have consulted Lewis and Short to determine what phrases Vida stole from the Latin language in general![42]

While the commonplace phrase is a stock-in-trade, often belonging quite as much to the genre, the period, or the language itself as to the author from whom one may learn it, the echo derives from and depends on the original work. The echo is a phrase or line reminiscent of a Vergilian phrase or line, used in a passage which is not crucial and echoing a passage which is itself not crucial. Vida's echoes are clearly identified with Vergil's *Aeneid*; the identification is important, for the echo serves to stamp the *Christiad* as the offspring of the *Aeneid*, to suggest various kinds of connection with the *Aeneid*, and to indicate the appropriate response.

The closing line of *Christiad* III,

> Pontius haec; cuncti intenti simul ora tenebant.

recalls the beginning of *Aeneid* II,

> Conticuere omnes, intentique ora tenebant.

In Joseph's discourse,

> Forsitan et puero fuerit quae cura requiris.
> $\qquad\qquad\qquad\qquad\qquad\qquad$ (III. 896)

echoes Aeneas's

> Forsitan et Priami fuerint quae fata, requiras.
> $\qquad\qquad\qquad\qquad\qquad\qquad$ (II. 506)

Self-respect seems to demand of Vida that he change the lines slightly; there is no example in the entire *Christiad* of a line, or even a half-line, lifted bodily out of the *Aeneid*. At the same time, no attempt is made to hide the "imitation." Vida clearly wants easy recognition of the source. Here are more examples:

> Verus et aspectu patuit Deus ...
> $\qquad\qquad\qquad$ (Christ transfigured; I. 938)

> et vera incessu patuit dea ...
> $\qquad\qquad\qquad\qquad$ (Venus; *Aeneid* I. 405)

> ... arma ingeminant arma acrius omnes ...
> $\qquad\qquad\qquad\qquad\qquad$ (angels; V. 513)

> arma manu trepidi poscunt, fremit arma juventus,
> $\qquad\qquad\qquad\qquad\qquad$ (*Aeneid* XI. 453)

> (Mens adeo mihi laeva fuit!) ...
> $\qquad\qquad\qquad\qquad\qquad$ (Joseph; III. 400)

> et, si fata deum, si mens non laeva fuisset ....
> $\qquad\qquad\qquad\qquad$ (Aeneas; *Aeneid* II. 54)

Some echoes, less readily pinned down, are nonetheless clearly Vergilian:

> Tectum auratum, ingens, pictisque insigne tapetis
> $\qquad\qquad\qquad\qquad\qquad\qquad$ (II. 546),

which may be traced to

            tectum augustum, ingens, centum sublime columnis
                            (Latinus's palace, *Aeneid* VII. 170),

also suggests Dido's palace. Vida's lines about the rumor
of the resurrection and the Jews' attempts to stifle it—

    Sed non ulla datur verum exsuperare facultas.
    Quoque magis tendunt serpentem sistere famam,
    Amplius hoc volat illa, omnemque exsuscitat oram.
                                            (VI. 399-401)

But they could not conquer truth. The more they tried to
suppress the story, the more it spread and aroused every
corner of the country.

—derive from Vergil's passage on *Fama* in *Aeneid* IV and
elaborate especially on *viresque adquirit eundo.*

    The general function of the echo would seem to be
that of keeping the original poem generally in the reader's
mind, calling up not specific scenes and specific emotions
but rather suggesting the virtues of the original and associ-
ating the whole with them. Some echoes, however, may
function partially as allusions. Thus, these lines about
despairing Judas,

    Infelix abit; hinc amens, caecusque furore
    Multa putat, curae ingeminant, saevitque sub imo
    Corde dolor, caelique piget convexa tueri.
    Tum secum huc illuc flammantia lumina torquens,
    Heu! quid agam infelix?...   (V. 30-34)

In misery he departed. Gone quite mad, blindly raging, he
turned over many things in his mind. His growing anguish
and despair racked his inmost heart; he could not bear to
raise his eyes toward heaven. His blazing eyes rolling, he
groaned aloud: Miserable man, what can I do? ...

and much of the following scene suggest the despairing
madness of Dido in *Aeneid* IV; it may be that Vida
intended to draw parallels between Dido rejected by

Aeneas and Judas by the priests, Dido deceived by her own deception and Judas by his, but on the whole the possibilities of such evocation seem distant here.

A series of echoes at the beginning of *Christiad* IV, taken together, impart to the context not just the reflected glory of the *Aeneid* but suggestions of significance; the lines come from the opening of John's discourse to Pilate, as he speaks of the Father, the Word, and His Spirit:

> Principio pater omnipotens rerum sator et fons,
> Ingens, immensus, solus regnabat ubique ... (20-21)
>
> Haud olli terreni artus, moribundave membra ... (31)
>
> Omnipotens Verbum, finisque, et originis expers,
> Quo mare, quo tellus, quo constat maximus aether.
> (35-36)
>
>   .... Spiritum
> Afflantem maria, ac terras, caelique profunda ... (53)

These lines echo mainly the discourse of Anchises in Hades; the following lines, referring to the mystery of the Incarnation,

> Quid vero impulerit tantos adiisse labores,
> Atque haec ferre Deum, dum morti obnoxius erat ...
> (59-60),

clearly recall lines from the invocation of the *Aeneid*:

> Musa, mihi causas memora, quo numine laeso,
> quidve dolens regina deum tot volvere casus
> insignem pietate virum, tot adire labores
> impulerit ...   (I. 8-11)

Muse, tell me the cause: for what injury to her divinity, for what great grievance, did the queen of the gods force this man, so remarkable for his goodness, to brave so many perils, to undergo so many hardships ...

The description of the fallen state of man after original sin—

> Hinc durus generi humano labor additus: hinc fons
> Curarum, et tristis patefacta est janua lethi,
> Morbique, et dolor, atque fames, et turpis egestas,
> Cum genus humanum curis sine degere posset,
> Plurimaque in terris vivendo vincere secla.
> (Christiad IV. 101-105)

Hence has harsh travail been the lot of man: this was the source of all our troubles, the source of miserable sickness and death, of pain, hunger, and bitter poverty, when mankind without care might have lived and endured on this earth for many centuries.

—combined with lines from the end of *Christiad* III, especially

> Prima mali fuit hinc nobis scintilla ...   (969),

which refers to the envy of the priests at the wisdom of the youthful Christ, suggest individual passages from the *Aeneid*. These include:

> ille dies primus leti primusque malorum
> causa fuit ...   (*Aeneid* IV. 169-170)

and Vergil's description of the inhabitants of Orcus:

> pallentesque habitant Morbi tristisque Senectus,
> et Metus et malesuada Fames ac turpis Egestas....
> (Aeneid VI. 275-276)

The effect of such echoes is to suggest, far more effectively than the statements themselves might, the import of what is being narrated or revealed. John's opening *Principio* and echoes in what follows call into play the speech of Anchises—the explanation to Aeneas of the phenomena he had beheld, the answer to many of his questions—as John discourses to the questioning and wondering Pilate on the divinity and power of Christ. The various reminiscences suggest, too, the difference between the third and fourth books of the *Christiad*. In the third book, a number of echoes recall the second and third books of the *Aeneid*, but for the fourth book, the clear frame of reference is *Aeneid* VI—as if to say that John's continuation of Joseph's narrative is to be quite different. In such reminiscent passages, then, it is not only the elegant or well-turned language which Vida seeks; it is also the large and solemn impression.

The commonplace phrase creates, in general, the illusion of the epic style, weaving a texture suitable for the great deeds being unfolded. By drawing on the poetic diction developed by Vergil for the epic, Vida is assured of a language that is generally appropriate and metrically fit; by adapting the language skillfully, he makes a suitable exterior for his poem. By means of the echo, he makes perfectly clear the kinship of his work with Vergil's and draws on, or attempts to draw on, the large impressions created by the *Aeneid*. But neither the commonplace nor the echo, alone or in conjunction, is very effective if other qualities are lacking, specifically if the poem fails to evoke the masterwork. Reminiscence keeps the *Aeneid* constantly but also somewhat distantly in the background. As long as the relationship between the two works remains lineal, the danger of irrelevant comparison between them is very strong. Vida's own principles of imitation, however, call for evocative allusion, by means of which the *Aeneid* is brought into the *Christiad*, becoming a source of feeling and meaning as well as of language.

Evocative allusion may be generally defined as a correspondence in language which, by recalling a passage, draws on the emotions or meanings attached to that passage. It may operate by similarity of context, in which case the

11.

evocation adds to the desired effect; it may operate also by mutation, surprise, or contrast. Both the passages involved in an evocation must be important; an obscure allusion produces no impact, while an allusion to an important passage, if used for a trivial context, can be incongruous or repugnant. Furthermore, allusions cannot operate properly *in vacuo*; the original cannot be divorced heedlessly from its context or put to work in a context where it can have no proper meaning. This does not, however, imply that at every point an allusion and its original must be parallel, or that by using an allusion the poet intends such a parallel. Evocative allusions are delicate matters which depend for their success upon the poet's taste and his sense of striking associations, appropriate juxtapositions, effective contrast, and surprise.

The general workings of allusion may be exemplified by a line from *Christiad* IV. John has been relating to Pilate the promises which Christ made to the Apostles—promises of hardship and poverty, exile and even violent death; he concludes, *jubet nos ...*

> Pauperiemque pati, rebusque assuescere egenis.
>
> (829)

The first two words of that line unmistakably evoke Horace's ode on true manliness and the hardship of military life: *Angustam amice pauperiem pati ...* The points of contact between that ode and the context of Christ's words are many—the motives for poverty, for instance, or the military aspects of the Christian life.

Early in her lament beneath the Cross, Mary cries out:

> ... heu! quam nato mutatus ab illo,
> Cui nuper manus impubis, omnisque juventus
> Occurrit festam venienti laeta per urbem,
> Perque viam ut regi velamina picturata,

Arboreasque solo frondes, et olentia serta
Sub pedibus stravere, Deum omnes voce fatentes!
(V. 858-863)

Alas! how changed are You from the Man whom, just the other day, crowds of children and young people ran to meet so joyously. As you came through the city, they strewed the streets beneath Your feet with embroidered tapestries—as if for a king—and with leafy branches and fragrant garlands, and they all cried aloud, calling You God.

The allusion is to Aeneas' description of Hector appearing to him in a dream:

hei mihi, qualis erat! quantum mutatus ab illo
Hectore, qui redit exuvias indutus Achilli,
vel Danaum Phrygios iaculatus puppibus ignes!
squalentem barbam, et concretos sanguine crines,
vulneraque illa gerens, quae circum plurima muros
accepit patrios.   (*Aeneid* II. 274-279)[43]

Alas! what condition he was in! how changed from that Hector who came back in triumph, wearing the armor of Achilles, or after casting Trojan fire on the Greek fleet! His beard was matted, his hair clogged with blood, and his body disfigured by the many wounds he had received around his country's walls.

The description of Christ on the cross, as Mary sees Him,

Squalentem ut barbam, turpatum ut sanguine crinem
(V. 820),

along with many other details in lines 815-822, makes the connection between the two passages even more telling. The pathos of the crucifixion and Mary's lament becomes more profound with this evocation of Hector's fate and the parallelism between Hector's short-lived victory which brought on his death and Christ's triumphant entry into Jerusalem, similarly short-lived and an immediate cause of His death. Up to this point, indeed, Mary's lament is very moving, but the growing bitterness and rage, reminiscent of Dido in despair or the hysterical Amata, destroy what effect Vida achieved by the allusion.

In the fourth book, John briefly lists the twelve whom Christ selected to be His followers. With a few words, he indicates the character, trade, or duty of each Apostle, concluding with this line:

> ... et ipse mali fabricator Iudas.   (IV. 274)

The brevity and sharp contrast to what had gone before— the emphasis on the obscurity, ignorance, and poverty of Christ's chosen followers—is striking, but the allusion to *Aeneid* II, the list of warriors emerging from the wooden horse, pulls the reader up short; that list concluded with

> ... et ipse doli fabricator Epeos.   (*Aeneid* II. 264)

Nothing else in John's list even vaguely suggested the Greek warriors; the surprise caused by this final line gives the reader, as nothing else can, the feeling of the deceitful cunning of Judas and his relationship to the other Apostles, unsuspecting until this very night but nonetheless not wholly easy about him.

Peter's words to Simon, the bard whose upper room is to be the scene of the Last Supper—

> Rex, ait, est nobis, quo nusquam iustior alter,
> Aut pietate prior, Christum omnes nomine dicunt;
> $\qquad\qquad\qquad\qquad\qquad\qquad$ (II. 579-580)

We have a king, he said, whom no man ever equalled in justice or holiness. All men call Him Christ.

—allude to the words of Ilioneus to Dido, in tribute to the supposedly dead Aeneas:

> rex erat Aeneas nobis, quo iustior alter
> nec pietate fuit, nec bello maior et armis.
>
> (*Aeneid* I. 544-545)

Aeneas was our king, whom no man ever equalled in justice or goodness, nor in the arts of war.

For the reader, the devotion and respect of Ilioneus for his master are added to Peter's. But the allusion does not operate alone; like most of the allusions in the *Christiad*, this one belongs to a large pattern of allusions which reflect both feeling and meaning to each other. It may be noted here that the Trojan who speaks represents a group of exiles in a land whose potential hostility they do not suspect, all of which is significantly related to the exile status of Peter and the Apostles; further, there is a very close similarity in the passages until the end of the second line, where for the martial prowess of Aeneas Vida has substituted the symbolic name of Christ. The possibilities suggested here are reinforced by other allusions related to this one.

There are the allusions, for instance, in Christ's moving discourse on the good life, as related by John in Book IV.

> Mortales contemnite opes, contemnite honores (885)

recalls, by rhythm as well as wording, Evander's words to Aeneas:

> Aude, hospes, contemnere opes et te quoque dignum
> finge deo.   (*Aeneid* VIII. 364-365)

Shortly thereafter, Christ says:

> Vobis haud propriae hic sedes, concessaque longum
> Regna: manent meliora, graves ubi solverit artus
> Mors anima, vos stelligera pater optimus aula
> Protinus excipiet laetos melioribus oris,

Pax ubi tranquilla, et cunctarum opulentia rerum,
Et secura quies, numquam peritura voluptas.
(IV. 889-894)

You have no true home here; far off and far better are the
destined realms which await you. When death has freed your
souls from the burdensome flesh, your great Father in His
starry court will receive you, rejoicing in a better world, a
world of tranquil peace and overflowing abundance, of serene
rest and boundless joy.

These lines recall part of Christ's first address to the
Apostles:

... domus non haec data, non hae
Sunt vobis propriae sedes: vos aetheris alti
Lucida templa vocant, stellis florentia regna,
Pax ubi secura, ac requies optata laborum.
Hic domus, hic patria. huc omnes contendite laeti
Angustum per iter. vestras hic figite sedes.
(I. 54-59)

This is not the home destined for you, this is not your true
dwelling place. The bright temples of high heaven call you,
the star-studded kingdoms, where you will find true peace
and the reward of your labors. That is your home, that is your
fatherland; all of you strive for that, joyful though the way
be hard. Fix your hearts on heaven.

Both passages allude broadly to significant passages in the
Aeneid. In *Aeneid* III, the Penates explain to Aeneas in
a dream,

mutandae sedes. non haec tibi litora suasit
Delius, aut Cretae jussit considere Apollo. (161-162)

We must move on. This is not the land Delian Apollo meant;
he did not want you to settle in Crete.

Speaking of Italy, they tell him,

> hae nobis propriae sedes, hinc Dardanus ortus.
>
> (167)

Helenus reverts to the same theme in his prophecy:

> is locus urbis erit, requies ea certa laborum. (393)

And Aeneas, trying to clear himself with Dido, returns to it: *hic amor, haec patria est* (IV. 347.) Finally, when he has arrived in Italy and seen the surprising fulfillment of the omens predicted in the third book, Aeneas cries out:

> ... "salve fatis mihi debita tellus
> vosque," ait, "o fidi Troiae salvete penates:
> hic domus, haec patria est." (VII. 120-122)

"Hail, o land promised me by the fates," he cried, "and you, gods of Troy who have kept faith with me, hail! Here is our home, here our fatherland."

In the prayer to His Father on Mount Tabor, Christ refers to the exile of His followers and to the magnitude of their mission in these lines:

> Hos saltem, qui me patriaque suisque relictis
> Per varios casus lectissima corda sequuntur,
> Aspice, et immeritos caecis averte periclis.
> . . . .
> Tu genitor, tanto finemque impone labori,
> Si tantae est gens humanum caelo addere molis,
> Seclaque mutatis in pristina reddere rebus.
> (I. 846-848, 854-856)

Look upon these faithful ones who have abandoned country and family, and have followed Me through every kind of peril; preserve them, in their innocence, from unforeseen dangers.
. . . .
My Father, make an end to all this travail, if it must be so

great a burden to save the human race and, the old order
being changed, to restore the golden age.

The lines recall unmistakably both Aeneas's words of encouragement to his followers—

> per varios casus, per tot discrimina rerum
> tendimus in Latium, sedes ubi fata quietas
> ostendunt....   (*Aeneid* I. 204-206)

Through every kind of peril, through many harrowing adventures, we are still bound for Latium, the peaceful abode
which the fates have reserved for us....

and Vergil's

> tantae molis erat Romanam condere gentem. (I. 33)

The passages cited from the *Christiad* are clearly important ones, stating or suggesting key themes of the
poem; Vida's utilization of striking and pregnant Vergilian
passages, by evocation, increases the impact. The individual allusions are significant in themselves; cumulatively,
their effect is very great. When Christ, commissioning
Peter, says to him,

> Tu regere, et populis parcens dare iura memento.
> Summa tibi in gentes iam nunc concessa potestas.
> Jamque pios tege pace: voca sub signa rebelles.
>   (VI. 666-668)

Your commission is to rule and to make laws and show
mercy to the peoples. Supreme power over the nations is
hereby given you. Keep them faithful in times of peace,
and vanquish the insurgents.

one recalls instantly the magnificent pageant in *Aeneid* VI:
the great men of Roman history whom Anchises had been
showing to his wondering son, the mighty offspring for
whose sake Aeneas was called upon to establish a new

Troy in Italy. Vida's lines are an adaptation of Anchises's climax:

> tu regere imperio populos, Romane, memento—
> hae tibi erunt artes—pacisque imponere morem,
> parcere subiectis et debellare superbos.
>
> > (*Aeneid* VI. 851-853)

Your commission, Roman, is to rule over the peoples—these will be your special arts—and to instill in them the habit of peace; to be generous to the conquered and to vanquish the proud.

Vida's allusion, evoking this central passage, helps greatly to clarify the precise qualities of the mission of Christianity. Christ's discourse to Peter and the Apostles has been dealing with peace, the spread of the Church, the descent of the Holy Ghost, the trials to be borne, and the General Resurrection and Last Judgment. With the help of the allusion, the power vested in Peter becomes clearly a profoundly spiritual power, meaningful only in terms of the Holy Spirit and the grace of God; the Church's functioning in the temporal order must be subordinated entirely to this spiritual mission. At one and the same time, here and in the other allusions, Vida evokes the emotions attendant on the original and suggests, by shift in detail or tone, that his is the "higher argument" for which the ideals of Vergil and the grandeur of pre-Christian Rome were a preparation.

Intimately connected with this pattern of allusions is the complex allusion at the beginning of the *Christiad*. Vida prays to the Holy Spirit:

> Qui mare, qui terras, qui caelum numine comples,
> spiritus alme, tuo liceat mihi munere regem
> Bis genitum canere ...   (I. 1-3)

Spirit of love, Whose divinity fills the sea, the earth, and the sky, grant me Thine aid to sing the twice-born King ...

There are two important passages not in the *Aeneid* to which the first line apparently alludes. First, the opening lines of *De rerum natura*:

> alma Venus, caeli subter labentia signa
> quae mare navigerum, quae terras frugiferentis
> concelebras ...

Loving Venus, who, under the wheeling constellations of the sky, hast filled with life the sea that buoys up ships and the fruitful earth ...

The other is a passage from the *Messianic Eclogue*:

> adgredere o magnos (aderit iam tempus) honores,
> cara deum suboles, magnum Iovis incrementum!
> aspice convexo nutantem pondere mundum,
> terrasque tractusque maris caelumque profundum:
> aspice venturo laetentur ut omnia saeclo!
> o mihi tum longae maneat pars ultima vitae,
> spiritus et quantum sat erit tua dicere facta ...
>   (48-54)

O dearest offspring of the gods, mighty descendant of Jupiter, enter upon your high office—the hour has come. Look upon the world bowing its massive dome—the earth, the expanse of ocean, and the vast heavens; see how everything rejoices in the age that is coming! I pray that a ripe old age may yet be in store for me and enought breath to sing your glories ...

Lucretius's address to *alma Venus* as source of all being and as goddess of love is modified substantially by Vida; his *Spiritus alme*, of whom he begs that he may *mortali immortalia digno / Ore loqui*, emphatically points up the difference between the goddess of human love and the spirit of divine love. The implications of the *Messianic*

Eclogue need not be spelled out; even if Vida, like his contemporaries, did not fully accept the allegorical reading of that poem, his frequent allusions to it show that he did not reject it fully.

Two probable referents for the allusion occur in the first book of the *Aeneid*, both in the scene in which Jupiter enunciates his first great prophecy. One is in Venus's plea for the Trojans; she reminds Jupiter of his promise of their greatness:

> qui mare, qui terras omnis dicione tenerent,
> pollicitus.   (*Aeneid* I. 236-237)

In his reply, Jupiter prophesies:

> his ego nec metas rerum nec tempora pono,
> imperium sine fine dedi. quin aspera Juno,
> quae mare nunc terrasque metu caelumque fatigat,
> consilia in melius referet, mecumque fovebit
> Romanos, rerum dominos, gentemque togatam.
>   (278-282)

I will set no limits of either space or time on these men; I have granted them dominion without end. Even fierce Juno, who now out of fear plagues sea and land and sky, will change her mind for the better and, just as I do, will foster the Romans, lords of the world and people of peace.

Despite variations and similarities, it is impossible to say, in this case, that this or that passage is the only one alluded to; the matter seems even more complicated when it is pointed out that there are two more passages which may be relevant. One comes from another section of Lucretius's first book:

> sunt igitur venti nimirum corpora caeca
> quae mare, quae terras, quae denique nubila caeli
> verrunt, ac subito vexantia turbine raptant ...
>   (I. 277-279)

Therefore, there are clearly winds which as unseen bodies sweep through the sea, the earth, and even the clouds of heaven, and shake them with sudden violent whirlwind ...

The other occurs in the first book of Lucan, *De bello civili*; explaining the causes of the rivalry between Pompey and Caesar, Lucan says of fortune:

> quae mare, quae terras, quae totum possidet orbem,
> non cepit fortuna duos.   (110-111)

It is not unlikely that Vida's passage refers to all these.[44] Each is, in a different way, very relevant; for one who studied his classics as unceasingly and as affectionately as Vida did, and for one who believed in the humble discipleship of "imitation," such complex allusion would not be unusual or far-fetched. It produces a complexity which, kept within bounds, has outstanding merit: recognition of only one or two of the evoked passages improves Vida's lines immediately.

The pattern of allusions reaches its climax in the final line of the *Christiad*, proclaiming the true golden age:

> ... toto surgit gens aurea mundo,
> Seclorumque oritur longe pulcherrimus ordo.
>   (VI. 985-986)

While adapted clearly from the opening lines of the *Messianic Eclogue*, Vida's passage alludes in general to the whole poem. In earlier lines, Vida says about the Apostles going out into the whole world, that, as prophesied, their message would reach the ends of the earth:

> (ut vates cecinere futurum
> Antiqui) illorum vox fines exit in omnes.
>   (VI. 975-976)

And of the new race springing up, he says that their name, *Christiades*, derives from *Christus*. The whole concluding passage attempts to evoke the bright hope Vergil felt when he wrote in *Bucolic IV*:

> ultima Cumaei venit iam carminis aetas;
> magnus ab integro saeclorum nascitur ordo.
> iam redit et Virgo, redeunt Saturnia regna;
> iam nova progenies caelo demittitur alto.
> tu modo nascenti puero, quo ferrea primum
> desinet ac toto surget gens aurea mundo,
> casta fave Lucina: tuus iam regnat Apollo. (4-10)

The final era of the Cumaean prophecy has come now; the great cycle of ages begins anew. Now the virgin returns, and the reign of Saturn; now a new race descends from the heavens. But you, chaste Lucina, be favorable to the Child that is being born, in whose time the age of iron will end and the golden race will arise throughout the whole world. Your own Apollo now rules.

Some changes are evident—for the future *surget* Vida substitutes present tense; for *magnus ordo*, he says *longe pulcherrimus ordo*, with *ordo* the last word of the epic. Again he is emphasizing that Vergil's limited inspiration can be fully understood only in the light of Christian Rome.

Evocative allusion, extensively and effectively used throughout the *Christiad*, is the most important element in the Vergilian style of the poem. The commonplace phrase, like the diction in general, contributes to the Vergilian surface; the echo adds a luster that is sometimes dubious. But allusion well employed draws directly on the masterwork, bringing to significant or highly charged scenes the weightiness or the feeling associated with that work. Here, as in the similes, Vida shows something of his genius, genius hardly hinted by the notes of the *Ars poetica*. From the hexameter essay it is all too easy to conclude that only the glittering elegance of classical Latin

attracted him, but the advice from that treatise which he
followed most faithfully is this, so simple it may well be
overlooked:

> adi monimenta priorum
> Crebra oculis, animoque legens, et multa voluta.
> (*Ars poetica* III. 186-187)

As Vida demonstrates by his impressive use of the epic
simile and the evocative allusion, he did indeed go
frequently to the *Aeneid*, read it with his whole soul, and
achieve a large measure of understanding.

CHAPTER FIVE

CHARACTER, STORY, AND STRUCTURE:

DRAMATIC VS. ORATORICAL IMAGINATION

IN HIS presentation of Christ in Book I of the *Christiad*, Vida both follows and exceeds the suggestions of his *Ars poetica*. There, he counseled verisimilitude, development through action and speech, attention to the possibilities and the limitations of nature, and restraint lest too much be given away at once.[1] So, too, in his handling of Judas and Pilate, and, in lesser measure, of Joseph and Peter, Vida shows a dramatic sense in developing characters beyond anything the religious epic had done before. But he fails to make most of the characters cohere, to follow them through in the entire poem, or to produce a total dramatic impact.

When we first see Christ, He is serious, almost somber, but clear and purposeful. The enormous crowds which have been flocking after Him do not distract Him. His first words to the Apostles are self-contained and dignified, if somewhat obscure; his speech is incisive, full, completely coherent. Peter's confused reply does not upset Him; rebuking firmly but gently, He cuts through the mistaken assumptions. When He hears of Lazarus's death, He is moved deeply—another facet of the personality, magnetic and compelling, just displayed to Zaccheus. The combination of dignity and compassion marks the raising of Lazarus. Towards the sinner Maria, whose motives in

coming to Simon's house in Bethany were hardly attractive,
He is gentle and understanding. When He rides into
Jerusalem, in triumph, His sublime dignity contrasts effectively both with the wildly cheering crowd and with
the furious priests. His anger at the vendors in the temple
and His impassioned but sublime outburst are rendered
flawlessly.[2]

In the ekphrasis, Christ, as the fulfillment of all the
strange and wonderful things engraved in the temple,
appears majestic but still human. The following scene
shows a remarkable agility of mind in His answers to the
Pharisees, without obscuring the profound pity He feels
towards the adulteress. Christ's expostulations on the
Jews, like His earlier prophecy of the destruction of Jerusalem, are qualified by pure strength and compassion.

Up to this point Christ has been grandly impressive, the
unfaltering hero with a mission, girding Himself for the
great battle, and touchingly humane, the Savior of His
people. There have been hints of reluctance. In the prayer
on Tabor, at the end of Book I, the hints become clear
expressions of repugnance and fear—repugnance at what
He knows will happen, and fear for the frail disciples. But
neither the repugnance nor the fear are out of character;
the Christ of Book I is a hero, but a fully human one.

Vida's presentation in Book I is full and quite successful. The impressions remain throughout the rest of the
poem. But characterization as such virtually stops. The
youthful Christ in Book III may square logically with the
hero of the poem, but not dramatically. There are some
glimpses of the sharply delineated Christ of Book I
elsewhere in the poem—in the confrontation of the
soldiers in Book II, for instance, or in the healing of
Malchus; in the long discourse near the end of Book IV;
in the arrival at Calvary and, later, in the words to His
mother, uttered with immense composure and dignity. But

on the whole, the characterization of Christ in the remaining five books of the poem depends on the presentation in the first book.[3]

Joseph, the foster father of Christ, is sharply characterized by attitudes and interpretations during his long narrative (Book III); Vida's characterization, in fact, all but makes the reader overlook Joseph's very advanced age.[4] Joseph accepts his royal blood unaffectedly. What clearly has fitted him for the role of guardian of Christ and Mary is his practical sense combined with his profound faith. Though he is stirred deeply by the Nativity, he asks the shepherds very pointed and detailed questions; and after they have gone, he remarks:

> Nos vero interea, quamquam indubitabile Numen
> Novimus atque Deum nec opis, nec lactis egentem,
> Parvum alimus tamen, ut mortali semine cretum,
> Ubera siccantem matris; tenerumque fovemus,
> Invalidumque artus. Mortalem quippe creatus
> Mortali matris traxit de corpore partem.
>
> (III. 634-639)

And even though we were quite aware that He was God and had no need of care or of food, we fed the Infant, just like any other child born of man that sucks dry its mother's breasts, and we fondled those tender helpless limbs. After all, He took His mortal part from the mortal body of His mother.

"After all, He took His mortal part from the mortal body of His mother." This is uttered not as theological mystery but as a common-sense observation, conducing to practical action.

Joseph's exclamations, punctuating the narrative regularly, indicate that, even after so many years, he is still quite bewildered at what transpired, especially at his election. His faith is unshakable, but it is a rude kind of faith, accepting the incomprehensible while translating

12.

it into inadequate human terms. His interpretations of the
angel's prophecies or of the phenomena of Christ's life
are tinged with pathetic irony.[5] He offers a very simplistic
interpretation of the conflict between Christ and the
Pharisees, when he says about the boy Christ teaching
in the Temple:

> Prima mali fuit hinc nobis scintilla: puerque
> Ex illo formidata primoribus urbis
> Virtute invisus fuit, et corda aspera movit:
> Atque hoc deinde ingens succensa est fomite flamma,
> Inque dies gliscens furor, atque insania crevit.
>
> (III. 969-973)

That was the first hint of all the trouble we would have; from
that time on, the Boy was disliked and feared by the leaders
for His goodness, and they hardened their hearts against Him.
From such tinder was this fierce blaze kindled; their fury and
their rage has grown worse with time.

For Pilate's benefit, he adds:

> Orabam impavidum, ne vitae prodigus hosti
> Objiceret ...   (975-976)

The implications of his plea to Pilate for Christ's release
are that this is a matter of spite and jealousy; that the
Pharisees are evil and should know better, but if Pilate
will only let Christ go, Christ will mind His own business
and not meddle any more.

But Joseph leaves the poem at this point, and the
remarkable delineation of character becomes a cameo, not
fused with the dramatic whole.[6]

Mary, the Mother of Christ, has a larger role in the
poem. When we first meet her, in Book III, she is caught
in a painful dilemma: her mother, Anna, has received a
divine command to find a husband for Mary; Mary had
long before consecrated herself a virgin by similar divine
command.

In medio astabat lacrimans pulcherrima virgo.
(III. 177)

She is, indeed, frequently presented as weeping in Joseph's narrative,[7] though she has also her moments of radiant joy. The details of the betrothal and wedding, the Annunciation by the Angel Gabriel, the Nativity and events of Christ's early life are frequently charming and moving; there are idyllic qualities in the description of the flight into Egypt, and tragic qualities in the narration of the presentation in the temple. A typically subtle touch is "Dicam equidem, pater"—the shift in relationship from married couple to daughter-father, as Joseph had suggested when Mary told him of her vow to remain a Virgin. But the character of Mary never emerges clearly in the whole of Book III.

In the fifth book, Vida builds a lengthy scene around Mary. After the irony and the tragic foreshadowings of Book III, this would seem an attempt to cast Mary in the role of tragic heroine. Much of the scene is admirably done. The expansive simile conveys Mary's feelings as she looks for Christ:

> Ac veluti pastu rediens ubi vespere cerva
> Montibus ex altis ad nota cubilia, foetus
> Jamdudum teneri memor, omnem sanguine circum
> Sparsam cernit humum, catulos nec conspicit usquam,
> Continuo lustrans oculis nemus omne peragrat
> Cum gemitu: tum siqua lupi, siqua illa leonis
> Raptoris signa in triviis conspexerit, illac
> Insequitur tota observans vestigia silva,
> Perque viam passim linquit pede signa bisulco:
> (V. 773-781)

As when a deer, returning in the evening from grazing high in the mountains, to her familiar lair, already thinking for quite a while about her fawn, finds the ground all about spattered with blood, but no trace of her young. Immediately, she looks all around and hurries through the whole wood, groaning aloud. Then if she sees at a crossroads any signs of a marauding wolf or lion, she follows hard on, searching for tracks in the woods, and leaving everywhere her own tracks, imprinting the trail with her cleft hoof.

This graphically expresses anxiety, motherly instinct, self-forgetfulness and single-minded concern for the son. The detail of the deer's tracks, in line 781, is particularly touching. The effect of her bursting through the crowd and seeing, suddenly, the Cross and its burden is dramatically expressed in the line—

> ... propiusque in vertice conspicitur Crux   (813)

—the monosyllabic ending of which pulls the reader up short, while the sudden change of pace in 814—

> Ingens, infabricata, et iniquis aspera nodis.—

conveys the full impact. The following details render precisely Mary's reactions and feelings; again a simile—Mary is immobile as a rock on an Alpine peak—but one brief enough to be effective.

But from here on, Vida loses control. Mary's lament becomes an outpouring of extravagant bitterness, its pathos marred by excess and the dignity of Mary virtually destroyed by the intemperance of the statements. It is no improvement that, after almost fifty lines of outcry, Vida says:

> Hos virgo atque alios dabat ore miserrima fletus.
> Nec comites possunt flentem illam abducere fidae.
> (892-893)

Such laments and more the sorrowful Virgin poured out, and her closest friends could not manage to draw the weeping woman away.

There is stark strength in the figure of Mary, seated on

cold stone and silent, while the dead body of Christ is hastily removed from the cross at the beginning of Book VI:

> ... late reboant plangore propinqui
> Foemineo montes: responsant flebile saltus:
> Omnia flere putes sola lamentabile letum.
> Ipsa sedet vivo genitrix moestissima saxo
> Aegro corde, comis passis,
> . . . .
> Frigida, muta silet, gelidoque simillima saxo.
> . . . .
> Indulgent omnes lacrymis, tristique ululatu
> Cuncta replent: vix inde viri divellere possunt.
> . . . .
> Et magnam comites genitricem in tecta reportant.
>
> (VI. 77-81, 86, 93-94, 98)

Far and wide the mountains echo with the women's wailing, and the dells reecho plaintively. One would think that the whole earth was weeping over this sad death. But the sorrowful mother sat on a cold stone, her heart heavy, her hair dishevelled ... cold and silent, as if she herself had turned into stone....

All of them give way to their tears, filling the whole area with their sad lamentations: so that their husbands could hardly tear them away....

Finally, her companions assisted His noble Mother home.

However impressive this is, the lament at the end of Book V has made it impossible for the reader to accept the "magnam genitricem." Zumbini suggests that the lament expresses the grief of all womankind, all motherhood; the lament recalls, he says, the grief of Evander in the *Aeneid*. He rebukes two translators of Vida, Perrone and Bartolini, for their arbitrariness in excising portions of the lament. The pious Perrone, be it noted, shows his hand when he excuses Vida for these lines: " ... ponno solo

condonarsi al dotto, e pio Autore, come expressioni pura-
mente poetiche." But Zumbini fails to see that the essential
quality of Mary's lament is the bitterness, derived not
so much from Evander as from Dido, Amata, and the
mother of Euryalus. This is a distinct case of Vida's
failure to assimilate his models thoroughly because of an
inadequate dramatic conception.[8]

Two other women, who play small but striking parts in
the narrative, may be noted here.[9] The *peccatrix* of Book I,
known only as Maria and obviously distinct from Mary
Magdalene, achieves in a few lines fairly definite characterization. Vida gives us her background, her attitudes,
her desires and motives, and goes on to describe her
appearance in a brief but excellent passage. Her confrontation of Christ and her conversion are both convincing.
Then she disappears from the story completely. The Magdalene of Book VI, who runs to the tomb and finds
it empty, is not described at all; she weeps at discovering
that Christ's body is gone, but she has a burning confidence
that all will be well. Her radiance during the wordless
meeting with Christ is well conveyed in the simile of the
rose.[10] But again, she comes briefly into the story, has her
episode, and is gone.

One of the more effective characters in the epic is Peter.
In his reply to Christ's prophecy, he speaks impetuously
and incoherently: "haud linguae, vocive pepercit." (I. 62)
Except for the neat "tui miserere, tuum miserere" (72),
Peter's speech stumbles without order or consistency; and
Christ's lucid rebuke serves partly to make Peter even
more sympathetic. At the Last Supper, when he asserts
that he will stay by Christ to the very end, his blunt
sincerity and courage are impressive: "Who is the
traitor?" he cries:

> Faxo hodie numquam nobis illudat inultis.
> Non adeo effugit cum sanguine vivida virtus

Pulsa annis, nec dextra mihi tam frigida languet.
. . . .
Foeda alios servent fuga: nec tu me ante timoris
Argue, quam terga urgenti dare videris hosti.
Quo te cumque feres, adero. sequar ultima tecum.
Nulla tuis poterit me vis abjungere rebus.
(II. 707-709, 727-730)

This very day I will see to it that he will never mock us unavenged. My strength has not yet left me, though I am getting old and lack my former vigor; my right arm has not yet become lifeless.
. . . .
Let others flee like cowards, but don't accuse me of timidity until You see me turn tail before the enemy. I will follow You wherever You lead, to the death. No power on earth can tear me away from You.

The changes from St. Luke's text add vividness to the portrayal, as may be seen by citing the relevant lines of Juvencus:[11]

Respondit Petrus: "Cunctos, si credere fas est,
Quod tua labenter possint praecepta negare,
Sed mea non umquam mutabit pectora casus."
. . . .
At Petrus: "Duram mortem mihi sumere malim,
Vox oblita suum quam deneget ista magistrum."

Peter answered: "I can't believe they would, but let all of them fall away and deny Your teaching, nothing will ever affect my loyalty...."
But Peter said: "I would prefer to endure bitter death than that this voice should forget and deny its master."

Tested, Peter fails:

Nec jam scit subita turbatus imagine rerum,
Quid faciat, quo se vertat, quas advocet artes:
(*Christiad* II. 929-930)

Confused by the startling turn of events, he did not know where to turn, what to do, what tricks to try ...

Vida shows Peter as *latebras foventem*; at the end of the denial passage, he mentions the legend:

> Quin illum hanc perhibent mox semper flesse sub
> [horam
> Admissi memorem, dum vixit. eum aethera pandens
> Saepe oriens, solis saepe ater vesper in antris
> Invenit luctu indulgentem, eademque querentem,
> Dum nulla admittit moesto solatia amori.
> Deserti subeunt monita usque novissima regis,
> Ac se perculsum muliebri voce recursat.   (957-963)

The story goes that for the rest of his life, he commemorated with tears the hour that recalled his guilt. Often the rising sun, spreading its light through the sky, or the dark evening, found him in a cave, bewailing his crime and sorrowing again and again, allowing himself no comfort in his desolate affection. Always the last warning of his King sounds in his ears; always he returns to the spectacle of his weakness before a maid's voice.

The tenseness of feeling beneath the smooth, polished lines enlarges the conception of Peter effectively.

In Book VI, Peter has more stature among the Apostles; his clear leadership of the band is reflected in the fishing episode, and his maturer devotion to Christ in his reactions to the apparition of the Master and in the commission Christ gives him.[12] For all his importance in the narrative, Peter however is not fully enough developed.

Except for Christ, all the characters discussed so far lack this fullness of development and coherence with the entire poem. Two characters, however, do stand out in the poem for fullness of development and some measure of coherence: these are Judas and Pilate. With these two, Vida could feel freer, since they are not so clearly developed in the Gospel accounts and they partake more readily of common humanity.

Judas[13] had begun, Vida tells us, as fervent and willing as any of the others:

> ... incertas quascumque paratus
> Ire vias, talique necem pro rege pacisci. (II. 78-79)

But his zeal cooled in time; he began to yearn for his former ease and freedom:

> ... durique laboris
> Paullatim pertaesum.   (80-81)

He had been one of the less obscure and poor in the select company.

This is conventional enough; it is when Satan comes to Judas in his sleep, in the guise of Ioras, a kinsman, that Vida shows his skill.[14] Judas is compared to a hind, Satan to a "Getulus leo ... exsultans animis" (89-92), suggesting the softening-up process already accomplished by Judas's pride and his desire for luxury. Satan, playing upon a sore spot, the disapproval by Judas's family of Christ, develops precisely those details of discipleship which were rankling:

> ... Tu nocte silenti
> Montibus in solis erras, insane, potesque
> Ultro saeva pati sub nudo frigora caelo:
> Atque tibi alterius sub nutu degitur aetas,

In the still night, you wander about the barren mountains, you fool, and ungrudgingly put up with bitter cold under the open sky and waste your life for the whims of another ...

and emphasizes Judas's own rationalized doubts about the value of such hardship:

> Dum sequeris (quis te tantus furor incitat?) istum
> Elatumque animis, eversoremque sacrorum,

> Quem tantum illuvies adeunt teterrima gentis
> Feminei coetus, et semiviri comitatus?
>
>   (II. 95-102)

While you follow this fanatic—what kind of madness drives you so far?—this subverter of religion, this demagogue favored only by rabble and the scum of earth, by silly women and effeminate men?

Finally, he adduces the desirability of being on the winning side:

> ... jamque ille furorem
> Vesanum expendet: cedet fiducia tanta.   (104-105)

The appearance of Judas in the midst of the worried and angry priests surprises them, but they rise to the occasion. Having determined to do away with Christ, they are concerned how to avoid trouble:

> Omnibus idem animus; sed qua ratione quibusve
> Id fieri occulte queat artibus, exquirebant.
>
>   (II. 255-256)

Though they are *trepidi* and *dubiis animis*, they give Judas a place of honor and listen to his proposal. Judas's brief address reveals both his careful assessment of the situation and the motives for his action. Feeling that he is in full control, he shows superior contempt to the priests, and, offering no proof of his trustworthiness, he declares abruptly, "omnia solus ... dispendia tollam," and takes both their money and their obsequies:

> Dimittuntque alacres, atque extra limina ducunt.

The next line expresses the unspoken details:

> Ille petit montes iterum, sociosque revisit. (271-272)

At the Last Supper, Judas is confident and self-assured, while playing along with what he now considers to be a farce:

> Dissimulans ... vultu mentitur amorem.   (650)

He enjoys his superiority, especially when Peter protests Christ's prophecies of betrayal and denial and draws his sword with bravado. Later that night, he leads the soldiers to the garden of Gethsemane according to his own plan:

> Hortator vero scelerisque inventor Iudas
> Composito interea vocat hostes vertice ab alto.
> (765-766)

Kissing Christ while betraying Him, he demonstrates his own fearlessness and audacity to the soldiers, and perhaps to himself also. But his moment of victory is brief. Christ's words,

> Haec vero meruit, comitum fidissime, noster
> Oscula amor? Tanton' scelere ulla ad praemia
> [tendis?— (798-799)

Most trusted of My companions, has My love deserved these kisses? Will you stoop to such crime for any gain?—

and His subsequent demeanor towards the soldiers break through the facade of rationalization; developments during the next hours show Judas the horrible implications of his deed. Trying to save his self-respect, he rushes to the priests,

> Vociferans: Vestrum hoc argentum, haec munera
> [vestra:
> Accipite. en scelerum pretium exitiale repono.
> . . . .
>   ... vera Dei ille
> Progenies, verusque Deus: nunc denique cerno.
> (V. 22-23, 25-26)

Crying out, This money, this price is yours—take it! Look, I am returning the fateful wages of sin. ... He is the true Son of God, very God Himself. Now at last I see.

The priests merely laugh:

> Olli autem flentem risere, ac sera videntem.   (29)

In this last line, Vida underlines the treachery of the priests, the blindness and weakness of Judas, and the pathos of his circumstances.

Infelix abit. Neither the former easy life nor the decency of following Christ is now possible; he has rejected both sides. In the next fifty lines, Vida develops the tormented state of Judas and his final suicide: the possible alternatives and the appalling quality of each; the yearning for death, but fear of it; the hope of peace, the wild images which conflict in Judas's mind, and the growing darkness all about him. He goes out, to a dark wood; hesitates, speculating idly about the various means of death—mainly to avoid contemplating the blackness within; then sees a noose suspended from a limb, and hangs himself. The presentation is masterful; even the final detail of the furies—

> Informem prona nectentes arbore nodum—   (77)

in a balanced line which suggests the inevitability of the event, adds to the grimness. The dramatic narrative is more effective for being presented through Judas's mind; even at the end, Judas hangs himself *ut meritus.* The characterization of Judas arouses interest and sympathy, yet neither condones nor condemns him.

The course of Judas is plotted in some degree by the inexorable end of it; that of Pilate, not really reaching an end, allows more maneuvering. We first meet him on Holy Thursday night:

> Illo Judaeam frenebat tempore missus
> Caesaris imperio Tiberi Pilatus opimam
> Pontius insigni Romanus origine gentis ...
>
> (II. 968-970)

At that time, Pontius Pilate, by commission of Tiberius Caesar, ruled over rich Judea, a Roman of outstanding family ...

His background is left vague, after this clear identification as a noble Roman and this sharp contrast with the *furibunda manus* of the Jews. They have dragged Christ before Pilate, intent on His condemnation; amid all their clamor and tumult, Pilate scans Christ's features closely:

> Ille autem juvenis procero in corpore fixos
> Intentusque oculos, intentusque ora tenebat.
> . . . .
> Insolitam speciem, insolitos miratur honores
> Oris, et expleri nequit. hunc e stirpe fatetur
> Aut divum, aut saltem magnorum e sanguine regum.
> (976-977, 979-981)

But he kept his eyes fixed earnestly on the noble form of the Youth, and earnestly on His face ...
He marveled at the unusual beauty, the unexpected attractiveness of His countenance, and he could not drink his fill of gazing. He is sure this Man is either of the race of gods or at least of the line of great kings.

His first impulse is to help, though the motive is ambiguous. When he questions Christ, it is as a counselor not as a judge, and Christ's answer, brief and legally proper, neither offends Pilate nor deters his interest; so stirred is he by Christ that he takes Him inside, to get away from the crowd and examine Him at great length.

The appearance of Joseph and John at the court is precisely what Pilate wished, but in his great delight, he does not neglect to be courteous to the suppliant: "Depositumque senem molli locat ipse sedili."[15] Gradually, Vida unfolds a character of striking nobility and decency; by subtle ironic contrast, for instance, he shows Joseph and John coming in some ignominy to the palace which had once belonged to their own kings, expressing their doubts about the likelihood of mercy or pity from a foreigner, and planning to slant their appeal, to play down Christ's divinity—the very thing Pilate was most interested in learning about. It is noteworthy that, in the course of his narrative in Book III, Joseph becomes warmer and easier towards Pilate.

Pilate speaks to Joseph and John with deference, setting them at ease, asking many and sincere questions, pouring out honestly and freely his own impressions, and even apologizing for Christ's unwillingness to talk about himself.[16] Overcome, perhaps a bit humbled, John whispers to Joseph:

> Omnia sublatis aperi jam nubilus ultro.
> Pone metus, et rumpe moras. video omnia tuta.
> (III. 103-104)

Joseph's long tale only stimulates Pilate more. Not completely clear about the nature of Christ, but deferring to Joseph's obvious weariness, he graciously suggests that John accede to Joseph's request and tell what he can.

When the long tale is at last done, Pilate concedes to himself, "Omnia respondent auditis." He has been critically weighing these accounts and is now convinced of Christ's divinity. The crowd has become more restive, outside the palace, but Pilate scornfully bids them to calm down and choose someone to present their case civilly and reasonably. Their spokesman, Annas, contrasts sharply with the poised Roman. Pilate, going out to the crowd, speaks briefly and to the point: "Nil dignum morte repertum.... Ne regem vestrum ignorate volentes." Annas's lengthy and sophistic answer bristles with distortions and *non sequiturs*, but Pilate rebukes their malice:

> Quare agite, o odiis miseri desuescite iniquis:
> Ne frustra pugnate, Deum sed discite vestrum.
> (V. 173-174)

Come now, you wretches, give up this miserable hate. Do not struggle so futilely, but acknowledge your God.

Relentlessly, the Jews press their demands; taken off-balance, Pilate plays for time. Here, in human terms, is the mistake Vida imputes to him: the cleavage between his intellectual clarity and his weakness of will. Pilate dispatches Christ to Herod; when that fails to satisfy them, he tries the Barabbas affair; then he further compromises by flogging Christ. Finally, assaulted by the possessed mob outside and by Timor and Ignavia within, he yields, all the while sharply condemning the Jews and protesting his own innocence. His moral collapse is ironically pointed up by the washing of hands, a clearly symbolic act which is relevant to Vida's characterization of Pilate.

Pilate is generous, honest, sincere, humane; his weakness, it is clear, is a redeemable weakness, prompted by fear which is only partially his own responsibility, for he is battling against foes he cannot fully understand or cope with, forces against which intellectual clarity is not enough. In Book VI, Joseph of Arimathea comes to Pilate and says:

> Fama pias servasse manus, caecumque furorem
> Adversus totis nequicquam viribus isse.   (15-16)

Everyone says that you kept your hands pure, and that you opposed their blind fury with all your strength, even if in vain.

Sympathy and rebuke are mingled in the remark. Without dodging the rebuke, Pilate answers:

>   ... Ut potius concedere vivum
> Nunc corpus cuperem! vos veri conscia testor
> Numina, tentavi versans mecum omnia, siqua
> Insontem morti excipere, ac dimittere possem.
> Et nobis pietas colitur, sanctique penates;

Sed nihil invita tandem profecimus urbe:
Crudelis vicit gentis furor: ite, sepulchro,
Muneribusque pii exanimum decorate supremis.

(23-30)

Would that I could now give you His living Body! You gods,
who know the real truth, I call upon you: I tried; I tried
every way I could find to save that innocent Man from death
and to set Him free. For we too have our gods and our
standards. But we could do nothing against this perverse city.
The wicked frenzy of this mob overcame us. Go, and reverently prepare the Body for burial as best you can.

In Pilate, Vida has availed himself of the freedom to
make a full character, but only up to a certain extent.
Pilate is the most human of the characters and, next to
Christ, the most fully drawn; yet Vida has invested him
with a symbolic significance of great importance to the
discussion of thematic interpretation. Without deviating
from the main lines of the Gospel story, he has rearranged
the details, dropped some, added more, and, as with Judas
though for different reasons, has produced an effective
characterization.[17]

Vida's narrative is as uneven as his characterization was.
Individual episodes are generally effective, occasionally
brilliant in execution; the total poem, however, does not
cohere as a narrative unit.

Christ's opening address to the Apostles suggests the
major narrative lines of the poem. He is going to Jerusalem because His hour has come; His death is, with
respect to His antagonists, an event both feared and desired. The conflict is both over His life and over the
meaning of His death. But He tells the Apostles clearly
that He will die at the hands of the Jews and that they
themselves will eventually welcome death in His name;
theirs is the lot of exile.

Throughout the first and second books, the narrative proceeds with vigor and certainty; skillfully, Vida arouses both our admiration for Christ and our hope that He will foil the plots of His enemies. Peter's impetuous rebuke of Christ's folly, for being so easily resigned, excites hope while simultaneously Christ's penetrating answer, contrasting *mortalia* and *immortalia*, evokes sympathy for Christ's fate and suggests the larger dimensions of the conflict. Throughout the rapid and graphically told episodes which follow, suspense grows: the demons in hell are intent on destroying Christ but unaware of the irony in their vague plans; the extent of Christ's goodness, humility, and power is made more evident in the incidents of the raising of Lazarus, the conversion of Maria, the triumphal entry into Jerusalem, the curing of the sick man at the pool, the driving out of the vendors, and the encounter with the scheming priests over the adulteress.

When the Jewish leaders meet in hell-inspired council, their irrationality and wickedness combined with their impotent bewilderment make Judas seem a towering figure, far superior to them in his cool grasp of the situation and his ability to cow them. The terror evoked by the demonic activity is heightened by Judas's participation; against this background, the majestic figure of Christ, now solemn and sublime, becomes more appealing. After the hushed Last Supper and the poignant prayer in the garden, during which scenes Peter's energy and then the Apostles torpor excite hope and despair, the arrival of the soldiers to arrest Christ and their reluctance evoke great uncertainty. Caiaphas condemns Him and sends Him to the Roman governor to be executed, but such a travesty of justice cannot be supported. The tide is moving against Christ; yet there are so many variable forces, and Pilate's first impressions are so genuinely sympathetic and noble, that one cannot escape the illusion that Christ will be released.

13.

In tension with that illusion is a sense of inevitability, generated primarily by the prophecies of the first two books. Christ's own words are clear enough; the prophecies referred to in the council of devils—that the day was nearing when an avenger would come and release the souls of the just—and those which Christ himself calls attention to in the scenes of the ekphrasis support those words. God the Father speaks of the benefits of Christ's death; at the Last Supper, Christ predicts that one will betray Him, another deny Him. But the certainty is confounded by the strength of Christ as against the bumbling weakness and darkness of His foes; when Peter jumps up and draws his sword, the reader responds immediately to his rousing words.

Thus, as Christ stands before Pilate and Book II ends, a really critical point has been reached in the narrative. It is not all over; there is still hope, as Joseph and John also observe when they reach the palace—the priests and the mob are seething with anger at Pilate's stay of execution.

At this point, the recapitulation occurs, occupying virtually the whole of Books III and IV. Much new and relevant information is imparted; Joseph tells Pilate about the human lineage of Christ and His first public signs, and John tells him about the public life, the miracles, the widespread respect in which Christ is held, and the sublime message He gives to the people. Both of these narratives illuminate the conflict, deepen the certainty, yet also feed the hope that all will be well. Both books are well managed. Joseph's tale has variation of incident, description, prophecy, and marvels, shifts in emotional tone, some highly colored passages of undeniably beauty; the simplicity, tact, and subtly delivered attitudes of Joseph engage the reader's attention. In the prophecies, especially that of Simeon, there is that curious double effect: clearly Joseph's interpretation is wrong, the prophecies do not mainly refer to the massacre of the innocents and the flight into Egypt, and yet one hopes that they do. John's tale, though largely discursive, has strong narrative interest also. The Baptist's confession of Christ and Christ's self-effacing baptism are moving episodes; the feeding of the five thousand in the desert and the conflict with the demons at Gerasa are vividly told, and the long comprehensive discourse of Christ from the boat is a graphic rendering of His teaching.

Yet when the main thread of the story is resumed and Pilate confronts the Jews with his decision that Christ is innocent, the original suspense has been irrevocably lost. The recapitulation has been too long and has gone too far afield; with respect to narrative, too much of it is neither new nor relevant enough to keep the story line intact. Vida attempted to justify his two middle books in the same way Vergil justified Aeneas's long narrative of the sack of Troy and the seven years' journeying, namely by providing a character whose interest in the recount is convincingly deep. But Pilate was brought into the poem too late: he is not able to win the reader as Dido did. Further, the books themselves are too late; too much is already known about Christ to justify these books as revelation of character, and the action has already advanced to a highly critical point, where retardation in effect destroys the impact.

In the first third of Book V, the conflict between Pilate and the Jews is excitingly rendered, as is the episode of Judas's suicide. It is easy to be caught up in Pilate's quandary, to sympathize with his sincere goodwill, and to feel pity for him when he finally gives way. The following large scene of the mobilization of the angels is also well told; its energy and sweep are impressive, and its colors vivid. But the figure of Christ, which ought to be at the dramatic center of these events, has become obscured; in the long retardation of the narrative, the emotions aroused in the first two books have become vague. Christ regains much of His vitality in the Harrowing of Hell, a scene pervaded by strength and joy; in the commission to Peter and the Apostles, He is confident and almost triumphant. In the apparition to Magdalene, and to the various Apostles, however, the character is again lost. What has happened in the last two books is that the focus of narrative has shifted, first from Christ to Pilate and to the angels—a shift that is clearly unintentional—and then to the Apostles and their mission. All attempts to keep Christ at the center of action have been doomed to failure by the diffuse recapitulation.

What has been said so far indicates Vida's skill in handling character and narration, as well as the basic weaknesses of his concept. Both technique and concept derive mainly from the study and interpretation of Vergil. There are, to be sure, variations and adaptations, but the main lines are clearly Vergilian.[18]

Like Vergil, Vida rarely gives us a detailed external description. It is impossible to say what Christ or Mary, Pilate or Judas looked like. The description of Maria in Book I is primarily aimed at evoking her whole appearance. In numerous brief touches, Vida establishes the general outlines of character, often providing details of breeding and background, as Vergil does. Though in Maria and Judas, such details help us understand motive and action, in most cases Vida is conforming to his precept, based on Vergilian practice, of providing appropriate and interesting persons and episodes.

In epic of the Vergilian model, enhancement is necessary for virtually everybody and everything, including unsympathetic personages. Vida scorns, in the *Ars poetica*, Thersites—

> Nec siquem indecoremque animi, pugnasque perosum
> Egregios inter memoras heroas in armis
> Castra sequi, cupidi exspectant audire legentes,
> Qua facie, quibus ille humeris, qualive capillo
> Incedat, captus ne oculo, an pes claudicet alter....
>
> (Ars poetica II. 179-183)

If there is a soldier among the great warriors who is base of soul and afraid to fight—a campfollower—remember that your readers are not interested in hearing what he looks like, what kind of physique he has, the color of his hair, and whether he is half blind or lame....

—and cites Drances as *aptior*:

> ... cui frigida bello
> Dextra quidem, sed consiliis non futilis auctor,
> Dives opum, pollens lingua, et popularibus auris.
>
> (186-188)

whose right arm was too stiff now for fighting, but who was wise in councils, wealthy, and held in high esteem by the people.

Mary and Joseph, Pilate and Herod are easy to render as regal, but Vida takes meticulous care to certify his incidental personages, like Lazarus, who

> ... Bethanes regna tenebat
> Dives opum, clarus genus alto a sanguine regum—

Simon the bard, *atavis clarus ... et prole beatus*; and Iarus, father of the dead child,

> Largus opum, pollens lingua et popularibus auris.[19]

Maria the sinner and Zaccheus, besides being of good disposition, are wealthy and comely.[20] The incongruity of

the practice is not relieved by the lowly origin of the
Apostles—for the Apostles are not crude or low, and
they are ennobled by their attachment to Christ and their
destiny as vessels of grace. But in emulating Vergil's im-
provements on Homer, Vida risks reducing his people to
faceless anonymity.

The episode of the angels' mobilization in Book V
manifests an even more troublesome preference for epic
enhancement over spontaneity and freshness. The mobilization does produce definite epic effects, but truth and
coherence are lost—not in the few awkward details, about
the angels assuming corporeal form or about the ekphrasis
on the portals of heaven, but in the decorum of the scene
and its pointlessness. In one respect, it recalls Lucan's
description of the marriage of Cato and Marcia, which
never actually comes off.[21] In its proportions, Vida's scene
is part of a tradition that begins with Apollonius of Rhodes
and reaches a kind of culmination in Milton—the tradition of improving by increasing the size. The stone which
Hector snatches up and carries along—

> ... two men, the best in all a community
> could not easily hoist it up from the ground to a
> [wagon,
> of men such as men are now, but he alone lifted
> [and shook it
> as the son of devious-devising Kronos made it light
> [for him—
> (*Iliad* XII. 447-450)

or which Achilles caught up,

> ... a huge thing which no two men
> [could carry
> such as men are now, but by himself he lightly
> [hefted it.—
> (XX. 286-287)

becomes in the *Argonautica* of Apollonius a stone "four stalwart young men could not lift." In the *Aeneid*, Turnus

> ... saxum circumspicit ingens,
> saxum antiquum ingens, campo quod forte iacebat,
> . . . .
> vix illud lecti bis sex cervice subirent,
> qualia nunc hominum producit corpora tellus;
> ille manu raptum trepida torquebat ...
>
> (XII. 896-901)

He sees a huge boulder, old and enormous, which happened to be lying there in the field ... Twelve men would hardly be able to raise it to their shoulders—men at least of the kind the earth produces nowadays; but he, quickly seizing it, threw it ...

Homer's detail was a perfectly natural one, illustrating graphically the furious energy of Hector or of Achilles; Apollonius, in trying to outdo Homer, loses truth, as does Vergil, enhancing the detail beyond all possible acceptance. Vida's angels, arming to no purpose, and Milton's combatants, hurling mountainsides at each other, both enhanced to fit the larger scale of their poems, are similarly Alexandrian in procedure and intent.

Oratory plays a large part in Vida's procedure. It is important to note here the difference between Homer and Vergil in this respect, and Vida's preference for Vergil. There is much talk in Homer, far more than in Vergil, but little of it is formal oratory. The spontaneous, impassioned, or rambling speech of Achilles, Hector, Diomedes, Andromache, Nestor, and others are rarely rhetorically organized. For this failing, Vida rebukes Homer, citing his repetitiveness, his garrulity, his lack of unity.[22] Vergil has less talk but admirable organization—set and often moving speeches, which are partly meant to reveal the speaker, not merely by the line of argument but by the tone, the attitude of the speaker, and his particular reaction to the matter at hand. About this, Sellar has made highly perceptive comments, much of which apply to Vida:

[Vergil's] power in dealing with human life consists generally in conceiving some state of feeling, some pathetic or passionate situation, rather than in the creation and sustained development of living characters.... We are more interested in what they say and in what happens to them than in what they are....

The oratory of the *Aeneid* ... cannot equal the vivid naturalness of the speeches of Nestor, nor the impassioned grandeur of those of Achilles.... The speeches in Virgil are stately and dignified in expression; they are disfigured by no rhetorical artifice of fine-spun argument or exaggerated emphasis; they are rapid with the vehemence of scorn and indignation, fervid with martial pride and enthusiasm, or, occasionally, weighty with the power of controlled emotion.

The exception to this, Sellar points out, is Dido, who seems

to acquire an existence independent of the experience and of the deliberate intentions of the author, and to inform this experience and mould these intentions as much as [she is] informed and moulded by them.[23]

The effectiveness of such a technique, predicated as it is on character-types and states of feeling, is quite limited. Its careful planning and its importance to the whole business of characterization produce, in the end, the effect of an oratorical rather than a dramatic imagination. Though Judas, like Dido, acquires an independent existence for a time, and Peter, like Mezentius, has brief moments of attractive spontaneity, the predominantly schematic procedure keeps the characterization under too tight control.[24]

It is possible to trace a detailed pattern of the effect of Christ on almost everyone else, not only on earth but in heaven and hell also.[25] The flocking crowds at the very beginning indicate his popular impact, and Peter's reaction to the first prophecy of death shows the magnetic personality. In subsequent scenes, Vida effectively juxtaposes the confused impressions of the devils in hell, the affection of Martha, the motives of Maria the sinner, and the reaction of the people and priests as Christ rides in triumph into Jerusalem.[26] To cite all the examples of the effect of Christ would be too long; every scene except the purely descriptive ones and the earlier sections of Book III, dealing with the events preceding the Incarnation, is concerned in some important way with the impact of the Messiah. In one sense, the sum total can be considered a mosaic, constructed slowly and patiently, revealing Christ fully through the medium of the people and beings whose lives or affairs He touched. Book V, in which Christ is a passive figure, moves from one point of view to another showing us Christ as perceived by Pilate, by Judas, by the priests and the mob, by the angels and the Father, by Mary, by the soldiers, by the thieves. The end result of all these impressions and reactions does not add substantially to the presentation achieved by Christ's actions and speeches in the first book. It does, however, indicate much about the impact of the Messiah. In showing Christ from numerous points of view, Vida fills in not character and narrative but significance, his thematic interpretation of the Incarnation.

According to Vida's notion of Vergilian characterization, characters in epic must be noble in person or circumstance or both. They possess a certain natural configuration which is to be revealed as interestingly, accurately, fully, and elegantly as possible; many serve for interest and pleasure, but they must not violate the integrity of the whole work;

character must always be subordinated to the larger theme, so that truncation is not without merit. It will be noted how thoroughly the concept is dominated by decorum—characters and action, are indeed, less important than their appropriateness.

By and large, Vida's people do not develop; the function of story is to reveal them as they are. To be sure, there are marked conflicts within Christ, Judas, and Pilate, all of which are finally resolved; there is a measure of change in Peter, though that is revealed, not dramatized. But the imitation of nature was for Vida the evocation of a circumscribed and comprehensible world, the penetration of which was postulated less on mystery than on order and hierarchy. While Vida is intensely interested in humanity and is quite capable of subtle psychological perception tellingly expressed, as both the *Ars poetica* and the *Christiad* demonstrate, he considers dramatic realization of character subordinate to the larger thematic interpretation of his material. The revelation of the person is mainly determined by the relevance of words and acts. Characters come, perform their function, and go. Episodes support not story but significance. The imaginative recreation of experience or the illusion of separate existence does not generally fit the *Christiad*, as it does not fit the *Aeneid*. That is why, in part, much of Joseph's narrative of the birth and youth of Christ fails to connect dramatically with the rest of the poem: the Christ we are presented in the first book, impressive and striking as He is, cannot be conceived of as existing outside the limitations of the poem.

Within the poem itself, virtually all the characters are disjointed. Mary's arrival on Calvary and her lamentation, for instance, give the reader the impression not of a mother seeing her son in agony, but of woman coming on a heart-rending scene. Similarly, the characters are

truncated: they exist in episodes but not in the whole.
It may be that Vida found this necessary for the
achievement of suitable distance, but in terms of characterization this practice virtually ruined his poem. He is
following Vergil's example, in the treatment of Dido,
Turnus, Amata, Nisus and Euryalus, Pallas, and Mezentius,
for instance, though none of his corresponding characters
can equal these.

Like the *Aeneid*, Vida's epic dwells not on the "vicissi-
tudes of individual fortunes and the play of human
passions and impulses," but on a "series of grave events,
bearing on a great issue and following an inevitable
course." Yet, however grave the events and great the
issue, Vergil

does surround the actors in his story with an environment
of religious belief and observances, of political and social life,
of material civilization, of martial movement and sea-ad-
venture, formed partly out of his poetical and antiquarian
studies, partly out of the familiar spectacle of his own age,
partly out of his personal sympathies and convictions. And
this representation, though it necessarily wants the vital
freshness and vigour of Homer's representation, has a peculiar
dignity and charm of its own.[27]

Much of this is true of the *Christiad*; what the reader
balks at is the gratuitous enhancement which detracts
from the story itself—as in the excesses of Book III—and
the emphasis on the part at the expense of the whole.
Vida's narrative is elaborated in much the manner of
Vergil; to cite only one more detail, the frequent prophecies of the poem, like their Vergilian antecedents, are
intended in part to unify all the elements of the narrative
and to keep the central character and the central event
constantly before us. What Vida was not able to do was
effect a cooperation between prophecy and narrative.

Narrative is attenuated after Book II, while prophecy is not fully realized dramatically. In the *Aeneid*, much of the prophecy has a concretized counterpart in, for instance, the character of Aeneas; in the *Christiad*, the disappearance of Christ as central character, and the lack of anyone else really to take His place, weakens the full effects of prophecy as a unifying force.

But if Vida's epic lacks a dramatically-unifying central character and a fully coherent narrative, it achieves a remarkable sort of unity in its intricately wrought structure. The *Christiad* consists of six books of fairly homogeneous length. The *Aeneid* had twelve, but the arithmetical difference is of minor importance. It may be noted that Statius also had twelve, that Valerius Flaccus apparently intended twelve for his *Argonautica*, and that Milton's revised edition of *Paradise Lost* would be arranged in twelve rather than ten books. But it must also be remembered that Vergil's master had twenty-four books in each of his epics, and one may, if one wishes, cite Vergil's procedure in imitating Homer as precedent for Vida's practice. Most probably, the truth lies in the simple suggestion that Vida's material fit most easily into six books.

The over-all arrangement of the *Christiad* and the structural patterns within that arrangement are of greater critical importance. As a recent scholar has pointed out in an elegant Latin eulogy, Vida's books alternate, the first, third, and fifth stressing the humanity of Christ, and the second, fourth, and sixth stressing His divinity.[28] The poem may be considered to have a division either into two large sections of three books each, or into three sections of two books, neither excluding the other. The first two books reveal Christ at full length as Man and as God, reaching a climax in the silent God-Man before Pilate. The next two describe in great detail His human lineage and His youth, His divine lineage and His divine mission on earth. In the last two, after the Passion and Crucifixion have been presented, the poem reaches its peak in the sublime and magnificent vision of the Ascension and the resultant descent of the Paraclete and establishment of the Church. This, for the tripartite division.[29] At the same time, the whole work pivots about John's revelation of the Verbum at the beginning of Book IV, the first three books being devoted to the drawing-up of the battle lines with only hints of the significance, and the last three to the Crucifixion as the fulfillment of the God-Man's mission and to a full-length presentation of the nature and significance of that mission.

In all these, the Vergilian precedent is obvious. Conway, Heinze and many other critics have demonstrated the alternating rhythm of Vergil's books; the odd-numbered books are generally lighter in content and import, while the even-numbered books are crucial. The division of the whole *Aeneid* into two sections of six books each or into three sections of four books each has been debated by scholars and critics for years, without either point of view satisfactorily excluding the other.[30]

Within Vida's general outline, there are a great many carefully devised parallels. A few of them are briefly schematized here:

Book I	*Book VI*
Christ going to Jerusalem (15 ff.)	Apostles going out into the whole world (973 ff.)
Inferno scene (121 ff.)	Harrowing of Hell (121 ff.)
Raising of Lazarus (236 ff.)	Resurrection (294 ff.)
Christ's revelation to Maria the sinner (300 ff.)	Christ's apparition to Magdalene (369 ff.)
Triumphal entry into Jerusalem (400 ff.)	Lonely apparitions to Apostles (437 ff.)

Jerusalem and its temple
(376 ff., 551 ff.)

Heaven (684 ff.)

Ekphrasis of creation
(591-673)

Hymn of Apostles to all
nature (726 ff.)

The Father's prophecy
(873 ff.)

The Father's prophecy
(845 ff.)

Transfiguration (932 ff.)

Ascension (709 ff.)

Book II

Book V

Judas and Jewish priests,
motivation and plans

Pilate and Jewish priests,
motivation and plans

Fall of Judas

Fall of Pilate

Crowds of the catalogue
(336-529)

Angels (509-703)

Song of Simon (607-642)

Improperia (721-742)

Last Supper (643-670)

Crucifixion (704-720)

Desertion by Apostles
(866 ff.)

Heedlessness of Mary (758 ff.)

Book III

Book IV

Lineage of Joseph and Mary
(104 ff., 140 ff.)

Lineage of Christ (20 ff.)

Prophecies of Messiah, born
of virgin (300 ff.)

John the Baptist, Precursor
(146 ff.)

Birth of Christ (571 ff.)

Baptism of Christ (199 ff.)

Hidden youth (800 ff.)

Public activity (315 ff.)

Teaching in the temple
(919 ff.)

Teaching in the boat (879 ff.)

In the first and sixth books, respectively, there is the vigorous human activity of Christ in the last days before His death, culminating in the Transfiguration, and the divine energyless activity of the last days before the Ascension, culminating in the descent of the Paraclete and the establishment of the church. Both Books II and V alternate between the activities of the demons and Jews, and of Pilate and Judas, on the one hand, and the figurative and actual sacrifice of Christ on the other. The human and charming narrative of Joseph in Book III, almost completely oriented as a paternal plea, is set off by the apocalyptic exposition by John in Book IV, virtually dispensing with argument and oriented in revelation.

From these brief observations, it is clear enough how carefully planned are the over-all structure and the individual parts of Vida's poem. The individual books are also carefully patterned. The first book, for instance, alternates rhythmically between action and imagery. The miracles, conversions, and conflicts with the Jews are interwoven with carefully chosen similes, images of temple and city, heaven and hell, and the constant polarity of light and dark. The pairs of conversions and miracles alternate with each other and are subtly parallelled and contrasted; the infernal scene, with its grotesque shapes, vaunting pride, and arrogant plans, is ironically juxtaposed with the raising of Lazarus. The two conflicts—with the vendors in the Temple and with the priests over the adulteress—are juxtaposed with the ekphrasis, that complex symbolic movement from the Old Law to the New, from which the incidents derive much of their full meaning. Finally may be noted a striking contrast. On the one hand, there are the surging crowds and the ephemeral popularity which Christ ignores, drawing His Apostles aside and trying to make them comprehend His impending death and their exile; on the other, there is the lonely Transfiguration at the end after the Father has detailed the meaning of that death and exile, and has prophesied the lasting esteem in which Christ will be held.

Book II has a simpler but nonetheless remarkable structure; it falls into four large sections—

Lines 1-272: the activities of devils, priests, and Judas;
273-529: the people of Palestine coming for the Paschal feast;

530-730: preparation and celebration of Christ's Pasch;
731-1001: arrest and condemnation of Christ by the Jews.

The first and last sections balance each other, as do the second and third; while the entire center section, lines 273-730, balances religion and worship, Old Testament and New Testament, against the human weakness, self-interest, and consummate evil of the first and last sections.

As a final example, Book IV has a tripartite structure which may be described as the Plan of the Incarnation, the Manifestation, and the Heritage, with a prologue (pre-time) and an epilogue (post-time):

(1-19: Introduction.)
20-58: Prologue: the Trinity and the Word.
59-274: Plan and preparation: Creation, Fall, prophecies, Baptist.
275-655: Manifestation: activity of Christ's public life.
656-980: Heritage: Christ's teaching.
981-1028: Epilogue: prophecy of the Last Judgment.
(1029-1047: Conclusion.)

The intricacy of the structure suggested by these brief analyses can be parallelled in the *Aeneid*; a suitable example is Book IV, whose passionate strength would seem to belie any carefully contrived organization. The whole falls into three major sections of generally similar length: Dido's passionate longing for Aeneas and their eventual "marriage" (1-218); Aeneas's decision to leave and Dido's furious attempts to have him stay (219-449); Aeneas's departure and Dido's despair and suicide (450-705). Dido's confidante, Anna, figures consistently in each of the three sections; around her, everything else changes in the rise and fall of action and passion. Dido's tormented ravings before she finally forsakes her vow, in the first section, and her rages in her final madness, ending in suicide, correspond with each other. Aeneas's defense, with its key words and phrases—*fas*, *pater*, *puer*, and *Italiam non sponte sequor*—occurs at the very center, as it is indeed the dramatic and the thematic focal point of the book.[31]

Such carefully executed structure, extending throughout the whole of Vida's *Christiad*, produces undeniable architectonic effects. The song of Simon is clearly linked not only to the *Improperia*, which it closely parallels, but also to other images and incidents to which it gives some meaning and from which it itself derives meaning. The context of that song—the Paschal Feast of the Jews, the Last Supper of Christ—indicates its bifurcation: it looks both backwards and forwards. The conventional look of its contents—the flight of the Israelites from Egypt, the manna in the desert, the water from the rock, and the sacrifice of Melchisedech—has puzzled at least one critic, who wondered how the erudite Vida could nod so badly as to collocate that last incident with the other three. But the *Improperia* in Book V, significantly adapted from the liturgical chant, suggest some reason.[32] There Vida counterpoints Judea's treatment of the Redeemer with His goodness: "He led you out of Egypt and through the Red Sea; He fed you in the desert; He gave you water from the rock; He exalted you."

The clear parallels speak for themselves. The exalted Chosen People whose main mission was to preserve the worship of the true God and thus prepare for the Messiah, is contrasted with the chosen people of the future, suggested in Melchisedech's figurative sacrifice of bread and wine, that is to say, the Apostles, at that moment hiding timorously; the contrast is mildly ironic but very telling. Both of these passages are further complemented by the symbolism in the last five scenes of the major ekphrasis, culminating in the image of the pelican; by the symbolism of Moses at the Transfiguration—

14.

> Isacidum Phariis genus alter duxit ab oris
> Dux profugum, legesque dedit, moremque sacrorum.
>
> (I. 951-952)

—and by the welcome which the expectant just give
Christ when He harrows Hell,

> Ignotasque vias aperis ad sidera caeli!   (VI. 245)

Among sections of Simon's song echoed or expanded in
other passages is this striking rendering: the Israelites
have just passed between the parted waters;

> A tergo tota ex Aegypto curribus hostes
> Quadrijugis vecti instabant fulgentibus armis.
> Iamque pios canit emenso pelago alta tenere
> Litora, litoreisque metu se condere silvis.
> Nulla mora est. iterum telo tellure recussa
> Divino, redeunt in se maria ...   (II. 616-621)

Behind them, the whole Egyptian host, in dazzling armor,
pressed hard on them in chariots pulled by four horses. Then
he sings how the faithful people passed through the sea and
reached the steep shores; in their terror, they took cover in
the woods. Immediately, the earth was smitten with the holy
rod, and the waters rushed back ...

The Israelites, in hiding but still *pios*, suggest the
frightened Apostles.[33]

It has been suggested that such contrivance, manifest
in both Vergil and Vida, is the offspring of Alexandrianism
combined with an oratorical imagination. Clearly, in
passages like those setting up the two grand prophecies
of the *Christiad* or those attempting to justify the excessive
length of the recapitulation in III-IV, such an observation
is reasonable.[34] But with respect to most of Vida's poem,
and needless to say of Vergil's, it is not. The implication
that the intricacy is there for the sake of the intricacy
misses the timber for the leaves. Vergil's parallels between

the earlier and later ravings of Dido indicate the accurate reading of his fourth book—in terms of *dissolvit pudorem* and *culpa*. Similarly, Vida's interweaving of passages, images, and incidents develops broad, carefully wrought themes, in the manner of a poet, not of a preacher. The contention that such architectural effects are achieved at too great a loss of spontaneity and naturalness is quite irrelevant; the *Iliad* and the *Odyssey*, cited from Vida's time to ours as exemplars of "free fury," have been shown to have surprisingly intricate construction.[35]

Curiously, while the *Ars poetica* treats epic mainly as narrative and offers varied suggestions on the breeding and nurture of characters, it says almost nothing about structure or thematic interpretation. In practice, however, the *Christiad* either ignores the rules or becomes defective by adhering to them. The few negligible lines in the *Ars poetica* about *sententiae* hardly prepare the reader for the overwhelming importance of theme in the epic poem. Bowra's remark about Aeneas applies fully to Vida's Christ: "Virgil has put so much into Aeneas that he has hardly made him a living man. But though he lacks human solidity, he is important as an ideal and a symbol."[36]

The difference in treatment of the two heroes, Christ and Aeneas, depends on the differences in material. Vergil's idealization of Aeneas, the model Roman, is clearly impossible in Vida's Christ. Christ is man but also God; the impact of the Incarnation on all human history and on heaven and hell, as theme, shifts the focus of interest from the center to the circumference. Christ's acts, like Aeneas's, are profoundly significant for the future of His people, but they are controlled to a greater extent by inexorable destiny. As a human being in almost continual conflict, Aeneas can be model or type; his battle with his own inclinations and with the human and super human forces around him can be translated into allegory. Christ is extensively prefigured, but the typology which Vida uses in his epic is allegory of a very narrow sort.[37] Beyond all these distinctions, the key fact is the conception of character and story as expressive functions of theme, and the operation of an architectonic structure as embodiment of the conception. In both poems, the antagonists are forces, symbolically represented in the *Aeneid* by the individual[38] characters—Dido, Turnus, Amata, Mezentius, and primarily Juno—and in the *Christiad* by the amorphous Satan, the Jewish priests (who are primarily puppets in his service), and the hapless Judas and Pilate. The differences between these and Homer's Achilles and Hector, Odysseus and Antinous, is clearly enormous.

Bowra's distinctions between Homeric and Vergilian epic may be illuminating here; his remarks make clear the large problems which faced Vida when, turning from his genial and broadly based notes on epic theory, he came to write his own epic and to discard most of what he had said. What Homer had done, Bowra points out, Vergil could not repeat; he was faced with a "new task," whose character he defined.

Because he wished to write a poem about something much larger than the destinies of individual heroes, he created a type of epic in which the characters represent something outside themselves, and the events displayed have other interests than their immediate excitement in the context.

Attempting, in a poem on the Roman character, to "bracket past and present in a single whole, and to give metaphysical unity to Rome," Vergil exalts the present as the fruition of a long, divinely ordained process.

The plan was bold, but there were no limits to its possibilities. .... Once we begin to grasp the various elements which make the complex art of literary epic, we are on the way to appreciate poetry of a special kind, which, though it claims to deal with a single subject, attacks it from different angles and at different levels. The mere story is less important than what it represents in the poet's vision of life.[39]

That Vida could deal very well with "mere story" is illustrated by episodes and characters of his epic, as well as by the earlier *Ludus scacchiae*, the sprightly mythological poem on the invention of chess. But in the *Christiad*, theme overwhelms narrative and characterization, and significance dictates architectural structure. We must now turn to this theme and this significance, and examine the "new character" which Vergil gave to the epic and which Vida took from him as his major inheritance.

CHAPTER SIX

THEMATIC DESIGN IN THE *CHRISTIAD*:
VIDA'S ESSENTIAL VERGILIANISM

IT MAY be accurately said that the *Ars poetica* treats heroic narrative in general and derives from the Vergilian version of the Homeric model. Had Vida adhered more closely to his own advice about narration and characterization, the *Christiad* as story would be better reading. However, between the time he versified his notes and the years of epic composition, Vida's views changed. In the *Ars poetica*, he saw Vergil as surpassing Homer because his narrative construction and his characterization were more decorous than Homer's, because his images were more refined and his diction more elegant. There, Vida concentrated on Homeric epic as improved by Vergil. But the *Christiad* is epic of a kind not treated in the *Ars poetica*, and not generally practiced in the tradition stretching from Statius to Sannazaro. Vida seems close to this tradition only in incidental matters of framework, style, or story; examination of elements like ekphrasis and prophecy, the epic simile, and evocative allusion shows how independent he can be. In both characterization and narration, he virtually discards all of his prior precepts, following Vergil in ways the tradition gives no hint of. The structure of the *Christiad*, totally and essentially Vergilian, supplies at least some clues to understanding what Vida was attempting.

For the *Christiad* is Vergilian epic in the profoundest sense, that is to say, symbolic or reflective epic, constructed on a grand design which is concerned more with theme than with story, in which theme engulfs both narrative and character. In the *Christiad*, Homer has been left completely behind. The naturalness of the Greek poet, the particularities of his technique, and the elements in which he is superior are forgotten in the attempt to embody a grand design as the *Aeneid* did. Between the *Ars poetica* and the *Christiad*, Vida moves from admiration for the elegance and polish of Vergil to understanding of Vergil's unique fusion of form and meaning. The definition of "heroic" changes for Vida, as it was changed in the history of epic by Vergil's practice. Whether Vida perceived the essential differences between Homer and Vergil before the writing of the *Ars poetica*, or ever indeed formulated them for himself at all, is of little importance here. The *Ars poetica* does have one passage which might suggest "grand design":

> Tuque ideo nisi mente prius, nisi pectore toto
> Crebra agites quodcumque canis, tecumque premendo
> Totum opus aedifices, iterumque, iterumque retractes,
> Laudatum alterius frustra mirabere carmen.
> Nec te fors inopina regat, casusque labantem.
> Omnia consiliis provisa, animoque volenti
> Certus age, ac semper nutu rationis eant res.
>
> (*Ars poetica* II. 156-162)

Thus, unless you think out your argument again and again, with your mind and your heart, unless you build the whole work with care and revise it over and over, you will find yourself forced to admire another man's success. Do not proceed by haphazard chance; plan your work carefully and with your mind fully alert, knowing exactly what you are doing; your reason must always be in control.

But this emphasis on coherence refers primarily, in the

context, to narrative and action; the *Christiad* is so pervaded by theme and so responsive, in its embodiment of theme, to the Vergilian epic that it seems to have quite forgotten the theory of the *Ars poetica.*

The differences between Homeric and Vergilian epic which are very important to an understanding of the *Christiad* must be considered here and an attempt made to define the essence of Vergilian epic. It may help first to compare briefly the opening of Vida's poem with the opening of the *Iliad*, the *Odyssey*, and the *Aeneid*. At the beginning of the *Christiad*, Christ is presented on His way to Jerusalem, followed by enormous crowds; drawing the twelve Apostles aside, Christ discourses to them on what is to happen shortly and why. The *Iliad* begins with the conflict between the commander of the Greek armies and the best of the Greek warriors. The *Odyssey* begins with two journeys—Odysseus attempting to get home, and Telemachus attempting to set out and find him. At the beginning of the *Aeneid*, Aeneas and his Trojans, on their way to Italy, are purposely deflected towards Carthage, after Juno's storm has failed to destroy them.

In the *Christiad* and the *Aeneid*, Christ's death and the achievement of Latium are real but also symbolic goals. The symbolism intended is reinforced throughout the poem and developed in supporting incidents and imagery. The conflict between Agamemnon and Achilles seems to have no broad significance beyond the narrative limits of the poem, and the attempts of Odysseus to reach home and of Telemachus to find his father, while they are clearly open to broad allegorical interpretation, are not intended as symbolic themes. A distinction must be made between allegory and symbolic design. In the one case, the *Odyssey*, there is a story which offers varieties of universal significance; in the other, the *Aeneid*, there is a story whose very texture is inextricably and intentionally interwoven

with the author's thematic interpretation of his material.
The fact that the *Aeneid*, like the *Odyssey*, may be read
allegorically does not affect the case; Landino's allegorization, or Vegio's, for instance, can be accomplished only
by the imposition of an organized pattern generally from
outside the poem itself.[1] But the thematic design depends
on the author's interpretation of his material, the vision
he is attempting to embody, and the clue to this design
lies in his own suggestions, such as this postscript to the
proposition of the *Aeneid*:

> tantae molis erat Romanam condere gentem. (I. 33)

The thematic design must be contained in and derived
from the major statements, incidents, characters, structure,
and imagery of the poem.

Some of the fundamental differences between Homeric
and Vergilian epic are indicated by the varying uses of
prophecy. In the *Iliad* and the *Odyssey*, prophecy contributes not only to heightening suspense and unifying the
poems by focusing interest on the central characters, but
also to expanding the limits of the narratives beyond the
central incidents. Thus, the death of Achilles and the fall
of Troy, and the further peaceful life and death of
Odysseus, convey the reader beyond the great duel and
beyond the restoration of Ithaca to its ruler. The first
prophecy in the *Aeneid*, however, has a different note:
manent immota tuorum fata tibi....

> bellum ingens geret Italia populosque ferocis
> contundet moresque viris et moenia ponet,
> tertia dum Latio regnantem viderit aestas,
> ternaque transierint Rutulis hiberna subactis.
> at puer Ascanius....   (I. 263-267)

Jupiter prophesied that after further warfare, Aeneas will
die before his kingdom is fully established in Italy, but

the effect is curiously different from the effect of the repeated prophecies regarding the short life of Achilles. Jupiter's words do not invest the hero of the *Aeneid* with pathos, nor do they urge a sense of sacrifice to a personal cause. These are the major concerns of Achilles in the *Iliad*: the choice emphasized by the prophecies of Zeus or the prophecies recalled by his mother, Thetis. Achilles's death is necessary if he is to achieve his heroic state, to enhance the dignity of the human condition by choosing consciously and fully the short life with glory over the long life with riches and peace.

The central interest of the prophecy concerning Aeneas's death is directed not to Aeneas himself but to the empire of peace and universal harmony which he is striving to establish. Prophecy in general in the *Aeneid* foretells far more than the outcome of the events the poem deals with; it projects the Trojans eleven centuries into the future and further, encompassing the high points of Roman history down to the days of Augustus, and it identifies the meaning of their enterprise.

The difference is seen also in the heroes of the poems. Homer's Achilles and Odysseus are versions of the heroic temper, from an individualistic age in which the glory and sacrifice involved in the chosen exploits bring honor to the hero and redeem the brevity and darkness of life, but the poet seems to attempt no broad interpretation of that life. Achilles is spontaneous. His free fury proceeds from sources neither he nor Homer analyzes; his actions are close to the surface and his deeds interesting mainly in themselves. He is deliberate, but with a deliberation based on a clearly defined heroic issue. Odysseus, also spontaneous and natural, also deliberate, presents a more complicated moral pattern, as the *Odyssey* is at once more tightly organized than the *Iliad* and more universal in suggestion. But neither hero and neither poem can be called diffuse or ambivalent; the light in which we see them is vertical, constantly brilliant, emanating from their activities and their characters.

Aeneas on the other hand is far more complex and more human, while also less individual than symbol; the events he moves and partakes in have far-reaching significance, rooted in the thematic design of Vergil's epic. As hero, Aeneas is more responsible to the abstract ideal of Rome than to himself. His furious reactions to the fires and battles in Troy reveal qualities which he must master. In a terrifying numinous scene, Venus purges Aeneas's natural vision and shows him the gods—Neptune, Juno, Minerva, and Jove himself—pulling down the walls of Troy; the pathos of Troy's fall is subsumed in the fuller perspective of a compelling Destiny, not fully understood as yet, but to whose urgency Aeneas must submit. When he realizes Creusa is missing, he rushes madly back into the Greek-infested city; the shade of Creusa, however, utters mysterious words, indicting his folly and emphasizing that compelling Destiny:

> non haec sine numine divom
> eveniunt; nec te hinc comitem asportare Creusam
> fas aut ille sinit superi regnator Olympi.
> longa tibi exsilia, et vastum maris aequor arandum ...
>
> (II. 777-780)

These things have happened only because of the will of the gods; you are not destined to take Creusa with you: the ruler of Olympus does not permit it. Your lot is distant and lengthy exile, broad expanses of sea to be furrowed.

Hardly hearing, Aeneas attempts to embrace her—

> ter conatus ibi collo dare bracchia circum;
> ter frustra comprensa manus effugit imago,
> par levibus ventis, volucrique simillima somno.
>
> (II. 792-794)

Three times then I tried to embrace her; three times, the phantom eluded by hands, my vain grasp, as might the gentle breezes, or, more accurately, a fleeting dream.

Then he returns quietly to the Trojan remnant:

> undique convenere, animis opibusque parati,
> in quascumque velim pelago deducere terras.
> iamque iugis summae surgebat Lucifer Idae,
> ducebatque diem; Danaique obsessa tenebant
> limina portarum, nec spes opis ulla dabatur:
> cessi, et sublato montes genitore petivi.
>
> (II. 799-804)

They had come from all over, as best equipped as they could manage, ready to go wherever I might decide to lead them over the sea. The morning star was already rising over the ridges of Mt. Ida and ushering in the day; the Greeks had the gates well guarded: hope of aid was there none. I ceased, and, picking up my father, I made for the mountains.

Much of the symbolism here is evident enough: the morning star and dawn of a new day evoking hope; the transitoriness of the life he had led at Troy—not his true city anyway, *Italiam poscimus matrem*. Later the symbolism is underlined and expanded—when, for example, lines 792-794 are exactly repeated about Aeneas's attempts to embrace the shade of Anchises, as prologue to Anchises's revelations of the future glories of Rome; or when the symbolic figure of Aeneas, *sublato genitore*, is evoked in the closing lines of Book VIII. In this latter scene, Aeneas has been looking at the shield made for him by Vulcan.

> talia per clipeum Vulcani, dona parentis,
> miratur, rerumque ignarus imagine gaudet,
> attollens umero famamque et fata nepotum.
>
> (VIII. 729-731)

These were the things he marveled at on Vulcan's shield, his mother's gifts; though he did not understand them, he was elated by the portrayal, and he took upon his shoulders the fame and the destiny of his descendants.

In the earlier book, Aeneas did not fully understand the import of the divine destruction of his native city, nor the value of his exile; yet, *cessi*—he ceased fretting about the ruins of Troy, about the demands of "honor," about the old life of his "native" city—and he took up his burden. Here, in the eighth book, Venus again has shown him marvels, which he is amazed by but cannot fully comprehend; still, with somewhat firmer faith, he takes up his burden again.

The fortunes of Aeneas make a pattern of renunciation throughout the whole epic—a pattern that surely had much to do with the endless allegorizing of the work. City, home, friends, wife, father, mistress, the ease of established life somewhere, all these must be yielded. Thus, when he bids farewell to Helenus and Andromache, settled in their colony on Epirus, he speaks with some firmness of purpose but with a wistful look behind as well:

> vivite felices, quibus est fortuna peracta
> iam sua; nos alia ex aliis in fata vocamur.
> vobis parta quies; nullum maris aequor arandum,
> arva neque Ausoniae semper cedentia retro
> quaerenda.   (III. 493-497)

May you live happily! you have accomplished your destiny, but we are to be bandied from one fate to another. You have won your rest; no longer need you furrow the face of the deep, no longer are you forced to pursue the ever-receding fields of Italy.

No sooner has Aeneas reached Italy than Cajeta dies, his old nurse, and virtually every bond with his former life is broken. Then commences the new bitterness of the war in Italy, a war Aeneas is forced into by divine decree on the one hand and, on the other, by human perversity, compounded by Juno's meddling. In this, too, there are renunciations and deprivations, of Pallas for instance or of brave young men like Nisus and Euryalus, losses which are part of the price, as the unwanted horrors of war also are part of the price which he must pay to fulfill his destiny. It is a destiny which is almost completely stripped of the personal and individualistic, for Aeneas will die before his kingdom is fully established, and the line which will spring from him will be not Trojan but Italian.

To distinguish the two kinds of epic, critics have, in different contexts, labeled the one primitive, natural, primary, or oral, and the other artificial, literary, secondary, or written. None of these terms suffices. Tillyard has suggested that Homer generally "sees events in a uniformly brilliant light, on the spot," whereas Vergil "constantly varies the distance and in this variety creates a varying scale of time.... Homer presented the contrasts comprised in a single world with incomparable force.... Virgil, on the contrary, is without a rival, in the subtle suggestion of different worlds of existence."[2] Elsewhere Tillyard says,

... the peculiar greatness of the *Aeneid* (and in this it surpasses all epics except the *Divine Comedy*) is that it also speaks for a whole change of human temper in the western world. Though cast in the form of the old heroic epic, the *Aeneid* is distant from the characteristic, unmitigated humanism of the Greek world before Alexander. The human race in the western world, or at least that part of it that was in the front of development and dictated the temper of the period, grew out of its stage of early manhood ... into the advantages and disadvantages of middle age. Just as in the growing man the time-sense suddenly asserts itself and induces the reflection that if he chooses this he must reject that, so in the race the attention is taken from a timeless interest in the immediate happening, and its mind suffers divisions. Life then presents itself less simply, and ... the sense of multiple worlds is created.[3]

This goes somewhat further than the limited distinction between "individual" and "national" epic. The *Aeneid* may be called national or institutional epic, as differentiated from the individual epics of Homer, only if institutional is understood as encompassing and celebrating not simply the Roman Empire but also the abstract ideal of Rome. The glory and sacrifice and achievements of the older heroes are then raised beyond personal gain to the level of a community in the broadest sense—the universal community—and the destiny which is imposed on the hero of an institutional epic, and which he is to carry out by a cooperation between his free will and the divine plan, transcends the principate of Augustus or any other principate, though it may be partially expressed therein. Destiny transcends the principate in the service of that abstract ideal, the quintessential Rome in Vergil's case, in which the divine power has vested the potential for full world order. In this sense, Vergil tolerates the battles of *Aeneid* VII-XII, while keeping his head averted, because he really could hope that the necessary evil symbolically presented might be a war to end all war.

It must be firmly underlined that when Jove says, *imperium sine fine dedi*,[4] not *imperium* but *dedi* is the key word. Vergil's epic embodiment of the ideal of Rome presents all the issues honestly and looks squarely not only at the sacrifices of Aeneas to social, political, and national cause, but also at the dangers inherent in the kind of empire Augustus was trying to build and at the cost involved. As such, Vergil's poem is less propagandistic than analytic. A propagandist would have been more rosily confident of the value of these present things than Vergil was—witness the moving scenes in *Aeneid* VI, the sheer astonishment of Aeneas that souls could want to forsake the reality of the Elysian Fields for the vaporous dreams of earthly life. A propagandist would have made Aeneas a less ambiguous, less fallible hero—witness the blood-lusty Aeneas of Books X-XI. Vergil is more concerned with the destiny which gives Rome an aura of divinity, than with the particular individual, however good, who at that given time was guiding Roman polity. He emphasized the spiritual self-realization and the profound rapport with the divine necessary for the fullest achievement of the Roman destiny. The golden age, enshrined in the *Aeneid*, remained an ideal to be striven for.

The *Aeneid* is reflective or symbolic epic, constructed on a thematic design which subsumes narrative and expands its meanings into cosmic proportions. Its art is far more intricate and operates on more levels than does the art of the Homeric epics.[5] Aeneas, at the center, symbolizes not only Augustus or the ideal Roman, but the very idea of the Roman operating in close harmony with the designs of Fate, something very like Christian Providence. The connection between gods and men is less intimate but much more real in the *Aeneid*; Jove is both more august and more concerned with human destinies than is Homer's Zeus. The opposition between Jove and Juno, between Juno and the Trojans, between Dido and Aeneas, and between Aeneas and Turnus, is less the basis for narrative incidents than it is the concrete manifestation of order vs. the irrational on a cosmic scale. This is how Vergil describes the cave of the winds in *Aeneid* I:

> hic vasto rex Aeolus antro
> luctantis ventos tempestatesque sonoras
> imperio premit ac vinclis et carcere frenat.
> illi indignantes magno cum murmure montis
> circum claustra fremunt; celsa sedet Aeolus arce
> sceptra tenens mollitque animos et temperat iras;

> ni faciat, maria ac terras caelumque profundum
> quippe ferant rapidi secum verrantque per auras.
>
> (I. 52-59)

Here in a huge cavern, Aeolus the king rules over the heaving winds and the roaring storms, and keeps them pent up and imprisoned. They fume and rage violently at their confines, and the mountain moans. But Aeolus sits in his lofty citadel, sceptre in hand, taming their spirits and curbing their passions; and if he did not, they would bolt off with the seas and the earth and the deep heavens, and whirl them rapidly through space.

These are the forces of disorder in the natural world, kept under control. Juno however, persuades Aeolus to loose the winds on Aeneas's fleet; Aeolus obeys and there is a terrific storm,[6] which is calmed by Neptune, angry at this insubordination in the celestial hierarchy. The simile Vergil uses here is profoundly different from the typical Homeric simile, as the whole scene is profoundly different in tone and scope and significance from the Homeric model:

> ac veluti magno in populo cum saepe coorta est
> seditio saevitque animis ignobile vulgus;
> iamque faces et saxa volant, furor arma ministrat;
> tum, pietate gravem ac meritis si forte virum quem
> conspexere, silent arrectisque auribus astant;
> ille regit dictis animos et pectora mulcet,
> sic cunctus pelagi cecidit fragor, aequora postquam
> prospiciens genitor caeloque invectus aperto
> flectit equos curruque volans dat lora secundo.
>
> (I. 148-156)

Just as, so often, when a crowd gathers and a riot begins, the rabble rages out of control, and clubs and rocks fly—for madness finds weapons—then, if they should see a man whom they respect for his goodness and his conduct, they stop and become quiet, listening carefully; and he, by his words, wins

15.

them over and calms their passions. Just so did the whole roaring ocean settle when Neptune gazed out over the face of the waters; under a cleared sky, he drove forth, giving the bit, as he flew on, to the willing steeds.

The simile makes the immediate point; more important, it expresses the conflict between order and disorder on three levels—the natural, the human and civil, and the celestial.

An important task for Aeneas throughout the poem is to conquer the irrational, particularly in himself. The audacity of Vergil's *Tum pius Aeneas* at the emotional crisis of Book IV, and the precise description of Aeneas amid the tears and frenzies of Dido—*Mens immota manet*—point up the conflict and its importance. Turnus in the second half of the poem is fiercely irrational— possessed by Allecto, defying the oracles, overruling the king, and fighting with the reckless abandon of the old-model hero. To Pandarus he cries,

> "incipe, si qua animo virtus, et consere dextram,
> hic etiam inventum Priamo narrabis Achillem"
> (IX. 741-742)

"If you have any courage at all, come ahead and fight; here too, you will tell Priam, you found another Achilles."

Trojans fall before him, in a rout which takes place mainly because the Trojans had neglected Aeneas's orders.[7] But Turnus's heroism is too anarchic and anachronistic:

> et si continuo victorem ea cura subisset,
> rumpere claustra manu sociosque immittere portis,
> ultimus ille dies bello gentique fuisset.
> sed furor ardentem caedisque insana cupido
> egit in adversos.   (IX. 757-761)

And had he, in his conquest, only kept sense enough to immediately break through the gates and let his comrades in, that day would have been the end both of the war and of the Trojan race. But his frenzy and his mad lust for slaughter drove him on against the enemy.

What defeats Turnus is his own bravery; he is beaten back by the rallying Trojans, now reorganized, and is forced to jump into the river and swim to the other side.

Many of these scenes are variations on the Homeric model; the variations are dictated primarily by the thematic design of Vergil's epic. Tillyard points out, about the Homeric storm Vergil used as model, the storm which washed Odysseus up on the Phaeacian beach: "Simply as a storm, and no more, the storm that throws Odysseus on to Phaeacia is superior to Virgil's; it has the certainty of unmixed reality. But it lacks the richness of Virgil's symbolism."[8]

Even more telling is Vergil's adaptation of the Hector-Achilles duel for the final scenes of the poem. Here are some details:[9]

> ...Achilleus went straight for him in fury, but Hektor fled away under the Trojan wall and moved his knees
> rapidly.
> They raced along by the watching point and windy
> fig-tree
> always away from under the wall and along the
> wagon-way
> and came to the two sweet-running well springs. There
> there are double
> springs of water that jet up, the springs of whirling
> Skamandros.
> One of these runs hot water and the stream on all sides
> of it rises as if from a fire that was burning inside it.
> But the other in the summer-time runs water that is like
> hail
> or chill snow or ice that forms from water. Beside these
> in this place, and close to them, are the washing-hollows

of stone, and magnificent, where the wives of the Trojans
                                                and their lovely
daughters washed the clothes to shining, in the old days
when there was peace, before the coming of the sons of
                                                the Achaians.
They ran beside these, one escaping, the other after him.
It was a great man who fled, but far better he who
                                                pursued him
rapidly, since here was no festal beast, no ox-hide
they strove for, for these are prizes that are given men for
                                                their running.
No, they ran for the life of Hektor, breaker of horses.

Zeus gathers the gods, for he does not know whether

to rescue this man or whether to make him, for all his
                                                valour,
go down under the hands of Achilleus, the son of Peleus.

But rebuked by Athene, he says to her,

"Act as your purposes would have you do, and hold back
                                                no longer."

. . . .

But when for the fourth time they had come around to
                                                the well springs
then the Father balanced his golden scales, and in them
he set two fateful portions of death, which lays men
                                                prostrate,
one for Achilleus, and one for Hektor, breaker of horses,
and balanced it by the middle; and Hektor's death-day
                                                was heavier
and dragged downward toward death, and Phoibos Apollo
                                                forsook him.[10]

The contrast evoked in the first passage exploits the
emotional possibilities of poetry to the extreme. But
despite the participation of the gods and the balancing of
the golden scales, the duel as a whole remains narrative,
a good fight between the greatest heroes of the war.

The duel between Aeneas and Turnus is purposefully arranged to resemble and differ from Homer's narrative. Turnus is the splendid individual hero, ready to do furious battle and achieve his ends. His arrogance contrasts with the solemn sacrificial ritual performed by Trojans and Latins. Juno interferes, provoking through Iuturna a breaking of the truce, and during the general melee Turnus rampages wildly. Aeneas, however, pursues only the duel, attempting to avert further bloodshed:

> solum densa in caligine Turnum
> vestigat lustrans, solum in certamina poscit.
> (*Aeneid* XII. 466-467)

To his son he has said,

> "disce, puer, virtutem ex me verumque laborem,
> fortunam ex aliis. nunc te mea dextera bello
> defensum dabit et magna inter praemia ducet:
> tu facito, mox cum matura adoleverit aetas,
> sis memor, et te animo repetentem exempla tuorum
> et pater Aeneas et avunculus excitet Hector."
> (435-440)

"My son, learn from my example what true courage and true effort are; others will show you the meaning of luck. Now my right hand will keep you safe in this war and will lead you to many rewards. But when your youth ripens into manhood, see to it that you remember us, that your spirit stir itself to recall your kinsmen—your father Aeneas and your uncle Hector."

When finally the duel does take place, it is a monumental conflict which men and gods watch in hushed solemnity. Jupiter hangs out the golden scales—

> Juppiter ipse duas aequato examine lances
> sustinet et fata imponit diversa duorum,
> quem damnet labor et quo vergat pondere letum.
> (725-727)

—in a parenthetical scene; and later, at the height of the duel, Vergil interrupts again, returning the action to Olympus, where Jupiter seals not only the fate of Turnus but the whole future destiny of Italy.[11]

Similarly, the third book of the *Aeneid* might be contrasted with the narrative of Odysseus to Alcinous.[12] Aeneas's wanderings have clear purpose and far-reaching significance; what there is of the fabulous, recalling Odysseus's tale, is subordinated to the revelations which Aeneas receives from Apollo, from the Penates, from his father, from Helenus, from the Harpies themselves, as well as to the unifying and dominating purpose: *Italiam poscimus matrem*. And *Aeneid* VI, despite its not wholly coherent theology, presents an attempt to view the universe and the particular destiny of Rome, while its counterpart, *Odyssey* XI, is a terrifying book, washed over with purple shades and teeming with distinct, uncomplicated emotions. The Shield of Aeneas, presenting an uncensored further view of Roman history and polity, contrasts with the Shield of Achilles, a panorama of beautiful and moving scenes but unrelated to any vast theme which dominates the poem.[13]

These representative examples should suffice to indicate the fundamental differences between the energetic, spontaneous, natural, heroic epics of Homer, and the reflective, symbolic, complex epic of Vergil, built on a vast thematic design in which character, incident, imagery, innumerable conventional devices are interwoven, in an intricate architectonic structure, into a symbolic whole whose significance absorbs everything else. C. S. Lewis has remarked that after Vergil epic poetry could not be the same again;[14] it is quite amazing how much the same it remained. Statius set the pattern, with a narrative poem so obviously imitative of the Vergilian model that it was easy to conclude that he had grasped the implications of Vergil's practice and was showing what imitation of Vergil must attempt. That is to say, a Vergilian epic must be an epic in which all the conventional devices, or as many of them as possible, are utilized for some purpose or other and are couched in Vergilian phraseology; in which someone must narrate a lengthy episode out of the past, and someone must descend into the underworld, and there must be banquets, journeys, great battles, and councils of war; in which the gods must be invoked often, omens must occur, and prophecies be made. Statius has no thematic design, indeed, no coherent structure, but no matter; he says himself that he is imitating Vergil.

After Statius, and Valerius Flaccus and Silius Italicus, who did much the same thing, Christian epic which assayed imitation of Vergil almost always was Statian, not Vergilian—a straight narrative adapted, or contorted, to the canonical elements and in the elaborately formal style redolent of the *Aeneid*. Juvencus's *Evangeliorum libri quattuor* has no recognizable structure beyond the Scriptural; the *Carmen Paschale* of Sedulius attempts some scope by its forays into Old Testament types and figures, but never ventures beyond the limits of conventional exegesis. These poems, it is true, have a sense of vitality and relevance which the Silver Latin poets never could achieve, but the essential weakness is seen in Arator's *De actibus Apostolorum*, which is neither poetry nor apologetics.[15] In the *Quattrocento*, immediacy itself was absent, and the feeble attempts at Christian epic, Vergilian in intent, rarely rose above the predominant chronicle form and automatic elegance. Girolamo Dalle Valli's *Jesuida* suggested some of the real dramatic possibilities in the material; Muzio's *De triumpho Christi* attempted to achieve real scope, for all its brevity. But neither the practice nor the theory of the *Quattrocento* penetrated Vergil's architectural design or understood the significance and function of the elegant style and the canonical elements in that design. The one exception, the allegorical epic which began with Prudentius, had an outstanding humanist representation in Marko Marulic's *Davidias*; allegory, however, is only partially relevant to Vida's aim. Finally, it may be noted that Lucan, the only epic poet who attempted the vastness of scope and grandness of theme which Vergil achieved, flaunted his break with the Vergilian tradition.

In writing the *Christiad*, Vida took over Vergil's epic style in its totality, constructing his poem on a vast thematic design. Few critics have recognized this. By and large, they have been hindered from even considering the possibility because they have too easily made one or both of these assumptions: that the *Christiad* was composed specifically along the lines laid down in the *Ars poetica*; that the *Christiad* is a simple retelling of the Gospel story, with frills added to make it resemble the classical epic of Vergil.[16] Bonaventura Zumbini would seem to be the only critic who began not with the *Ars poetica* or the Gospels, but with the poem itself. His perceptions about the scope of Vida's epic have point here:

Ch'egli sia stato il degno precursore del Milton e del Klop-stock non poteva sfuggire agli storici della letteratura: ma nessuno di essi, io credo, comprese appieno il valore di quel fatto, e anzi neanche seppe ben determinare in che propria-mente quel fatto consistesse. Ecco. Il Vida fu il primo a con-giungere col particolare soggetto del suo poema, ch'era la Passione, gli altri grandi fatti della storia ebraico-cristiana. Ho detto il primo, parendomi, che, pur fra i nostri migliori, non ci sia chi possa contendergli un si bel vanto. Non il Mu-zio, perché il suo *De Triumpho Christi* è come un solo epi-sodio della storia del Redentore.... Né tanto meno ... San-nazaro; il quale ... anche ricorrendo alle amplificazioni dei particolari, si tenne sempre stretto al suo determinato argomento. Ma la Passione, o qualsiasi altro fra i grandi fatti della storia sacra, tolto a soggetto del poema, allora può produrre i suoi maggiori effetti morali e poetici, quando ci sia presentato come parte integrale di quell'immensa epopea che va dalla creazione del mondo al giudizio universale. Cosí veramente quei fatti li vediamo adunati nel *Paradiso Perduto*, nel *Messia*, e cosí anche nella *Cristiade....*[17]

That Vida was the worthy forerunner of Milton and Klopstock could not escape the historians of literature; but I do not think any of them understood fully the significance of that fact, nor indeed were they able to determine what precisely that fact consisted in. Here it is. Vida was the first to unite with the particular subject of his poem, which was the Passion, the other grand facts of Hebraeo-Christian history. I say the first, because it seems to me that, among our better writers, there is no one to contest that title to fame. Not Muzio, whose *De Triumpho Christi* is, as it were, a single episode of the story of the Redeemer ... Much less ... Sannazaro, who, though at times he enlarges some particulars, is always bound straitly by his announced theme. But the Passion, or whatever other of the grand facts of sacred history, taken as the subject of the poem, can produce its major moral and poetic effects only when it is presented to us as an integral part of that immense epic which extends from the creation of the world to the general judgment. Thus truly do we see those facts united in *Paradise Lost*, in the *Messiah*, and thus also in the *Christiad....*

Though Zumbini does not examine the influence of Vergil on Vida's vast conception, he implies it clearly in his praise of Vida's unique classical-Christian fusion.[18]

Vida pointed out himself that the subject of his poem extended beyond narrative of the Passion. A good statement is that in the undisguised digression in his *Republic*, referring to Leo's commission; his aim was, he says, "quid efficere ... valerem in exprimendis, et versu explicandis rebus divinis, quae pertinent ad Christi insti-

tuta, totamque tam augustae religionis, ac sanctitatis
rationem." The key words are quite evidently "Christi
instituta, totamque ... religionis ac sanctitatis rationem."
He adds that much of the Gospel narratives had to be
omitted for reasons of length or relevance, and that the
poem he conceived could not encompass everything per-
taining to Christianity. Much of the remaining material,
he says, was used in the *Hymni*.[19]

Vida's epic is a religious poem if one refers to content
only. It is not lyrical or personal; despite the apostrophes,
Vida objectified his material, in contrast to the *Hymni*.
The *Christiad* attempts to depict the objective pattern of
things, the necessity and significance within all history of
the Incarnation; the cosmic story is set before us and we
are invited to look at it from the outside.[20] The *Christiad*
is not the poetic expression of religious experience. At
the same time, as an attempt to embody the Incarnation
with all its meaning,

> to apprehend
> The point of intervention of the timeless
> With time ...
> [Where] the impossible union
> Of spheres of existence is actual,
> [Where] the past and future
> Are conquered and reconciled...,[21]

the poem is a "raid on the inarticulate." The complexity
and abstractness of the subject are indicated in the invocation:

> Fas mihi, te duce, mortali immortalia digno
> Ore loqui, interdumque oculos attollere caelo,
> Et lucem accipere aetheream, summique parentis
> Consilia, atque necis tam dirae evolvere caussas.
>
> (*Christiad* I. 11-14)

The *Christiad* has as its major theme the Incarnation

in its cosmic significance, not only for earth, but for heaven and hell as well; not only for contemporary history, but for all human history, from the beginning of time to the end. Though this complex and ramified theme subsumes all the others, it may be well here to single out some. There is a distinct and important Roman theme, in which the impact of the coming of Christ on particular history is studied—Rome is set off against Jerusalem, Romans against Jews, the Christian destiny of Rome against both its own past and against the future of deicidal Judea. In the workings of this theme, Vida comments on Vergil and the ancient world: the golden age ideal of antiquity is set off against the truly golden age. There is also the theme of exile—not only the exile of Christ, without honor among His own people, but of the Apostles, in temporary exile from their true home on earth and their ultimate home in heaven. There is the theme of grace, the divine gift of God whereby man can participate in the supernatural life, nature can be raised, humanity and divinity united; grace, bringing on the true golden age, provides the *ordering* force of the universe, another theme.

These intricately interwoven themes, extensive and manifold in their significance, are less stated than expressed and embodied. The means chosen for this embodiment are diverse—the architectonic structure; the devices of ekphrasis and prophecy; the patterns of similes and of the running imagery; action on multiple levels; broad and skillful allusion; juxtaposition of characters and incidents with dramatic statement or with symbolic suggestion; and the use of shifting points of view. Like the *Aeneid*, Vida's epic is less active and heroic than complex, reflective, and symbolic.

In a number of passages, Vida seems to be hinting at the highly symbolic nature of his treatment. "Arcanis sed

cuncta notis," he remarks tersely about the major ekphrasis. Old Testament typology is much in evidence; John
says of Christ's teaching on fulfillment, not rejection, of
Law and Prophets:

> Verum alios longe ritus, moremque sacrorum
> Indicat obscura verborum ambage latere,
> Legiferique aperit voces animumque magistri.
>
> (IV. 795-797)

He shows them that far different ceremonies and rituals are
hidden in the mysterious words, and He explains to them
the words and the spirit of their lawgiver.

And John's summary description of Christ's teaching may
well refer to the whole epic:

> Nunc caecis vera involvens ambagibus ultro,
> Nunc manifesta palam claro sermone loquutus.
>
> (IV. 1031-1032)

Sometimes He would clothe the truth in mysterious statements; at other times, He uttered it simply and clearly.

Of Simon the bard we are told often, "Deo plenus ...
ventura canebat." Simon, having shown the upper room
to Peter and John, returns to his song with a highly
ambiguous statement:

> Interea adventu vestro intermissa sequamur
> Carmina, et antiquos patrum repetamus honores,
> Dum nigra roriferis nox terras obruat umbris.
>
> (II. 604-606)

Meanwhile, let us pursue the songs interrupted at your arrival,
and tell again the ancient glory of our fathers, while the dark
night hastens to cover the earth with its dewy shadows.

Whatever the state of the weather, it is clear from the
carefully selected details of Simon's song and their striking

parallel to the *Improperia* of Book V that the last two
lines refer to the coming Passion.

It may be recalled that in his general remarks on
metaphor in the *Ars poetica*, Vida suggested more than
his specific figures accounted for:

> Usque adeo passim sua res insignia laetae
> Permutantque, juvantque vicissim, et mutua se se
> Altera in alterius transformant protinus ora.
> Tum specie capti gaudent spectare legentes.
> Nam diversa simul datur e re cernere eadem
> Multarum simulacra animo subeuntia rerum.
>
> > (*Ars poetica* III. 58-63)

Often things cheerfully change their shape and form, and mutually support each other, interchanging and metamorphosing
into each other's appearance; and, taken with the beauty of
it, readers enjoy contemplating it. For it often happens that
from the same thing it is possible for many diverse images
of other things to occur to the mind.

Continuing with a rich image comparing the reader to
a *viator*, he indicates the larger possibilities of analogy:

> Ceu quum forte olim placidi liquidissima ponti
> Aequora vicina spectat de rupe viator,
> Tantum illi subjecta oculis est mobilis unda:
> Ille tamen silvas, interque virentia prata
> Inspiciens miratur, aquae quae purior humor
> Cuncta refert, captosque eludit imagine visus.
>
> > (*Ars poetica* III. 64-69)

Thus a traveler, sitting on a rock, contemplates the surface
of the quiet sea, and only the gentle ripples of the waves
are present to his eyes; nonetheless, as he gazes, he marvels
to behold the woods and the green meadows in the waves,
all of which the clear water reflects, creating an allusion
which holds the gazer spellbound.

If the *Ars poetica* allows broad freedom with truth and

fiction, the prophecy in the *Christiad* about the poets who
would celebrate Christ's passion insists on *veri vates*; the
whole passage is indeed redolent of Petrarch's famous
statements in the *Africa* and the *Contra Medicum*.[22]

The *Christiad* opens with Christ on His way to Jerusalem, a symbolic journey the significance of which He
suggests in His address to the Apostles.[23] This opening
address sets many themes. What Christ says is hard, as
Peter's reaction shows: it is impossible for Peter to accept
all this about impending death, exile, some sort of redemption. He argues impetuously that Christ's proposals
are misguided, that life is too good to give up, that they
will be left orphans. But Christ cuts through the argument
sharply:

> Non pudet ... mortalia semper
> Volvere nube oculos pressum, caelestium inanem?
>
> (I. 75-76)

The contrast between *mortalia* and *caelestia*, and its collocation with the image of darkness is not casual.[24] Earlier,
Christ said of His resurrection:

> Quum tamen expulerit tenebras lux tertia ...   (49),

and described heaven, their true home, as "aetheris alti /
Lucida templa..., stellis florentia regna."[25]

The polarity of light and dark operates generally
throughout the poem. Though usually the forces are in
balance, there is a definite movement from dark to light,
climaxing in the intensity of the last book. The conversion
of Zaccheus, for instance, is referred to as *luce recepta*;
the closeness of Christ's friendship with Lazarus is shown
by the detail,

> creberque domus indulsit amicae
> Hospitio, atque Deum posita se nube retexit.
>
> (I. 109-110)

To these is immediately contrasted the dark region of
hell, where abide the *lucifugi* amid *luctifucum fumum ...
et atros ignes*.[26] A similar contrast is set between the light
of God the Creator and the darkness of hell, in the major
ekphrasis, and between the darkness of Jerusalem and
the brilliant glory of the Transfiguration.[27] The simile in
the last scene compares the transfigured Christ to the
rising sun:

> Verus et aspectu patuit Deus, atque per auras
> Divinum toto spiravit vertice odorem
> Luminis aetherei specimen, genitoris imago.
> Nec secus emicuit roseo pulcherrimus ore
> Insolita circum perfundens omnia luce,
> Quam quum mane recens lucis fons aureus ingens
> Lumine Sol caelum exoriens rigat omne profuso,
> Oceani in speculo longe resplendet imago,
> Et croceae effulgent aurata cacumina silvae.[28]
>
> (I. 938-946)

And the Godhead was manifest in His countenance, and He
diffused a divine aura into the air of the mountain top. The
embodiment of celestial radiance, the image of the Father,
His beautiful countenance shone with a roseate glow, suffusing
everything around with a miraculous light, no less brilliant
than when the sun, new risen at dawn, the very fountain of
light, golden and mighty, touches the whole sky with its
splendor and is reflected in the mirror of ocean, and the gilded
woods reflect the golden mountain tops.

With Him appear Moses and Elias, the latter in his fiery
chariot; the heavens burst open and the choirs of angels
break out in song.

The second book opens with the powers of darkness
virtually in control of Jerusalem; the only witness to
Christ is Nicodemus, of whom we learn,

> ubi Numen
> Admonitus sensit, veluti de nocte profunda

> In lucem revocatus, ei se junxit amore. (II. 156-158)

Once he was moved to perceive the divinity present, like a man recalled from the dark night to the light, he bound his heart firmly to Him.

For the rest, there is darkness in place of light:

> Praecedunt dirae facies, facibusque nefandis
> Sufficiunt lucem, et summo dant vertice lumen,
> Terrificas capitum quatientes undique flammas.
> (II. 60-62)

Preceding them go the dire visages of hell, who provide light for the horrendous torches, illuminating the whole area with the terrifying flames they shake from the top of their heads.

At the center of the book is *lux sacra*, the Paschal Feast, celebrated by the throngs converging on Jerusalem and by Christ and the Apostles; but when the day is over, Christ is arrested, the Apostles are in flight, Judas is vaunting his success—all expressed in terms of darkness.

The darkness of the fallen Jews at the beginning of Book III and of the plotting priests at the end of Joseph's narrative pair off against the radiant center—particularly the description of Mary in ecstasy, and of the Incarnation and birth of Christ.[29] Similarly, in IV, John's references to the fall of angels and of man, and the longing of the Old Testament just; the darkness of the world of demons and of Christ's enemies—these are varieties of darkness, expressed in numerous ways and set off against the light of the Redeemer.[30] The fifth book is darkest of all, opening in dim twilight and closing in the unnatural darkness at Christ's death.[31] The bright scene of God's court and of the angels, in the middle of the book, sets off that darkness more sharply.

This polarity of darkness and light is developed not only through description and incidental images, but also through carefully selected similes. Central to these is the simile comparing John, rapt in ecstasy, to an eagle soaring aloft and gazing at the sun; John's own simile comparing God to the sun is pendant to this one.[32] John the Baptist is like the morning star, heralding the sunrise—a detail Vida added to the familiar passage.[33] Similes for Mary in Book III are of the moon or a star or the dawn; for the newborn Christ, of the rising sun or of an emerald in its setting; for the risen Christ in VI, sunlight penetrating into and illuminating a dark house.[34]

The conflict between heaven and hell is developed in every book. After the brief victory of darkness in Book V, the brilliance of VI embodies the victory of Christ not only over death but also over hell. In the Harrowing, Christ is the avenger, driving the demons further back into the darkness, and leading the waiting souls of the just to the light of heaven. Vida develops this scene at great length, comparing the brightness of the victorious Christ in two different but related similes to gleaming Roman legions, and, in a further simile,

> Nam Deus haud secus obscuris conspectus in antris
> Perstringens oculos divina luce refulget,
> Quam quum gemma ignes splendore imitata corusco
> In noctem thalamis lucet regalibus, atrasque
> Exsuperat tenebras, largo et loca lumine vestit,
> Purpurea circum perfundens omnia luce.
>
> (VI. 216-221)

For God, visible in the gloomy caverns, enters, His eyes shining with such divine light, as when a brilliant crown jewel beams its glittering radiance into the darkness in royal chambers and vanquishes the dark shadows, lavishing its full light everywhere and making the room glow with its regal brilliance.

16.

Christ leads them to heaven in glorious procession, described in part thus:

> Applaudunt volucres purum tranantibus aurae,
> Subsidunt Euri, fugere ex aethere nimbi,
> Arridetque procul clari liquidissima mundi
> Tempestas: caelo arrident rutila astra sereno.
> Assurgit matutinis Aurora volucrum
> Cantibus: assurgit rubefacta Vesper ab aethra.
>   (VI. 288-293)

As they traversed the air, the gentle breezes applauded; the winds quieted down, the clouds dispersed, and sun shed its liquid radiance over the whole bright world. The crimson stars smiled in the peaceful sky. Aurora rose with the matin-song of the birds; and Vesper rose in the glowing twilight sky.

The climax of the light imagery in the sixth book is reached at the Ascension, perhaps the most carefully worked out of all the scenes in the poem. There the brightness of the angels, the intense light of heaven, and the glory suffused on the Apostles below are all combined with celestial activity and the joyful hymn of the Apostles into a radiant symbol of the union of heaven and earth through Christ's redemption.

The themes embodied by this imagery are manifold and extensive. The conflict between Christ and Satan is clear enough, but the darkness which Christ seeks to dispel has more specific meanings. The Apostles were prepared to fight and die for Him—

> una socii cum rege parati
> Cuncta pati et juvenis sortem indignantur iniquam.
>   (I. 91-92)

—but Christ is forced to reprove them because they do not really know whereof they speak. They are blind to His truth—the truth of heaven's justice, not earth's; the truth of unworldliness against worldliness; the truth of humility and spiritual peace. He upbraids the Jews for their wickedness, but more sharply for their hypocrisy, their self-seeking, and their conveniently narrow religious notions. He insists on purity of motive and tries to show the way of love, not fear. The new law is what He preaches, the fulfillment of the old; particular conflicts spring up because His words threaten vested interests. When He rebukes the hardheartedness of the Jews, He does so because they refuse to distinguish between letter and spirit, because they are obstinate in their pride, because they try to trap Him and discredit Him from debased motives.[35]

These interlocked conflicts are dramatized by the structure of Book I, where the plans of the consulting demons are contrasted by juxtaposition with the converted Zaccheus, a miser who has become generous; with the noble Lazarus who uses his riches wisely; and with the penitent Maria whose wealth, once dedicated to satiating restless lust, is now poured out prodigally on Christ. The opening of Book I indicated Christ's great repute; His triumphal entry at the center shows how widely that repute extends. Though He singlehanded drives the greedy merchants out of the Temple, the priests are helpless to interfere. But the Christ who is followed by the multitudes is not impressed by those multitudes.[36] Accorded a splendid entry and fawned on by the wealthier citizens, He modestly goes aside to cure a helpless old beggar by the pool. In even sharper contrast to the cheering popularity is the Transfiguration, with its solitary glory and the Father's quiet approbation.

A few more details may show other aspects of the conflict and other concrete expressions. The accursed fig tree symbolizes nature deformed, made sterile; its improper function is emphasized in the line, "Luxurians

late circum tendebat opaca."[37] In the third book, Joseph
interprets freely the reactions to the youthful Christ's
teaching in the Temple: "Prima mali fuit hinc nobis scin-
tilla ..." (969); throughout the whole book, Joseph is
attempting to show the conflict in human terms. He sees
it as power politics, vested interests threatened, a local
squabble which Pilate need not bother about; sometimes
he suggests that the root of the trouble lies in a confused
civic sense on both sides. The episode of the possessed
youth of Gerusa, which John narrates as the last and
longest of a representative series, shows depraved nature
at its worst; among the symbolic details are not only the
herd of swine, from the Gospel account, but also the
shrieking metaphors of frenzied nature, conveyed in
grinding and harsh rhythms and sounds, and the debased
and sadistic rabble, now fleeing in terror, but once safe,
"gaudent longe spectare periclum." (487) The same rabble
acclaims Christ God when He exorcises the devils and
cures the youth, but that Christ knows them well,
His counsels show: "rumoresque vagos contemnite vul-
gi," (902)—and John's simile, comparing such crowds to
the camp followers of a triumphant army, their motive
"divus habendi amor," identifies them with the mob at
that moment clamoring outside Pilate's court.

In the passage describing Christ's walking on the waves,
there is a twofold movement.[38] The excitement and terror
of the Apostles induced by the storm are paralleled by
their excitement and bewilderment induced by the apparition of Christ. Christ calms both, gently rebuking the
Apostles for their lack of faith; the closing lines of the
passage convey the peace of both sea and Apostles. The
peace Christ imparts here is part of the large concept of
peace He discourses on, by statement and metaphor, at
the end of Book IV. That peace is based on the perma-
nence of heaven and on complete, abandoned trust in

God. The specific contrast between the militant Christian life and the violence of the world—"pacem inglorius hostibus opta" (909)—is itself dramatized in various details at the arrest of Christ in the garden.

In his canticle, the aged Simeon calls the infant Christ "In tenebris lux, Isacidos nova gloria prolis" (III. 715.) To the uncomprehending listeners, he stresses the redemptive meaning of Christ's coming; his point would appear unmistakable:

> Macte infans virtute, Dei indubitata propago,
> Mundi opifer, qui nostra venis, veterumque parentum
> Sponte admissa tui largo lavere amne cruoris,
> Et liquidas aperire vias ad sidera caeli,
> Exoptatus ades, nec me tua maxima fallunt,
> Summe pater, promissa. mori me denique fas est.
> Nunc o me nunc ad requiem, finemque laborum
> Corporis exutum vinclis dimittis, ut olim
> Pollicitus. jam viderunt mea lumina quem tu
> Auxilium mundo misisti, ut gentibus esset
> In tenebris lux, Isacidos nova gloria prolis.
>
> (III. 705-715)

Hail, Child, undoubted offspring of God, welfare of the world; You have come of Your own free will to wash away our sins and those of our forefathers in the generous river of Your blood, and to open the liquid paths to heaven's stars. Long yearned for, You have come. Heavenly Father, Your great promises have not been in vain; at last, now, I may die. Now, o now, You send me to rest, to the end of my labors, freed from the bonds of the body, as You once promised me. For my eyes have seen Him whom You sent into the world to save it, and to be light to the people who live in darkness, the new glory of the sons of Isaac.

By adding specific imagery and interpretation, Vida expands Luke's original into more than paraphrase; there is also a shift in emphasis. Here is Luke 2:29-32:

Nunc dimittis servum tuum, Domine, secundum verbum tuum
in pace: quia viderunt oculi mei salutare tuum: quod parasti
ante faciem omnium populorum: Lumen ad revelationem gentium, et gloriam plebis tuae Israel.

Vida's version, providing particular as well as general
interpretation of *salutare tuum* and *Lumen ad revelationem gentium*, points up the redemptive function of the
Messiah. The canticle itself is preceded by the sacrifice
of the calf and the doves, and is followed by an ambiguous
prophecy to Mary. In context, the calf symbolizes Christ's
death on Calvary, and the doves, Mary's suffering; the
prophecy to Mary, linked by the image of rivers of blood
to the water images in the canticle, suggests other elements of the Redemption. In imagery and statement, Vida
opposes Old Law and New; the irony of Joseph's misinterpretation and of the general lack of comprehension
underlines this. Simeon, speaking from the past, revealed
the future.[39]

Vida is concerned to give his poem the richest possible
significance by using all available means. To render the
nature of the Incarnation and its implications, he resorts
to various structural and symbolic devices. To express the
impact of the Incarnation, he utilizes a technique which
may be called the point of view, and a related motif of
the revelation of divinity through facial beauty.

Vida characterizes Christ according to Vergilian practice,
making Christ a symbolic figure, progressively less active
and less dramatic in the poem. Even in the first two books,
with their strong characterization, Vida is notably less
interested in delineating Christ Himself than in presenting
the reactions of others to Him; and in the course of the
whole poem, Vida varies the point of view to convey as
fully as possible the impact of the Incarnation. One of the
main patterns is the effect of Christ on the crowds[40]—like

that which surges after Him at the opening of I, that at
the triumphal entry, the crowds around Lazarus's tomb
and outside the house of Simon at Bethany. To them,
Christ is a fad, a popular hero, a curiosity; many of those
coming to the Paschal Feast are eager to see Him. He
could become a demagogue easily enough if He so wished;
the priests fear to move against Him because of the
people. But Christ keeps aloof, and when His hour comes,
He says nothing to affect the course of events.

More striking than these are the varying viewpoints of
specific individuals and specific groups. Peter's surprising
reaction to Christ's first words provides some insight into
the Apostles' feeling for Christ—warm but uncomprehending, knowing only that they are doing something
good but for reasons only half-understood, at times indeed
not even sure what it is they are doing. The same was
true of Christ's parents and relatives. There were ties of
humanity, there was a half-embarrassed reverence, there
were attempts to pierce the prophecies of old and understand what was coming to pass; but in Joachim and Anna,
in Elizabeth, in Joseph's father, there is always the
lingering incomprehension. Mary's understanding is limited, and Joseph's even more so. The Messiah looked for in
Book III, Joseph's narrative, is to be the great leader,
"Isacidos nova gloria prolis," in the misunderstood outcry
of Simeon. What Joseph and Mary best comprehend is
conveyed in this particular emphasis of the angel's words:

> Supra homines, supra aspicies se tollere et ipsos
> Caelicolas fama insignem, ac praestantibus ausis.
> Nam pater omnipotens atavorum in sceptra reponet
> Pristina regnantem late, regumque sedebit
> In solio: neque enim metas, neque tempora regni
> Accipiet. toto aeternum dominabitur orbe.
>
> (III. 344-349)

You will see Him rise above men and above the very angels, noteworthy for His glory and His great deeds. For the Almighty Father will restore to Him the ancient scepter of His people, and He will sit on the throne of kings. Of His kingdom, there will be no limits of space or of time; He will rule forever over the whole world.

To the scribes and priests, Christ represents a menace, whatever His claims or teaching. Not only in the third book, but in the fourth and first as well we find them incorrigibly resorting to the most devious methods to undermine His power—a power which He had no real interest in. He was a similar menace to Herod, whose methods of dealing with Him at least attempted to be more direct.

Maria the sinner comes to Christ for one purpose, but in the end conceives *alias flammas*. Judas sees Him as a source of adventure and interest. Satan knows of Him only as the potential avenger who will free the souls of the just unless He can be prevented—there is sharp irony in Satan's plans to turn the Hebrew leaders against Christ, have Him killed, and thus avert catastrophe.

Even in the fifth book, the reader is kept at the periphery of the circle, seeing the suffering Christ now through the eyes of the mob, now through Pilate's, now through the despairing Judas's or from the standpoint of the angels in heaven, or of the Father. And in the sixth, the avenging Christ, the risen Christ, and the glorified Christ are shown less directly than through the reactions and feelings of the demons and the just, Magdalene and the individual Apostles, and the angels.[41]

Among the most striking and revealing reactions are Pilate's. At their first meeting, Pilate's sympathy and interest in Christ are profoundly aroused. The Jewish leaders thought of Roman Pilate as a natural enemy of Christ, easy to sway; they expected Apostles and people to be their problem. But the people are easily turned into rabble, the Apostles flee in terror; it is Pilate who turns out to be the stumbling block. He finds in Christ a mystery which is overwhelming. He is moved, almost far enough to foil the deicides, though he cannot go that far; like Turnus, he is a tragic figure caught in world-shaking events beyond his control. But even when he has compromised, he repents and shows the repentance honestly. Vida indeed contrives his narrative so that Christ brings out the very best in Pilate.[42]

Pilate is particularly moved by the beautiful countenance of Christ. The Jews cry out for Christ's death;

> Ille autem juvenis procero in corpore fixos
> Intentusque oculos, intentusque ora tenebat.
> . . . .
> Insolitam speciem, insolitos miratur honores
> Oris, et expleri nequit. hunc e stirpe fatetur
> Aut divum, aut saltem magnorum e sanguine regum.[43]
> (II. 976-977, 979-981)

But he kept his eyes fixed earnestly on the noble form of the Youth, and earnestly on His face.... He marvels at the unusual beauty, the unexpected attraction of His countenance, and he cannot drink his fill of gazing. He is sure this Man is either of the race of the gods, or at least of the line of great kings.

When Joseph and John come to him, Pilate exclaims about Christ:

> non ille creatus
> Stirpe humili, mihi si verum mens augurat. ut se
> Incessu gerit! ut vultuque, et corpore toto est
> Humana major species! ut lumina honorum
> Plena! ut regifici motus! verba inde notavi;
> Nil mortale sonat. sensi illo in pectore Numen.
> Aut certe Deus ille, aut non mortalibus ortus.
> (III. 87-93)

He was not begotten of lowly stock, if my mind senses accurately. How erect He bears Himself! The beauty of His face, and indeed of His whole person, seems far more than mortal man's. How full of majesty are His eyes! how royal His movements! I have marked His words well: they have nothing of mortal sound in them. I felt a divinity in that breast. Certainly, either He is God, or not of mortals born.

Pilate sees yet does not see the divinity; grace is not fully given. Though he assents intellectually, the time has not come for the Roman acceptance of Christ; but Pilate is symbolic witness that it will come.

With his nobility and willingness, embodied in his reaction to the divinity of Christ expressed through facial beauty, Pilate is pivotal. Maria, the harlot of Book I, perceived fully. It is remarkable that Vida, for all his description of Maria, confined himself to her external accoutrements; about her own beauty he says simply, "forma insignis cultuque puella" (I. 305). She has come to the house of Simon for the specific purpose of conquering Him who is reputed to be the comeliest of the sons of men—

> Ergo laeta virum praestanti corpore postquam
> Accepit venisse, Deum quem fama ferebat,
> Nullam passa moram studio correpta videndi
> Venerat.   (I. 338-341)

So, overjoyed to know that a man exceedingly handsome had come, who, as rumor had it, was also God, she hastened without delay, driven by a strong impulse to look on Him.

But, having confronted Christ—

>   ast ubi conspicuos deperdita vultus
> Hausit, et egregiae divinum frontis honorem,
> Divinosque oculos ardentis pabula amoris,
> Diriguit, penitusque animo sententia versa est,
> Atque alias longe concepit pectore flammas.
>   (I. 341-345)

But when she, damned by her handsome features, had her fill of gazing on the divine glory of that remarkable face, and those divine eyes, glowing with love, she stopped cold, and abandoned her original purpose. Far different flames were kindled within her breast.

Her conversion is complete.[44]

The importance of this motif is indicated by the stress placed on it at the beginning of Book IV. As III closes, Pilate asks John to continue Joseph's narrative. Book IV opens:

> Hic juvenis, facie quo tum non gratior alter,
> Puberibusque annis erat ingrediente juventa ... (1-2)

Such references to the facial beauty of characters other than Christ are limited to contexts like this one, in which there is contact with the divine: here, John is rapt in ecstasy. In similar terms, Joseph describes Mary just after the Incarnation:

> O illa a solita quantum mutata figura!
> Quantus honos oculis, quantus decor additus ori!
> (III. 265-266)

As she tells Joseph of the angel's appearance, "ora Deo propior" and "pulcherrimus ore"—her eyes shine. At the birth of Christ, Mary's face is again depicted in glowing terms, by a simile whose connection with other image-patterns is unmistakable:

> Astrorum qualis facies rorantibus umbris
> Post imbrem, siccis Boreas ubi frigidus alis
> Ingruit, ac caelum populans cava nubila differt;
> Talis virgineo species accesserat ori. (III. 587-590)

The kind of beauty that one sees in the face of the stars when cold Boreas has dispersed the dewy shades and dried them with his wings, raging through the sky and scattering the hollow clouds—such beauty suffused the Virgin's face.

The major application of this motif is to Christ. While there is no complete description of Christ's physical appearance, the divine countenance is prominent. It shines like the sun at the Transfiguration; its radiance is perceived by the children at the triumphal entry, and by Jethro at the pool; the shepherds gaze on the radiant face of Christ newborn.[45] The boy Christ, communicating with His Father, has a sublime beauty of countenance. In the temple, His radiant visage, bright eyes, and golden hair are prominent;

> Nam quocumque caput circum torsisset honestum,
> Luce recens orta, vel sidere pulchrior aureo,
> Laeta serenato ridebant omnia mundo,
> Et toto dulcem jactabat corpore amorem.
>
> (III. 960-963)

For wherever He turned His comely head, fairer than the sun rising or than a golden star, everything laughed and was joyful in a serene world. His whole body radiated the sweetness of love.

Even on Calvary, notable emphasis is placed on the divinity which shines through the clotted blood, the sweat, and the dirt.[46]

Pilate's halfway state sets off the full perceptions against the complete lack of perception. Nicodemus and Lazarus perceive that beauty fully, as do the just in Limbo and Magdalene at the tomb. In the remarkable apparition of Christ on the beach, while the Apostles are fishing, John recognizes the Master:

> Sensit Joannis hic Numen, et Heus, prior inquit,
> O socii, ne fallor, adest Deus, ille magister
> Ille quidem. agnosco divinos oris honores.
> Laetitiam ut jactat vultuque, oculisque decoris!
>
> (VI. 615-618)

John was the first to sense the presence of God, and he cried out, Comrades! I am certain God is here, the Master, the Master Himself! I know the divine splendor of His countenance. See how He radiates joy in His face and His shining eyes!

But Satan and the demons never perceive that beauty; though the devils which possessed the Gerasene youth admit Christ's divinity, this is only an admission, not an apprehension. Neither do the Jewish priests and leaders perceive, or the soldiers on Calvary, or the traitorous Judas. In the admission of Christ's divinity, which precedes his despair, Judas is indeed analogous to the devils who will admit but not serve. The whole motif and the crucial difference between knowledge and love is stated by John in a significant passage towards the end of his discourse:

> Nam quem non moveant, nisi prorsum aversa voluntas,
> Tanta viri virtus, tot facta ingentia, talis
> Oris honos? ipse ut vidique, hausique loquentem
> Et dulcem toto jactantem corpore amorem,
> Fortunas, patriam, genitricem, cuncta reliqui.
> Id socii fecere. neque hunc me deinde secutum
> Poenituit. verum quantum ingens saepe favilla
> Surgit ab exigua, semperque fit acrior ignis,
> Hujus amor tantum visus mihi crescere in horas,
> Et mage cor dulci semper flammescere cura.
>   (IV. 806-815)

For who, unless his will was obstinately perverted, would not be moved by this Man's great goodness, by so many great deeds, by such divine beauty? I myself, when I first saw Him and drank in those words and that sweet love radiating from His whole person, I relinquished fortune, fatherland, family, everything. So did the others. I have never regretted being His disciple. Indeed, just as a huge blaze grows from a tiny spark and the fire becomes hotter and hotter, so did my love for Him seem to grow by the hour, and my heart take fire with sweet concern.

This is, interestingly, part of the only polemical passage in John's entire revelation. There is irony in it, in the facial-beauty motif—it was specifically "talis / Oris honos" which moved Pilate profoundly, but not enough to stir up divine love. In the preceding passage, John has been emphasizing that the priests who were now demanding Christ's death, knew well enough who He was and what he had come to do:

> Unus qui nobis caeli invia claustra recludat,
> E tenebrisque pios vehat alta ad sidera manes,
> Id patribus promissum, omnes id volvere vates,
> Hunc animis certi exspectant. miseri quibus atris
> Non datur in tenebris praesentem agnoscere lucem,
> Et mediis largi sitiunt in fluminis undis!
>
> (IV. 800-805)

The only One who could reopen for us the gates of heaven, and could lead the souls of the just out of darkness and up to the stars—this was promised to our fathers; this was revealed by all the prophets; Him they await with deep confidence. O wretched ones, who are not able though in darkest shadows to know the light that is at hand, and who thirst amid the flowing waters!

The irony of John's argument seems almost to unite Pilate with the priests, but, Vida would have us understand, the difference remains that the Jews were offered grace and refused it; Pilate has not yet had his chance.[47]

The modes of poetic expression discussed thus far do not readily yield to summary or brief exposition. Implied in them is the difference between the countenance of Christ and that of the Father, too severe to behold. In scenes like the Transfiguration and Ascension, the intense light imagery attempts to suggest the ineffable. There are connections too between the facial-beauty motif and the fire images—the radiantly beautiful youth, for instance, is frequently attended by mysterious tongues of fire which surround Him or rest on His head; the star which heralds the Epiphany and leads the three kings to the Infant Christ is compared to comets portending war or the death of monarchs.

Some of the terms in these manifestations recall Vergil or even allude to the *Aeneid*. The tongues of flame evoke the flames which, resting on the head of Ascanius, made unmistakable Aeneas's future course. Vergil's Homeric "os umerosque deo similis"[48] and the light imagery in *Aeneid* II and VIII particularly are frequently recalled or alluded to. Relevant also is this passage from Book IX:[49]

> Nisus erat portae custos, acerrimus armis,
> . . . .
> et iuxta comes Euryalus, quo pulchrior alter
> non fuit Aeneadum Troiana neque induit arma,
> ora puer prima signans intonsa iuventa.
> his amor unus erat, pariterque in bella ruebant;
> tum quoque communi portam statione tenebant.
> Nisus ait: "dine hunc ardorem mentibus addunt,
> Euryale, an sua cuique deus fit dira cupido?
> aut pugnam aut aliquid iamdudum invadere magnum
> mens agitat mihi, nec placida contenta quiete est."
> (IX. 176; 179-187)

Nisus, the very valiant warrior, was guarding the gate ... and beside him was his friend Euryalus, a stripling with the full bloom of youth on his smooth cheeks: no more handsome soldier was there in the whole of Aeneas's army. One love bound these two; together they would charge into battle. At the time, they were doing joint sentry-duty. Nisus said: "Is it a god who fills my spirit with this ardor, Euryalus, or does our own fierce passion become its peculiar god to each of us? For a long time, my soul has been aching for battle, or at least to do some noteworthy deed; and it will not rest quiet with this inactivity."

In part, the interlocked motifs of Vida's epic are commentary on these lines and on the whole Nisus-Euryalus episode, with its poignantly tragic heroism.[50]

Vida's oblique devices achieve a distancing of Christ and of the whole action. Christ and His deeds are kept at arm's length—perhaps the proper distance. The point-of-view technique renders it possible to get the face of God in profile, thus making the material poetically viable; to have attempted to get "inside" Christ would have meant, as Vida was well aware, to write mystical, not epic, poetry. It would have been indeed in the nature of religious experience.[51] The technique also makes it possible to see the face of man in profile. The varying reactions to Christ suggest natural human experience. While Christ Himself is, in part, an image of perfected humanity, it is in the impact of Christ on such characters as Lazarus, Zaccheus, Maria, Nicodemus, Peter, and Joseph that the proper measure of humanity can be taken. Pilate is in the middle, fully the natural man, though the suggestions are clear that he will inherit the land. As for the Jewish priests, the inevitable destruction of Jerusalem is penalty not only for deicide but also for their denaturalization by the perversions underlying their whole attitude to Christ, their dishonorable scheming and plotting to foil and discredit Him.

Finally, the many misconceptions about Christ's Messianic mission provide intellectual as well as emotional drama. In the interplay of statement and action, imagery and theme, the poem does move, though on a level more metaphysical than the narrative level. The misconceptions cancel each other out because of the inexorable realities of the Passion, the Harrowing of Hell, the Ascension, and the coming of the Paraclete, and because of the indirect but very certain force of the interpretative prophecies and the large symbolic scenes or "spectacles" as Zumbini called them: [52]

Si può tenere per fermo ... l'intento [scil. of Vida] di suscitare nel nostro pensiero una serie di spettacoli, piú o meno lontani, i quali con l'immediato soggetto del poema, facciano uno spettacolo solo e immenso....
Appunto da quell'aggruppamento di scene cosmiche e terrene, celesti e infernali, dovevano procedere i maggiori effetti della vastissima rappresentazione.

We may accurately regard as Vida's intention to arouse in our minds a series of spectacles, more or less distanced, which, with the manifest subject of the poem, form a single and immense panorama....
Precisely out of that grouping of scenes cosmic and earthly, heavenly and infernal, were supposed to emerge the major effects of the greatest significance.

Within the framework of the intricate structure, Vida's vast scenes impose a massive unity of feeling on the whole epic. As Vergil did in the *Aeneid*, Vida attempts to balance symmetrically masses of material which, commenting mutually, extend the imagery and embody thematic statements. At the same time, the spectacles attempt, and sometimes grandly achieve, broad epic effects.

The battle between heaven and hell is most forcefully depicted in the interplay of large scenes. The Inferno of Book I, presenting one of the shapes of evil, sets off a chain of vast scenes which reach their dramatic resolution in the Ascension. The lengthy description of the regions of hell and its inhabitants prepares for the action of the Harrowing of Hell in Book VI; the devils are intended to contrast sharply with the angels, particularly those in the

17.

mobilization scene of Book V; and hell itself is seen in fullest perspective against the serenity of the reaches of heaven as described in Book V. Not by coincidence both the devils of I and the angels of V are determined to do something about Christ—the former to destroy Him and thus avert catastrophe of one sort, the latter to save Him and thus avert catastrophe of another sort. They are both wrong, but the difference in their wrongness is crucial. Crucial, too, is the difference in their views, both wrong, of the fall of Lucifer. To the demons, this was a manifestation of God's envy and fear, the result of unfortunately inferior tactics and equipment; to the angels, this is a reminder of their tested and proven fidelity and of the inevitable superiority of being on the right side. But when both the plans and the viewpoints of both sides are measured against the divine plan and the divine viewpoint, as enunciated by God the Father, the angels are seen to merit only a mild rebuke for their haste, while the blind pride and thorough evil of the demons is repulsive.

In the brightness and splendor of the Ascension, the full antithesis between heaven and hell is expressed. It is a crowning scene, rich with symbolism, glorious with light and music; Vida pulls out all the stops in this attempt to express the full power and meaning of the act. The Ascension is implicit in every large scene, from the infernal council and the triumphal entry into Jerusalem through the Harrowing of Hell, and including particularly the scenes of enthusiasm, violence, and spacious activity. The crowds converging on Jerusalem in Book II are envisaged symbolically: trying to enhance the reality, Vida puts aside the bustle and the confusion and orders his material to relate it to scope and theme by cataloguing the cities and tribes of the Jews and by summoning up much of Old Testament history. Relevant, too, are the crowds which forced Christ to get into a boat for His comprehensive discourse; the crowds at Pilate's court and on Calvary; the mobilizing angels; the yearning souls of the just in Limbo; and the crowds reached by the Apostles' preaching after they have been filled with grace. The Ascension gathers in all of these, resolving them in the symbolic union of divinity and humanity.

The expression of so much through vast scenes enlarges the scope of the action, not as a titanomachia, but as a panorama against which the specific action is most meaningful.[53] The celestial-infernal enmity interlocks with the action on earth, both through the selective imagery and through the grouping of scenes in such a way that their relevance to each other cannot be missed.

The sadness of nature at Christ's death, and the rejoicing of nature at the procession of the souls of the just to heaven, are part of the pattern by which the symbolic implications are suggested. Pivotal to the whole are the twin images, at the center and at the end of the poem—the first, for the Incarnation, the impregnation of the earth in springtime; the second, for the descent of the Paraclete, the effect of rain on parched soil.[54] Vida uses fierce images—wolves and lions, storms and floods—to express the violent, disorderly, uncontrolled nature of evil, and serene, tame images for the forces of good; but in the hymn of the Apostles at the Ascension, the whole of nature is subjected to His power. In Book V, the enraged Jews are compared to a river in flood, and in another simile during the same episode, Pilate collapsing is compared to a ship's captain yielding before a storm.[55] Related to these are two of the last similes in the poem, describing Christ as He gives His commission to the Apostles:

> Talia mandabat terras, hominesque relinquens.
> Sic natis moriturus oves, et ovilia pastor

Commendans caris, furta, insidiasque luporum
Edocet, et pecori contraria pascua monstrat.
Sic sociis aevo jam fessus nauta biremem
Credit, inexpertosque docet varias maris oras,
Et brevia, et syrtes, et navifragas Sirenas.

(VI. 677-683)

Such was the mandate He gave as He was taking leave of
the earth and of His Apostles. Just so a shepherd, about to
die, commends his sheep and his sheepfolds to his sons,
warning them against the cunning thievery of wolves and
indicating the fields which are unhealthy .Just so also does
a sea captain, weary with age, turn over his ship to his
comrades and teach them, since they lack experience, the
various coasts of the sea, and the shoals, and the Syrtes, and
the shipwrecking Sirens.

One controls the forces of nature by understanding them
and knowing how to guard against them: there is no
hint here of eliminating them. Most important are the
sheep and the boat. These two similes, taken in conjunction with other similes of seafaring, the pastoral life,
and nature in general, are a concise parable of one aspect
of the Christian life.

The curious structure of the fifth book is a good illustration of how the action on all levels interlocks. The
book divides into three large sections. The first is the
conflict between Pilate and the Jews, ending in Pilate's
abdication of responsibility and the *Via Crucis* (to 447);
the second is the scene in heaven, the mobilization of
the angels and the Father's speech (to 703); the third is
the scene on Calvary, ending in the death of Christ. The
central scene is dislocated. If we take Vida's *Ars poetica*
as guide to *Christiad* V, the central scene is nothing but
digression, fantasy, relief. But ignoring that, we may
discover what Vida is really trying to do. The scene
contrasts shockingly in tone with the other two. The first

is by turns shrieking, cruel, pathetic, and confused, but
heaven is broadly drawn as serene, majestic, and orderly:

> In medio pater omnipotens solio aureus alto
> Sceptra tenet, lateque acie circum omnia lustrat
> Totus collucens, totus circum igne corusco
> Scintillans, radiisque procul vibrantibus ardens.
>
> (V. 469-472)

In their midst, the almighty Father holds His scepter on His
high throne, Himself golden and radiating light all about;
His whole being glows with light and shines with shimmering
fire and blazes with quivering rays.

The whole central passage retards the action and sets it
in perspective: against the detached coherence of Eternity,
what is going on in Jerusalem properly appears insane.
The event on earth is characterized as frenzied and demonic; so do the women react to it, weeping for Christ,
and so do the angels, putting on their armor. But Christ
speaks to the women, the Father speaks to the angels,
and some measure of perspective is restored. Christ arrives
on Calvary in a scene which is parenthetical, briefly inter-
posed between the description of heaven and the mobilizing of the angels; once there, He looks on crowd, cross,
and heaven. "Patriam ... reminiscitur aetheris aulam"
emphasizes the unity of the various levels. Christ and His
Father are at the center of the two spheres of action; the
identity between them is explicitly brought out and helps
to define the significance.

The broad effects suggested here are achieved partly
by the many connections between the three scenes—the
helplessness of weeping women, angels, and Christ's
followers; the Father's grim prophecy of impending destruction for Jerusalem echoing the outcry of the Jews,
and the prophecy's fulfillment presaged in the terror
brought on Jerusalem by the unnatural darkness at the

end;[56] angelic ordeliness contrasting with the confusion of Jews and of soldiers. Primarily, however, the broad effects are achieved by the separateness yet harmony of the three large scenes, taken individually and all together.

Contributing also to the vastness of scope is the stretch of time the poem encompasses. Deliberately, Vida includes the creation and fall of the angels, the creation of the world, the fall of man, and much Old Testament history, through various devices; as well as the Apostolate and spread of Christianity, the rise of Rome as center of Christendom, and the end of the world and Last Judgment. Now the fall of man is to be expected. As an important cause of Christ's death, it could not be omitted, no matter how the author limited his work. Vida, however, takes pains to give prominence to that incident and others. The fall is presented graphically in the major ekphrasis and again in the beginning of John's narrative. In the first, its implications are explored amid figurative scenes from the Old Testament which suggest further meanings; in the second, John explicitly relates the fall and the history of the Chosen People to the redemptive mission of Christ. Then, by ending his discourse with the prophecy of the Last Judgment, he expands the implications. It will be useful here to examine briefly John's revelation to Pilate and its function in the whole epic.

The fourth book of the *Christiad* appears to be a continuation of the third and part of the canonical recapitulation, like *Aeneid* II and III. But John's narrative is significantly different in shape and tone from Joseph's; it functions rather like the sixth book of the *Aeneid*.[57] In Book III, Joseph presented the human aspects of Christ and interpreted the conflict with the Jewish leaders in civic and social terms. His narrative was, in effect, an argument for the release of the prisoner. But John's discourse is revelation, not argument. It commences with the nature of God and of the Trinity, and extends to the Last Judgment. It probes the creation and the fall to show Christ's redemptive mission. The lyrical closing lines have none of the polemical tone of Joseph's conclusion:

> Nunc se principium rerum, finemque canebat,
> Nunc veri fontem, atque hominum lucemque, viamque.
> Nos fortunatam prognatam hoc tempore prolem,
> Nos felix tellus, nos saecula laeta tulere.
> Nobis divinam vocem, divina loquentis
> Verba haurire Dei propius saepe obtigit unis.
>
> (IV. 1034-1039)

Now He would speak of Himself as the beginning and end of all things, and again as the fountain of truth, and the light of men, and their way. We are indeed fortunate to be alive now, in this blessed place, and at this time of joy; it has been our unique lot to hear so often His holy voice, to drink in the sacred words of God.

The two books might be likened to two of the Gospels, the one resembling somewhat Luke's, with its detailed narration of Christ's life, while the other is like John's own Gospel, more concerned to reveal that life's meaning, beginning "In principio erat Verbum," and replete with mystic discourse. John's narrative to Pilate, defined by the soaring simile of the eagle and by the profound catechism with which it begins, is an inspiring outpouring of the hypostatic union and its meaning, a revelation of the unique Godhead of Christ.

As such, it attempts to present doctrinally the themes of the poem, as Vergil's sixth book does for the *Aeneid*. There are important differences between the terrible God of thunder of the Old Testament and the sentence on Adam and Eve in the first part of the book; the manifestation of the Incarnate Christ, compassionate, redemptive, the friend of sinners, in the second part; and the judging Christ, presented in the simile of the shepherd, at the end. That final judgment depends on the long and dramatic discourse which precedes it, the discourse in which Christ epitomizes the Christian life. In this discourse, Christ presents a sacramental view of life, certainly one of the final causes of the Incarnation, the expression, that is, of divinity in humanity; and while the sacramental view gives tone to most of the fourth book, its symbolic focus is the central narrative of the loaves and fishes.[58] The miracle of the loaves and fishes is related in each of the four Gospels, with slightly varying details, but Vida's organization of the material and addition of details make his incident distinctly thematic. He changes the length of time the people had been without food from one day to three; he expands the brief mention of Christ's "raising His eyes to heaven" into an invocation of the Lord of creation, emphasizing God's power over earthly things; he says pointedly and a bit surprisingly, if one considers verisimilitude, that the people's desire for food *and drink* is satisfied; he gives the fish, with its traditional symbolism, much more prominence. Intentionally, no doubt, he uses the name of Christ in this episode for the first time in the poem since Joseph explained the meaning of the name. Thus, by detail and suggestion, Vida has worked into the incident the symbolism of the Eucharist and the Mass, compressing in it much of the doctrine in John's Gospel about the "living bread" and uniting the whole episode to the pelican image in the major ekphrasis, the song of Simon before the Last Supper, and Christ's two major discourses—that from the boat and that preceding the Ascension.[59]

In his fourth book, Vida has distilled a great deal of theology while expanding the limits of his subject to encompass the whole of time as well as space. The vast sweep of the poem is predicated on more than material causality. While the causal relationship between the fall and the crucifixion is obviously important, clearly Vida is attempting a poetic vision of the city of God. The Incarnation as the fullness of time is presented as a kind of radiant center of all time and space, the point at which all levels of existence, divine, human, and natural, can meet. Now, though the theology may derive from the Fathers and Doctors of the Church, particularly St. Augustine and St. Thomas, the impulse to celebrate his subject in such large poetic terms came distinctly from Vergil's *Aeneid*.

Vergil's panoramic view of Rome takes in explicitly eleven centuries, between Aeneas and Augustus, and extends in space to the celestial and the infernal. There are also, however, suggestions which exceed even these vast limits:

> "his ego nec metas rerum nec tempora pono:
> imperium sine fine dedi."
>
> (*Aeneid* I. 278-279)

Rome's destiny was ordained long before the fall of Troy; the ideal of Rome which Vergil enshrines has a partial fulfillment in the empire of Augustus:

> "nascetur pulchra Troianus origine Caesar,
> imperium Oceano, famam qui terminet astris,
> Iulius, a magno demissum nomen Iulo
> hunc tu olim caelo spoliis Orientis onustum
> accipies secura; vocabitur hic quoque votis.
> aspera tum positis mitescent saecula bellis."
>
> (*Aeneid* I. 286-291)

"Of this noble line will be born Trojan Caesar, called Julius, from the name of great Iulus, whose empire will extend to the limits of Ocean, and whose glory as high as the stars. One day you will full willingly receive him in heaven, laden down with Eastern spoil; and he too will be honored with prayers. Thus, the rough ages shall grow gentle and wars shall cease."

But the complete fulfillment of that ideal transcends the Augustan Age. Vida's expansion of Vergil's scope derives both from the material he had, more massive and weighty than Vergil's, and from the necessity he felt to make explicit the sacramental meaning of the Incarnation. He could not, indeed, end his poem with the death of Christ, as Girolamo Dalle Valli did, or with the Ascension, as Macario Muzio did, or even with the descent of the Paraclete. There had to be the Apostolate, the dispersal of the twelve into the whole world, teaching all nations and ushering in the true golden age.

Christ's discourse at the close of the fourth book is significantly echoed in the final discourse, just before the Ascension, in which He commissions the Apostles to go out in His name and preach the Gospel. The connection between the two is important. It is the latter which seems derived from Anchises's vision of Roman greatness at the end of *Aeneid* VI, but actually both discourses are related to Anchises's and both offer commentary on it.

In the first, easily mistaken for a trimmed version of the Sermon on the Mount, Christ surveys the Christian life. He teaches charity, meekness, trust in God; He dissects the vices of fraud, lust, sloth and hypocrisy. The whole is pervaded with the theme of peace and the ideal of perfection. The peace that surpasses understanding is both necessary for this ideal life and the result of it. At the end, Christ teaches them how to pray, and then prophesies the Last Judgment.[60]

In the discourse before the Ascension, the theme is again peace. Christ's advice here is more specific, dealing with the trials the Apostles will face in establishing the Church and with the specific mission of the Church. Again

He speaks of the Last Judgment, with particular reference this time to the glory of the Apostles, who will judge the nations with Him. He commissions Peter as His vicar—

> Tu regere, et populis parcens dare jura memento.
> Summa tibi in gentes jam nunc concessa potestas.
> Jamque pios tege pace: voca sub signa rebelles.
> (VI. 666-668)

Your commission is to rule and to pass laws and show mercy to the peoples. Supreme power over the nations is hereby given you. Keep them faithful in peace; vanquish the insurgents.

—and gives him the sword of the spirit, emphasizing the spiritual duties and spiritual weapons that are proper to His kingdom.[61]

In both discourses, Vida has taken the theme of peace, drawn particularly from the Gospel of John, "Pacem relinquo vobis, pacem meam do vobis...," and has made more explicit its sacramental character.[62] It is peace in exile, the peace that makes exile endurable:

> Placidam super omnia mites
> Pacem optate viri....
> Mortales contemnite opes, contemnite honores,
> . . . .
> Vobis haud propriae hic sedes, concessaque longum
> Regna: manent meliora, graves ubi solverit artus
> Mors anima, vos stelligera pater optimus aula
> Protinus excipiet laetos melioribus oris,
> Pax ubi tranquilla, et cunctarum opulentia rerum,
> Et secura quies, numquam peritura voluptas.
> (IV. 882-883, 885, 889-894)

Above all other things, my friends, humbly search for tranquil peace, and put by the excesses of pride .... Despise mortal treasures and mortal glory ....
You have no true home here; far off and far better are the

destined realms which await you. When death has freed your
souls from the burdensome flesh, your great Father in His
starry court will receive you, rejoicing in a better world, a
world of tranquil peace and overflowing abundance, of serene
rest and boundless joy.

The exile theme is a multiple one, expressed in various
ways. Life itself is exile from heaven. For Christ, Incarnation meant exile from heaven to earth—

> ... e superi qui sede parentis,
> Virginis intactae gravidam descendit in alvum,
> Mortalesque auras hausit ...   (I. 3-5)

—while it was also the resolution of mankind's exile
from God:

> ... ut genus ultus
> Humanum eriperet tenebris, et carcere iniquo
> Morte sua, manesque pios inferret olympo. (I. 5-7)

As prophet without honor in His own country, Christ is
in exile; the theme is broadly elaborated and needs no
stress here. But it has a further aspect: Jerusalem itself is
an exile for Christ and the Apostles because the true
earthly home of Christendom will be Rome.[63] Thus, the
Apostles who are sent out to convert the whole world
and lead the "sanctum genus ... ad astra" (VI. 648) are in
exile both from heaven and from Rome.

The theme was emphasized by Christ in His first address
to the Apostles:

> domus non haec data, non hae
> Sunt vobis propriae sedes. vos aetheris alti
> Lucida templa vocant, stellis florentia regna,
> Pax ubi secura, ac requies optata laborum.
> Hic domus, hic patria. huc omnes contendite laeti
> Angustum per iter. vestras hic figite sedes.
>   (I. 54-59)

This is not the home destined for you, this is not your true dwelling place. The bright temples of high heaven call you, the star-studded kingdoms, where you will find true peace and the reward of your labors. That is your home, that is your fatherland; all of you strive for that, joyful though the way be hard. Fix your hearts on heaven.

The broad allusions to the *Aeneid* in this passage and in the similar one at the end of Book IV evoke Vergil's exile theme. Various images and incidents support it—the traditional image of the Church as a ship, for instance, or Christ's birth in a hovel, or the forced flight into Egypt. Christ's prayer for the Apostles begs constancy for them in their exile.[64]

The theme is best dramatized in the Exodus motif, recurring in allusions to the wanderings of the Israelites and in the waiting souls of the just in Limbo. The major ekphrasis alludes to the historical Exodus, in a scene depicting Moses raising up the brazen serpent, a type of the crucifixion. At the Transfiguration, Moses is identified as the leader and the lawgiver:

> Isacidum Phariis genus alter duxit ab oris
> Dux profugum, legesque dedit, moremque sacrorum.
> (I. 951-952)

The long catalogue of Book II is preceded by an explanation of the background of the Paschal Feast and by a relevant remark on the present state of Palestine: "Nunc tellus deserta jacet." Summoning up much Old Testament history and typology, the catalogue symbolizes the Old Law, as the subsequent Last Supper symbolizes the New. The vatic song of Simon celebrates the favor which God showed to the wandering Israelites, but collocates that strikingly with symbolic references to the Eucharist and the Church. Both meanings are expanded in the *Improperia* in Book V, which parallel Simon's song with added stress on the Jews' infidelity to their heritage.[65]

The exile of the just in Limbo, counterpointing the historical Exodus by underlining the real mission of the Messiah, is also first expressed in the major ekphrasis. Christ's comment is revealing:

> En nostrum deposcunt ista laborem.
> In me nulla mora est. ego tantae debitus irae
> Morte mea eripiam hos tenebris, et claustra refringam.
>
> (I. 688-690)

Behold these things call for My passion. I shall not delay. A debtor to this great wrath, by My death I will break open their prison and free these souls from darkness.

The same view is emphasized by John in his survey of the spiritual history of the Chosen People. He unites the exile of the just, waiting in Limbo—

> Casti autem interea manes, animaeque piorum
> Sub terram umbrosa exspectabant valle sedentes.
>
> (IV. 123-124)

—to the broader meanings of the Old Testament: "Jam vatum memores numerabant tempora" (125). The Harrowing of Hell dramatically resolves this exile and symbolizes the resolution of all exile.

At the same time, as long as the Apostles are in the world, they live in a kind of exile. But the fulfillment of the Old Testament types—the manna, for instance, which nourished the Israelites and fortified them in their wanderings, fulfilled in the Eucharist, the abiding presence of Christ on earth—indicates that this new exile is only apparent. Of old, too, there were angels who frequently came down from heaven to the Holy Land; Vida lays stress on this in the lines preceding the catalogue. The angels helped bridge the distance between heaven and earth; when Christ came, the angels were constantly in attendance on Him—the extent of their activity in Book

III and IV is remarkable. But in the fifth book, God restrains them from going to Christ's aid, and in the sixth, they function only as joyous escorts for the souls of the just and for Christ ascending. Heaven is open now; when the Apostles' mission is about to begin, God sends the Paraclete to fill them with divine life, to unite heaven mystically to earth. The Apostles go forth, to bring the fruits of Christ's redemption to the whole world and to establish the seat of God's worship at the Eternal City of Rome.

At least three times in the first book, imagery of exile and the Roman theme are collocated. At the Transfiguration, the description of Moses as *dux profugum* follows the Father's prophecy of the grandeur of Rome. The imagery of exile in the major ekphrasis is preceded by Christ's prediction of the destruction of Jerusalem and its temple, and of the transfer of the center of worship to another land. The third of these Roman references comes at the very beginning, in the simile of the Po and the allusion to Aeneas and the Trojan remnant; this suggestion, read with the others and collocated with Christ's words on exile, becomes thematically meaningful.[66] Christ's reference, in His prediction, to "another land" is not itself specific, but the Father's prophecy develops it:

> Atque adeo gravida imperiis Roma illa superba,
> Apenninivagi quae propter Tybridis undam
> Ingentes populos frenat pulcherrima rerum,
> Summittet fasces, et, quas regit, orbis habenas.
> Illic relligio, centum illic maxima templa
> Centum arae tibi fumantes, centumque ministri
> Quique viris late, atque ipsis det jura sacerdos
> Regibus, et summo te in terris reddat honore.
>
> (I. 911-918)

And even proud Rome, that rules many great nations from its seat on the Tiber, Wanderer of the Apenines, even that

magnificent city shall yield to You her dominion over the
world. There shall be the center of worship, there many
great churches and altars burning incense to you, there armies
of priests. There, one high priest shall lay down laws for
men and for kings themselves far and wide, and be Your
honored vicar on earth.

The prominence given to Rome in the statements of
the poem is supported by suggestive incidents, pregnant
allusions, imagery, parallels, and contrasts. The two long
books of recapitulation are, in effect, the first teaching
of the Gentiles, and as such a more dramatic embodiment
than the briefly summarized dispersal of the Apostles.
Joseph's tale, relating the human genealogy of Christ and
attempting to explain His divine origin, is tailored to,
while it helps expand, the capacity of his hearer.[67] Often
it sounds like a grand myth about a mortal born of gods,
corresponding to one half of Pilate's exclamation: "Aut
certe Deus ille, aut non mortalibus ortus." The limited
narrative arouses Pilate's further curiosity, and he turns
to John with many questions; but when John has done,
Pilate is left somewhat perplexed. "Nec jam obscurum
genus esse deorum."

John's revelation is masterfully constructed for cate-
chetical purposes. He begins blandly but sublimely, discoursing on the Godhead and the Trinity, gently showing
the differences between the true God and the gods Pilate
knows. His reference to God's omnipotence—"solus reg-
nabat ubique" (21)—is acceptable to Pilate, of the generation after Vergil; so is much that follows. But gradually,
John asserts truths about the equality of Father, Son, and
Holy Ghost, about the simultaneous transcendence and
immanence of God, and "quove magis mirere," about the
union of the prisoner with His Father. When he does
touch on the humanity of Christ, he speaks mainly of
Christ humble and meek, offensive to the leading Jews

and tempted by devils; not of the Messiah so central to Joseph's narration. He presents the Christ come to save and to teach, and as such Christ is accepted by Pilate.

But Rome remains the city of the future and Pilate an instrument, necessary in God's present plan. The Roman theme devolves around the various conflicts between the spiritual city of the present and that of the future; there is a political conflict, a moral conflict, and a spiritual conflict—the third implied in and subsuming the other two. Vida may have had this theme in mind when he began his poem with the vague similarity between Christ going to Jerusalem and Aeneas to Carthage. Certainly the points of resemblance between Jerusalem and Carthage are not wholly accidental. The Roman theme also provides the best explanation for the long catalogue in Book II. The catalogue is hardly according to formula. In *Ars poetica* III. 316-328, Vida laid special stress on avoiding names difficult to fit into the hexameter, and in his letter to Botta, his commentator, he remarks on the difficulties the catalogue gave him. The names of the Apostles would have been more suitable metrically, but there is no catalogue of the Apostles. Apparently, then, Vida is using the tribes and cities of Palestine as a final commemoration of the land where Christ lived and the land favored by God in the past, and as a graphic distinction between that past and the future—a point sharply made in lines 305-309.

The earlier description of the city and the temple, the details of their history, give no hint of any glory or importance remaining to either except from the past. The guilt of deicide falls on the whole nation. In the council scene preceding the catalogue, Caiaphas states his main argument thus:

> Hinc quae tot nobis annos tam prospera cessit

18.

Relligio, eversis actutum desinet aris.
Tum metuo, ne Romulidae non talia passi,
Quidquid adhunc juris superest, a gente reposcant,
Et profugos patria jubeant decedere terra.
Unum pro multis detur caput: Unius omnes
Expiet ac tutos mors tanto in turbine praestet.

(II. 244-250)

Henceforth, our altars destroyed, all the prosperity which our religion has brought us for so many years will suddenly end. Furthermore, I fear that the Romans, intolerant of such matters, may take back from our people what little authority remains to us, and may order us out of our fatherland into exile. Let one head be sacrificed for the people, let the death of one man atone for all and preserve our safety in such troubled times.

The irony here consists not only in the double meaning of "unum pro multis...," but also in Caiaphas's positing the Roman as enemy and in Caiaphas's belief, obviously demon-bred, that the destruction of Christ is a defense of their religion and their altars. Vida stays close enough to the Gospel version of Caiaphas's words, but the shift in emphasis is sufficient.

When restraining the angels, God grimly prophesies the destruction of Jerusalem; He says nothing of any guilt on the part of the Romans. In a passage used in the liturgy of Good Friday, St. Augustine discusses the meaning of a verse from Psalm 63: "Exacuerunt tamquam gladium linguas suas."[68]

Non dicant Judaei: Non occidimus Christum. Etenim propterea eum dederunt judici Pilato, ut quasi ipsi a morte ejus viderentur immunes. Nam cum dixisset eis Pilatus: Vos eum occidite: responderunt: Nobis non licet occidere quemquam. Iniquitatem facinoris sui in judicem hominem refundere volebant: sed numquid Deum judicem fallebant? Quod fecit Pilatus, in eo ipso quod fecit, aliquantum particeps fuit: sed in comparatione illorum, multo ipse innocentior. Institit enim quantum potuit, ut illum ex eorum manibus liberaret: nam propterea flagellatum produxit ad eos. Non persequendo Dominum flagellavit, sed eorum furori satisfacere volens: ut vel sic jam mitescerent, et desinerent velle occidere, cum flagellatum viderent.... At ubi perseveraverunt, nostis illum lavisse manus, et dixisse, quod ipse non fecisse, mundum se esse a morte illius. Fecit tamen. Sed si reus, quia fecit vel invitus: illi innocentes, qui coegerunt ut faceret? Nullo modo. Sed ille dixit in eum sententiam, et jussit eum crucifigi, et quasi ipse occidit: et vos, o Judaei, occidistis. Unde occidistis? Gladio linguae: acuistis enim linguas vestras. Et quando percussistis, nisi quando clamastis: Crucifige, crucifige?

Let the Jews not say, We have not killed Christ. They turned Him over to Pilate to judge, precisely so that they might appear innocent of His death. For when Pilate said to them, You kill Him, they answered, It is not lawful for us to kill anyone. They wanted to pass on the guilt of their crime to the human judge: but did they deceive the divine Judge? By the very fact that he did what he did, Pilate was involved to some extent in what he did, but in comparison with them, he is far more innocent. For he tried as hard as he could to deliver Him from their hands; that was why he had Him scourged and then brought Him before them. He scourged the Lord not to persecute Him, but hoping to allay their mad frenzy, hoping that they might have some compassion, and give up their determination to kill Him, when they saw how He had been scourged.... But when they persisted, you know how he washed his hands and said it was none of his doing, he was innocent of His death. Yet he did it. But if he is guilty, because he did it quite unwillingly: are they then innocent who forced him to do it? Hardly. But he passed sentence and condemned Him to be crucified, and as it were killed Him himself: but you, O Hebrews, killed Him. How did you kill Him? With the sword of your tongue: for you sharpened your tongues. And when did you strike Him down, except when you shouted: Crucify Him, crucify Him?

Much of Vida's Roman theme is shaped by this. When Christ upbraids the priests and predicts the destruction of Jerusalem and the transfer of the center of worship, it is in terms of their blindness and their wickedness. He knew their hearts, John says, and, in a passage quoted earlier, He indicts their willful rejection.[69] The mob which cries out for Christ's crucifixion is identified by John with the crowds which surged after Him and uncomprehendingly accepted Him, and with the crowds from all over Palestine which have come to Jerusalem for the Paschal Feast.

In one striking simile, John describes the crowds as camp followers:

> Haud secus ac bellum sicui rex maximus urbi
> Indixit, jamque arma ciet, jamque agmina cogit,
> Cladem orae, exitiumque ferens, populisque ruinas,
> Non tantum jurata manus, lectaeque cohortes
> Incedunt: sed praeterea quos dirus habendi
> Duxit amor varia cupidos ditescere praeda,
> Agglomerant multi, atque injussi castra sequuntur.
>
>   (IV. 847-853)

Just so, when a mighty king having declared war on some city, mobilizes his forces and deploys them, and wreaks havoc on the land and visits death and destruction on the people: it is not only the regular army and the conscripted legions that march against the city, but many others also gather, drawn by miserable avarice, intent on enriching their greedy selves with booty, and, though not under orders, follow the army.

An earlier simile of John's described the future followers of Christ as the foreigners who would have to be called in when the natives were inadequate.[70] Both of these are inextricably bound to three important similes in the sixth book. The first illustrates the joy and excitement of the waiting just in Limbo when Christ comes, by comparing them to the citizens of a besieged city:

> Sicut ubi cives longa obsidione tenentur
> Urbem intra, et vallum, portarumque objice tuti,
> Dum circum sonat, atque in muros arietat hostis,
> Tum si forte acies procul auxiliaribus armis
> Adventare vident socias e turribus altis,
> Consurgant, animosque alacres spe ad sidera tollant.
> (VI. 192-197)

As when the citizens are kept by long siege inside a city, and are safe only because of the barricades of the ramparts and of the gates, while the enemy moves about outside and battles at the walls—then, if they happen to see from their towers the approach of reenforcements, they rise up in a spurt of great hope and lift their hearts to the stars.

The second, not long after this, compares the reactions of the demons at Christ's arrival to barbarians,

> ... quae celsis habitantes alpibus Euros
> Semiferae gentes semper petiuntur, et imbres,
> Romanas si forte procul fulgentibus armis
> Ora exsertantes antris videre phalangas,
> Fumosa extemplo palantes tecta relinquant,
> Dispersique jugis, siqua altius exit in auras,
> Rupe sedent, longeque duces mirantur euntes.
> (VI. 229-235)

who, dwelling high up in the Alps, are constantly exposed to winds and rain; and if, emerging from their caves, they should ever catch sight of the Roman phalanxes bright with flashing armor, they would immediately leave their smoking dens and scatter over the ridges at the higher peaks, and there sit amid the crags and admire the passing rulers from a distance.

The third occurs at the Ascension. In it, Vida attempts to convey the rejoicing of the angels as Christ ascends by comparing the whole scene to a Roman triumph:

> Non aliter sunt ingressi volucri agmine contra
> Concentu vario, et multisono modulatu,
> Quam, prolapsa Remi quum nondum urbs alta jaceret,
> Tarpejaeque arces starent; lateque subactis
> Jura daret populis rerum pulcherrima Roma;
> Consul victor, ovans pugnatis undique bellis,
> Intrabat rediens, Capitoliaque alta subibat.[71]
>
> (VI. 701-707)

They flew in formation to meet Him, with varied harmony and melody, just as in the days when the great city of Remus was still standing, and the Tarpeian rock, and Rome most magnificent of all cities, promulgated laws to many subject nations—the consul, victorious in many wars, returned in triumph and ascended the lofty Capitol.

Taken all together, these similes provide on one level an analogy of Christ's mission and extend its significance to the Christian destiny of Rome. In the total context, the reference to the *past* earthly glory of the city of Remus is important.

Vida focuses his treatment of the Roman theme in the characterization of Pilate. He portrays the Roman in broad strokes, concentrating on his decency and his good will towards Christ, showing him even more sympathetically than Augustine did. Though Pilate eventually weakens, he stands out against the other characters involved in Christ's death. At the end of Book II, Vida juxtaposes the flight of the Apostles, the denials of Peter, the arguments of Caiaphas, and the willing interest of Pilate, all to Pilate's advantage. At the beginning of Book V, he inserts into the narrative of Pilate's conflict with the Jews the episode of Judas's suicide, contrasting the base motives and despair of the one with the sincerity and the eventual repentance of the other. For even after he has given way, Pilate is contrite and lends his aid to Christ's followers. The sharp distinction between Pilate's calm self-control and the furiously demonic anger of the Jews persists through the first part of Book V. Pilate's brief, rational speeches counterpoint the irrelevant hysteria of Annas, *fandi doctissimus*—the epithet is appropriate to the high-pitched shrieks which hiss through his tirades. In the context, it is ironic that Annas takes up the argument of Caiaphas:

> Quae nova tempestas? ea ne inconstantia caelo?
> Dede neci, ne turicremas, quibus imminet, aras
> Destruat, et posthac non ausit talia quisquam.
> Dede neci. poenas sceleri impius hauriat aequas.
> A sacris prohibe infandos altaribus ignes.
>
> (V. 147-151)

What new marvel is this? Is heaven so fickle? Condemn Him to death, before He destroys our incense-burning altars as He threatens! so no one else will ever make so bold again. Condemn Him! Let the villain pay the just penalty for His crime. Keep those terrible fires from our sacred altars.

Pilate's decency is also set off in relief by Herod's quick scorn. Both receive virtually the same response from Christ, but where Pilate was moved by the divine beauty of His countenance, Herod is offended.

In the Gospel of St. John, Christ says to Pilate: "Non haberes potestatem adversum me ullam, nisi tibi datum esset desuper. Propterea qui me tradidit tibi majus peccatum habet." (19:11) Without quoting or paraphrasing this statement, Vida dramatizes it, with every resource at his command. He goes as far as he may to minimize Pilate's guilt and exalt his character. When Pilate yields, it is before forces he can neither understand nor cope with. Passionately, the Roman bids the Jews:

> Quare agite o odiis, miseri, desuescite iniquis.
> Ne frustra pugnate; Deum sed discite vestrum.
> Dixerat. at magis, atque magis violentia gliscit

Omnibus. ingenti clamore insistere, et una
Infreni saevire, humerisque abscindere amictum.
Nec secus increvere animis ardentibus irae,
Quam quum Athesimve, Padumve undis laeta arva
                                              [parantem
Diluere, agricolae subiti compescere tendunt
Aggeris objectu, praeceps magis aestuat amnis
Insultans, victorque altas ruit agmine moles.
                                      (V. 173-182)

Come, now, you wretches, put by this wicked hate. Stop
struggling so futilely and acknowledge your God. Thus he
spoke; but their violence grew more fierce, and with a loud
shout they stamped and raged uncontrollably, even tearing
their garments at the shoulder. Rage grew in those furious
hearts, just as when the Adige or Po rises and threatens to
flood the sunny fields, and the farmers hurry in a effort to
check the waters with dams, but the river seethes and foams,
and rushes on, until finally, victorious in its attack, it roars
over the high mounds.

In the passage, rhythm, sound, and simile cooperate to
suggest the quality of the conflict. The hisses of the Jews
recall the council scene in Book II, a council called together and presided over by devils; it is particularly relevant that amid similar hisses and similar anger Nicodemus
was thrown out of the chamber after daring to bear
witness for Christ.[72] The simile suggests the disordered,
irrational forces surging around Pilate.

When the possessed crowd proves unable to overcome
Pilate, Satan sends Timor and Ignavia to weaken him
internally. Under their influence, "nec jam superantibus
obstat / Amplius." (V. 345-346). The rage of the Jews
is an "insanus furor," which Pilate cannot comprehend;
he is like the captain of a ship caught in a storm—

Ceu quum rostratae se se opposuere triremi
Protinus adversi mediis in fluctibus Euri,

Luctatur primum celsa de puppe magister,
Hortaturque viros validis insurgere tonsis;
Demum ubi se niti contra intolerabile caelum
Incassum videt, ac ventos superare furentes,
Vertit iter, quocumque vocat fortuna per aequor
Multivium, atque auris parens subremigat aeger.

(V. 348-355)

As when the south winds clash right against a trireme in the midst of the waves; first the captain struggles from his top deck, calling to his crew to lay on boldly with their oars. But then finally he realizes that he is struggling vainly against an unyielding sky, and that the raging winds are getting the better of his ship, and so he steers wherever fortune leads over the many-laned sea, wearily sailing at the whim of the winds.

But the ship does not sink; Pilate's symbolic yielding before "intolerabile caelum" seems to have very broad significance. Turning on the Jews, Pilate says,

Verum, Vincor, ait; nec habet vestra ira regressum.
In me nulla mora est. moriatur crimine falso
Damnatus. vos triste manet, speroque propinquum
Supplicium vos sacrilego, serique nepotes,
O miseri, meritas pendetis sanguine poenas.

(V. 357-361)

Yes, I yield, he said; for your wrath knows no turning back. I will not hold you any longer. Let Him die, convicted of a false charge. As for you, a miserable end awaits you—soon, I trust. You and your offspring, cursed people, will pay the just penalty called for by this sacrilegious shedding of blood.

The Father's speech to the angels, later in this book, echoes these lines unmistakably. It echoes, too, the grim outcry of the Jews. That the Romans are to carry out God's sentence, to replace the angels in effect, is of some relevance when that political fact is seen in the context

of Christ's earlier prophecies, the references in the catalogue to Palestine's fate, and the Father's prophecies about
Rome's futue greatness.

Vida does not apostrophize Pilate, though he does
apostrophize pathetic Judas, the Jewish leaders, Satan and
the demons. He does not mitigate Pilate's guilt, but he
makes clear that it must be considered relatively. Pilate
was conquered by forces beyond his ken. The implied
contrast between the Roman *arbiter* and the Judge of
the world whom he is forced to judge suggests the essential barrier: pre-Christian Rome is not yet ripe enough
spiritually. But, as action and imagery indicate, Pilate's
hour and Rome's will come.

This sympathetic Roman is drawn by Vida partly as a
comment on the *Aeneid*. Pilate is a Vergilian man, evolved
morally as well as politically from those centuries of development, under divine guidance, towards the Roman
ideal. He embodies the Vergilian hope of the golden age.
His weakness is essential; any other course, given the
context of the *Christiad*, would have demanded an un-
historical full conversion. As the last of the pagans, Pilate,
lacking grace, is easy prey to the devils. Though he is
not as sublime as Dante's Vergil, and though his attempt
to rise is necessarily limited, it is still a noble and
praiseworthy attempt. Pilate is both a comment on the
old and a presage of the new.

In the first book, Christ, upbraiding the Jews for their
formalism, speaks of the "new sacrifice":

> Nunc pater omnipotens, pecudum, volucrumque cruori
> Parcere vos posthac jubet, ac fumantibus extis.
> Vos diversa manent mutatis orgia sacris;
> Discite justitiam tantum, puraque litate
> Mente, Deumque piis precibus placate volentem.
>
> (I. 530-534)

Now the Almighty Father commands you henceforth to spare the blood of animals and birds, and the steaming entrails. New rites, new sacrifices are to be yours. Turn your thoughts to justice and pray with pure heart and placate God's will with your humble prayers.

The justice of which He speaks is the justice of Rome transmuted, as the Father's prophecy at the end of the first book shows. Through this justice, the true golden age will come. A typical connection between the two is made by John the Baptist as he preaches the coming of Christ:

> Discite justitiam interea, atque assuescite recto,
> Et duce me scelus infectum lavite amne liquenti.
> Ipse autem aetherea divinitus eluet aura
> Omne malum, ac veteris penitus contagia culpae:
> Seclaque mutato succedent aurea mundo.
>
> (IV. 193-197)

Meanwhile learn justice and accustom yourselves to goodness. Follow my example and wash away your sins in the flowing stream. For He, with His heavenly breath, will miraculously cleanse all evil and the infection of the ancient sin. And when the whole world has turned to Him, the golden age will begin.

Justice is the necessary preparation for the full acceptance of Christ. It is postulated on a universal world order, which itself is based on a combination of the Vergilian universe and Christian tradition. The Trinitarian hierarchy, the orderliness of the angelic hosts, the sharp contrasts between the conduct of the angels in scenes of exuberance and the confusion of the devils in parallel scenes, the contrasts between the calm of Christ and the confusion of the devils at the incident at Gerasa, and between the self-possession of Pilate and the frenzies of the Jews—all these are expressive of the theme of order.[73]

The theme of order is announced in the complex allusion with which the poem begins, an allusion which is significantly echoed at crucial points throughout the poem; and the epic closes with further references to the golden age, significantly adapted from the *Messianic Eclogue.*[74] Many incidents and images develop the theme, not the least of which is the careful use of numbers. Most important is the climactic scene of the Ascension; to understand that fully, a brief further consideration of the Roman prophecy may be helpful.

When He has enunciated the greatness of Christian Rome, the Father adds these words:

> Siquae tamen paullatim annis labentibus aetas
> Decolor inficiet mores, versisque nepotes
> Degeneres surgent studiis; per dura, laboresque
> Exercens lapsam revocabo in pristina gentem.
> Illa malis semper melior se tollet ad astra.
> Saepe solo velut eversam, excisamque videbis,
> Quam modo praedixi, populorum incursibus urbem:
> Verum quo magis illa malis exercita, semper
> Altius hoc surgens celsum caput inseret astris,
> Moeniaque in melius semper recidiva reponet.
> Nec nisi subjecto passim sibi desinet orbe.
> Sic placitum. nostri sedes ea Numinis esto.
>
> (I. 919-930)

But if, as the years pass, a perverted age gradually undermines morality and, through abandonment of your teachings, unworthy successors seize power, I will visit them with hardship and travail and will recall the erring people to their proper goodness. That city will always arise from its miseries more glorious than before. Often You will see that chosen city virtually destroyed, razed to the ground, by the attacks of its foes. But the more it is beset with evils, the higher will it rise in glory, to raise its mighty head among the stars and rebuild its shattered walls mightier than before. And it will not yield until the whole world is subject to it. This is My will: that city shall be the seat of Our Godhead.

The divine plan is clear, and so are the dangers which Rome must avert to achieve its Christian maturity. Vida is no doubt alluding here to some contemporary problems; taken with the insistence on peace and spiritual values in other passages, *versis studiis* appears a reminder to the politically embroiled Clement VII of his primary duties. But the view is broader, referring as much to the destruction of Rome by the barbarians as to that by Charles's mercenary armies, and to the various spiritual crises through which Rome passed.

Vida's Roman theme is, of course, limited; for a poem celebrating universal redemption, such nationalism is far less appropriate than it was in the *Aeneid.* The weakness here, and the weakness in the golden age theme—presented with too much complacency—, is mitigated somewhat by the insistence on human cooperation. The divine plan has stringent necessity, but even the death of Christ must be accompanied by a stripping of His divine power and a conflict within Him out of which issues His full consent. Both Isaiah's "Oblatus est quia ipse voluit," and Paul's "Semetipsum exinanivit formam servi accipiens, in similitudinem hominum factus.... Humiliavit semetipsum, factus obediens usque ad mortem," are central to Vida's view of the crucifixion.[75] Vida stresses both less to "humanize" Christ than to express dramatically the vital theme of grace, God's gift which, given the cooperation of men, can order all things.

The central symbol for the ordering of nature by grace is the Ascension. In the first section of it, Vida describes at length the joy of the angels, their song and their activity. Amid all the exuberance and enthusiasm there is an order almost choreographic; for instance,

> ... ter patris ad solium pernice chorea
> Indulsere choris, ter ludo lucida regna
> Lustravere, polique e vertice decurrere ...
>
> (VI. 698-700)

Accompanying Christ, the angels bear the "caedis moni-
menta nefandae." Meanwhile, the Apostles stand below,
bewildered, until a voice from heaven reassures them;
but only then do they hear the angels' song:

> Nec mora. carminibus caeli domus ardua longe
> Auditur resonare, modisque per astra canoris,
> Contra etiam plausere, atque haec alterna canebant
> Laeta viri, caelumque oculis, animisque petebant.
>
> (VI. 732-735)

Immediately, the whole heavens were heard to resound with
songs and melodious strains amid the stars. The Apostles, for
their part, also clapped, scanning the heavens with eyes and
hearts, and sang this song in joyful response.

Vida seems to be suggesting that only when the Apostles
understood, could they hear the heavenly songs. Their
alternate hymn extends further the symbolism of the
Ascension.

The Apostles' lengthy hymn is very carefully organized.[76]
Calling upon all men, all creatures, and all nature to
rejoice and praise Christ, they detail His attributes—
without beginning, Creator, God omnipotent, and source
of all order. That order is detailed—in the sun, moon,
and stars; in fire and water; in the earth and her inhabitants; in sickness, disease, and death, and even in the
depths of hell. The hymn presents an epic view of creation
and of the God-Man's rule over all things, manifested both
in their natural existence and in miraculous diversions
from the ordinary. In the first half of it, the natural order
is stressed, the chain of creation, as all proceeding from,
dependent on, and given order by God Incarnate; in the

second, the control exercised and demonstrated in various ways climaxes in the conquest of death and hell. The two halves are distinguished. In the first, existence itself is to praise Christ for simply being; here, hell is absent. In the second, Christ's power is stressed and its self-imposed limits implied:

> Salve, opifex rerum, vastique salutifer orbis,
> Aspice nos propius, propius genus aspice nostrum,
> Morte tua patet aetherei cui janua olympi.
>
> (VI. 797-799)

Hail, creator of the great world and its redeemer. Look down upon us, look down upon our race, for whom the gate of heaven has been opened by Your death.

In the whole scene, the Incarnate Christ radiates as the timeless center of all human history and as the ordering focus of all human existence. Brought to bear on this scene is all the rich symbolism of the reopening of heaven by Christ's death and the theology which connects that death to the mission of the Apostles and of the Church.

The water and fire imagery used here resonate elsewhere in the poem as particular symbols of grace. The fire of the Spirit which purifies and strengthens the Apostles is suggested both by the tongues and by the accompanying simile:

> ... tum innoxius ignis
> Omnibus extemplo supra caput astitit ingens,
> Et circum rutilis incanduit aura favillis;
> Stricturis veluti crebrae crepitantibus olim
> Dissiliunt scintillae, acres dum incudibus ictus
> Alternant Chalybes, robustaque brachia tollunt
> Candentem curva versantes forcipe massam.
>
> (VI. 919-925)

Then the great harmless flame was suspended over their heads, and the air glowed as from golden embers. Just so do showers of sparks fly from the clattering iron bars as the Chalybes rhythmically hammer with sharp beats, and raise their robust arms, turning the glowing mass with curved tongs.

The advent of grace is powerful and overwhelming:

> Infunduntque viris Numen. Deus ecce repente
> Ecce Deus. cunctis divinitus algida corda
> Incipiunt afflata calescere, Numine tacti
> Implentur propiore viri, sacrumque furorem
> Concepere; Deumque imis hausere medullis.
> Nec mora, nec requies ter scintillantibus igneis
> Terrifico radiis fulgore, ter alitis aurae
> Turbine correpti blando flammantur amore,
> Ignescuntque animis; atque exsultantia cunctis
> Exercent acres stimulis praecordia motus.
>
> (VI. 928-937)

They pour out Their Godhead on the men. And lo, suddenly and swiftly God was present. Their cold hearts, feeling the breath of God, warmed; seized by the Godhead, they were filled full with divine frenzy, as God pierced to the very marrow of their bones. Nor is there any delay; thrice the flames with shooting rays and terrifying glow, thrice caught up in the swirling whirlwind, their hearts catch fire and blaze with divine love, and the sharp thrusts invigorate their pulsing hearts.

But that is precisely what they were praying for. Earlier, they were erring, weak, often helpless; only their good will redeemed them. In a poem full of aristocrats, the Apostles alone remain unenhanced. Their helplessness is graphically presented in similes; they are like little girls who are deserted, dogs who have lost their masters, sheep frightened by fierce animals, doves fleeing before a hawk.[77] Even after their inspired song at the Ascension, they go back into hiding, pray without perfect faith, and kill time by speculating on Judas's replacement. Only after the frightening descent of the Spirit are they really ready for their mission:

> ... animosaque leti
> Spes magis atque magis viget acris Numinis haustu.[78]
>
> (VI. 966-967)

The fire imagery of the descent is foreshadowed in the fire of love of which both Joseph and John speak, in the fire which plays about Christ's head, in the pillar of fire which guided the Israelites in the desert, and particularly in the star of the Magi, which Vida daringly likens to that pillar of fire:[79]

> Ceu quondam patribus deserta per avia nostris
> In patriam tandem Pharia redeuntibus ora
> Praecurrens monstrabat iter nocte ignea lampas
> Desuper, et mirum spargebat lucida lumen.
>
> (III. 749-752)

Just as once, a blazing fire, coursing the sky above, shed a miraculous light to guide our ancestors through the pathless desert as they returned home from the land of Egypt.

Interlocked with the imagery of fire is the water imagery. Christ speaks of Himself as the living water:

> Ipse ego fons veluti liquidam purissimus undam
> Sufficiam. properate ad aquas. haurite liquentem,
> Matres, atque viri, sitientes protinus amnem.
> Ferte pedem huc omnes. nec opus potantibus auro,
> Argentove. mei fontis patet omnibus unda.
>
> (IV. 959-963)

I Myself, the well of purest water, will furnish abundant water. Hurry to the well and drink of the flowing stream, all you men and women who thirst; come to Me and drink: there is no need for gold or silver. The water of My spring flows for all.

19.

Recurrent references—to the water from the rock, at Christ's baptism in the Jordan, in Simeon's prophecy of rivers running blood, in the blood and water which flow from Christ's side when it is pierced by Longinus—elaborate the Christian meanings. Water also functions in its conventional significance as the element of life, as in the passage of the Israelites through the Red Sea, the ark of Noah, the frequent similes of ships at sea and of storms. But even in this, the theme of grace is obliquely developed. That Christ can control the forces of nature without destroying nature is suggested often—nowhere more potently than in the incident when, walking on the waves, He stills both the raging storm and the Apostles' fear.

The effects of the blazing descent of the Spirit are compared to the effects of water on parched earth:

> Haud secus ac crebris quum rimis terra dehiscit,
> Quum sitit omnis ager, tum quae morientia languent
> Gramina, caeruleus si caelo venerit imber,
> Continuo attollant rursus capita, arvaque ponant
> Squalorem, redeatque decor suus omnibus agris.
>
> (VI. 968-972)

Just so, when the earth is rutted with many cracks and every meadow is parched, if a sweet shower should suddenly fall, the drooped and withering grasses would straightway raise up again, and the fields would put aside their barren look, and gladness return to the whole earth.

This simile, effective in its sound and rhythms, is most significant for the allusion to Gideon's fleece, a well-known Old Testament type; in Book III, Joseph, speaking like an exegete, explained the relevance of the type to Mary.[80] The fleece prefigures the humility of Mary, the chosen one, who received the Messiah; in Vida's context, it suggests further the effect of the Incarnation and of grace. Indeed, in describing the Incarnation itself, Vida uses the image of the earth impregnated in springtime, here not only alluding to Gideon's fleece but also transforming the myth of Persephone into a symbol, completely Christian, of the operation of grace.[81]

This chapter has attempted to indicate the multiple poetic devices with which Vida embodied the themes of his poem. His conception of the Christian epic is truly large and his approach profoundly Vergilian. The practice of the *Christiad* demonstrates conclusively how far Vida's understanding of the *Aeneid* goes beyond the inchoative notes of the *Ars poetica*. We can only speculate to what extent Vida was influenced by the commentators on the *Aeneid* and the Scriptures; much of his imagery can be traced directly to the liturgy, at least for its raw state. But manifestly his poem is too complex to be reduced to sources, and the important point here is his Vergilian treatment of his material. Not only the treatment; in the themes of exile and the golden age, in the conflict of rational and irrational, in the hierarchic order of his universe, he has taken over and transmuted much of Vergil's matter. His imitation of Vergil, far from being a linear and obtuse servility, is in the best traditions of creative transformation.

CHAPTER SEVEN

CREMONA'S TRUMP

THE YOUNG John Milton perceived more than he may have
realized when he wrote the line,

Loud O'er the rest Cremona's trump doth sound.

As an estimate of the *Christiad* compared to other attempts at Christian epic, this is clear, comprehensive, and
accurate. The admiration implied suggests the possibilities
of Vida's influence on the poet of *Paradise Lost*. At the
same time, the image of the "trump" helps to set Vida's
achievement in full perspective.

Compared with the quasi-Vergilian poems which span
the fifteen centuries since Vergil, from the works of
Statius and Valerius to Muzio, Sannazaro, and Bona,
Vida's *Christiad* is virtually the only attempt at Christian
epic that succeeded. It may be called, indeed, the only
true Christian epic in the Vergilian tradition. Vida was a
giant among the pygmies in his understanding of Vergil's
structure and thematic design, in his architectonics, in his
transformation of many of the canonical elements, in his
sensitive employment of evocative allusion, functional
similes, interwoven patterns of imagery, and other devices
to embody theme, and in his vast conception nobly executed. The *Christiad* is a fundamentally Christian epic
which manages to remain profoundly true to its classical
model. Even the narrative, diction, and characterization,

faulty in many respects, are superior to anything the preceding centuries produced.

Vida's perception of Vergilianism went far deeper than either *Quattrocento* humanism or his own *Ars poetica*, legacy of the *Quattrocento*, could promise. In many ways, Vida was suitable heir of *Quattrocento* humanism. The teachings of the pedagogues and the inchoative insights of the critics clearly contributed to shaping that genius which reconciled *Aeneid* and Scriptures. The allegorists also belong here for helping to shape a tradition in which Vida could see poetically the relationship between the story of Moses and the story of Aeneas and could gauge the potential inherent in Christian typology. But as my examination of the connection between *Ars poetica* and *Christiad* has attempted to demonstrate, Vida's creation was not the result of theory. Vida followed the *Quattrocento* and his own poetic where they cannot really be followed—that is, in the severe command to contemplate and absorb the masters, in making his model into an exemplar, in transforming his original, and in imitating in such a way that the inventive genius does what it will and what it must.

Vida's achievement undoubtedly affected the whole epic genre. The following centuries saw many attempts to do again what Vida had done, often with the same results which attended quasi-Vergilian poetry from Statius to Sannazaro. It may be that the *Christiad* could only be done once in Vergilian Latin; to do it again with the same kind of perceptions would be work of supererogation. Such, at least, is the conclusion suggested by Ceva's *Puer Jesus* or Lebrun's *Ignatiad*, two typical seventeenth-century Latin epics which derive from Vergilian Vida. In a sense, Vida had brought the humanistic-Vergilian form to its perfection, established a classic, and destroyed the mould, all at once.[1]

Less dependent poets may well have profited greatly from Vida. Many critics, like Gatta, Zabughin, and Zumbini, have asserted his distinct influences on Tasso, Milton, and Klopstock, not only in matters like the infernal council scene, the battle in heaven, the methods of characterization, and individual incidents or images, but also in conception, scope, and structure.[2] The critics who have disagreed with these suggestions, like Tillyard and Kirkconnell, have proceeded on the notion that Vida's poem is devoid of structure or of scope—an amazing notion, to say the least.[3] Hence, their negative view is hardly convincing. I believe that it is quite plausible to maintain that Vida's massive transformation of Vergil cleared the way for these poets. In *Paradise Lost*, for instance, there are too many large similarities to the *Christiad* to argue coincidence. The threefold movement, each with its own center of gravity; the vast scope; the rich unity of structural organization, with its "symbolic patterns of repetition and recurrence that knit the fabric of the epic together..., and its innumerable correspondences"—these elements are far from unlike the *Christiad*.[4]

Two fundamental differences, however, separate Vida and Milton. One is Milton's "answerable style;" the other is that Milton was fully equal to his high argument. The sustained magnificence of *Paradise Lost* leaves Vida far behind. Vida's style is consistently elevated but only infrequently inspired. His inattention to diction[5] affected the texture of his poem, which could not quite stand the strain imposed by theme and structure. The Alexandrian quality is only too clear in the narrative organization, in some of the characters—particularly the artificial Mary—, in the disturbing overelaboration, and in the lack of a firm foothold on reality.

In the end, it is perhaps this last flaw which kept Vida's poem from the front line of epic poetry. In a crucial sense,

the *Christiad* is something of an anachronism. The Roman
theme which Vida makes so central raises problems which
are not adequately solved. By his insistence on that theme,
Vida framed an argument to whose implications he was
not equal. The hierarchy of the early *Cinquecento* and the
Lutheran heretics had, together, opened a chasm which
yawned before the Church, but Vida seems to have
partially averted his eyes. In this, he badly misread Vergil.
Vergil dreamt of and celebrated the golden age majestically, with a toughness and an honesty that have
misled critics into believing the *Aeneid* a tragedy; in
Vida's hands, this golden age becomes a mirage. The
ending of the *Christiad* suggests not the demands which
the Church's mission must make but the ease with which
that mission will be fulfilled; such complacency is brutally
ironic in the light of Rome's spiritual history during the
earlier sixteenth century.

Unlike Milton, who virtually drives his reader to grapple
with the theme of liberty in very concrete terms, so that
the final image of *Paradise Lost* is powerful and stirring,
Vida defeats himself in his conclusion. In its thematic
design, the *Christiad* is a large theological-historical vision,
but the conclusion does not equal the vision. Here are the
last fourteen lines:

> Ergo abeunt varias longe, lateque per oras
> Diversi, laudesque canunt, atque inclyta vulgo
> Facta ducis, jamque (ut vates cecinere futurum
> Antiqui) illorum vox fines exit in omnes.
> Audiit et siquem medio ardens aethere iniquo
> Sidere desertis plaga dividit invia terris,
> Quique orbem extremo circumsonat aequore pontus.
> Continuo ponunt leges, moremque sacrorum
> Urbibus. infectum genti lustralibus undis
> Eluitur scelus, et veteris contagia culpae;
> Relligioque novas nova passim exsuscitat aras.

Protinus hinc populos Christi de nomine dicunt
Christiadas. toto surgit gens aurea mundo,
Seclorumque oritur longe pulcherrimus ordo.

                                   (VI. 973-986)

So they traveled far and scattered broadly through many parts
of the world, proclaiming to the people the glories and the
marvelous deeds of their Lord; and so, as the prophets of
old had foreseen, their voice went out into all countries. They
were heard—even by men living in the pathless tracts of the
wilderness, burning under the fierce sun which hangs high
in the heavens, and around whose lands the far ends of the
ocean roar. Immediately, they laid down laws and religious
practices in cities; with purifying waters, the taint of sin is
washed away, and the effects of the original sin. Everywhere,
the new faith calls forth new altars. Henceforth, by reason
of Christ's name, His followers are called Christians. Through
all the earth a golden race arises, and the most splendid order
of all time is born.

The passage gains something in significance from the
cumulative effect of multiple allusions, but the passage as
a whole is too pat. Earlier allusions had stressed both
hope and effort, in contexts which were not so sure
of themselves; here, a facility with phrases and a desire
to wrap up the poem neatly make many of the lines vapid
and complacent. The thematic structure of the poem
demanded some struggle with the early age of Christianity
and with the apostolic character of Christ's Church, but
both of these are virtually glossed over. Thus the closing
allusions to the *Messianic Eclogue* fall flat: they lack
human conviction and so, whatever logical appropriateness
they have, they are not triumphant.

In some ways, Vida out-Vergils Vergil. He leans heavily
on the oblique, diluting action and drama. In his inattention to narrative and his use of multiple devices in a
complex thematic design, he is even further from Homer

than Vergil was. The *Christiad* sometimes seems so loaded with significance that it almost does not stand up; perhaps only a poet with the genius of Dante or Milton could do what Vida attempted. Perhaps too, to succeed fully, such a poet would have to have the fierce independence, from Pope or Presbyter, which these poets had. If Vida's massive epic escaped greatness, it may well be in part because he was too close to those for whom he was writing the poem—the Medici Popes and his fellow humanists—to have full perspective. But when all these criticisms have been set down, the *Christiad* of Marco Girolamo Vida remains an impressive epic poem that informed literary history and the epic tradition in ways that have escaped notice all too long.

SUMMARY OF THE *CHRISTIAD*

Book I

THE POEM opens with invocation and brief statement of theme. It is shortly before the Paschal Feast. On the way to Jerusalem, Christ draws the twelve Apostles apart, prophesies His death, and encourages them to face their own trials boldly. Dining at the house of Zaccheus, they hear that Lazarus is dead and immediately go to Bethany.

Meanwhile, at a council of devils, Satan announces that the day is coming on which an avenger is to harrow hell. Discoursing on God's fear and envy as causes of their fall, Satan proposes to subvert the divine plan by doing away with Christ. In some disorder, the devils set forth for Jerusalem.

At Bethany, to the amazement of the crowd of onlookers, Christ raises Lazarus; the bewildered man attempts to convey some notion of his experiences among the dead. Later, while Christ is dining at the house of Simon, a notorious woman, Maria, comes to seduce Him of whose handsomeness she had heard so much. Christ's divine beauty, however, converts her.

After healing many, Christ proceeds to Jerusalem, whose founding and history are briefly related. In humble triumph, He enters the city, cures the man at the pool, drives the vendors out of the temple (thus infuriating the helpless priests), and predicts the destruction of Jerusalem and the transfer of the center of worship to another land.

At the Apostles' request, He comments on the scenes depicted in marble on the temple walls—scenes of the Creation and the Fall, and figurative scenes from Old Testament history. Outside, an adulteress is dragged before Him; one of the priests asks Christ's advice. He urges whoever is without sin to cast the first stone. Priests and mob disperse.

Turning to the Apostles, He discourses on the Old Law, dwelling with emphasis on the hardheartedness of the Jews. That evening, on Mt. Tabor, Christ prays to His Father for the Apostles. The Father assures Him that only one will fail, that His own death will bear great fruit, and that Rome, the future center of worship, will be a great city, devoted particularly to religion. The heavens open and Christ is transfigured between the figures of Moses and Elias.

Book II

The devils are at work. Some, disguised as ministers of the temple, summon a council; others assault the Apostles. Satan himself, in the guise of a kinsman, appears to Judas asleep and wins him over by arguing expediency.

The Jewish priests, in demonic council, drive out the loyal Nicodemus and, following the advice of Caiaphas to seek the good of the nation, plot Christ's death. As they cast about for means, Judas comes and offers to deliver Christ to them for a price.

Here, Vida briefly describes the history and ritual of the feast; a lengthy catalogue follows, detailing the tribes of Israel and their cities.

Preparing for the Last Supper, Christ sends Peter and John to the house of Simon, a noble rustic and bard. They find Simon singing of ancient times. Simon shows them a large, well-furnished upper room, and orders preparations to be made. Then he resumes his song, now dealing with the exodus of the Israelites, the manna, the water from the rock, and the sacrifice of Melchisedech.

The Last Supper, briefly narrated, is followed by the washing of the feet and the prediction of betrayal and denial. On Mount Olivet, Christ prays, but the Apostles sleep. Judas comes, leading soldiers, who after some delay, arrest Christ and drag Him before Caiaphas. To the high priest's questions about His divinity, Christ answers firmly; enraged, Caiaphas sends Him to Pilate to be condemned. Peter, meanwhile, recognized by a maidservant, vehemently denies Christ, whereupon he hears the cock crow and goes out weeping bitterly. The legend of Peter's tears is briefly related.

At the Roman court, Pilate is impressed by Christ's bearing and countenance, and, ignoring the mob, he has Christ led inside for further questioning.

Book III

Joseph and John come to Pilate's court, deriving some hope from the apparent frustration of priests and mob outside. Throwing himself at Pilate's feet, Joseph begs mercy for Christ, but Pilate, not receiving any response from Christ to his urgent questions, seeks all the information he can get from them. Joseph hesitates, but John, sensing Pilate's sincerity, urges him to reveal everything.

Joseph begins by tracing briefly his own lineage and stating his precise relationship to Christ. He details the lineage of Mary and the unusual circumstances of her marriage: how a divine command called for it; how he, already an old man, came at the request of Mary's father, Joachim, his kinsman; how, in an inspired frenzy, Anna singled him out as the divinely-chosen groom. He explains Mary's vows of virginity, their proposed father-daughter relationship, and the difficulties he experienced. With lingering amazement, he narrates the story Mary told him of the apparition of the angel, the Annunciation, and the Incarnation. His own doubts, he says, were great, but were finally dispelled by an angel.

There follows the trip to Elizabeth's house, the signs and wonders, the decree of Augustus, and the journey to Bethlehem, where Christ was born. Shepherds came to adore; after forty days, Joseph brought the child to the temple, where he heard the ambiguous prophecies of Simeon. Wise men from the East came to adore Christ, but Herod plotted His death; warned by an angel, Joseph took the child and His mother to Egypt.

At this point, Joseph suggests that he is getting weary and his tale long; briefly, he tells of Christ's youth, His modest character, the first sign to the people—His teaching in the temple at the age of twelve—and the first signs of opposition, and finally of his first public miracle at the wedding in Cana. For the rest, he refers the fascinated Pilate to John, who has firsthand information about Christ's public life.

Book IV

But John, unable to begin, is rapt in ecstasy; then the words rush out and he discourses on the nature of God and of the Word, and explains the difference between the Trinity and the pagan gods. To show why the Word became man, he recounts the creation and rebellion of the angels, the creation of man and his fall, and the plan of redemption.

Briefly describing the life and role of John the Baptist, he narrates the baptism of Christ at the Jordan and the calling of the twelve Apostles, most of them fishermen and all but one of humble and obscure origin. John surveys the numerous miracles of Christ's public life, relating a few in detail: the raising from the dead of the widow of Naim's son and of the daughter of Iarus; the episode of the loaves and the fishes; the cursing of the barren fig tree; Christ's walking on the waters; the miraculous coin in the fish's mouth; and the exorcism of the Gerasene youth.

To show Christ's human nature, he tells of Christ's trials and joys, of the persecution by His enemies, and of the temptations in the desert. John illustrates Christ's qualities—His charity for all; His kindness to sinners, for which He was rebuked by priests and Pharisees; His great and often incomprehensible humility; and His purity of motive. To His followers, Christ offered hardship, exile, and violent death; yet they remain with Him. Despite opposition, He was enormously sought after. Once the crowds became so great that he had to get into a boat in order to preach to them.

John recounts that particular discourse at length, from the counsels of peace, charity, and forgiveness, to the sublime prayer which Christ taught and the prophecies of the end of the world and the final judgment.

As John concludes with some general remarks, the crowd bursts through the outer doors, demanding that Christ be condemned. Joseph and John go to tell Mary what has happened.

Book V

Impressed by all he has heard, Pilate wishes to save Christ. At the same time, Judas is disturbed by the turn of events and takes the money back to the priests, attempting to extricate himself from complicity in the crime. The priests scorn him. Now an outcast, Judas despairs and, in a dark wood near Pilate's court, he hangs himself.

Scornful and confident, Pilate fences with the Jews. When Annas, in a long and furious speech, indicts Christ as a danger to the community, Pilate reaffirms the man's innocence. But the unabated frenzy shakes Pilate. To gain time, he sends Christ to Herod; Herod sends Him back. Now Pilate invokes the yearly custom of releasing a prisoner; when the mob chooses Barabas, Pilate has Christ scourged, hoping thus to appease them. His wife relates a portentous dream she has just had and implores him to release the prisoner and avoid God's wrath.

But Pilate, undermined by devils and by the shrieking mob, unable to find any further evasions, washes his hands of the whole affair and delivers Christ to the Jews. Christ is mocked, crowned with thorns, and led off to be crucified. Though it is hardly morning, crowds of people flock out to watch; to women who mourn His plight, Christ offers words of consolation.

From heaven, God and the angels watch. As Christ reaches Calvary, He cries out to the Father. God hears but remains impassive. The angels, however, gather from all over heaven and earth, and, taking on corporeal form, arm themselves and mobilize behind the archangel Michael. Intent on saving Christ, they march to the gates of heaven, where, engraved on the portals, they see scenes from the ancient war with the rebel angels. But God sends Clementia and Pietas to restrain them; with a rebuke, He reminds them of His power and explains the plan of redemption.

Christ's hands and feet are nailed to the cross; an inscription is placed over His head; two thieves are crucified with Him. At this point, Vida breaks into the *Improperia*, a chant-like apostrophe enumerating God's favors to Judea and counterpointing to these Judea's treatment of Christ.

Seeking her son, Mary has hastened to Jerusalem. From

the top of Olivet, she sees the surging crowd and hastens towards it; Jewish women attempt to console her, but she rushes on and finds Christ at last, on the cross. Her long and bitter lament recalls details of Christ's youth and the predictions of His greatness.

The soldiers mock Christ, but He begs forgiveness. To one thief, He promises a place in heaven. The soldiers cast dice for his tunic. Darkness descends on the land, the veil of the temple is rent, Christ bows His head and dies.

Book VI

When Joseph of Arimathea comes boldly asking permission to bury Christ's body, Pilate readily grants the request. The corpse is reverently removed from the cross, washed and anointed, and buried in a new tomb. Fearful of a resurrection-plot, the priests set armed guards over the tomb.

Free of His body, Christ descends into hell, where the souls of the just await. The devils attempt to stop Him, but fall back in terror at His approach, and the gates of hell crash open. Wild with joy, the just hail Christ, who leads them to heaven amid songs of joy.

Early in the morning, Magdalene and other women go to the tomb. It is empty. Magdalene, sitting alone, sees on the wall of the tomb a representation of the story of Jonah. As she contemplates it, Christ appears briefly to her.

Word of the resurrection spreads. Later in the day, Christ appears to the Apostles; when the absent Thomas returns, he disbelieves their story. Cleophas, a disciple, bursts in and recounts how Christ walked with him and a companion, talking with them, and they did not recognize Him until He broke bread at Emmaus. Thomas still does not believe. Christ comes to them again and invites the doubter to touch Him.

During forty days, Christ is frequently with the Apostles, teaching them and preparing them for their mission. At the last apparition, Christ addresses them at length on the subject of peace and fortitude. He prophesies the descent of the Holy Ghost, the spread of the Church, the general resurrection, and the last judgment, and He commissions Peter head of the Church. Thereupon, He ascends slowly into heaven. The angels sing gloriously, but the Apostles watch in fear, until a voice from heaven tells them not to fear, and they join in the angels' song.

On the tenth day, Christ asks His Father to send the Paraclete to strengthen the timorous Apostles. Responding, God prophesies the spread of the Church and the future poetic celebration of Christ's passion. The Paraclete descends. Tongues of fire settle on the heads of the Apostles. No longer afraid, they speak out boldly in Christ's name. Then they go forth, preaching the Gospel all over the earth and establishing Christ's Church. A new golden age has dawned for mankind.

NOTES

ABBREVIATIONS

Aen.	*Aeneid*
AP	*Ars poetica*
B	*Bombyx*
Chr.	*Christiad*
Com.	Cominiana edition of Vida's works
LS	*Ludus scacchiae*
Rep.	*De reipublicae dignitate dialogi*
AJP	*American Journal of Philology*
ASL	*Archivio Storico Lombardo*
BSC	*Bollettino Storico Cremonese*
CJ	*Classical Journal*
EETS	*Early English Text Society*
GSLI	*Giornale Storico della Letteratura Italiana*
HSCP	*Harvard Studies in Classical Philology*
IMU	*Italia Medioevale e Umanistica*
PMLA	*Publications of the Modern Language Association*
RCLI	*Rassegna Critica della Letteratura Italiana*

Chapter One: Life and Works

1. Giraldi, *De poetarum historia* (Basel, 1548), Dial. 4. 148; M. Pauli Tartessii *In M. Hieronymi Vidae poeticam praefatio* (Cremona, 1559), available in Com. II, xv; full text, vii-xvi.

2. Francesco Novati, "Il Virgilio Cristiano," *A ricolta* (Bergamo, 1907), pp. 101-102. The brief sketch which follows, a reduced version of the first chapter of my dissertation (Columbia, 1960), uses only clearly documented data. The docu-

ments are abundant but incomplete; the most important collections are those by Tommaso Vairani, *Monumenta Cremonensium Romae Exstantia* (Rome, 1778), and Novati, "Sedici lettere inedite di M. G. Vida," *ASL*, XXV (1898), 195-281, and XXVI (1899), 1-59. I have in preparation inventories of Vida's letters and documents, published and unpublished. Two biographies, though neither fully accurate nor complete, have been of some service: Hazel Stewart Alberson, *Marcus Hieronymus Vida*, dissertation, Wisconsin, 1935, and Vincenzo Cicchitelli, *Sulle Opere Poetiche di M. G. Vida* (Naples, 1904). A full biography of Vida remains a desideratum.

3. The year of Vida's birth has been argued hotly, and sometimes wildly: see Cicchitelli, pp. 2-3; *GSLI*, XLVI (1905), 406 f.; William Roscoe, *The Life and Pontificate of Leo the Tenth*, ed. and rev. by T. Roscoe (London, 1876), II, 189. The size of Vida's family is not clear; one brother, Giorgio, and two sisters, Lucia and Helena, are mentioned by name, and at least one more sister and "other" brothers are referred to: Novati, *ASL*, XXVI (1899), 51-60.

4. He may also have studied under Pietro Marcheselli di Viadana and Battista Fiera. Lucari was educated by Pietro Manno, a fervent follower of Vittorino: see Franciscus Arisius, *Cremona Literata* (Parma, 1702-6), I, 359, 362; II, 101; and Cicchitelli, pp. 4-5; Luigi Cisorio, "Niccolo Lugari e la scuola Cremonese...," *BSC*, I (1931), 155-172; V. Finzi, "Di Niccolo Lugari," *ibid.*, pp. 111-122. For Marcheselli, see Novati, *ASL*, XXV (1898), 233, and N. Salvatore, *L'arte poetica di M. G. Vida* (Foligno, 1912), p. 116; for Battista Fiera, see C. Dionisotti, *IMU*, I (1958), 401-448.

5. Published in *Collectanea* (Bologna, 1504), a volume to Serafino's memory, ed. by Filoteo Acchillino; the signature "Marcantonio" indicates that Vida had not yet joined the Canons Regular when he wrote these, probably in 1500-1501. On Vida at Mantua, see Cicchitelli, pp. 7-10, and Luzio-Renier, "La Coltura di Isabella d'Este," *GSLI*, XXXIV (1899), 325-326, and *Mantova ed Urbino* (Turin, 1893), pp. 89-94. Vincenzo Lancetti asserted dogmatically that Vida studied also at Padua and Bologna, but can cite only the line from *Parentum*

manibus as proof: "Atque ideo doctas docilem misistis ad urbes" (63). *Della vita e degli scritti di M. G. Vida* (Milan, 1840), p. 9. Cf. Novati, *ASL*, XXV (1898), 233.

6. Nothing more is known of the *Felsineid*: see Leon Doréz, *La Bibliothèque privée du Pape Jules II* (Paris, 1896), p. 17: N. 31, "Hieronymi Vidae Felsinaidos, ex memb., in velluto rubeo."

7. The subject was urged on Vida by Castiglione, to whom he dedicated the work. Giraldi had detailed information about it (*De poetis nostrorum temporum*, ed. K. Wotke [Berlin, 1894], pp. 15-18, 30), as did Paolo Giovio (*De vita et rebus gestis Consalvi* [Rome, 1547], p. 223). The surviving fragment of 894 hexameters was first edited by Luigi Cagnoli (Milan, 1818) and more recently by Luigi Canesi, who also translated it and embarked on a lengthy study: "La sfida di Barletta nel *XIII pugilum certamen* di M. G. Vida," *BSC*, Vols. VIII through XII (1938-1942). For critical observations, see Cicchitelli, pp. 462-483, and Vittorio Cian, *Scritti Minori* (Turin, 1936), II, 147-151.

8. Letters and texts of both poems are given by Vairani, II, 36-60. Tadisi's contention that the *Juliad* was published in 1511 is mistaken: *Vita di Monsignore Vida* (Bergamo, 1788), p. 55. On the *Quercens*, see Cicchitelli, pp. 457-462. The John Rylands Library and the Bodleian possess undated quarto editions of the poem.

9. *Carmina Coryciana,* ed. Blosius Palladius (Rome, 1524). The occasion was the building of a chapel by Sansovino at Goritz's expense. My citations are from Com. II, 157-160. The erudite company of such Academy members as Sadoleto, Bembo, Giovio, Pierio Valeriano, and Gianmatteo Giberti was, no doubt, salutary for Vida, up to a point; it is easy to make too much of this, as Cicchitelli does (pp. 36-37). See Ludwig von Pastor, *Geschichte der Päpste*, IV (Freiburg, 1906), 425-490.

10. The chronology of these poems is difficult to establish. Cicchitelli advances various dates from "internal evidence," but ignores Vida's own testimony in a letter to Mario Equicola, Isabella's secretary, dated January 15, 1520, in which

only the odes are not specifically mentioned as ready for publication: *GSLI*, XXXVI (1900), 343. The principle of organization seems to be size.

11. Cicchitelli, p. 419; G. Carducci, *L'Aminta di T. Tasso* (Florence, 1896), p. 17. On the identification of Corydon, see Cicchitelli, *Sulle Opere in Prosa di M. G. V.* (Naples, 1909), Introduction. Giberti, 1495-1543, brilliant and energetic diplomat and scholar, was secretary to Cardinal Giuliano de' Medici (later Clement VII), and member of the Roman Academy. In 1527 he became Bishop of Verona.

12. The *AP* passage referred to, II. 558-603, is later than the rest of the poem.

13. *Rep.* (Com. II, part 2), pp. 46-48. The reflection on old age may seem premature and affected. But though Vida was in his forties when he wrote this ode, if my conjecture of 1524-1525 is accurate, the recent death of his parents (1523) and a more recent illness had left a strong impression: see *Parentum manibus* and *Scipioni Vegio medico*, Com. II, 143-148 and 154-155.

14. The *LS* and the *B* were both originally composed around 1513; for discussion of a variant text of the *LS*, see T. von der Lasa, *Zur Geschichte und Literatur des Scaachspiels* (Leipzig, 1897), pp. 184-186. Some useful notes on the *LS* may be found in Cicchitelli, pp. 173-196; for a summary, Alberson, pp. 83-87. Imitators of the *Scacchia*, including Marino in the *Adone*, are discussed by Cicchitelli, pp. 196-202. Both Isabella and Leo were devoted chess players: Castiglione, *Il Cortegiano*, II. xxxi; Luzio-Renier, *Mantova ed Urbino*, p. 64. On Vida's place, apparently important, in the history of chess, see H. J. R. Murray, *A History of Chess* (Oxford, 1913), Chap. XI.

15. Belloni purports to find "intento didascalico," then carps that the intent is never fulfilled: *Il Poema Epico e Mitologico* (Milan, n.d. but 1912), pp. 354-355. Jules Lefèvre-Deumier, furiously and almost pathologically anti-Vida, attacks the poem as worthless, frivolous, dull, and useless to one who wants to learn how to play chess: *Études Biographiques et Littéraires* (Paris, 1854), pp. 262-264.

16. Belloni, *ibid.*, observes that Vida has created a new myth and calls the *LS* one of the most notable of the mythological "poemetti" of its time. Critical admiration in general has been extensive, as Cicchitelli attests, while himself misreading it (pp. 174-179, 181); Cicchitelli assigns to it an "aspetto grave" and links it with the abuse of pastimes in Leo's age. He considers the *LS* a rebuke to degeneracy and a call to more genteel pastimes. Flamini sums up his own discussion laconically: "è uscito egregiamente!" (*Il Cinquecento* [Milan, n.d. but 1903], p. 113) Toffanin is the most nearly accurate: "nello *Scacchia ludus* un brivido di sorriso illumina il contrasto fra la sostenutezza del tono e la frivolità del contenuto." (*Il Cinquecento*, 4th ed. [Milan, 1945], p. 47.) For the multiple literary effects—lightness of rhythm, alliterations, apt similes, surprising apostrophes, figurative language, and the almost inexhaustible stock of descriptive words and phrases—see Cicchitelli, pp. 190-195, and Alberson, pp. 76-83. Good examples of light lines are *LS* 50, 69, 225, 305, 339, 369; of alliteration, *LS* 155, 247, 396, 513.

17. Cicchitelli, pp. 187-189; on 187 and 190, C. also notes some "imitations" of Homer.

18. *Poetices* (Basel, 1561), VI, 309. A lengthy summary of the *Bombyx* is given by Alberson, pp. 53-67. Cicchitelli's extensive treatment (pp. 204-281) manages to say strikingly little about the poem itself.

19. Alberson, p. 51 and notes.

20. Letter of June 17, 1519; see *GSLI*, XXXVI (1900), 339. On Lazarelli's *Bombyx* and Giustolo's *De Sere*, see Flamini, p. 586, Cicchitelli, pp. 218-250. On Lazarelli himself, see P. O. Kristeller, *Studies in Renaissance Thought and Letters* (Rome, 1956), pp. 221-248.

21. Vida was not in search of a patroness. By 1519, when he despatched the revised manuscript to her by Castiglione's hand, he was well-established at Frascati and had also a house and a priory in Rome: see Novati, *ASL*, Vol. XXV. Isabella read the manuscript and found it pleasing enough to warrant publication, but it is not clear whether the complicated ne-

gotiations of 1519 and 1520 actually resulted in the undated quarto edition listed by J. G. T. Grässe, *Trésor de livres rares...* VI, 2nd ed. (Dresden, 1867), 303. The University libraries of Cambridge and Munich possess exemplars of this edition. See *GSLI*, XXXVI (1900), 340-342, for the correspondence and details.

22. Mainly Vergil, Ovid, and Lucretius: see Cicchitelli, pp. 227-235, and Alberson, pp. 69 ff.

23. Cicchitelli, pp. 87-173, gives a useful introduction and detailed summary. N. Salvatore, *L'arte poetica*, is thorough on sources, especially pedagogical; his work is derived (without credit) in part from J. A. Vissac, *De Marci Hieronymi Vidae Poeticorum Libris III* (Paris, 1862). Tommaso Sorbelli's "Chiose alla Poetica di M. G. Vida," *BSC*, XIV (1944-1945), 45-75, is a good examination of the *AP* as poetry.

24. On mystery, see, e.g., I. 545-563; II. 367-394, on the poet carried away; II. 395-444, on inspiration; III. 355-363. On spontaneity and genius, see, e.g., I. 55, 244, 276, 318, 435; II. 212, 226-227; III. 349. On importance of deep love of poetry, see I. 84-88; II. 216-231; and the famous closing hymn to Vergil.

25. George Saintsbury, *A History of Criticism* (New York, 1902), II, 32-33. For some parodies, see *AP* I. 154; III. 127, 146-147. For other examples of tongue-in-cheek, II. 20-29; III. 16, 76, 117.

26. On the Cremonese letter, Com. II, v. Hessus, *Epistolae Familiares* III, 64: "Vidam ... tanti facio, ut anno superiori eius tres de poetica libros formis excudi curaverim et publice praelegerim." (1532) See also Hessus, *Carmina* (Halle, 1539), Book V, p. 272; Book IX, p. 830. For Tartessio, Com. II, vii-xvi. See also A. Baldi, "Die *Ars Poetica* des M. Hieronymus Vida," in Carl Ludwig Urlichs, *Festschrift* ... (Würzburg, 1880), pp. 199-212; Arisius, *Cremona Literata* (Parma, 1706), II, 101 ff.

27. Scaliger, *Poetices*, IV, 310-311, VII, 338. Luigi Baldacci, *Il Petrarchismo Italiano nel Cinquecento* (Milan, 1957), p. 4 and n. 4.

28. Saintsbury, II, 26-33. For less antipathetic but simi-

larly wrongheaded notions, see C. Trabalza, *La Critica Lette-raria* (Milan, 1915), pp. 55, 57-58; P. Bernay, *Poétique de Marc-Jérôme Vida* (Paris, 1845), Introduction. See also C. S. Baldwin, *Renaissance Literary Theory and Practice* (New York, 1939), pp. 155-158. There were many editions of the *AP* in 18th-century England. Pope praised it highly, published it, and encouraged Pitt to translate it; Pitt's translation went through dozens of editions and reprintings. A full bibliography, listing editions and translations of Vida's works, is in progress.

29. Alberson, p. 106. For similar comments: Lefèvre-Deumier, pp. 282 ff.; Paul van Tieghem, *La Littérature Latine de la Rénaissance* (Paris, 1944), p. 126. All the matters discussed here will be taken up in more detail in Chapter Two.

30. Giraldi, *De poetis nostrorum temporum*, p. 30. Tartessio, in Com. II, xii. See also Faballo, *ibid.*, part ii, 143-144.

31. Toffanin, pp. 36-48, passim. The implications for Christian epic are developed provocatively by Bonaventura Zumbini.

32. For details on Frascati, the history of the priory, and Vida's tenure there, see G. Tomasetti, "Della Campagna Romana," *Archivio della R. Società Romana di Storia Patria*, XXVIII (1905), 115-124.

33. Sannazaro's poem, fruit of twenty years of labor, was published in 1526. For details on his relationship with Leo, see Toffanin, pp. 42-43, and Giulia Calisti, *Il De Partu Virginis di Jacopo Sannazaro* (Città di Castello, 1926), Chapter II.

34. Clement gave Vida active financial support, including the capitular church of San Lorenzo in Monticelli d'Ongina, near Cremona, in 1524; in 1531 he made Vida a canon of the cathedral in Cremona, and in 1532, archpriest of the church of SS. Maria and Dalmazio. See Novati, *ASL*, XXVI (1899), 26-30, and *passim*; Vittorio Osimo, "La prepositura di Monticelli d'Ongina," *GSLI*, L (1907), 105 ff., and LI (1908), 231 ff.

35. See, e.g., letters of Girolamo Negri, in Ruscelli, *Lettere de' Principi a Principi*, I (Venice, 1564), 95-97 and 107; Augurellus and Zanchius, quoted in Com. II, 162-163, and

164; Georg Ellinger, *Italien und der Deutsche Humanismus* ... (Berlin, 1929), p. 206.

36. M. H. *Vidae Christias*, B. Botta interprete (Pavia, 1569), a large folio work; for a commentary by Girolamo Marcheselli da Lugo, see Com. II, 175 n. On school use, see Botta, "Praefatio"; Faballo, Com. II, part. 2, 145. For Sabinus's comments, see his *Carmina* (Leipzig, 1563), III, p. 91; for Lotichius, see *Bibliotheca poetarum*, II, p. 184. A few years after Vida's death, Nicholas Reusner wrote one of the neatest couplets praising Vida:

Mantua Virgilio, Vidaque Cremona superbit,
Vates hic Christi, Caesaris ille fuit.

(*Poemata* [Jena, 1593], III, p. 190). Zuichemus's letter: *Opus Epistolarum... Erasmi* X, edd. H. M. Allen et H. W. Garrod (Oxford, 1941), 286.

37. For the date, see Osimo, *GSLI*, L (1907), 113.

38. "Il Virgilio Cristiano," p. 106. In the remainder of this chapter, I touch only the high points. I have tried to avoid the confusion of Cicchitelli and Mrs. Alberson, who often read backwards and forwards too easily and impose upon the earlier poetry views which ripened in a new ambience. The political, ecclesiastical, and theological activities in which Vida was involved help to illuminate his character but not his epic. Vida himself lost sight of his original conception of that poem and unwittingly fostered the intentional fallacy; the distinction he made in *Hymn* I, cited *infra*, becomes blurred in later pronouncements.

39. All references to *Hymni* are by numbers; the entire final canon, including three of those in the 1527 edition, is contained in the first volume of the Cominiana, and in standard editions.

40. Com., II, part 2, pp. 47-48. For letter to Bembo, p. 137, and Vairani, II, 30. See also Novati, *ASL*, Vol. XXVI (1899), *passim*.

41. *ASL*, XXVI (1899), 216-217, 220-221, and notes; Com. II, 153-154. The affair is the subject of Vida's touching epigram, *Telluri*.

42. For correspondence with du Bellay, *ASL*, XXVI (1899),

223-224, 228-230, 235-241. Cicchitelli, pp. 58-66, gives more details and references. For Vida's own description of the defense of Alba, see *Orationes tres* ... (Venice, 1764), p. 156. The exact chronology of the years from 1542 to 1562 is difficult to establish. Vida was in Alba a number of times, and though he lived mainly at Cremona or at his San Bassano villa, he was not an absentee prelate. His correspondence indicates conclusively that he was far more effective, under the prevailing conditions, interceding directly in Milan than he could have been in Alba. See Novati, "Delle antiche relazioni fra Trento e Cremona," *ASL*, XXI (1894), 20; and *ASL*, XXV-XXVI (1898-1899), *passim*; Osimo, *GSLI*, L (1907) and LI (1908).

43. Cicchitelli makes the charge: p. 69. Cf. Novati, "Il Virgilio Cristiano," p. 101. In *Gerolamo Vida e la Cristiade* (Palermo, 1900), Lorenzo Gatta writes (pp. 17-19) of the apathy which beset Vida in his episcopal career, but Gatta's notions are founded on an impossible dating of various odes. Vida's close friends, Sadoleto and particularly Giberti, were too closely involved in the problems of reform; the bitter reactions of Sadoleto and others to the Sack of Rome are echoed in Vida's epigram, cited *infra*. That Vida's energetic attack on the heretic problem, as seen in his letters to Paul III and his secretary Marcello Cervini (the future Marcellus II); in his communications with du Bellay; in the hymns he wrote and the reforms he undertook, culminating in the *Constitutiones Synodales*—that all this was not the work of a Johnny-come-lately is indicated sufficiently by letters preceding his taking over Alba: see Novati, *ASL*, XXI (1894), 26 n., and Amadio Ronchini, "Marco Girolamo Vida," *Atti d. R. dep. di storia p. per le prov. Modenesi e Parmensi*, Vol. IV (1866), documents I and II.

44. "Il Virgilio Cristiano," p. 99.

45. *ASL*, XXV (1898), 270-273. In a letter to du Bellay, Vida urges the viceroy not to be half-hearted in handling a fugitive from Alba, a man indicted for preaching heresy: "Non potes hostiam meliorem Deo immortali immolare" (*ASL*, XXV [1898] 235-236). There are at least two cases on record

in which Vida was responsible for a heretic's execution: see
Ronchini, pp. 80-83; F. Gabotto, "Girolamo Vida e una con-
segna al braccio secolare," *Biblioteca delle Scuole italiane*,
IV (1892), 218 ff.; Novati, *ASL*, XXI (1894), 26 n. 1; P. Ri-
voire, "Jérôme Vida et les hérétiques du diocèse d'Alba,"
Bulletin Soc. d'histoire Vaudoise, XLVIII (1926), 107-111.

46. Vairani, II, 32. Novati, "Il Virgilio Cristiano," pp. 99-
100, quotes from an unedited 1546 letter in which Vida
speaks his mind on absentee prelates.

47. The full text of this admirable document was first
given by Novati, *ASL*, XXI (1894), 21-25.

48. Novati, *ASL*, XXI (1894), 27. See also Cicchitelli, pp.
79-80 and notes. At the very end of Vida's long life, Pius V
indicated his intention of making him a cardinal, in recognition of his integrity: see the letter from the Pope's Secretary, dated February 16, 1566, in Vairani, II, 33.

49. *Marci Hieronymi Vidae Cremonensis Albae Episcopi
Poemata omnia tam quae ad Christi Veritatem pertinent quam
ea quae haud plane disiunxit a fabula utraque seorsum ab
alteris.* In a postscript to this edition, Vida insisted on the
unconditional veto he had exercised: "Siquid forte praeterea
ullo umquam tempore adjectum fuerit, adulterinum censeto,
ab aliquo aut maligno, aut in re aliena nimis officioso, ac
diligente adinventum." (Com. II, 156.)

50. Paul Van Tieghem has an interesting comparison of
Vida's elegy with a similar one by Janus Pannonius, written
in 1466: *La Littérature Latine de la Rénaissance* (Paris, 1944),
p. 100.

51. See Georg Ellinger, *Italien und der Deutsche Humanismus* (Berlin, 1929), pp. 206-207.

52. Ellinger points out the amazing impact of these hymns
on German humanism. The long hymns to the Persons of
the Trinity are the closest Germany and Italy come to each
other in humanist lyric; they could almost have been written
by a German humanist, "und an ihrer grossen Wirkung auf
die neulateinische Poesie Deutschlands ist nicht zu zweifeln"
(p. 208.) See also pp. 206-207, 253, 268, 322-323.

53. *Hieronymi Vidae dialogi de rei publicae dignitate* (Cre-

mona, apud Vincentium Contem, 1556). The entire text is given in Com. II, part 2. Toffanin, *L'Umanesimo al Concilio di Trento* (Bologna, 1955), appends a truncated text with Italian translation by A. Altamura (pp. 77-228). Cicchitelli, *Sulle Opere in Prosa di M. G. Vida* (Naples, 1909), pp. 59-128, is the fullest treatment. Alberson, pp. 211-225, gives a detailed summary. The work was dedicated to Cardinal Pole.

54. Pages 67, 84 ff., 102.

55. The work was published anonymously in 1550: *Cremonensium Orationes tres contra Papienses* (Cremona), but sufficient documents on the commission by Cremona, Vida's acceptance, and Vida's composition are extant to prove his authorship. See Ronchini, Documents XII and XIII (pp. 89-91); Vairani, II, 28; F. Gabotto, *Cinque lettere inedite di M. G. Vida* (Pinerolo, 1890), pp. 13-15; Luzio-Renier in *GSLI*, XXXVI (1900), 344 n. The handiest edition of the work is *Orationes tres pro Cremonensibus quae in Cominiana editione desiderantur* (Venice, 1764), ed. by G. C. Bonetti. Cicchitelli, *Prosa*, pp. 2-58; Novati, "Il Virgilio Cristiano," pp. 112-113.

56. See especially pp. 210-219, 1764 edition.

57. From prefatory letter, Com. II, part 2, p. 134. Cicchitelli, *Prosa*, pp. 129-143. The best study is V. Osimo's "Le *Costituzioni Sinodali* di Girolamo Vida," *GSLI*, LVII (1911), 332-347.

58. Osimo, *GSLI*, LVII (1911), 332. Some of the details of Vida's work are drawn from previous works of this kind—e.g., that by Giberti; Vida's constitutions were, in turn, drawn on by Borromeo: Toffanin, p. 49. Clearly enough, Vida has a broad stock not only of experience but also of theological and juridical training, both canon and civil. For his continuing interest in law and theology, see, *inter alia*, remarks in the *Republic*, Com. II, part 2, p. 46, and his letter to Antonio Cuccho, *ibid.*, pp. 135-136.

59. Cicchitelli, *Prosa*, pp. 85-100. The argument was stoutly maintained by Giuseppe Ferrari, *Corso di Scrittori Politici Italiani* (Milan, 1862), pp. 288 ff., but refuted convincingly,

I believe, by Paolo Treves, "Un falso precursore del Rousseau," *La Cultura*, X (1931), 57-62.

60. *Hieronymi Faballi, in M. Hieronymi Vidae... laudem oratio* (Cremona, 1561), cited from Com. II, part 2, p. 147.

61. Lorenzo Giampaoli edited it in 1890: *Orazione Inedita di Marco Girolamo Vida, recitata nel primo concilio provinciale di Milano* (Ferrara, 1890); virtually everything but the text is useless, since Giampaoli assumes, as if unable to read what is before his eyes, that Vida and not Cardinal Borromeo delivered this oration; his erudite notes make amazing suppositious references to Vida's "movements" in the 1560s. The work is studied briefly by Cicchitelli, *Prosa*, pp. 144-148, who finds it "uno degli esempi piú belli di quell'eloquenza che ... ritorna all'antica semplicità dell'Evangelio."

62. See the thirty-seven letters edited by Osimo in *GSLI*, L (1907), 105-115, and LI (1908), 231-250.

63. Cremona, December 8, 1552. Text of both letters: Ruscelli, *Lettere...*, III (Venice, 1577), 219-221; Com. II, part 2, pp. 131-132.

64. See Osimo, *GSLI*, LVII (1911), 333-334. "Il monumento modestissimo è sormontato dall'imagine, assai mediocremente sculta, del Vida e fregiato con il suo stemma familiare e con gli emblemi convenzionali della facoltà poetica."

Chapter Two: Vida's Ars Poetica *and Vergilian Humanism*

1. *Poetices*: see *Epistola ad Sylvium* and *Hypercriticus* IV. 310-311, VII. 338. A useful discussion of *Poetices* as criticism is E. Lintilhac, *De J.-C. Scaligeri Poetice* (Paris, 1887). Actually, Scaliger's intent is to prepare the reader for a demonstration of his own superiority to Vida and, consequently, to Horace and the others.

2. C. S. Baldwin's criticism that the *AP* was "hardly" meant "to interpret what was already too well known" misses the point: *Renaissance Literary Theory and Practice*, p. 158. As both Toffanin and Trabalza point out, the poem was important as the culmination of *Quattrocento* views:

Toffanin, *Cinquecento*, p. 50; Trabalza, *La Critica Letteraria*, pp. 57-58.

3. See especially *Inst.* I. i-iii, v, vi, viii; III. i-iv; VIII. iii, vi; X. i-iv; XI. iii. Plutarch was available in Guarino's Latin version. For Vergerio and Piccolomini, see the English translations in W. H. Woodward, *Vittorino da Feltre...* (Cambridge, 1905). Salvatore, *L'arte poetica di M. G. Vida* (Foligno, 1912) assumes also that Vida knew St. Basil, in Leonardo Bruni's translation, *De legendis libris gentilium*: pp. 12-40. Quintilian is more appropriate than appears at first sight. His ideal of the perfect man and his exaltation of poetry won the affection of both the Renaissance humanists and the Middle Ages: see Eugenio Garin, *Prosatori Latini del Quattrocento* (Milan, 1953), pp. x-xvi, and E. R. Curtius, *European Literature and the Latin Middle Ages*, transl. Willard Trask (New York, 1953), pp. 436-438. The thesis that Horace was Vida's main source was first advanced by A. Pircher, *Horaz und Vida* (Merano, 1895), was picked up by J. E. Spingarn, *A History of Literary Criticism in the Renaissance* (New York, 1908), p. 106, and has been cited as recently as Baldwin, p. 155; but Bruno Cotronei had totally demolished that thesis in *GSLI*, XXX (1897), 459-466. There is no evidence, internal or external, that Vida knew Aristotle's *Poetics*: see Salvatore, pp. 43-47.

4. *AP* I. 459-465. On the acceptance of the practice, see C. S. Lewis, *English Literature in the Sixteenth Century* (Oxford, 1954), p. 357; Alexander Barclay, *Eclogues*, ed. Beatrice White (*EETS*, 1927), p. 1. E. K. says of Spenser that, in writing *The Shepheardes Calender*, he was following "the example of the best and most auncient poetes, which devised this kind of wryting, being both so base for the matter, and homely for the manner, at the first to trye theyr habilities, and, as young birdes that be newly crept out of the nest, by little first to prove theyr tender wyngs, before they make a greater flyght. So flew Theocritus, as you may perceive he was all ready full fledged. So flew Virgile, as yet not well feeling his winges. So flew Mantuane, as being not full somd. So Petrarque. So Boccace. So Marot, Sannazarus,

and also divers other excellent both Italian and French poetes, whose footing this author everywhere followeth." Edmund Spenser, *Works: The Minor Poems*, Volume I, edd. C. G. Osgood et al. (Baltimore, 1943), p. 10.

5. *Vita Donati*, 23-24, in *Appendix Vergiliana*... rec. R. Ellis, ed. C. Hardie (Oxford, 1955).

6. Much of the *AP*'s influence is due to this combination: Vida's moderation, his genial and elegant hexameters, his virtuosity, and the integrity of his life as cleric and Bishop and the acceptability, in the post-Tridentine world, of his classicizing practice.

7. For definition of humanism, P. O. Kristeller, *The Classics and Renaissance Thought* (Cambridge, Mass., 1955), pp. 10-11.

8. *Inferno* VII. 3, VIII. 7; *Purgatorio* XXVII. 130-142. J. B. Fletcher, *Literature of the Italian Renaissance* (New York, 1934), pp. 7, 30-34, 74; Georg Voigt, *Die Wieder-belebung des klassischen Altertums*, 3rd ed. (Berlin, 1893), I, 11-16.

9. Le *Familiari*, Vol. IV per cura di U. Bosco (Florence, 1942), XXIII, 19; see also V, 2. Remigio Sabbadini, *Storia del Ciceronianismo* (Turin, 1885), pp. 7-8. In the letter quoted, Petrarch uses the bee image, familiar in Seneca, *Epistolae* 84.3 and 5; Plutarch, *Moralia* 41F; and Macrobius, *Saturnalia*, Preface. A common image in the Renaissance, its function and meaning differ with each author. See also *Invectiva contra quendam magni status hominem...*, per cura di Pier Giorgio Ricci (Florence, 1949), p. 10.

10. A cura di Nicola Festa (Florence, 1926). See, e.g., II. 299-307; IX. 448-457.

11. There is no need to document Petrarch's fondness for Vergil; abundant references are cited by Vladimiro Zabughin, *Vergilio nel Rinascimento Italiano* (Bologna, 1921-1923), I, 21-38; see also B. L. Ullman, *Studies in the Italian Renaissance* (Rome, 1955), pp. 35-37, 126, 130; and P. de Nolhac, *Pétrarque et l'humanisme* (Paris, 1907), I, 11, 59, 123, 180.

12. Fletcher, pp. 6-7. On Petrarch's patriotism, Voigt, I, 51-64; on *Africa*, A. Belloni, *Il Poema Epico e Mitologico* (Milan, n.d. but 1912), pp. 64-86, and E. M. W. Tillyard,

The English Epic and Its Background (London, 1954), pp. 186-191. The fullest work on the *Africa* appeared too recently for use in this study: Aldo S. Bernardo, *Petrarch, Scipio, and the* Africa (Baltimore, 1962).

13. A cura di P. G. Ricci (Rome, 1950), pp. 69; 66-67, 74. On the general problem, Sabbadini, "Se si possono leggere i poeti antichi," in *Storia del Ciceronianismo*, pp. 92-99; E. K. Rand, *Founders of the Middle Ages* (Cambridge, Mass., 1928), Chaps. I and II.

14. *Epistolario di Coluccio Salutati*, a cura di Francesco Novati, 4 vols. (Rome, 1891-1911), I, 298. On the controversies waged by Salutati over pagan poetry, see Zabughin I, 109-140; V. Rossi, *Il Quattrocento*, 6th ed. (Milan, 1956), pp. 54-59.

15. *Epistolario*, I, 321-323. G. Toffanin, *Storia dell'Umanesimo* (Naples, 1940), p. 142. Voigt, I, 205 f., II, 164.

16. The full text of the letter, written *circa* 1405, is given in Ullman, *Studies*, pp. 251-254; in preceding pages, Ullman sets forth the probable chronology of the Dominici-Salutati correspondence (249-251). *Epistolario*, IV, 170-205, gives the full text of Salutati's answer. Leonardo Bruni, touching on the problem in *De Studiis* (1425), also invokes the name of Lactantius; see Woodward, pp. 130-131, 212-213.

17. Ullman, pp. 249, 251. On the relationship of Dominici and Salutati, see Novati's notes, *Epistolario*, IV, 205-212; on Dominici, see Rossi, *Quattrocento*, pp. 56-57 and n. 90. The *Lucula* was edited recently by Edmund Hunt (Notre Dame, 1940). Garin says of the work that the author's opinions were sincerely and profoundly felt: *L'Educazione umanistica in Italia* (Bari, 1953), pp. 19-20, n. 1.

18. "The matters of Latin usage, grammar, and spelling ... are far more important and significant than might at first sight appear.... The direction the Renaissance was to take was partly determined by these early forays." Ullman, p. 260. See also pp. 34-35, 257-258. Zabughin calls the work a "bewildering patchwork of citations," I, 111. See *Epistolario*, IV, 83-84.

19. *Epistolario*, IV, 229-230; full text, 205-240. Salutati

21

died before completing it. See also *De laboribus Herculis*, ed. B. L. Ullman (Zurich, 1951), I. iii-iv.

20. Garin, *L'Educazione umanistica*, pp. 19-20, 29-38; *Prosatori*, Introduction. Rossi, pp. 57-58, denies the depth of Salutati's moral concern.

21. *Epistolario*, I, 268, 301.

22. Zabughin, I, 120, and nn. 79, 81; Voigt, I, 554-555; Sabbadini, pp. 96-98; *Epistolario di Guarino Veronese*, ed. Sabbadini (Venice, 1915-1919), II, 519-534.

23. Woodward, *Vittorino*, 1-92, 179-250; *Studies in Education during the Age of the Renaissance* (Cambridge, 1906), pp. 1-78. Rossi, pp. 46-54.

24. P. O. Kristeller, *Studies in Renaissance Thought and Letters* (Rome, 1956), pp. 553-583.

25. *The Classics and Renaissance Thought*, p. 80. Rossi, p. 56, dates the translation as roughly 1401. Woodward says the target of Bruni's translation was Giovanni Dominici's *Regola del Governo di Cura Familiare*, which "set the temper of the Dominicans for the next century" (p. 120). But Rossi shows, p. 59, that, with the gradual easing of tensions, the friars adopted quite different positions by mid-century. The defenses in the middle third of the *Quattrocento*, Rossi suggests, were really "voci di vittoriosi."

26. *Le Quattrocento* (Paris, 1901), I, 212.

27. See Curtius, pp. 436-438; Woodward, pp. 10-27. Piccolomini demanded "fruitful activity"; to Vergerio's mind, there was always the danger of speculative thought becoming too self-regarding: Woodward, pp. 155, 110.

28. Zabughin, I, 177; 140, n. 75. Vegio, *De perseverantia religionis*, I, 1, quoted by A. C. Brinton, *Maphaeus Vegius and His Thirteenth Book of the Aeneid* (Stanford, 1930), p. 3. Vegio, *De educatione liberorum*, ed. M. W. Fanning (Washington, 1933), II, 9; 18; 19; Woodward, pp. 45, 165; 149; and see Zabughin, I, 122-125, and nn. 95-122.

29. *De studiis et literis*, in Woodward, pp. 125, 129, 131-132.

30. *De liberorum educatione*, in Woodward, p. 151; *De ordine docendi et studendi, ibid.*, pp. 170, 168, 175.

31. Angeli Decembrii Mediolanensis, *De politia literaria libri septem* (Basel, 1562). I am grateful to Professor Kristeller, who loaned me a microfilm of this edition. The *Politia* is discussed briefly by Sabbadini, and by Karl Vossler, *Poetische Theorien in der Italienische Frührenaissanz* (Berlin, 1900); Anita della Guardia treats it in some detail in a monograph, misleadingly titled *La Politia literaria di Angelo Decembrio e l'umanesimo a Ferrara* ... (Modena, 1910); this study is mainly concerned with the life of Leonello d'Este, one of the participants. It is useful for details about some of the characters, pp. 41-65; the *Politia* itself receives only cursory treatment, pp. 67-78. Trabalza analyzes the work briefly, *La Critica Letteraria*, pp. 25-33. Zabughin's treatment is concentrated but helpful: II, 3-10 and 36-46, nn. 3-53. The major participants are Guarino Veronese, Leonello, Tito Strozzi, and the author. The seven books run to a total of 103 chapters and 674 octavo pages. The work was dedicated to Pius II (Piccolomini).

32. *Politia* is derived from *polire*, an unclassical usage justified at length in the second chapter.

33. Pages 5-8, 16-20, 21-29, 40. The Vergilian fervor here is, in part, Angelo's reply to his brother, Pier Candido, who glorified Homer at Vergil's expense: Zabughin, II, 3, and nn.

34. Pages 41, 50-51, 54. The Greek authors are discussed generally in terms of the Latin translations available.

35. Chapters 32-51.

36. See Woodward, pp. 45-47, 229-230, 234.

37. Chapter 69.

38. Chapter 64, pp. 471-475. While the rejection of Dante is becoming anachronistic, it shows a frame of mind common to many Latinists down to Vida. See, e.g., Bruni's *Dialogi ad Petrum Histrum*, in Garin, *Prosatori*, pp. 44-99, for major statements which persist long after they have been generally discredited. The rejection of Greek was similarly a rear-guard action. See also Rossi, pp. 105-110.

39. Page 40.

40. Cf. Zabughin, I, 200-201.

41. Pages 480-481; 48, 50, 516, 518, 520.

42. Pages 67-74.

43. Pages 21, 29. This is a strange judgment, unless by *materia* is meant detail of epic composition—battles, journeys, similes, the descent, etc.

44. Noteworthy that in these discussions *Aeneid* IV is singled out as "una Vergilii pars praestantissima"—a judgment shared by Landino, Pontano, Vida, and Ronsard, among others.

45. Pages 480-482, 530-531.

46. Page 300.

47. Pages 67-74; pp. 471-475.

48. *Africa*, IX. 90-102. See also Boccaccio, *De genealogia deorum*, XIV. On Petrarch, Boccaccio, and Landino, see Sabbadini, "Sull'allegoria dei poeti, specialmente di Vergilio," *Storia*, pp. 103-111.

49. Salutati, *De laboribus Herculis*, IV (tractate 2), x. 14 (p. 582); I. ii. 12 (p. 13); II. ii. 14 (p. 86). Cf. *Epistolario*, IV, 49.

50. I. ii. 19 (pp. 15-16).

51. I. xii. 11 (pp. 64-65). The fourth book of *De laboribus* is devoted largely to allegorical interpretation of the sixth *Aeneid*—pp. 449-582.

52. Woodward, *Vittorino*, p. 130.

53. *De educatione liberorum*, II, 18-19.

54. *Aeneid* I. 198-207; Vegio, *De perseverantia*, translated by Brinton, *Maphaeus Vegius*, p. 28.

55. Brinton, p. 2.

56. *Interpretationes in P. Vergilium* (Florence, 1487); *Disputationes Camaldulenses* (Basel, 1577). The discussions took place in the summer of 1468 at Camaldoli; the first edition was apparently published in 1480. On the *Disputationes*, see Zabughin, I, 194-202 and 214-225, nn. 67-118; Rossi, pp. 334-335.

57. Zabughin, I, 198, and n. 96; see *Interpretationes*, proem; *Disputationes*, 3051.

58. Zabughin, I, 199; *Disputationes*, 3004.

59. *Disputationes*, 3026-3032.

60. See M. Y. Hughes, *Virgil and Spenser* (Berkeley, 1929), pp. 402-405.

61. Zabughin suggests, I, 194-196, that Landino's commen-

tary is medieval in tone and cites some Dantean readings and the rigorous approach to detail; he does not recognize the advance that the *Disputationes* represents: Landino "sente Vergilio attraverso Dante." The remark distorts context. Zabughin does admit that "egli seppe affinare il proprio giudizio estetico, le facoltà critiche" (p. 201).

62. Rossi, p. 335. In *Disputationes*, 3029, Landino declares that Dante showed his understanding of Vergil's allegory by his admirable imitation of it, and elsewhere he suggests the approval of Petrarch, but he differs essentially from both, as well as from the medievalizing Filelfo. See Zabughin, I, 198-199, 220-221, 223-225, nn. 98, 100, 117; Sabbadini, *Storia*, pp. 105-107.

63. Hughes, p. 406. On his influence, Hughes, pp. 399-402.

64. *Disputationes*, 3023, 3024. Compare Vida's letter to the Patres of Cremona, and the concluding passage of *AP* III. The meaning Vida would give "allegory" is problematic; certainly, the *Christiad* is constructed on a design that has some elements in common with allegory. But any suggestions of "influence" here must be very tentative; Vida's only remarks on the matter are those discussing the decadence of certain obscure and confusing poets, gratuitous displayers of their erudition: *AP* II. 191-204.

65. Bruni, *Ad Petrum Histrum*, in Garin, pp. 68-74, 84-96.

66. The remark is still being made in Erasmus's time. See Voigt, I, 381-385; for full discussion of Dante and Petrarch in the *Quattrocento*, see W. Binni, *I Classici Italiani nella Storia della Critica* (Florence, 1954), I, 18-26, 97-106, and references there.

67. See Sabbadini, p. 15-31; Voigt, II, 139, 448; 147-150, 462-466. Ferruccio Ulivi, *L'Imitazione nella Poetica del Rinascimento* (Milan, 1959), pp. 10-11; Rossi, pp. 87-90 and nn.

68. In Garin, *Prosatori*, p. 596. On Bembo and Pico, see G. Santangelo, *Il Bembo Critico e il Principio d'Imitazione* (Florence, 1950), pp. 46-60; Ulivi, *L'Imitazione*, pp. 16-22, 27-32, 35-47; Sabbadini, pp. 26-31, 33-42. See also Lefèvre-Deumier, *Études Biographiques*, pp. 256-258; Fletcher, *Italian Renaissance*, pp. 244-248, discusses some interesting results.

69. The *Oratio* is available in Garin, *Prosatori*, pp. 870-884; for the *Sylvae*, Angelo Poliziano, *Le Selve e la Strega*, per cura di Isidoro del Lungo (Florence, 1925). *Ambra*, third of the four *Sylvae*, prefaced Poliziano's course on the *Iliad* at the Studio Fiorentino, 1485-1486. A devotee of Homer, Poliziano never joined the anti-Vergil party however. See Zabughin I, 122-124; II, 20-25.

70. *Manto*, 351-352, 353, 362; *Inferno* I. 87; II. 67. Compare the conventional praises by Benedetto Colucci, humanist of Pistoia, in his *Oratio ante lectionem Virgilii* (early 1470's): "Divinus poeta...; divini vatis artificium insigne." Benedetto's theme: "quo juvenes... huius artificium vigiliis ac laboribus quaeritantes libentiore animo assequantur." *Scritti inediti... a cura di A. Frugoni* (Florence, 1939), pp. 57-60.

71. For the letters, Garin, *Prosatori*, pp. 902-910. Cf. Petrarch: "Multo malim meus michi stilus sit, incultus licet atque horridus..." (*Fam.* V, 2.); speaking of Vergil, whom he loves above all, "Curandum imitatori ut quod scribit simile non idem sit.... Utendum igitur ingenio alieno utendum coloribus, abstinendum verbis; illa enim similitudo latet, hec eminet; illa poetas facit, hec simias.... Ex multis et variis unum fiat, idque aliud et melius." (*Fam.* XXXII, 19.)

72. *Le Epistole "De Imitatione" di Giovanfrancesco Pico della Mirandola e di Pietro Bembo*, a cura di Giorgio Santangelo (Florence, 1954), pp. 28, 31-33, 36. The debates from which these tracts are derived took place in 1512. Pico's letter is dated September 19, 1512; Bembo's answer, January 1, 1513.

73. *De Imitatione*, pp. 27, 42-43; pp. 54, 56, 57-60.

74. Giovanni Pontano, *I Dialoghi*, a cura di C. Previtera (Florence, 1943), pp. 146-147, 161; see Vida on variety, *AP* III. 23-43. *Actius*, the longest of Pontano's dialogues, was published posthumously by Summonte at Naples in 1507.

75. *Dialoghi*, pp. 202-203; cf. *AP* III. 217-222 and 257-262.

76. F. J. E. Raby, *A History of Christian-Latin Poetry* (Oxford, 1953), 2nd ed., pp. 61-63; 17; 108-109. Pierre de Labriolle, *Histoire de la Littérature Latine Chrétienne* (Paris,

1947), 3rd ed., pp. 716-720; 468, 471-472; 732-736. The early *Cinquecento* saw a kind of culmination of the interest in these poets and others, e.g., Arator for his *De actibus Apostolorum* and Avitus for his short epics on the creation and the fall. In 1500 Fausto Andrelini, lecturing at Paris, chose Juvencus for his text, and subsequently edited the poem; his introduction to that edition attempted to recapture the sense of conflict that had animated the poet. See Belloni, *Il Poema Epico*, pp. 329-330; Watson Kirkconnell, *The Celestial Cycle* (Toronto, 1952), p. xix.

77. The work was dedicated to Bessarion. See Zabughin, *Vergilio nel Rinascimento*, II, 180-181 and 207-209, nn. 2-13. *Crisias* II. 233-237; cf. II. 168-171, 175-177, all quoted in Zabughin.

78. *Crisias* II. 79-83, quoted in Zabughin II, 209. See also the remark about the allegory of Hercules' labors and how it applies to Christ:

Virtutis cultor: vitiorum ultor severus

Usque fuit passus graves durosque labores

Alcidae laudabit iter.... (*Crisias* II. 175-177)

79. Ed. Josep Badalic (Zagreb, 1954). Kept from publication by certain heterodox details, the work circulated in MS. Another edition has appeared recently (Merida, Venezuela, 1957), edited by Miroslav Markovic from the same MS. On Marulic and another Croatian humanist, Jakov Bunic or Jacobus de Bona, see Ante Kadic, "Croatian Renaissance," *Studies in the Renaissance*, VI (1958), 28-35.

80. *Davidias*, ed Badalic, p. 213. Marulic may have known Salutati's *De laboribus*, but he certainly knew Bona's *De raptu Cerberi*, and allegorical-mythological poem influenced by Salutati, published in Rome, 1490, and later in Venice, 1500, and Basel, 1538. See Badalic, p. 228. While the details of Bona's epic follow Seneca's tragedy *Hercules*, the language is wholly Vergilian: Kadic, *Studies*, 32-33.

81. Cicchitelli, *Sulle Opere Poetiche di M. G. Vida*, pp. 117-119; Zabughin I, 279, 287-302, 313-345, nn. 69-217; *idem*, *Un Beato Poeta* (Rome, 1917), pp. 21-22; Belloni, Chapter IV, *passim*. Noteworthy that most of these humanists

preferred the latter six books of the *Aeneid* for their model.

82. Belloni, pp. 27-31, 35-54, discusses all these in detail. Only the *Berengarius* attempts to be epic in the true sense— not adhering conspicuously to historical detail, it attempts epic scope. Even Mussato attempted an historical epic: Belloni, pp. 59-60.

83. In the *Gesta Federici*, the "least" classical of these, Belloni reports 500 examples of verses plagiarized or semi-plagiarized, 450 of them from Vergil: p. 47. The cento-form, incidentally, was completely out of favor in the *Quattrocento*.

84. Rossi, *Quattrocento*, pp. 284-286; Giulia Calisti, *Il De Partu Virginis di Jacopo Sannazaro: Saggio sul poema sacro nel Rinascimento* (Città di Castello, 1926), pp. 12-13.

85. Calisti, p. 13; see also Belloni, p. 327. The attitude of Ugolino Verino, contemporary of Buonincontri and Corella, seems not untypical; in advancing years, he renounced the profane poetry of his youth and attempted a paraphrase (never completed) of parts of the Old and New Testament. In 1491 he wrote to Savonarola, inveighing vehemently against those who preferred pagan vanities to Christian substance, elegance to piety, and erudition to knowledge: "inflati non dico scientia, sed vano dicendi fuco depicti, nihil arbitrantur posse diserte loqui, si quod Christianitatis nomen attigerint, velut sit barbarum abhorrent.... Jovem quam Christum, tyrsum quam crucem, Junonem et Bacchum quam Mariam et Johannem malunt nominare." Quoted from A. Lazzari, *Ugolino e Michele Verino* (Turin, 1897), p. 103, in Calisti, pp. 13-14.

86. Belloni, p. 328. On the numerous MS. copies and printed editions of the *Antonias*, see Zabughin, *Vergilio* II, 207. For its humanist characteristics, Rossi, pp. 283-284; Cicchitelli, pp. 116-117.

87. The *Jesuida* was completed *circa* 1445; Dalle Valli lived *circa* 1420-1472. For the MS. copies, Zabughin, II, 207; there were at least five printed editions between 1509 and 1517, but the poem lost favor by the middle of the sixteenth century; the last edition was published in 1559. See Roberto Cessi, "Un poemetto cristiano del secolo 15," in *Raccolta di Studi ... a Fr. Flamini* (Pisa, 1918), pp. 681-691.

88. Cicchitelli, p. 119; Zabughin, *Beato Poeta*, p. 19; *La Partenice Mariana di Battista Mantovano*, con introduzione, traduzione metrica, e note di Ettore Bolisani (Padua, 1957), p. 7.

89. Zabughin, *Un Beato Poeta*, p. 21; *Vergilio*, I, 287-302. Zabughin studies at length the curious influence of the Middle Ages—especially Dante and the vision-poems—on Mantuan's work, and the indirect way this influence might have been exerted on Vida and Sannazaro.

90. Zabughin, *Un Beato Poeta*, p. 37; Giraldi, *De poetis nostrorum temporum*, p. 10; Zabughin, *Vergilio*, I, 243-246, and 269-272, nn. 76-98.

91. Belloni, pp. 328-330; B. Zumbini, *Studi di Letteratura Comparata* (Bologna, 1931), p. 39; A. Feliciangeli, "Notizie sulla vita e sulle opere di Macario Muzio," *Scritti Storici* (Venice, 1915), pp. 230 ff. Gaetano Moroncini, *Sulla Cristiade di Marco Girolamo Vida* (Trani, 1896), pp. 45-49.

92. L. Gatta, *Vida e la Cristiade*, pp. 34-39; Moroncini, pp. 42-45. Cf. Bruno Cotronei, *GSLI*, XXXI (1898), 364-365, who cites two minor connections.

93. "Tanta parte di quella mitologia... tratta dietro a sé non l'argomento cristiano, ma piuttosto la forma che il poeta avesse scelto a trattarlo." Zumbini, p. 72. Zumbini's entire discussion of the *De Partu* (pp. 63-72) is admirable. But cf. Saint-Marc Girardin, on both Vida and Sannazaro, in *Tableau de la littérature française ... suivi d'études sur la littérature ... de la Rénaissance* (Paris, 1862), pp. 237-269. For detailed discussion of epic and classical qualities in the poem, see Belloni pp. 331-337; Zabughin, II, 181-187 and 210-223, nn. 16-57.

94. Rossi, pp. 282-283.

95. Moroncini, pp. 20-23.

96. *Cinquecento*, p. 106. See also Toffanin, *Cinquecento*, pp. 41-42.

97. Belloni, p. 329.

98. Rome, 1526. See Zabughin, II, 188-190 and 224-225, nn. 64-70. Calisti, p. 16, remarks: "Bona chiama suo maestro

Virgilio.... Il suo racconto ha un andamento epico, ma i fatti
sono troppo diluiti per avere forza drammatica... e le situazioni
non sempre indovinate."

99. Carlo Dionisotti in *IMU*, I (1958), 401-418; of Fiera's
Audina (1537), which celebrates Italy and the person and
poetry of Vergil allegorically, Dionisotti remarks: "È docu-
mento notevole della persistenza di una interpretazione alle-
gorica in età che sempre piú volgeva a una imitazione rigoro-
samente stilistica" (p. 410). See Moroncini, p. 126.

100. "Un poemetto cristiano," pp. 684, 690.

101. Otello Andolfi, *Il poema del cristianesimo* (Rome,
1907), discusses possible influences of Juvencus on Vida:
pp. 22-30. Calisti, pp. 60-61, suggests some minor influences
on Vida by Paracleto Fosco dei Malvezzi's *Passionis Dominicae
libri duo*, an unedited epic of the fifteenth century, by Mantuan, and by Bona.

102. Cicchitelli, p. 120.

103. In the *Politia literaria*, chap. 57.

Chapter Three: The Vergilian Framework

1. A detailed summary of the *Christiad* is given in the
appendix. I do not propose to trouble the reader with detailed
comparisons between Vida's epic and the innumerable Vergilian epics from Statius to Sannazaro; my major point of
departure will be the *Aeneid*. We can fairly assume that the
author of the *AP*, who scorned so majestically the attempts
of lesser poets, went directly to the master for guidance. Once
we have determined Vida's strategy vis-à-vis the *Aeneid*, it
will be possible to examine with some value the relationship
of Vida's achievement to the body of the tradition.

2. Lucretius, *De rerum natura* I. 1-43. Vida probably considered the *Aeneid* not completely revised; this is suggested
not only by his conclusion but also by the absence of Vergilian
half-lines. Donatus's statement on the matter was widely interpreted in Vida's time as referring to the half-lines and
repetitions as well as the conclusion of the *Aeneid*: "Ac ne
quid impetum moraretur, quaedam imperfecta transmisit, alia

levissimis versibus veluti fulsit, quos per iocum pro tibicinibus interponi aiebat ad sustinendum opus, donec solidae columnae advenirent." *Vita Donati*, 24. But the incompleteness is mainly stylistic; at most, Vida would have considered only a few lines necessary after the death of Turnus. See Karl Büchner, *P. Vergilius Maro* (Stuttgart, 1958), columns 402-404. See also *infra*, on Vegio's *Supplementum*.

3. Eduard Norden, *Aeneis Buch VI* (Leipzig, 1903), ad VI. 264. In *AP* II. 25-29, Vida cites genially the necessity for frequent invocations to the appropriate tutelary deities.

4. *Iliad* XVI. 112-113; *Argonautica* III. 1-5; *Aen.* VI. 264-267; VII. 37-45; IX. 525-529; *Chr.* II. 316-322; V. 200-210; VI. 110-120.

5. Compare Milton in *Paradise Lost* IX. 13-47, announcing his

> Sad task, yet argument
> Not less but more heroic than the wrath
> Of stern Achilles ...

and asking from his "celestial patroness... answerable style" for the "higher argument."

6. *Aen.* IX. 446-449. T. E. Page considers XII. 500-504 apostrophe rather than invocation: *The Aeneid... Books VII-XII...* (London, 1955), p. 446. Vida has eight apostrophes.

7. *Chr.* V. 721-742; *Aen.* VI. 883-886. Cf. Lucan, *De bello civili* I. 7-32, the apostrophe to Rome, or VIII. 823-872, the apostrophe to Egypt which betrayed Pompey.

8. *Chr.* V. 211-224, *De bello civili* VII. 1-44; *Chr.* II. 119-132, *De bello civili* I. 183-212.

9. E. M. W. Tillyard, *The English Epic and Its Background* (London, 1954), pp. 6-8.

10. *Chr.* II. 316-322. See *Iliad* II. 484-493, which Vergil imitates in *Aen.* VII. 641-646; see also *Aen.* X. 163-165.

11. *Chr.* II. 356-383; 515-517; 405-421; 518-529. Cf. Cicchitelli, *Sulle Opere Poetiche di M. G. Vida*, pp. 305-306. The discussion of such elements as the catalogue in *AP* II. 232-238 and 191-204 invokes the authority and practice of Vergil.

12. The Apostles get 24 lines in Book IV, mainly devoted to highlighting their humble origin; the devils get even less in Book I.

13. E.g., the founding of Carthage and the establishment of the temple there: *Aen.* I. 338-368, 441-449.

14. III. 800-870. *La Cristiade*, tr. Tommaso Perrone (Naples, 1733), pp. 157-158, nn. 50-58. Botta, *ad loc.*

15. Cf. *Ludus Troiae* in *Aen.* V. 545-603. *Chr.* II. 663-670, V. 412-419.

16. The history of the feast and Simon's song provide preparation; the scene itself consists merely of Christ's words over the bread and wine, the washing of the feet, and the predictions of betrayal and denial.

17. *Chr.* II. 556-642; see *Aen.* I. 740-746. The song about Hercules in *Aen.* VIII is even less relevant.

18. *Chr.* III. 190-196; *De partu virginis* III. 331-497. Cicchitelli, pp. 314-315.

19. Perrone cites the view of many commentators that an angel was sent to Pilate's wife Portia in a dream, to speed on the work of redemption: p. 249, n. 22.

20. III. 405-445. Joseph says of himself: "Mens adeo mihi laeva fuit," and of the angel:

> Verum eadem in somnis pueri redeuntis imago
> Visa mihi, vultusque, habitusque simillimus illi
> Ipsa sibi modo quem memorabat sponsa loquutum.
>
> (405-407)

As for the revelations by the angel:

> Meque ipsum incuso amens: et lux reddita menti,
> Inque dies magis, atque magis caeli alta patescunt
> Consilia, antiquis quae vatibus omnia quondam
> Obscuris vera involvens Deus ostendebat.
>
> (452-455)

He goes on then to detail the types of Mary from the Old Testament which he finally understood.

21. II. 93-112. Satan-Ioras finds Judas *insomnem*, but the apparition has the character of a dream. The form, and some of the language, most resembles Allecto's apparition to Turnus in *Aen.* VII. 406-459; Turnus, however, is fully skeptical

of the preternatural qualifications of this apparition and has to be convinced.

22. *Aen.* II. 270-301; III. 147-171; IV. 554-570. See A. H. Weston, "Three Dreams of Aeneas," *CJ*, XXXII (1937), 229-232. Weston cites the "curious lapse of memory" in Aeneas's dream of Hector, and the shouts, screams, and clash of arms of which he is aware (II. 299-301) before he awakes. The "essential principle" involved in dreams is clearly recognized in Cicero's *Somnium Scipionis.*

23. *Chr.* IV. 462-465; IV. 308; V. 306.

24. Reminiscences like *concilium horrendum* (I. 134—see *Aen.* III. 679) are very minor. There are some details for the citizens of hell in *Aen.* VI. 285-289; Satan, however, resembles Claudian's Allecto (*In Rufinum* I. 28 ff.) Cicchitelli hunts too vigorously for *attinenze* (pp. 340-347). On the traditional view of the mythological deities, Augustine's *Civitas Dei* would seem the major authority.

25. *Chr.* I. 666-673; II. 22-64, 133 ff., 196-215; V. 101 ff., 175 ff., 255-281, 306-325; IV. 604-655; 439-531.

26. Gatta compares Vida's underworld scenes with Dante's: "Il suo limbo ... è topograficamente quello dell'Alighieri e una parte degli abitatori è accennata quasi con le stesse parole del IV dell'*Inferno*...." He goes on with other points of contact between the Italian and the Latin poet, emphasizing particularly Vida's Christ descending into hell to free the souls of the just, and suggests that Milton's vast architectonic conception was derived from Vida's scenes: "Quanta somiglianza ha il Cristo del Vida con quello che Dante ci fa immaginare parlando dell'alta vittoria, che il Salvatore aveva riportato sulla porta, la quale senza serrame ancor si trova!... Ciò ... è la prima volta che ci vien data dell'Averno una descrizione, che ha la misura e la solennità delle concezioni architettoniche del Milton, il quale intorno all'impalcatura ed ossatura dell'edificio del Vida sovrapporrà i materiali ed animerà gli abitatori col fuoco dell'anima sua ardente e vigorosa." (*Vida e la Cristiade*, pp. 50-51.) For Dante's Harrowing, *Inf.* IV. 25-63. The just evoke faintly Vergil's blessed in the Elysian fields: *Aen.* VI. 637-638.

27. Some angels are derived from the Gospels: the angel stirring the waters at the Pool of Siloe (I. 452-461); consoling Christ in the garden (II. 760-764); announcing the Incarnation, explaining to Joseph, appearing to the shepherds (III. 319-398, 405-455, 608-625). Others are traditional: the angels who minister to Mary in her pregnancy, guide the Holy Family through Egypt, minister to the youthful Christ (III. 516 ff., 849-870, 896-918). The splendid angels of the Ascension (VI. 684-800) need no source. That Vida's own century highly approved of his angelology is apparent from frequent imitation—Tasso's in the *Gerusalemme* (IV. 1-19), Valvasone's in the *Angeleida.* Zabughin goes so far as to suggest that Vida's example spurred the development of a full-scale angelology and demonology: *Vergilio* II, 192-194, and nn. on 246-250 and 231-235. For Milton's use of this scene, see Cicchitelli, p. 360.

28. *Chr.* I, 693-724; II. 359-383. See Perrone, p. 107, n. 167.

29. Cicchitelli, pp. 359-361. Gatta, pp. 66-75, considers this passage Vida's best; he sees in it the germs of those "wonderful books" of *Paradise Lost.* Moroncini, *Sulla Cristiade*, pp. 78-81, finds the scene "epicamente inefficace," a judgment with which Bruno Cotronei sharply disagrees: *GSLI*, XXXI (1898), 367.

30. Petrarca, *Invective Contra Medicum*, ediz. crit. a cura di P. G. Ricci (Rome, 1950), III, 300-305 (p. 67). See also *Africa* IX. 90-105.

31. Saint-Marc Girardin, *Tableau de la littérature française...*, pp. 237-269. To a lesser extent, Girardin's confusion informs and vitiates much of the criticism of Cicchitelli, Gatta, Moroncini, and C. S. Lewis.

32. *Chr.* I. 943-946. The striking simile is expanded from the suggestion in Matthew 17:2—"resplenduit facies ejus sicut sol."

33. P. Papini Stati *Thebais et Achilleis*, rec. H. W. Garrod (Oxford, 1906), XII. 810-815. Petrarch, *Africa*, IX. 229-238. More lines of similar burden follow. One critic has attempted to defend Vida's passage as showing both his pro-

found piety and his feeling for his native city: "Essa ci mostra non solo la profonda religiosità del poeta e del pastore, ma ben anco l'amor suo per la patria Cremona." Guido Bigoni, "Per un poema sacro del Cinquecento," *Ateneo Veneto*, XIX (1896), 139. Bigoni is apparently thinking of the suggestion, *AP* II. 232-238, that poets should praise their homeland; that hardly excuses this lapse in taste. Vergil's oblique reference to Mantua in the *Aeneid* is hardly comparable here.

34. For general discussion, see George E. Duckworth, *Foreshadowing and Suspense in the Epics of Homer, Apollonius, and Vergil* (Princeton, 1933), and Clifford H. Moore, "Prophecy in the Ancient Epic," *HSCP*, XXXII (1921), 98-175, whose scope is broader than Duckworth's, but whose treatment is far less perceptive.

35. Christ's death foreshadowed: I. 38-45, 684-724, 842-845; II. 656-662, 681-683; III. 720-728. Related events: II. 684-691 (betrayal), 714-724 (denial); III. 146-158; 337-349, 356-368, 612-615, 806-815.

36. I. 687-724; II. 405-422, 518-529; IV. 817-829.

37. E.g., the destiny of Rome is first hinted at in I. 579-580; the trials of the Apostles are suggested in I. 51-59, 890-896; the betrayal by Judas is first hinted in I. 880 ff.

38. Helenus—*Aen.* III. 374-462; Venus—II. 598-623; Hector—II. 268-297; Creusa—II. 771-791; oracles and omens—III. 84-120, 147-191, 527-547.

39. *Chr.* V. 367-368; VI. 161-197; IV. 981-1028; VI. 640-647.

40. *Chr.* I. 591-724; V. 589-617; VI. 349-368.

41. Perrone, p. 46, n. 52.

42. *Iliad* XVIII. 483-608; *Aen.* VI. 724-751. See also Hesiod, *Shield of Herakles*, 140-317. On the style, see Cicchitelli, pp. 301 ff., where he shows the particular importance of Lucretius' last book. The most striking adaptation from the shield of Aeneas passage, *Aen.* VIII. 626-731, is Vida's use of the symbolic closing lines:

> dona parentis
miratur, rerumque ignarus imagine gaudet,
attollens umero famamque et fata nepotum.

Chapter Four: The Vergilian Style

1. *Chr.* V. 457, 555, 781; VI. 105, 628, 698, 806. See *AP* III. 267-293. The breeding is important, though exotic or unusual words from barbaric tongues need not be excluded. Vida exemplifies by incorporating words like the Gallic *essedum* or *sarissa* (*AP* III. 290-291). Cf. Horace, *Ars poetica* 48-72.

2. See the exemplary passage in *AP* III. 295-298:

licet tua, sancta vetustas,
Vatibus indugredi sacraria. saepius olli
Aetatis gaudent insignibus antiquai,
Et veterum ornatus induti incedere avorum.

To this he adds, *his modus adsit.*

3. Compare Vergil's use of *olli* in *Aen.* VI. 321; IX. 740; XII. 18, 537; and his use of *quoi* for *cui* in *Aen.* I. 267; VI. 812; XII. 225, 392. See also *queis* for *quibus* in *Chr.* III. 731; IV. 242; V. 171. Cf. *Aen.* I. 95; VII. 444; VII. 742.

4. Cf. *Aen.* VII. 464, *aquai*; IX. 26, *pictai*. See Ennius, Fragment 99: *terrai frugiferai.*

5. Cf. *Aen.* IV. 493, *accingier*; VII. 70, *dominarier*; VIII. 493, *defendier.*

6. *Institutiones Oratoriae* VIII. iii. 25.

7. The exception is *Aen.* VI. 103. See M. N. Wetmore, *Index Verborum Vergilianus* (New Haven, 1911), s.v. See also Page, *The Aeneid...* I-VI (London, 1955), p. 159, where he cites Conington's disapproval of Vergil's use of *heros* and the statistical observations of A. Calvert.

8. See II. 144, 335, 414, 580.

9. I. 256, 266; 405; 516; 961. See also 936 (the transfiguration itself)—*Christus.*

10. II. 149, 776; IV. 392, 492, 608, 667, 704, 856; VI. 322, 438, 471, 489.

11. See also III. 342.

12. II. 533, 580; 991. IV. 364. VI. 538.

13. *English Literature in the Sixteenth Century* (Oxford, 1954), p. 26. See also Gatta, p. 79; Cicchitelli, pp. 316 ff.,

416-418; to these compare Zumbini, *Studi di Letteratura Comparata*, pp. 44-46, 60, 67-68.

14. The scorn of J. A. Symonds is echoed by Tillyard, *The English Epic and Its Background*, p. 220. See also Lewis, pp. 24 ff.

15. Vida's use of periphrasis is occasionally Statian: cf. the injunction in the *AP* to avoid naming the hero. The Statian manner appears in this passage, when Vida thus identifies the two figures who join Christ at the Transfiguration:

> ... quorum alter adivit
> Flammifero quondam invectus caeli ardua curru,
> Et tranavit, equis insultans, aeris auras:
> Isacidum Phariis genus alter duxit ab oris
> Dux profugum, legesque dedit, moremque sacrorum.
>   (I. 948-952)

Another periphrasis of this sort is more recondite: the leader of the mobilizing angels in Book V is identified, in part, as *dux*

> Nuper Iapygii Gargani, e vertice vectus
> Armipotens...   (V. 578-580)

Perrone identifies Iapygius Garganus as the mountain where the archangel Michael was venerated because of his apparition there at the time of Pope Gelasius I (p. 251, n. 30). Clearly, the erudite allusion is an attempt at pleasing variation and surprise, with some enhancement deriving from the formalism of the manner.

16. *The Christiad of Vida*, translated... (Cambridge, 1768). The almost contemporary translation by Edward Granan (1771), which I have inspected cursorily, seems somewhat more adequate and stylistically consistent. Vida's *atros* is reasonably appropriate for a description of water being *turned into* wine.

17. For other examples, see *amicum* (III. 17) or *pater* (III. 294).

18. The same technique is employed in Joseph's description of the Nativity, III. 571-594, and, in lesser degree, in the description of hell and its inhabitants, VI. 128-160.

19. Cicchitelli, p. 303; Gatta, pp. 79-80.

20. A few of the morning descriptions occur in II. 964-

22.

965; III. 301-302; V. 82; V. 420. The translation of V. 429
in the text was adapted from Gertrude Georgina Coyne's
translation, in *An Edition of the Christiad with Introduction,
Translation, and Notes....* Dissertation, Cornell, 1939. See also
her note on the passage.

21. *Institutiones oratoriae* VIII. vi; IX. i; IX. iii. 2.

22. *AP* III. 44-115, 116-169, 294-328.

23. *AP* III. 116-169. Add to these grammatical figures
(294-328) like tmesis and aphaeresis, archaism and periphrasis.

24. Lorenzo Gatta considers Vida's similes excessive: pp.
78-79. See also Moroncini, *Sulla Cristiade di Vida*, pp. 96-
98. In a lengthy and acute review, Bruno Cotronei suggests
that the abundance is caused mainly by the limitations of
Vida's material; like Petrarch in the *Africa*, Vida was able to
release his fancy mainly in the similes: *GSLI*, XXXI (1898),
368; and see Bonaventura Zumbini, *Studi sul Petrarca*
(Florence, 1895), pp. 143-144. But Cicchitelli finds some of
the "best passages" of the poem in the similes—pp. 382-383;
he is bothered only by what he calls the excessive and mechanical imitations of Vergil—pp. 377-380.

25. There are twelve similes in Book I, nine in II, fifteen
in III, thirteen in IV, ten in V, and fifteen in VI; eight of
these are just under three lines long. Curiously, all the books
except the second have roughly the same number of lines used
in similes—sixty-six. The abundance of similes in the recapitulation books is "non-Vergilian"; in *Aeneid* III, for
instance, there is only one simile. As to the length of individual similes, there are five of nine lines each, seven of seven
lines each, and eleven of six lines each; almost half are four
or five lines long. The average length is almost exactly five
lines.

26. I. 436-510. The similes are 458-461, 469-473, and 505-
510. Of the snake simile, Gatta says justly that it may be
attributed to "un capriccio di descrivere cose nuove" (p. 78).

27. IV. 439-531. The similes are bunched together in a
space of twenty-six lines: 481-483, the howling of the possessed youth is compared to the howling of a bull being led
to the altar; 494-496, the devils shriek like wolves; 497-502,

the devils' howls are louder than the noises made by Velinus' waters in flood bursting against the rocks. A number of shorter similes occur in 503-506:

Nunc caeli crepitus imitantur, quam superum rex
Fulminat, et tonitru quatit aetheris aurea templa:
Nunc ferri sonitum, aut ruptarum mole catenarum
Ingenti horrificum stridorem, aut murmura ponti.

Another example of clutter is VI. 418-450, containing fourteen lines of similes.

28. Anna Cox Brinton has remarked (*Maphaeus Vegius and His Thirteenth Book*, p. 11) that the general style of Vegio is Vergilian in flavor, like the style of the Puritan which begins to sound biblical from long association with the Bible; the statement would seem even more appropriate to Vida. The hunt for imitations can easily lead astray; Cicchitelli's claim that *Chr.* I. 545-550 derives from *Aen.* II. 355-358, and *Chr.* II. 30-33 from *Aen.* VI. 311-312; *Chr.* II. 89-92 from *Aen.* X. 721-728, among other *attinenze*, needs careful modification (pp. 377-380). H. S. Alberson is more prudent and more perceptive: "... this hunt for similarities is... always elusive and unsatisfactory.... The more persistently one tries to trace the indebtedness in its details the more surely one arrives at the conclusion that it is the broad aim of that other master that has been his high inspiration." "Lo Mio Maestro," *CJ*, XXXII (1937), 207.

29. *Chr.* VI. 968-972; Judges 6: 36-40. See also *Chr.* III. 460 ff. For other uses of Scripture, see the daring combination of the star of the Magi with the pillar of fire: *Chr.* III. 749-752, Exodus 13: 21, Matthew 2: 2, 9; and the variation on the parable of the Good Shepherd: Luke 15: 4-7, *Chr.* IV. 695-703.

30. *Chr.* IV. 931-938, Matthew 6: 25-30; *Chr.* VI. 524-528, Matthew 21: 33 ff.

31. *Studi di Lett. Comparata*, pp. 44-45. It is no coincidence that Zumbini is the only major critic who has some notion of the *Christiad's* scope and true subject; cf. the "simple retelling of the Gospel narrative" line taken by Moroncini, Gatta, Cicchitelli, and Alberson, among others.

32. V. 528-533, 571-573, 694-702. This last and the simile comparing the sick at the pool to athletes (I. 469-473) may be oblique attempts to suggest the epic games.

33. V. 773-781; II. 30-33; V. 490-493.

34. W. Y. Sellar, *Virgil* (Oxford, 1877), p.406.

35. VI. 381-386 (cf. *Inf.* II. 127-129); VI. 306-312; 568-572.

36. *Chr.* VI. 922-925.

37. The sun as image of God is part of a complex pattern of interrelated similes and of the light-dark polarity which Vida employs in his epic; the subject will be discussed in Chapter Six.

38. Virtually every critic has gone at least partway up this blind alley. See, for instance, Alberson, dissertation, p. 106; Cicchitelli assumes the relationship in most of his study, as does Moroncini. Zabughin, *Vergilio nel Rinascimento Italiano*, who takes Saintsbury and Spingarn to task precisely for this error, is himself guilty of appallingly superficial readings based on application of this principle. See also Paul Van Tieghem and Jules Lefèvre-Deumier, cited in Chapter One, n. 29.

39. *AP* III. 185-263.

40. *The Iliad of Homer*, translated with an Introduction by Richmond Lattimore (Chicago, 1951), pp. 37-38.

41. *AP* II. 325-338.

42. An especially ludicrous list is provided by Pircher in his *Horaz und Vida*, pp. 25-26. Out of the first fifty examples of "imitations" which he cites, more than half are mere commonplaces. Cicchitelli, less extreme, abounds with examples like the following (p. 341): from *Aen.* VII. 513-515,

> cornuque recurvo
> tartaream intendit vocem, qua protenus, omne
> contremuit nemus et silvae intonuere profundae.

and XI. 45, Dat signa rauca cruentum buccina...,

the following passage of the *Christiad* is derived (I. 135-138):

> ... ecce igitur dedit ingens buccina signum.
> Quo subito intonuit caecis domus alta cavernis
> Undique opaca, ingens: antra intonuere profunda
> Atque procul gravido tremefacta est corpore tellus.

But the connection is obviously very slight. For other examples, Cicchitelli pp. 348-349, 365, 416.

43. This same passage is alluded to by contrast in *Chr.* III. 266. Joseph is describing Mary in ecstasy:

O illa a solita quantum mutata figura!

Solita, referring to the Mary who had been all tears again and again the day before, contrasts with Aeneas's *illo Hectore*, the gleaming and heroic figure resplendent with Achilles's armor. But the surprising reversal is only mildly effective.

44. As the first line in the poem, the line would obviously be important. In the *Christiad*, Vida gives it prominence by repetition, sometimes with slight variations: see, e.g., IV. 36, 43, 921; V. 203-204.

Chapter Five: Character, Story, and Structure: Dramatic vs. Oratorical Imagination

1. *AP* II. 304-324, 455-525; 40-50; 98-123. What the *AP* says on character is generally secondary, subsumed under discussions of decorum, suspense, and the resources available to the poet.

2. *Chr.* I. 32-130, 236-367, 400-435, 511-550.

3. II. 776-848; IV. 858-1028; V. 481-503; V. 830-845. Cf. Gatta: "Quel Cristo, che gli apostoli vedono comparire improvvisamente e svanire dinanzi agli occhi, sfugge anche dal guardo del poeta, che non lo può seguire." (*Vida e la Cristiade*, p. 52) Cicchitelli considers three scenes outstanding for their "grand" portrayal of Christ: the adulteress scene (I. 725-792), the Last Supper (II. 643-730), and the long discourse (IV. 825-1028). But his suggestion that Christ is unheroic in the agony and death, and that the characterization is marred by "docetist" heresy, is far-fetched: *Sulle Opere Poetiche*, pp. 322-331.

4. Joseph informs Pilate, III. 163, that at the time of betrothal to Mary, he was already advanced in age, in fact a contemporary of Joachim, Mary's venerable father. See also III. 199, 248, 250.

5. One example, approximating tragic irony, may be cited

here. In III. 717-728, the aged Simeon predicts to Mary that
she will suffer great sorrow because of her child; he hints also
at the Jordan running with "kindred blood." Immediately
afterwards, he dies. Joseph suggests that events which oc-
curred soon after this are those referred to, but adds:

> Ni nobis majora etiam nunc vulnera restant,
> Atque alia ex aliis semper graviora parantur.
>
> (737-738)

In III. 816-817, he interprets the Flight into Egypt as the
great sorrow, and in 886-887, he interprets the Massacre of
the Innocents as the event predicted ambiguously. The irony
was missed by Vida's translator, the learned cleric Tommaso
Perrone; he suggests, modestly enough but firmly, that *Vida's*
interpretation of the prophecies is not quite accurate: *La
Cristiade*, p. 156, n. 42.

6. It may be that Vida's gentle and sympathetic treatment
of Joseph and his attempts to render the "magna Mater" have
their source partly in his religious feeling, demonstrated in
many of the *Hymni*. And there is the notion, set forth in the
AP, that passages dilating on homeland and heroes are proper
in epic; but even there he insists that such passages be carefully related to the unity of the whole work (*AP* II. 191-246,
156-159; see also Tillyard, *The English Epic*, pp. 219-220).
Book III in general is not completely fused with the epic.

7. See III. 187-188, 204, 208, 225-226, and 814-815, 876-
877, 933-939.

8. Zumbini, *Studi di Letteratura Comparata*, pp. 51-56;
Perrone, p. 252, n. 39. D. Bartolini, *La Cristiade di M. G.
Vida*, tradotta in ottava rima (Naples, 1833), II. 225, cited
by Zumbini, pp. 55-56. Cicchitelli argues that the weak characterization of Mary derives from Sannazaro, *De partu virginis*,
especially I. 344-367, and from the bond both Vida and
Sannazaro have with "il mondo pagano." But he does not
justify his contention that Vida makes Mary "priva di fede" on
these grounds. The problem there lies rather in the initial
inability of either poet to conceive or execute a tragic characterization. Both succeed with the radiant and joyous virgin—
see especially *Chr.* III. 254-349; but both overdo the laments.

9. *Chr.* I. 300-367 and VI. 313-391. On the various Mary Magdalenes, Perrone has a detailed discussion: pp. 42-44, n. 38.

10. VI. 374-387. Gatta considers it superior to Dante's: "Ecco un'altra gemma caduta dalla penna del Vida. In poche pagine non si poteva dir piú e meglio. Quanta soavità nella figura della Maddalena, che si strugge nell'adorazione di Gesú e quanta delicatezza nella similitudine della rosa." (p. 54)

11. Luke 22:33, 38. C. Vettii Aquilini Juvenci *Libri Evangeliorum IIII*, rec. C. Marold (1886), IV. 467-469, 475-476.

12. *Chr.* 611-613, 666-668. See also Peter's vivid and moving narration of the apparition of Christ, VI. 440-486.

13. Cicchitelli states that Vida has drawn Judas "con arte incomparabile," but in the following fifteen-page discussion of Judas, he neglects to demonstrate this, showing rather parallels and contrasts (some spurious) between Vida's poem and Claudian's *In Rufinum*, and the use Klopstock made of Vida's Judas and of Claudian's poem: pp. 340-355. Gatta concedes much skill in the delineation of Judas, but, curiously, considers it all wasted because Judas never achieves tragic stature: p. 43. Zumbini, more disciplined and perceptive, analyzes the portrayal of Judas at length, dwelling particularly on the "vera passione" and the "sentimenti contrari ... nel cuore di Giuda," and examining Vida's free adaptation of the Gospel texts: pp. 45-50.

14. The dream is clearly psychological in character (see chap. III). It is important to stress that Judas was not subverted overnight, and that he was not possessed before Holy Week. The latter is made clear by the vagueness of Satan's plans in the council scene.

15. III. 76. See also 1018-1019:

> ... namque hunc in corpore vires
> Deficiunt, teque auxilio jubet ipse subire.

16. Note the excitement conveyed by rhythm and by the irregular shape of the lines in 88-90:

> ... ut se
> Incessu gerit! ut vultuque, et corpore toto est

> Humana major species! ut lumina honorum
> Plena! ut regifici motus!—

and the pensive quality of 92-96:

> Nil mortale sonat. sensi illo in pectore Numen.
> Aut certe Deus ille, aut non mortalibus ortus.
> Dicite vos. nam me scitantem avertitur ipse,
> Et vix responso tacitus dignatur amicum,
> Contemtorque illi est animus lucisque, meique.

17. The liberties Vida has taken with the Gospel text are not in strict matters of detail but in the elusive tone. (A major exception: VI. 99-109, where Vida removes from Pilate the responsibility for setting the guard on the tomb. Cf. Matthew 27: 62-66.) Cicchitelli notes that Vida has followed the apocryphal *Epistola Pontii Pilati* in some respects, and compares his Pilate with Klopstock's. The latter is disdainful, demanding good reasons before he will surrender the body of Christ, reflecting on his own judges Rhadamantus, Eacus, and Minos; only Portia's intercession ends the bickering. Cicchitelli, pp. 338-339.

18. Though Vida borrows from Vergil traits and descriptive details for his characters, these are incidental and need not be considered here. Similarly, allusion to Vergilian scenes or episodes in the handling either of character or of relationships between characters is not relevant here, as not contributing essentially to characterization. It would be impossible here to acknowledge all the scholars and critics who have helped shape my ideas on Vergil's characterization. Some debts are cited below; reference may be made in general to Viktor Pöschl, *Die Dichtkunst Virgils: Bild und Symbol in der Aeneis* (Innsbruck, 1950), to T. R. Glover, *Studies in Virgil* (London, 1904), and to Henry W. Prescott, *The Development of Virgil's Art* (Chicago, 1927).

19. *Chr.* I. 102-106; 476-477; II. 556, 561-563; IV. 347-348. Joseph of Arimathea, who plays quite as small a role as these, is described as intelligent, handsome, courageous, and wealthy:

> ... egregiusque animi, praestansque juventa,
> Et bellis assuetus, agri ditissimus idem,

Atque auri. is Christi miratus maxima facta
Addiderat comitem ...   (VI. 5-8)
Granted that there is a contrast between his riches and his
decision to follow Christ, the nobility here is mainly a matter
of certification.

20. I. 316 ff., 90 ff.

21. *De bello civili* II. 349-371.

22. *AP* II. 304-338. For Vida's views on oratory as an
important resource for the epic poet, see *AP* II. 496-525.
While rejecting Homer, Vida is quite aware of his superiority
in creating "natural" characters. The essential difference
between the Greeks and the Romans, he says, is that the
Greeks had the imaginative faculty in abundance but were
inferior craftsmen, while the Romans perfected the Greek
inventa by *cura* and *arte*. The Greeks, after all, were far less
serious than the Romans:

Multa tamen Grajae fert indulgentia linguae,
Quae nostros minus addeceant graviora sequentes.
                                    (II. 189-190)
The lack of "invention" will be made up for by "art." On
the stylistic influence of Cicero on Vergil, see E. Fränkel,
"Vergil und Cicero," *Atti e Mem. d. r. Accad. Virgiliana di
Mantova*, XIX (1926), 217-227.

23. W. Y. Sellar, *Virgil* (Oxford, 1877), pp. 399-401; see
also pp. 387-389. R. Heinze, *Virgils Epische Technik*, 3rd ed.
(Stuttgart, 1957), pp. 403-435.

24. The speech in Judas's dream, II. 95-112, is perhaps
the most subtly revealing of all. Various effects are achieved
by other speeches—e.g., Christ's in I. 38-59; Nicodemus's in
II. 163-195, and Caiaphas's, II. 216-254; Pilate's, V. 92-100
and 157-174; and Annas's, V. 105-151.

25. For the technique of indirect characterization, cf. especially Homer—the revealing words spoken by the old men
on the walls about Helen; Helen's remarks about the slain
Hector; Briseis's lament over Patroclus (*Iliad* III. 150-160;
XXIV. 763-775; XIX. 282-300.)

26. *Chr.* I. 15-31, 60-70, 90-367, 400-435.

27. Sellar, pp. 355, 358.

28. Maria Leopizzi, *Marci Hieronymi Vidae "Christias"* (Cremona, 1935), pp. 19-20. Dr. Leopizzi's stimulating observations on structure stand almost alone not only in her essay (marred by blanket generalizations and by errors of fact) but in the general history of Vida scholarship.

29. Leopizzi, pp. 16-19. Cicchitelli (pp. 293-296, 303 f., 316 f.) considers the structure of the poem "noble" but wholly simple, and excoriates Vida (pp. 305 ff.) for too mechanical an imitation of Vergil's structure. Gatta (pp. 45-46, 51, 75-76) sees no structure at all in this "simple retelling of the Gospel story." His entire study, generally acute, insists on considering Vida's work only piecemeal.

30. R. S. Conway, "The Architecture of the Epic," *Harvard Lectures on the Vergilian Age* (Cambridge, Mass., 1928), pp. 129-149; Heinze, *Virgils Epische Technik*, pp. 261 ff. Prescott, *Virgil's Art*, pp. 360 f., 440. J. Perret, *Virgile: L'homme et L'œuvre* (Paris, 1952), pp. 111-120. The best study of structure is Duckworth, "The Architecture of the *Aeneid*," *AJP*, LXXV (1954), 1-15, which builds brilliantly on Conway.

31. Many more details of interweaving could be adduced. Further, much of *Aen.* IV echoes and parallels II, the narrative of the Sack of Troy, as if Vergil was attempting, consciously or not, a city-maiden motif. Cf. B. Fenik, "Parallelism of Theme and Imagery in *Aeneid* II and IV," *AJP*, LXXX (1959), 1-24.

32. *Chr.* II. 607-642. See Cicchitelli, p. 308 and n. 2. He is particularly scandalized at Vida's "confusion" of the Salem where Melchisedech offered sacrifice (Genesis 14) with Jerusalem. Vida's omission of certain of the Improperia—the scourging of Egypt, the pillar of cloud, the smiting of the Chananite Kings—is not inadvertent. See *Liber Usualis*, edd. Benedictines of Solesmes (Tournai, 1945), pp. 706-708.

33. Also related to Simon's song are such items as John the Baptist's outcry,

> ... Deus, ecce, Deus, qui crimina nostra,
> Turicremas agnus veluti mactatus ad aras,
> Morte luet...   (IV. 232-234)

and the *agnus candidus* which Pilate's wife sees in her dream.

It is notable that virtually everything used in the passages under discussion derives from the Bible. For further examples of architectonics, one might note the striking changes of pace and tone between the end of each book and the beginning of the next (except III); the careful selectivity employed in the narrative of Christ's miracles, IV. 315-531, on which see also Alberson, "Lo Mio Maestro," pp. 204-205; the contrasts between the frenzied scenes at Pilate's court and on Calvary in the first third of Book V, and the calm, majestic description of heaven in the second third; the contrast in tone of the parallel details in the narrative of the massacre of the innocents and the joyous hymn of nature at Christ's coming into Egypt (III. 800-870). The extent to which Vida goes beyond his own earlier suggestions on structure and variety (see *AP* II. 239 ff., 339 ff.) demolishes any notion that the *Chr.* is simply a putting into practice of the *AP's* limited theory.

34. It is possible to document fully, and somewhat convincingly, Pilate's "interest" as structural justification for the length of III and IV; such proof would be merely logical, however. Pilate is brought in too late in II to attain convincing dramatic existence; in the tedious length of the recapitulation, one completely forgets Pilate and his curiosity and interest. Moroncini finds the recapitulation much too long (*Sulla Cristiade*, pp. 82-85), but his critic, Bruno Cotronei, suggests irritably that the whole tradition of recapitulation books is at fault and blames Homer for having begun the practice (*GSLI*, XXXI [1898], 367).

35. See Tillyard, *English Epic*, pp. 21-30; C. M. Bowra, *Tradition and Design in the Iliad* (Oxford, 1930); Cedric Whitman, *Homer and the Heroic Tradition* (Cambridge, Mass., 1958).

36. Bowra, *From Virgil to Milton* (London, 1945), pp. 69-70. See also Heinze, pp. 271-280.

37. Maffeo Vegio's *Supplementum* was intended to perfect the allegory of Aeneas. Very popular, Vegio's thirteenth book was often printed in conjunction with the *Aeneid* and favored with a full commentary by Badio Ascensio, first appearing in the 1500 edition of Vergil. But for Vida and his contempo-

raries, the commoner view was that of Aldo Manuzio, first suggested by his reluctant publication of the thirteen-book *Aeneid* in 1505 (see Preface to that edition) and sharply expressed in his letter to Bembo prefacing the 1514 Vergil. That edition, Aldo points out, properly omits the unfortunate *Supplementum*. It may be added that severe critique of Vegio, for all his competence and fluency, goes back to Guarino in the *Politia literaria*. Vida's peers generally disliked allegory, and a poem about Christ can be handled allegorically only by violent dislocation.

38. Even the Greeks who destroy Troy are operating according to divine plan: see Venus' revelation to Aeneas, II. 589-623, concluding,

> apparent dirae facies, inimicaque Troiae
> numina magna deum.

39. *From Virgil to Milton*, pp. 15, 31.

Chapter Six: Thematic Design in the Christiad: *Vida's Essential Vergilianism*

1. A typical allegorical poem of Vida's time, imitative of Vergil, is the *Davidias* of Marko Marulic (ed. Josep Badalic [Zagreb, 1954]), which the author furnished with a detailed *Expositio Tropologica* pp. 213-215. But Camoens and Milton, both profoundly influenced by Vergil's *Aeneid*, are innocent of large-scale allegory in their epics, while these clearly have symbolic design.

2. *The English Epic and Its Background*, pp. 72, 78-79.

3. Page 87. Cf. Bowra, *From Virgil to Milton*, pp. 15, 31, 34-38, 56-84; Lewis, *Preface to Paradise Lost* (Oxford, 1942), pp. 6-8, 26-38; T. S. Eliot, "Virgil and the Christian World," *On Poetry and Poets* (London, 1957), pp. 121-131.

4. *Aen.* I. 279.

5. Distinction, not denigration, is intended in these remarks; Homer's art is highly mature. Lewis' illuminating comments in his *Preface* are occasionally marred by misrepresentation of Homer. I insist on the thematic "simplicity" of Homer's epics,

but do not discount their intricacy of structure. See Tillyard, Bowra, and Whitman, cited in Chapter Five, n. 35.

6. The Homeric model for this storm is *Odyssey* V. 291-456.

7. See *Aen.* IX. 38-46.

8. Tillyard, p. 76. The comment is extreme.

9. Translation by Richmond Lattimore (Chicago, 1951).

10. *Iliad* XXII. 143-161, 175-176, 185, 208-213.

11. Iuturna's interruption of the duel is clearly blasphemous—see lines 283-286; the words of *pius Aeneas* lay emphasis on that—see lines 311-317. Noteworthy too is the function of Amata's madness in the twelfth book; she is a symbol of the irrational. The miraculous cure of Aeneas's wound is similarly expressive of theme. Jupiter's solemn *ventum ad supremum est* (803) is significantly used by Vida in Christ's opening speech: *Chr.* I. 38.

12. See Heinze, *Virgils Epische Technik*, pp. 82-114, for detailed study of Aeneas's wanderings and comparison with *Odyssey* IX-X.

13. *Aen.* VIII. 608-731; *Iliad* XVIII. 478-616.

14. *Preface to Paradise Lost*, p. 38.

15. Raby suggests that this poem, too dependent on Christian as well as classical antecedents, heralds the decadence of empty classicizing: *Christian Latin Poetry*, pp. 118-120. For all these poets, postclassical and fifteenth century, see the discussion in Chapter Two, above, and the authorities cited there.

16. E.g., Gatta, pp. 46, 61-63; Moroncini, pp. 39-40, 64-65; Andolfi, *Il Poema del Cristianesimo*, pp. 31-32; U. A. Canello, *Storia della Letteratura Italiana del secolo XVI* (Milan, 1880), p. 158; Lefèvre-Deumier, *Études Biographiques*, pp. 282-284; Van Tieghem, *La Littérature Latine*, pp. 125-126. The learned and detailed commentary of Bartolommeo Botta, though concerned mostly with matters of grammar and theology, looks through the surface enough to suggest some intricacies of structure and theme. Ezio Lopez-Celly, *La Cristiade di M. G. Vida* (Alatri, 1917), announces his concern for significant contemporary themes in the

Christiad, but talks almost entirely around the poem, never about it. Lopez-Celly considers the poem an important Counter-Reformation document, though he never quite lets the reader know what he means by that or why he thinks so. See the detailed critiques of Lopez-Celly by P. Carli, *GSLI,* LXXIV (1919), 152-156; T. Sorbelli, *Archivium Romanicum* (1919), 319-320, and Cicchitelli, *RCLI,* XXIII (1918), 95-101.

17. *Studi di Letteratura Comparata,* pp. 39-40. See also pp. 42, 44, 67-71.

18. Zumbini, pp. 79-86. Alberson, "Lo Mio Maestro," approaches understanding until she postulates that the *Christiad* is an "excellent demonstration of the relation of theory and practice" (p. 195). Neither her dissertation nor her essay suggest any awareness of the poem's structure.

19. Com. II, part 2, p. 47.

20. See Lewis, *Preface,* whose remark about Milton's epic is appropriate here: "It is feigned, for the moment, that we, as readers, can step aside and see the faces of God and man in profile" (p. 128).

21. T. S. Eliot, *The Dry Salvages,* in *Complete Poems and Plays* (New York, 1952), p. 136.

22. *Africa* IX. 90-105; *Contra Medicum* III (pp. 66-67). See the discussion in Chapter Two, above.

23. The similarity of Christ's journey to the journey of Aeneas is obvious. But such similarities must be kept in proper context; they should not be mistaken for attempts at *parallelism.* Christ is not a retouched Aeneas; Jerusalem is not a translation of Carthage; the Jews are not paraphrased Greeks or Italians. Vida's method of imitating and using the *Aeneid* is very much like Vergil's method of imitating and using the Homeric epics. He borrows, he echoes, he alludes evocatively, and he comments obliquely. Such a practice, not uncommon among modern poets, seems to have been virtually unknown to Latin epic poets between Vergil and Vida.

24. Often, Vida employs word-position suggestively, whether or not the meaning is strictly relevant; it is a technique he learned from Vergil. Thus, *Chr.* II. 533, "Affatur socios *Christus: Lux* sacra propinquat." Other examples:

"*mortali immortalia* digno / Ore loqui" from the invocation; from the apostrophe to Christ, Who "toti advenies olim datus *arbiter orbi.* / *Pontius* ut vinctum..." (V. 224-225); at the beginning of Book II: "At Solymi trepidi rerum, et formidine *caeci* / *Noctem* illam ..." See also the curious order in V. 1, "Insonti ... Romanus ... capto," and the juxtaposition of *Sol luce* in VI. 595.

25. I. 55-56. In Christ's speech *lux* is used in three meanings, all related: *infanda lux* (39), referring to the day of His death; *lux* (49), referring to morning and resurrection; *lucis* (52), referring to life.

26. I. 140, 150-151. See also I. 121—"mundi regnator opaci"; 136-137—"caecis domus alta cavernis / Undique opaca..."; 164-165—"opaca / Regia, rex donec nigram igne tricuspide..."; 178—"tenebris ... sub imis"; and 228—"obscurum per inane."

27. Note also the reenforcing details: the description of sun and stars, "ceu mundi vigiles" (624), and the simile of the star for the angel at the pool (458-461).

28. More than illustration, this simile intentionally uses the symbolic sun, light of creation, and interlocks with many other similes. The detail of *oceanus* is also important in connection with the water imagery of the poem. The translation of lines 940-942 was adapted from Coyne, *An Edition.*

29. See III. 254 ff., with its double meaning for *tenebris* in 254 and *nigras umbras* in 255. Passages referred to: III. 277-349; 373-398; 571-594. See also angelic activity throughout Book III: besides passages cited, also 673-674; 740 ff.; 779 ff.; 904-907; 955-968.

30. Dark: IV. 79, 124, 131; 183-184; 803-804; 879-880; Light: 54-58; 187-189; 216-224; 686-687; 714-715.

31. V. 27; 61-64; 207-212; 268-272; 278-281; 285 ff. See also 471-472; 752-757; 959 ff.

32. IV. 10-15; 54-58.

33. IV. 187-189.

34. III. 181-183, 265, 587-589; III. 630-633, 964-968; VI. 568-572. See also VI. 218-221, 301-305, 381-386, 544-545.

35. I. 525-535 and 793-829.

36. Christ pointedly takes the twelve aside and rebukes them for their blindness.

37. IV. 395. Vida's changes from the Gospel account are significant. Matt. 21:18 ff. attaches a moral; Mark 11:12 says it was not the season for figs. Adapting the incident to theme, Vida contrasts the tired and hungry Christ with the immediately preceding episode—the feeding of the five thousand—and stresses that the tree was barren.

38. IV. 399-426. The contrast between this episode, showing Christ's power over nature, and the immediately preceding episode of the barren fig tree would be strange unless both were read symbolically.

39. For the sacrifice: III. 653-704; the prophecy: 716-728. Other noteworthy details, among many: the number symbolism; the remark that the calf's sacrifice was "ut sontis populi commissa piaret" (658); the imagery of sword and fire; the death of Simeon—convenient and useful, in that it leaves the prophecy necessarily ambiguous, but intended also as symbolic of the end of the Old Law.

40. *Chr.* I. 22-23,

>Olli se innumeri jungebant usque parati
>
>Jussa sequi, vellet quascumque abducere in oras,

echoes curiously *Aen.* II. 799-800, where Aeneas is describing the remnant of Trojans gathering outside the city:

>undique convenere animis opibusque parati
>
>in quascumque velim pelago deducere terras.

On first reading, Vida's lines seem hyperbolical and thin; considered in the full context of the poem, and especially in the whole crowd-motif, both the detail and the allusion are ironic.

41. A typical example of the point of view technique: Joseph's description of the Nativity (III. 571-594). Awakened by intense light, Joseph enters the hovel, sees Infant, donkey, cow, and then Mary, his main emotional concern; not until line 590 does the whole event register on him. The psychological truth of the passage is impressive, but more impressive is the almost wordless presentation of Christ. Other examples:

Satan, in I, does not know who Christ is (185 ff.); in context, his account of the temptation of Christ is superbly out of focus. The bruises and wounds of Christ on Calvary are described more than once, with important shifts of emphasis, depending on who is looking—the crowd, for instance, or Mary, or the soldiers. Christ's own standpoint unites all the others of Book V. Arrived at Calvary, He looks about, finds Himself completely alone amid the crowd; looks at the Cross and shudders; looks up to Heaven and prays (481 ff.); line 500 unites the scene with the preceding description of the heavenly court: Vida is determined that no reader will miss the various levels and viewpoints. In Book VI, the three similes in the Harrowing of Hell passage all illustrate the *effects* of Christ's coming; other details (239, 276-293) present further reactions of devils and nature. Vida's passing over the Resurrection so briefly recalls Guarino's opinion in the *Politia literaria* (Chapter 11, pp. 67-74) that there was no need for Vergil to describe the funeral of Turnus or the nuptials of Aeneas and Lavinia, since such matters would be repetitious; the critique, directed at Vegio's *Supplementum*, defends the perfection of Vergil's twelve books. For Vida's themes, the Resurrection could add nothing not adequately symbolized in Transfiguration, Harrowing, and Ascension. The Ascension scene itself concentrates more on the immediate effects than on specific description: see especially VI. 698 ff. For the effects of the Resurrection on Magdalene, VI. 369-391; on Peter, 445 ff.; on Cleophas, 487 ff.

42. Contrast the reaction of Herod to the prisoner Christ with Pilate's. Eager to see Him, Herod questions Christ, receives no answer, immediately scorns Him and sends Him back to Pilate. The point of view technique is used in other respects. There are, for instance, three views of the fall of the angels: that of Satan (I. 167-179); that of John (IV. 70-79); that of the mobilizing angels (V. 589-617). The three are fully resolved when God the Father explains the divine plan (V. 651 ff.), and that resolution is dramatically realized in the Harrowing of Hell.

43. To emphasize that Christ's brief answer does not put

off Pilate, Vida stresses the motif of the revelation of divinity through beauty of countenance: "Haec tantum. ille autem admirans *decus oris honesti...*" (996).

44. The comma after *Hausit* in line 342 seems to me mistaken; *conspicuos vultus* in 341 is best read as accusative of respect with *deperdita.* Though there is syntactical simplicity in considering *vultus, honorem,* and *oculos* all objects of *Hausit,* a literal rendering of "forehead" for *frons* seems to me exceptional; the term is rather synecdoche for "face." If my reading, reasonably giving Vida the benefit of the doubt here, is correct, the contrast between the *conspicuos vultus* of Maria, by which she is specifically *deperdita,* and the shining countenance of Christ is telling. Coyne's *Edition* (1939) specifies no variants for this passage.

45. I. 420—"placida ora" (triumphal entry); I. 485, 498—"placido ore" (to Jethro). For the radiant Infant, III. 626-633; e.g., "Fulgebat puer ore, oculis, ac corpore ab omni / Divino longe circum loca lumine complens."

46. For boy Christ: III. 900 and 903 ff. The simile used for Christ's face as He hangs on the cross is particularly interesting:

> Qualis, qui modo caerulea perfusus in unda
> Lucifer astrifero radios spargebat olympo,
> Si mundi species violetur clara sereni,
> Et subdita incipiat caelum pallescere nube,
> Nondum omne occuluit jubar, obtusaque nitescit
> Pulcher adhuc facie, et nimbo tralucet in atro.
>   (V. 752-757)

In this motif, Vida alludes broadly to Isaiah 53: "non est species ei, neque decor: et vidimus eum, et non erat aspectus, et desideravimus eum: despectum, et novissimum virorum, virum dolorum, et scientem infirmitatem: et quasi absconditus vultus ejus et despectus, unde nec reputavimus eum. Vere languores nostros ipse tulit, et dolores nostros ipse portavit: et nos putavimus eum quasi leprosum, et percussum a Deo et humiliatum..." For other details: V. 326; VI. 199, 239 ff., 374 f.

47. In the Gospel of St. John, Christ reminds the Pharisees

that they are particularly guilty because of their special knowledge: John 9:41; and in a more outspoken passage, states bluntly that if He had not come they would have no sin: John 15:22-25. It is remarkable how much Vida avoids quoting Scripture texts; that fact ought to be a clue to his procedure—not an attempt to paraphrase or gloss over the "lowness" of the Gospel story, as Lewis calls it (*Sixteenth Century*, p. 24), but rather an effort to embody poetically whatever is relevant to his design.

48. *Aen.* I. 589 ff. The Homeric original is *Odyssey* XXIII. 156-162, and VI. 229. Heinze remarks about the Vergilian passage and its originals: "Aussere Mittel, Bad, Salbung, und Kleidung zu der Erhöhung der Leiblichkeit führen, die das Ergreifen der Athena sozusagen nur anschaulich macht. Bei Virgil ist wie so oft das Motiv verinnerlicht und darum weniger unmittelbar überzeugend..." *Virgils Epische Technik*, p. 122, n. 1. Vida's imitation is here even more distinctive, bound up with traditional imagery derived from the Old Testament, especially Isaiah, and from the liturgy of the Church.

49. Cf. the opening lines of Vida's *Hymnus... Spiritui Sancto*, and note the pervasive light and fire imagery there.

50. It is impossible to believe that Vida was completely free of Dante's influence. There is some similarity of subject matter, but this and the exigencies, for both poets, of rendering the spiritual in concrete human terms do not account for all the points of contact between them. The growing intensity of light in *Chr.* VI is not accidentally reminiscent of the growing intensity of light in the *Paradiso*. The patterns of imagery in the *Christiad* are more evident, perhaps, than those in the *Aeneid*, but certainly not than those in the *Commedia*. Vida's relationship to Vergil is, in one sense, very like Dante's—both find Vergil leading them far, but not quite all the way. At some point, they must leave their guide behind and proceed on their own, taking all they have learned and assimilating it somehow with all the other elements in their tradition, elements which would be quite foreign to their guide. Despite the unphilosophical cast of

Vida's mind, Landino, with his *Disputations* and his *Commentary*, may well have been the intermediary here.

51. With respect to Vida's characterization of Christ, two major criticisms curiously cancel each other out. One, most sharply articulated by L. Gatta, maintains that Vida does not present Christ, that Christ disappears too often and too easily from the reader's view; the other, best articulated by Cicchitelli and Moroncini, maintains that Vida overly humanizes Christ, to the point of theological ambiguity—and even of heresy, according to Cicchitelli. Both are to a certain extent correct, but neither recognizes what Vida was trying to do by means partly of the point-of-view technique. In an apostrophe, Vida exclaims (V. 207-210):

> Haec animi victus quoties evolvere tento,
> Omnia me circum nigrescunt: pallida cerno
> Astra, caputque atra roseum ferrugine Solem
> Occulere, et moestum in lacrimas se solvere caelum.

He is pleading a virtual helplessness to transform such matter into poetry, as he contemplates the impending Crucifixion. The references to nature are not only thematic but compositional—the transmutation into concrete human and natural terms, the viable means of poetry, is his only resource; and even so, at this point, he is suggesting that he is unable to preserve the distance, to stand far enough outside nature and outside Christ to be a poet.

52. *Letteratura Comparata*, pp. 42, 44.

53. See IV. 76-78 and V. 613-615: the battle is essentially with man.

54. III. 389-392; VI. 968-972.

55. V. 178-182, 348-355.

56. The Jews (V. 367-368):

> Deus haec nobis, gnatisque reservet,
> Instauretque graves poenas, quascumque meremur.

The Father, to the angels (V. 686-688):

> At sinite, adveniet (neque enim mora longior) urbi
> Tempus ei, frustra hunc quum magno optaverit emtum
> Haud tetigisse...

And see V. 980-991: Vida makes the Scriptural "velum templi scissum est" into a terrifying anticipation of the destruction of Jerusalem: "sceleris mens conscia cuique est" (982).

57. See Chapter Four for some detailed echoes of *Aen.* VI in *Chr.* IV.

58. IV. 351-388. For the Gospel accounts—Matt. 14:15-21; Mark 6:35-44; Luke 9:12-17; John 6:4-13.

59. Connected also are the Last Supper itself, the manna symbolism in Books I and II, and the symbolic breaking of bread by the risen Christ at Emmaus in Book VI.

60. IV. 882-1028. Cicchitelli, pp. 323-324, aptly characterizes this discourse as "grande e maestoso."

61. VI. 629-676. For the allusion to *Aen.* VI, see Chapter Four.

62. John 14:27. See the whole of chapters 13-17, the Last Supper discourse, which Vida has transformed broadly by image and incident.

63. I. 579-580, 911-930.

64. See especially the prayer at the end of I and after the Ascension in VI; both have further allusions to the exile theme of the *Aeneid*. Both prayers precede grand prophecies about the spread of the Church, the exaltation of Rome, and the golden age. The selling of Joseph by his brothers (I. 707-710) is a type of the betrayal of Christ. See Christ's comment, I. 687-692; and III. 1-2.

65. For detailed comment, see Chapter Five, and notes 32-33. The star which leads the three kings is compared to the pillar of fire which guided the Israelites: a further detail in the Exodus-motif. III. 749-752.

66. I. 951-952 and 911-930; 564-581 and 674-686; 20-31 and 51-59. For the allusions to the *Aeneid*, see above, note 40.

67. Note III. 505-515, Joseph's reference to Rome and, presumably, to the *Fourth Bucolic*; a little far-fetched, this is nonetheless skillfully handled. The simile, however, of the "polished image" (III. 268-272) is very awkward.

68. Ad Matutinum, in II. Nocturno, Lectio VI.

69. IV. 800-815, quoted above.

70. IV. 560-564.

71. The procession of the just to heaven is described in

terms analogous to those used for a Roman triumph: VI.
267-293.

72. II. 133-150, 196-215. See also V. 101 ff.

73. A few other specific passages indicating confusion: II.
30-33; 54-59; 259-261. For the Trinity, Vida's number
symbolism is significant—e.g., III. 617 ff.; IV. 20-59, 64-65,
356-357; V. 578, 649, and 464-465; VI. 363, 698, 699, 926-
928, 933, 934. A more subtle example: the patterned apostrophe, V. 200 ff. While the number symbolism is in the
Christian tradition, the symbolic conflict of rational and irrational is distinctly Vergilian.

74. The allusions are discussed in detail in Chapter Four.
For other specific references to the golden age, see III. 312,
538; VI. 648, 868.

75. Isaiah 53:7; Philippians 2:7.

76. Perrone, p. 298, traces parts of the hymn to Psalms,
Exodus, Josue, and Daniel.

77. II. 845-848, 867, 931-937; V. 490-493; VI. 806-809.

78. When Christ was still with them, they could work
miracles in His name, but even then there were limits. When
they could do nothing with the possessed man, Christ rebuked
them gently, pointing out their imperfect faith and their need
for grace: IV, 536 ff.

79. See also the imagery of fire in the episode with Maria
the harlot, I. 300-367. For compressed fire, water, and light
imagery from the Old Testament, see IV. 129-144.

80. III. 460 ff. See Judges 6-36-40.

81. III. 389-392. The union of heaven and earth is broadly
suggested in the attendant details.

Chapter Seven: Cremona's Trump

1. See the cursory survey of classical Latin poetry from the
sixteenth century to our own time in Tomasso Sorbelli, "Relazioni fra la letteratura italiana e le letterature classiche,"
Letterature Comparate, Volume IV of *Problemi ed orientamenti critici...*, ed. A. Momigliano (Milan, 1948), pp. 338-

366, and bibliography cited there. See also Watson Kirk-connell, *The Celestial Cycle, passim*, for many other examples.

2. On Tasso and Milton, Gatta, pp. 65-75, and Zumbini, *Studi di Lett. Comparata*, pp. 41-46, 77-86, who also discusses Klopstock, *passim*. In general, Zabughin, II, 192-195 and notes, 295-306 and notes. Detailed *attinenze* between Vida and Tasso are given by Giulio Guastavini in *Discorsi et Annotationi* (Pavia, 1592); see also Cicchitelli, pp. 384-415.

3. Tillyard, *The Miltonic Setting* (London, 1938), pp. 178-179; Kirkconnell, pp. xxii-xxiii.

4. See Kirkconnell, pp. xxiii-xxiv, and works cited there.

5. But cf. the highly laudatory discussion of Vida's diction in Coyne, *An Edition*, pp. 86-103.

SELECTIVE BIBLIOGRAPHY

OF VIDA'S WORKS

Principal editions

Marci Hieronymi Vidae Cremonensis, De arte poetica libri
III..., de Bombyce libri II..., de ludo scacchorum liber I...,
hymni..., bucolica. Romae, L. Vicentinus, Majo, 1527.

—— Christiados libri VI. Cremonae, Ludovicus Britannicus,
Oct. 1535.

—— Poemata omnia tam quae ad Christi veritatem pertinent
quam ea quae haud plane disiunxit a fabula utraque seorsum
ab alteris. Duo voll. Cremonae, J. Mutius et B. Locheta.
1550.

—— Orationes tres contra Papienses in controversia prin-
cipatus. Cremonae, in aedibus divae Margheritae. 1550.

—— Dialogi de rei publicae dignitate. Cremonae, apud Vincentium Contem. 1556.

—— Constitutiones Synodales eidem civitati ac dioecesi
praescriptae. Cremonae, apud Vincentium Conctum. 1562.

Editions used

—— Poematum... pars prima, continens de arte poetica libros
tres, bucolica, et epistolam....Pars altera, continens bomby-
cum libros duos, scacchiam ludum, et carmina diversi gene-
ris. Edidit Thomas Tristram. Oxonii, 1722.

—— Christiados libri VI, edidit Edwardus Owen. Oxonii,
1725.

—— Hymni de rebus divinis, edidit Edwardus Owen. Oxonii, 1733.

—— Poemata Omnia quae ipse vivens agnoverat. Editio... emendatissima, curantibus J. A. et C. Vulpiis. Dialogi de reip. dignitate, epistolae nonnullae, testimonia, appendix. Duo voll. Pataviae, 1731. Excudebat Josephus Cominus. (Cominiana edition.)

—— Orationes tres pro Cremonensibus quae in Cominiana editione desiderantur. Edidit G. C. Bonnetti. Venetiis, 1764.

—— Epicaedion in funere Oliverii Cardinalis Caraffae. (In Vairani, *Monumenta*, II, 37-45.)

—— Carmen pastorale, seu Quercens, in quo deploratur mors Julii II. (In Vairani, *Monumenta*, II, 47-60.)

—— XIII Pugilum Certamen: Frammento di un poemetto inedito... ed. Luigi Cagnoli. Milano, 1818.

—— Orazione inedita... recitata nel primo concilio provinciale di Milano. Pubblicata da Lorenzo Giampaoli. Ferrara, 1890.

Commentaries and translations

—— Christias, Bartolomeo Botta interprete. Ticini, 1569.

—— La Cristiade... trasportata dal verso Latino all'Italiano da Tommaso Perrone... con annotazioni.... Napoli, 1733.

—— The Christiad... translated from the Latin... by John Cranwell. Cambridge, 1768.

—— An Edition of the Christiad with Introduction, Translation, and Notes, by Gertrude Georgina Coyne. Dissertation, Cornell, 1939.

—— De arte poetica libri tres. Autoris vitam premisit, et annotationes adjecit T. Tristram... Ed. sec. Oxonii, 1723.

—— De arte poetica libri tres. Commentarium de poetae vita et carminibus addidit Christ. Adolphus Klotzius. Altenburgi, 1766.

—— De arte poetica, in Abbé Batteux, *Les Quatre Poétiques: d'Aristote, d'Horace, de Vida, de Despreaux*, avec des traductions et des remarques. 2 vols. Paris, 1771. (Commentary on Vida by P. Oudin.)

—— Poétique... traduite en vers français, texte en regard... avec une introduction... et des notes. Par P. Bernay. Paris, 1845.

—— Art of Poetry, translated by Christopher Pitt into English verse, in Albert S. Cook, *The Art of Poetry*, Boston, 1892. (With commentary.)

GENERAL BIBLIOGRAPHY

(Note: Except for items on Vida, I have omitted works cited only occasionally, common editions, and editions in the Oxford Classical Texts and Loeb Classical Library series.)

Alberson, Hazel S. "Lo Mio Maestro," *Classical Journal*, XXXII (1937), 193-208.

—— *Marcus Hieronymus Vida.* Dissertation, Wisconsin, 1935.

Andolfi, Otello. *Il poema del Cristianesimo.* Rome, 1907.

Arisius, Franciscus. *Cremona Literata*, 2 vols. Parma, 1702-1706.

Baldi, Alexander. "Die *Ars Poetica* des M. H. Vida," *Festschrift für Ludwig Urlichs...*, pp. 199-212. Wirzburg, 1880.

Baldwin, Charles S. *Renaissance Literary Theory and Practice*, ed. Donald L. Clark. New York, 1939.

Belloni, Antonio. *Il Poema Epico e Mitologico* (Storia dei Generi Letterari Italiani). Milan, n.d. but 1912.

[Bembo]. *Le Epistole "De Imitatione" di Giovanfrancesco Pico della Mirandola e di Pietro Bembo*, a cura di Giorgio Santangelo. Florence, 1954.

Bigoni, Guido. "Per un poema sacro del Cinquecento, la *Cristiade* del Vida," *Ateneo Veneto*, XIX (1896), 134-140.

Bissolati, Stefano. *Le Vite di Due Illustri Cremonesi.* Milan, 1856.

Bowra, Cecil Maurice. *From Virgil to Milton.* London, 1945.

—— *Tradition and Design in the Iliad.* Oxford, 1930.

Brinton, Anna Cox. *Maphaeus Vegius and His Thirteenth Book of the Aeneid.* Stanford, 1930.

Büchner, Karl. *P. Vergilius Maro: Der Dichter der Römer* (Pauly-Wissowa Realencyclopädie). Stuttgart, 1958.

Calisti, Giulia. *Il De Partu Virginis di Jacopo Sannazaro.* Città di Castello, 1926.

Canesi, Luigi. "La sfida di Barletta nel *XIII Pugilum Certamen* di Marco Girolamo Vida," *Bollettino Storico Cremonese*, VIII (1938), 5-65, testo e traduzione; studio storico-critico, *ibid.*, IX (1939), 35-64; *ibid.*, X (1940), 81-127; *ibid.*, XI (1941), 52-90; *ibid.*, XII (1942), 62-95.

Cessi, Roberto. "Un poemetto cristiano del sec. 15," *Raccolta di Studi di Storia e Critica Letteraria dedicati a Fr. Flamini...*, pp. 681-691. Pisa, 1918.

Cian, Vittorio. "XIII Italorum pugilum certamen," *Scritti Minori*, Vol. II, pp. 147-151. Turin, 1936.

Cicchitelli, Vincenzo. *Sul "De Reipublicae Dignitate" di M. G. Vida.* Naples, 1900.

—— *Sulle Opere Poetiche di Marco Girolamo Vida.* Naples, 1904.

—— *Sulle Opere in Prosa di Marco Girolamo Vida.* Naples, 1909.

—— Review of Lopez-Celly, *Rassegna Critica della Letteratura Italiana*, XXIII (1918), 95-101.

Colucci, Benedetto. "Oratio ante lectionem Virgilii," *Scritti inediti di B. Colucci da Pistoia*, a cura di Arsenio Frugoni, pp. 57-60. Florence, 1939.

Cotronei, Bruno. Review of Pircher, *Giornale Storico della Letteratura Italiana*, XXX (1897), 459-466.

—— Rev. of Moroncini, *ibid.*, XXXI (1898), 361-369.

Decembrio, Angelo. *De politia literaria libri septem.* Basel, 1562.

Della Guardia, Anita. *La Politia Literaria di Angelo Decembrio e l'Umanesimo a Ferrara nella prima metà del secolo XV.* Modena, 1910.

Dionisotti, Carlo. "Battista Fiera, Umanista Mantovano," *Italia Medioevale e Umanistica*, I (1958), 401-418.

Dominici, Giovanni. *Lucula Noctis*, edidit Edmund Hunt, University of Notre Dame Publications in Medieval Studies, Notre Dame, 1940.

Duckworth, George E. "The Architecture of the *Aeneid*," *American Journal of Philology*, LXXV (1954), 1-15.

—— *Foreshadowing and Suspense in the Epics of Homer, Apollonius, and Vergil.* Princeton, 1933.

Eliot, Thomas Stearns. "Virgil and the Christian World," *On Poetry and Poets*, pp. 121-131. London, 1957.

Ellinger, Georg. *Italien und der Deutsche Humanismus in der Neulateinischen Lyrik.* Berlin, 1929.

Finzi, V. "Di Niccolo Lugari," *Bollettino Storico Cremonese*, I (1931), 111-122.

Flamini, Francesco. *Il Cinquecento.* Milan, n. d., but 1903.

Fletcher, Jefferson B. *Literature of the Italian Renaissance.* New York, 1934.

Gabotto, Ferdinando. *Cinque Lettere di Marco Girolamo Vida.* Pinerolo, 1890.

—— "Girolamo Vida e una consegna al braccio secolare," *La Biblioteca delle scuole Italiane*, IV (1892), 218-220.

Garin, Eugenio, *L'Educazione umanistica in Italia*, Testi scelti e illustrati..., 2a. edizione. Bari, 1953.

—— *Prosatori Latini del Quattrocento.* Milan, 1953.

—— "Umanesimo e Rinascimento," *Problemi...* ed. A. Momigliano: Vol. III, *Questioni e correnti di storia letteraria*, pp. 349-404. Milan, 1949.

Gatta, Lorenzo. *Gerolamo Vida e la Cristiade.* Palermo, 1900.

Giraldi, Lilio Gregorio. *De poetarum historia dialogi.* Basel, 1548.

—— *De poetis nostrorum temporum*, ed. Karl Wotke. Berlin, 1894.

[Guarino]. *Epistolario di Guarino Veronese*, a cura di Remigio Sabbadini, 4 vols. Venice, 1915-1919.

Guastavini, Giulio. *Discorsi et annotationi.* Pavia, 1592.

Heinze, Richard. *Virgils Epische Technik*, 3rd ed. Stuttgart, 1957.

Hughes, Merritt Y. *Virgil and Spenser*, University of California Publications in English, Vol. II. Berkeley, 1929.

Juvencus, C. Vettius Aquilinus. *Libri Evangeliorum IIII*, rec. Carolus Marold. Leipzig, 1886.

Kadic, Ante. "Croatian Renaissance," *Studies in the Renaissance*, VI (1958), 28-35.

Kirkconnell, Watson. *The Celestial Cycle: The Theme of*

Paradise Lost in World Literature.... Toronto, 1952.

Kristeller, Paul Oskar. *The Classics and Renaissance Thought,* Martin Classical Lectures, Vol. XV. Cambridge, Mass., 1955.

—— *Studies in Renaissance Thought and Letters.* Rome, 1956.

Labriolle, Pierre de. *Histoire de la Littérature Latine Chrétienne.* Paris, 1947.

Lancetti, Vincenzo. *Della Vita e degli Scritti di Girolamo Vida,* 2a ediz. Milan, 1840.

Landino, Cristoforo. *Disputationes Camaldulenses....* Basel, 1577.

—— *Interpretationes in P. Virgilium.* Florence, 1487.

Lattimore, Richmond. *The Iliad of Homer,* translated with an introduction. Chicago, 1951.

Lefèvre-Deumier, Jules. *Études Biographiques et Littéraires.* Paris, 1854.

Leopizzi, Maria. *Marci Hieronymi Vidae "Christias."* Cremona, 1935.

Lewis, Clives S. *English Literature in the Sixteenth Century.* Oxford, 1954.

—— *A Preface to Paradise Lost.* Oxford, 1942.

Lopez-Celly, Ezio. *La Cristiade di M. G. Vida,* poema della riforma cattolica. Alatri, 1917.

Luzio, Alessandro, and Rodolfo Renier. "La Coltura e le relazioni letterarie di Isabella d'Este Gonzaga," *Giornale Storico della Letteratura Italiana,* XXXI (1900), 325-349.

Mambelli, Giuliano. *Gli annali delle edizioni virgiliane.* Florence, 1954.

Marulic, Marko. *Davidias,* edidit Josep Badalic. Zagreb, 1954.

Momigliano, Attilio, ed. *Problemi ed Orientamenti Critici di Lingua e di Letteratura Italiana,* 4 vols. Milan, 1948. (See Garin and Sorbelli.)

Moore, Clifford H. "Prophecy in the Ancient Epic," *Harvard Studies in Classical Philology,* XXXII (1921), 98-175.

Moroncini, Gaetano. *Sulla Cristiade di M. G. Vida.* Trani, 1896.

Nolhac, Pierre de, *Pétrarque et l'humanisme,* 2nd. ed., 2 vols. Paris, 1907.

Norden, Eduard. *Aeneis Buch VI.* Leipzig, 1903.

Novati, Francesco. "Delle antiche relazioni fra Trento e Cremona," *Archivio Storico Lombardo*, XXI (1894), 1-78.

—— "Il Virgilio Cristiano," *A ricolta*, pp. 97-115. Bergamo, 1907.

—— "Sedici lettere inedite di M. G. Vida, Vescovo d'Alba," *Archivio Storico Lombardo*, XXV (1898), 195-281; *ibid.*, XXVI (1899), 1-59.

—— "Sulla *Cristiade* di M. G. Vida," *Cultura*, XVI (1897), 212-213.

Osimo, Vittorio. "La prepositura di Monticelli d'Ongina," *Giornale Storico della Letteratura Italiana*, L (1907), 105-115.

—— "Ancora sulla prepositura...," *ibid.*, LI (1908), 231-250.

—— "Le 'Costituzioni Sinodali' di M. G. Vida," *ibid.*, LVII (1911), 332-347.

—— Review of Cicchitelli, *Prosa*, *ibid.*, LVI (1910), 223-226.

Pércopo, Erasmo. Review of Moroncini, *Rassegna Critica della Letteratura Italiana*, I (1896), 113-117.

Perret, Jacques. *Virgile: l'Homme et l'œvre.* Paris, 1952.

Petrarca, Francesco. *L'Africa*, a cura di Nicola Festa. Florence, 1926.

—— *Le Familiari*, Vol. IV, per cura di Umberto Bosco. Florence, 1942.

—— *Invectiva contra quendam magni status hominem sed nullius scientiae aut virtutis*, edizione critica per cura di Pier Giorgio Ricci. Florence, 1949.

—— *Invective contra Medicum*, testo latino e volgarizzamento di Ser Domenico Silvestri, edizione critica a cura di Pier Giorgio Ricci. Rome, 1950.

Pircher, Alois. *Horaz und Vida.* Meran, 1895.

Poliziano, Angelo. *Le Selve e la Strega*, prolusioni nello Studio Fiorentino (1482-1492), per cura di Isidoro del Lungo. Florence, 1925.

Pontano, Giovanni. *I Dialoghi*, edizione critica a cura di Carmelo Previtera. Florence, 1943.

Pöschl, Viktor. *Die Dichtkunst Virgils: Bild und Symbol in der Aeneis.* Innsbruck, 1950.

Prescott, Henry W. *The Development of Virgil's Art.* Chicago, 1927.

Raby, F. J. E. *A History of Christian-Latin Poetry from the Beginnings to the Close of the Middle Ages,* 2nd ed. Oxford, 1953.

Ratti, Achille. "Marco Girolamo Vida, Vescovo d'Alba," *Scritti Storici,* pp. 253-257. Florence, 1932.

Ronchini, Amadio. "Marco Girolamo Vida," *Atti d. R. dep. di storia patria per le provincie Modenesi e Parmensi,* IV (1866), 73-96.

Rossi, Vittorio. *Il Quattrocento,* sesta ristampa..., con supplemento bibliografico (1932-1956) a cura del Prof. Aldo Vallone. Milan, 1956.

Ruscelli, Girolamo. *Lettere de' Principi a Principi.* Vol. I, Venice, 1564; Vol. III, Venice, 1577.

Sabbadini, Remigio. *Storia del Ciceronianismo....* Turin, 1885.

Saint-Marc Girardin. *Tableau de la littérature française au XVIᵉ siècle, suivi d'études sur la littérature du Moyen Âge et de la Rénaissance,* pp. 237-269. Paris, 1862.

Saintsbury, George. *A History of Criticism and Literary Taste in Europe,* Vol. II. New York, 1902.

Salutati, Coluccio. *De laboribus Herculis,* edidit B. L. Ullman, 2 vols. Zurich, 1951.

——— *Epistolario di C. S.,* a cura di Francesco Novati, 4 vols. Rome, 1891-1911.

Salvatore, Nicola. *L'Arte Poetica di Marco Girolamo Vida.* Foligno, 1912.

Sannazaro, Jacopo. *De partu virginis,* edizione critica a cura di A. Altamura. Naples, 1948.

Santangelo, Giorgio. *Il Bembo Critico e il Principio d'Imitazione.* Florence, 1950.

Scaliger, Julius Caesar. *Poetices libri septem.* Basel, 1561.

Sedulius, Coelius. *Opera Omnia,* recensuit... J. Huemer, Corpus Viennense 10. Vienna, 1885.

Sellar, W. Y. *The Roman Poets of the Augustan Age: Virgil.* Oxford, 1877.

Sorbelli, Tommaso. "Chiose alla Poetica di M. G. Vida," *Bollettino Storico Cremonese,* XIV (1944-1945), 45-75.

24.

—— "Relazioni fra la letteratura italiana e le letterature classiche," *Problemi...* ed. Momigliano: Vol. IV, *Letterature Comparate*, pp. 329-376. Milan, 1948.

—— Review of Lopez-Celly, *Archivium Romanicum*, III (1919), 319-320.

Spagnuoli, Battista. *La Partenice Mariana...*, introduzione, testo latino, versione metrica, e note, a cura di Ettore Bolisani. Padua, 1957.

Spingarn, Joel E. *A History of Literary Criticism in the Renaissance*, 2nd ed. New York, 1908.

Stebbing, Henry, "Marco Girolamo Vida," *Lives of the Italian Poets*, Vol. II, 2nd ed., pp. 365-379. London, 1832.

Tadisi, Jacopo Antonio. *Vita di Monsignore Vida*. Bergamo, 1788.

Tillyard, E. M. W. *The English Epic and Its Background*. London, 1954.

—— "Milton and the Epic," *The Miltonic Setting*, pp. 141-204. London, 1938.

Toffanin, Giuseppe, *Il Cinquecento*, quarta edizione. Milan, 1945.

—— *Storia dell'Umanesimo*, 2a ediz. Naples, 1940.

—— *L'Umanesimo al Concilio di Trento*. In appendice: M. G. Vida, *De rei publicae dignitate*, testo e traduzione di Antonio Altamura. Bologna, 1955.

Tomasetti, G. "Della Campagna Romana," *Archivio d. R. Società Romana di Storia Patria*, XXVIII (1905), 115-124.

Trabalza, Ciro. *La Critica Letteraria del Rinascimento*, Storia dei Generi Letterari Italiani. Milan, 1915.

Treves, Paolo. "Un falso precursore del Rousseau," *La Cultura*, X (1931), 57-62.

Ulivi, Ferruccio. *L'Imitazione nella Poetica del Rinascimento*. Milan, 1959.

Ullman, B. L. *Studies in the Italian Renaissance*. Rome, 1955.

Vairani, Tommaso. *Monumenta Cremonensium Romae Exstantia*, 2 vols. Rome, 1778.

Van Tieghem, Paul. *La Littérature Latine de la Rénaissance*, Bibliothèque d'Humanisme et Rénaissance, Vol. IV. Paris, 1944.

[Vegio]. *Maphei Vegii... de educatione liberorum et eorum claris moribus libri sex*, ed. Sister M. Walburg Fanning, Catholic University Studies in Medieval and Renaissance Latin, Vol. I. Washington, 1933.

[Vergil]. *P. Vergili Maronis Opera*, recognovit Fredericus Arturus Hirtzel. Oxford, 1900.

—— *Virgilius*, cum commentariis... Servii, Landini, A. Mancinelli, Donati, Domitii.... Venice, 1493.

—— *Virgilius*.... Aldus, Venice, 1505.

—— *Virgilius*.... Aldus, Venice, 1514.

—— *P. Vergili Maronis opera omnia...*, cum commentariis A. Mancinelli, B. Ascensii... et M. Vegii Landensis libro.... Venice, 1544.

Vissac, J. A. *De Marci Hieronymi Vidae Poeticorum libris tribus*, thesim Facultati Litterarum Parisiensi proponebat.... Paris, 1862.

Voigt, Georg. *Die Wiederbelebung des klassischen Alterthums...*, 2 vols., 3rd ed., ed. Max Lehnerdt. Berlin, 1893.

Weston, Arthur H. "Three Dreams of Aeneas," *Classical Journal*, XXXII (1937), 229-232.

Wetmore, Monroe Nichols. *Index Verborum Vergilianus*. New Haven, 1911.

Whitman, Cedric. *Homer and the Heroic Tradition*. Cambridge, Mass., 1958.

Woodward, William H. *Studies in Education during the Age of the Renaissance*. Cambridge, 1906.

—— *Vittorino da Feltre and Other Humanist Educators*. Cambridge, 1905.

Zabughin, Vladimiro. *Un Beato Poeta*. Rome, 1917.

—— *Virgilio nel Rinascimento Italiano: Da Dante a Torquato Tasso*, 2 vols. Bologna, 1921-1923.

Zumbini, Bonaventura. "Dell'epica cristiana, italiana, e straniera, e particolarmente dei poemi del Vida e del Sannazaro," *Studi di Letteratura Comparata*, pp. 39-86. Bologna, 1931.

—— "Un'osservazione sulla *Cristiade* del Vida," *Per il Giubileo Sacerdotale del Card. Alfonso Capecelatro*, pp. 350-353. Caserta, 1897.

—— *Studi sul Petrarca*. Florence, 1895.

GENERAL INDEX

Achates, 120-21

Achilles, 186-87, 188, 200, 204-7
passim, 215-26, 218; shield of,
112

Aeneas, 96-97, 101, 108, 112, 145,
148, 152-56 *passim*, 183, 196-200
passim, 204-18 *passim*, 259,
321*n*, 337*n*, 338*n*, 340*n*; shield
of, 323*n*

Agamemnon, 204

Alberson, Hazel S., quoted, 327*n*,
338*n*

Alberto da Sarzano, 65

Alcinous, 218

Allecto, 97, 210, 320*n*, 321*n*

Allegory, 57 ff., 72-83 *passim*,
336*n*; and symbolic design,
204-5, 336*n*

Allusion, *see* Evocative allusion

Amata, 152, 170, 191, 200, 337*n*

Anchises, 91, 112, 147-48, 156-57,
208, 218, 254

Andromache, 209

Angels, 100-2, 186-87, 189, 236,
320*nn*, 322*n*

Anna (mother of Mary), 95, 97,
113, 235

Anna (sister of Dido), 196

Annas, 178

Antinous, 200

Apollo, 218

Apollonius, *Argonautica*, quoted,
187

Apostles, 108-9, 112, 119, 125,
136-37, 152-57 *passim*, 160, 180,

184, 186, 197-98, 204, 226,
230-31, 232, 235-36, 247-48,
254-57, 258-59, 274-78; hymn of,
274-75

Apostrophe, in epic, 91, 319*nn*;
used by Vida, 91, by Lucan, 91,
319*nn*, by Petrarch, 91

Appellations, *see* Epithets

Arator, *De actibus Apostolorum*,
219, 337*n*

Archaic forms, in *Christiad*, 116-17

Ariosto, Lodovico, 65

Aristotle, 50, 53; *Poetics*, 22

Ars poetica (Vida), vii-viii, 4, 12-24,
40-86, 130-32, 164, 199, 300-1*nn*,
329*n*; relation to *Christiad*, 24,
83-86, 128-30, 130-32, 140-41,
141-42, 220, 225-26, 328*n*; influences on, 40; sources, 40-41,
307*n*; departures from, in *Christiad*, 114 ff.

Ascanius, 243

Ascension, 246-47, 265-66, 272 ff.

Athena, 100, 101, 216

Augustine, St., 45, 50; quoted,
262-63

Authors, Latin, preferred to Greek
by humanists, 43-53 *passim*

Background, historical, in *Christiad*,
92-93

Baldwin, C. S., 306*n*

Banquets, in epic, 94

Bard, in epic, 94-95

Barzizza, Gasparino, 49

INDEX OF MAJOR QUOTED PASSAGES

This index is confined to quotations from the *Aeneid*, the *Ars poetica*, and the *Christiad*. Other quotations are entered under the name of the author or the work in the General Index.